The Sacred Oral Tradition of the Havasupai

FIGURE 1:
Manakaja, who became
Big Headman after the
death of his uncle, Navajo.
He narrated Havasupai
traditional stories to
Leslie Spier between
1918 and 1921 and to
Erna Gunther in 1921.
Photograph by George
Wharton James, 1899.
Photograph courtesy
of the Havasupai Tribal
Collection.

FIGURE 2:
Sinyella, who served
as one of five Lesser
Headmen. He narrated
Havasupai traditional
stories to Leslie Spier
between 1918 and 1921
and to Erna Gunther
in 1921. Photograph by
Karl Moon, ca. 1910.
Photograph courtesy
of the Havasupai Tribal
Collection.

The Sacred Oral Tradition of the Havasupai

As Retold By Elders and Headmen
Manakaja and Sinyella 1918–1921

Translators:
Tribal members Mark Hanna, Lillie Burro,
Jess Chickapanega, and West Sinyella

Anthropologists and Transcribers:
Leslie Spier, Ph.D., and Erna Gunther, Ph.D.

Contributors:
Robert C. Euler, Ph.D.,
and Douglas W. Schwartz, Ph.D.

Contributors and Editors:
Frank D. Tikalsky, Ed.D.,
Catherine A. Euler, Ph.D.,
and John Nagel, M.D.

UNIVERSITY OF NEW MEXICO PRESS | ALBUQUERQUE

LIBRARY OF CONGRESS CATALOGING-IN-PUBLICATION DATA

The sacred oral tradition of the Havasupai : as retold by elders and headmen Manakaja and Sinyella 1918–1921 / editors, Frank D. Tikalsky, Ed.D., Catherine A. Euler, Ph.D., and John Nagel, M.D.
        p. cm.
Includes bibliographical references and index.
ISBN 978-0-8263-4931-6 (cloth : alk. paper)
1. Havasupai Indians—Folklore. 2. Havasupai mythology. 3. Tales—Arizona.
4. Oral tradition—Arizona. I. Tikalsky, Frank D. II. Euler, Catherine A. III. Nagel, John.
E99.H3S23 2010
398.209791—dc22

2010028599

Funding for color illustrations by Dave and Roma McCoy.

Appendix One: Havasupai (Yuman) Texts was originally published in Leslie Spier, Havasupai (Yuman) Texts. *International Journal of American Linguistics*. Vol. 3, no. 1 (July 1924), pp. 109–16.

DESIGN AND COMPOSITION: Melissa Tandysh
Composed in 10.5/14 Sabon LT Std
Display type is Chaparral Pro Light

To all the Yuman-speaking peoples of the Americas, both north and south of the modern border, whose forebears and elders carried versions of these and other stories for hundreds of unknown migratory generations;

To yesterday's Havasupai elders, whose geographical isolation and oral memory combined to preserve and protect these stories;

To today's Havasupai, and to all future generations of Havasupai, a people whose challenge it is to balance the positives and negatives of American modernity with traditional cultural vitality. These are the stories that, interspersed with many, many songs, your ancestors told and sang to their children and grandchildren in the wintertime, up on the plateau, during the blizzards, as they sat together in a shelter protected by sage, warmed by a juniper or piñon fire, eating venison and rabbit, or squash, or piñon stew. May your grandchildren find their way to sharing the essence of these experiences.

To the well-intentioned pioneering anthropologists who helped to preserve these meanings following a period of brutal conquest, foreign sickness, and doubtful cultural survival;

And to all cultural scientists of integrity who have since helped humanity to better understand and appreciate the Havasupai heritage of story-telling, desert-thriving, dream-singing plateau- and canyon-roaming gatherers, hunters, farmers, and warriors.

FIGURE 3: Robert C. Euler with former Havasupai Tribal Chairman Lee Marshall in the 1970s. Lee Marshall was one of Manakaja's grandsons. Photo by Frank D. Tikalsky.

FIGURE 4: The view from Hilltop, close to the entrance of the seven-mile dirt trail to Supai, the village where the Havasupai live at the bottom of the Grand Canyon, Arizona. They also utilize the resources of the desert and forest environments on the plateau above and behind this view. Photographer and date unknown.

All readers, please take note: These stories are closely linked to traditional Havasupai beliefs. There is a strong Havasupai preference that these stories be told aloud *only* during the winter months. Some tribal elders have specifically asked that readers honor this request. Thank you.

Profits from the sale of this book will be equally divided between the sovereign Havasupai Nation and the Robert C. Euler Anthropology Scholarship fund at Northern Arizona University, Flagstaff.

CONTENTS

LIST OF MAPS

HAVASUPAI TRIBAL COUNCIL

P.O. Box 10 • Supai, Arizona 86435
(928) 448-2731 ~ Fax (928) 448-2551

June 8, 2009

Frank D. Tikalsky
2488 CR 500
Bayfield, Colorado 81122

Mr. Tikalsky,

The Tribal Council is in receipt of a letter dated May 31, 2009, which requests approval from The Havasupai Tribal Council for publication of stories that you and your colleagues have collected.

During a Special Tribal Council meeting held on June 05, 2009, your request for publication of Havasupai stories has been approved.

If you should required additional information, please feel free to contact my office or the Vice-Chairman at the administration building.

Signed,

For: Don E. Watahomigie,
Tribal Chairman
Havasupai Indian Tribe

Cc: Tribal Council (7)
       File

PREFACE

THE 1918–1921 FIELDWORK OF ANTHROPOLOGISTS LESLIE SPIER and Erna Gunther preserved one of the earliest, most complete translations known of an entire precontact Native American oral tradition. In the early twentieth century, these Columbia University, Franz Boas–trained anthropology graduate students hiked to the bottom of the Grand Canyon to learn about and record living Havasupai culture. In the process, they asked two Havasupai leaders and elders for every story they could remember. These were translated by native speakers and transcribed first by Spier and later by Gunther. Yet for unknown reasons Spier never published the whole collection of forty-eight stories—some of which are duplicates because both elders remembered the same story. Spier passed the manuscript on before he died in 1961 to anthropologist and Havasupai scholar Dr. Robert C. Euler, who before he died entrusted the stories to his friend and colleague, psychologist Dr. Frank Tikalsky. They are a cultural library and a cultural treasure, and reflect an ancient Yuman-language mythological tradition. Following periodic consultations with the tribe over the past five years, the Havasupai Tribal Council gave permission for their publication. It is our great honor to finally be able to restore them in published form to the People (Pai/Pa/Pah) from whom they arose. Some readers may choose to skip the multidisciplinary contextualizing information in this Preface and in Part I and move directly to the stories themselves, found in Part II.

Ninety years have passed since anthropologist Leslie Spier conducted investigations of the Yuman-speaking peoples along the Colorado River and its tributaries. During these nine decades the Havasupai have undergone extensive cultural change and they continue to face multiple challenges, requiring adaptation to their own and to the mainstream culture. Some of their youngest representatives can now move fluidly and confidently between the two cultures and the two languages. But the challenges over the last one hundred years have been enormous. A rapid shift has been made between being a completely self-sufficient, intermittently migratory stone-tool-making community of family-based bands practicing agriculture, gathering, and hunting to being a settled community whose members practice paid work in both outside and tribal economies, the latter based now largely on tourism.

In recent years the tribe has built a modern K–8 educational facility and is teaching the Havasupai language in the school. Yet some elders worry that the young people are losing their native language skills, which, in comparison to those of other southwestern indigenous youth, appear considerable, with over 93 percent of those under twenty speaking Havasupai in 2006. Today no tribal member *has* to speak English in the village, but almost all can. One sees satellite TV and hears reggae and rap music in Havasu Canyon, yet the oral tradition is still carried on as well as it can be, and many of the old songs and stories are still repeated from memory—if not always in the long, detailed versions recorded by researchers between 1918 and 1921. There are several tribal members of various ages who try, in the face of change, to preserve and renew the cultural and linguistic traditions of their people, including songs and dances. We sincerely hope this published collection of what were always considered sacred/religious stories will contribute to that effort.

It has been about thirty years since the Havasupai language was assigned its own alphabet, and the Bible and other texts have been translated into it. Havasupai itself is a subgroup of Yuman, which linguists tell us is one of the oldest language groups in North America. The precontact Havasupai had a thriving oral tradition, as do many preliterate societies. Precontact and preliterate (in the sense of having and writing an alphabet) are coterminous descriptors of all tribes in southwestern U.S. prehistory. The establishment of literacy in the twentieth century had a particularly profound impact on the preservation of the sacred stories of the Havasupai. Simply put, literacy is not always an advantage in the preservation of what is essentially an oral, verbal tradition. Universally, when humans begin to write things down, they slowly stop using their memory in the same way, and cultural information stored only in memory begins over time to fade and become endangered. Some authors have also suggested that the transition to writing may profoundly impact cultural perceptions of the environment and its inhabitants, cultural perceptions of time structures such as past, present, and future, as well as cultural perceptions of shamanic religion and healing.[1] One researcher has suggested that a move from an oral to a written world impacts cultures in more precise ways, such as altering the relative valuation given to the masculine and feminine, arguing that almost all preliterate societies are more egalitarian.[2]

At the beginning of the five-year consultation period, it initially seemed to some tribal members that publication of these stories might in itself be contrary to traditional beliefs. Yuman cultural tradition indicates that these kinds of stories carry power, and that they should only be retold during the winter. Elders knew that if the written form was available, people could potentially tell the stories at any time of year. Yet after manuscripts were made available, it was clear to modern elders that, as much as they had tried to pass on the oral tradition, many of the stories were not being told. No elder can now remember all of these stories, nor in as much detail as when told by Chiefs Manakaja and Sinyella. After much discussion, the tribe decided that publication was more in the interest of traditional cultural preservation than not. The consultation period also made it clear that our original title, *Myths and Tales of the Havasupai*, had more unnecessary western cultural overlays than simply *The Sacred Oral Tradition of the Havasupai*, which thus seemed to us also more accurate. While "myths" and "stories" are also used throughout this text, those words carry more distancing western meanings, whereas these stories emerge from a people for whom they continue to have immediate spiritual, cultural, and emotional impact.

The unique isolation of the Havasupai at the bottom of the Grand Canyon fed Spier's obsession to record what he perceived as a disappearing and endangered culture. It is probable that these 1918–1921 transcriptions reflect the preconquest, prehistoric oral tradition more accurately than stories recorded later in the twentieth century. This may be so because of the extremely limited cultural contacts among Europeans and Havasupai between 1776 and 1918, (discussed in Chapter 3).

If we can judge from Spier's account (1928) as well as Hirst's (2006), our storytellers, the headmen Manakaja and Sinyella, were in their late seventies around 1920. The Spanish had never fully controlled northwest Arizona, and the United States did not begin to achieve control until around 1870, by which time our storytellers would have been at least twenty. By 1918 Sinyella had learned a little English, but neither man learned writing. Thus, the memory of these storytellers was *always* oral. Their memory and recall had not been impacted by literacy, and they had learned the stories before contact.

These stories may also reflect the authentic precontact oral tradition because the community as a whole was never forcibly relocated as were so many other tribes. This caused less disruption to traditional cultural transmission. However, it has been argued that in 1880, when the U.S. government restricted the Havasupai to a small part of their traditional range, Cataract Canyon, reducing access to their traditional winter storytelling environment on the plateau above, this impacted normal cultural oral patterns.[3]

For reasons not stated, Spier and Gunther chose Manakaja and Sinyella as storytellers, probably because they knew the stories best, because of their age, and as part of their tribal leadership role. Spier described them as chiefs, or they could be called headmen or possibly band leaders, each linked to groups of families within the community. Tribal members told Spier that Manakaja was the "big chief," and Sinyella was one of five "lesser chiefs." Because neither man spoke much English, the then much younger Havasupai Mark Hanna, Lillie Burro, Jess Chickapanega, and West Sinyella were chosen as translators. Some had attended the village-based government school, and they spoke English relatively well. This collection of forty-eight stories remains exactly as it was when translated and transcribed in the field, except for some punctuation corrections and more modern and consistent spellings of tribal surnames.

A few of the stories have been published in other forms in other places (e.g., Cushing, 1882; Spier, 1929; Euler and Smithson, 1964, 1994). Yet this is the first time the entire collection of all forty-eight of the earliest remembered traditional stories has been published in its entirety. When one considers the gap in time between the transcription of these stories and their full publication, most readers will of course ask, "Why so long?" There is no simple answer; all we can do is share what we know.

Spier and Gunther were the first anthropologists to conduct serious, extensive ethnographic studies of the Havasupai (although Cushing's 1882 account, *The Nation of the Willows*, is extremely important). Both were graduate students of Franz Boas at Columbia University, as Euler was later Spier's graduate student at the University of New Mexico. Before his death in 1961, Spier asked his colleague, friend, and former student Robert Euler to assume responsibility for publishing these Havasupai stories. Spier probably thought Euler was a good choice for monitoring the publication process, since the focus of his dissertation was on the nearby rim-dwelling colingual Hualapai, among whom he had worked since the 1950s. By 1961, when Spier died, Euler had also analyzed many prehistoric archaeological sites near Havasu Canyon, in Glen Canyon (prior to its flooding in 1963), along the Little Colorado River, and had begun his major life work of surveying and recording hundreds of sites within the Grand Canyon.

In addition, Spier may have selected Euler as the anthropological guardian and caretaker of these manuscripts because the Havasupai themselves had selected Euler as their anthropological advisor and expert witness to assist them in their federal land claims case. Euler was recommended for the land claims task by Florence Ellis (a distinguished anthropologist and colleague of Leslie Spier). In the late 1950s and early 1960s Euler worked closely with Havasupai tribal officials and their legal representatives. In the course of that work, he and Lee Marshall, the Havasupai tribal chairman, met with U.S. Congressional committee members who were considering the validity of the Havasupai land claims.[4] Euler's research and findings were crucial in the final determination in the Indian Land Claims case, which permanently acknowledged an aboriginal Havasupai claim to more than 2.25 million acres, and in 1969 resulted in a trust-fund compensatory "payment" to the tribe of 55 cents an acre or $1.24 million. Twenty-five percent went to individuals, with $651.37 eventually distributed to each of 425 adult members in 1973. In addition to the land claims settlement, *indeed in spite of it*, the Havasupai leadership continued to press for the return of as much of their ancestral plateau territory as possible. After many battles, and despite the initial opposition of the Sierra Club, they did actually win back free use of 251,000 acres in the Grand Canyon Enlargement Act of 1975, one of the largest tribal land returns in U.S. history.[5] The determination of Chairman Lee Marshall was crucial in this process.

Aside from the fact that Euler was a former graduate student of Spier's at the University of New Mexico and deeply involved in scholarly research on the prehistory of Colorado River peoples, it is important to emphasize that the theoretical anthropological views of Spier and Euler were also congruent, and this probably also influenced Spier's decision. Basehart and Hill comment:

> The conception of scientific method fostered by Boas and Spier stressed rigorous empiricism, induction, objectivity, and extreme caution in the interpretation. In this conception, theory was equated with an anthropological stance that conspicuously failed to exhibit these necessary characteristics of method; . . . to Boas and Spier [theory] had made the field a secure refuge for all varieties of speculation buttressed by anthropological fact in the service of preconceived notions. The corrective for adventitious formulations consisted in first hand, disinterested inquiry yielding an accumulation of carefully attested facts. There was no pressing need for broad generalizations from these data; while in principle the possibility of developing laws of culture was not denied, the mandate was to gather data. Eventually, comparative studies might unveil uniformities in culture processes and growth.[6]

Boas favored rigorous empiricism, induction, objectivity, and caution in interpretation, as did Spier as well as Euler.[7] Thus, since Spier offered no theoretical interpretation of the stories he and Gunther collected, and out of deference to his theoretical position, we, too, have tried to refrain from theoretical speculation on these specific texts. We have, however, included an introduction to the scientific study of myth for readers who want to pursue this (Chapter 4).

In the middle 1960s Robert Euler and Frank Tikalsky began several decades of discussions about Grand Canyon human history generally and the Havasupai in particular. Tikalsky, a psychologist, assisted Euler in doing interviews with the Havasupai, focusing on their beliefs and views related to traditional land use. Tikalsky and Lee Marshall met on several occasions to discuss these topics. Ultimately, at Marshall's suggestion, Tikalsky and Euler explored the Hopi-Havasupai trail, examining material cultural elements that, in some instances, could be related to the stories collected by Spier.

The editors have come to the project in different ways. In the late 1960s psychiatrist John Nagel joined Euler and Tikalsky in discussions concerning the Havasupai and personality and culture theory. These discussions led to an examination of the Havasupai stories left to Euler by Spier. In the late 1960s Euler's wife, Elizabeth Magee Euler, with the assistance of native translators and family members, spent three summers recording the memories of the oldest Havasupai, Hualapai, and Yavapai then living. Those recordings, collected from 1968–1970, remain in the archives of the Museum of Anthropology at the University of Arizona in Tucson.[8] As a child, Catherine Euler lived in Supai village for two of those summers, partly listening to the elders, but mostly playing in the canyon with Havasupai children. She was asked to join the project in 2003 to help honor her father and because of her history, editing, and consulting skills. As a group, the editors decided to refrain from taking any royalties for their work, instead dedicating half of these to the Robert C. Euler Anthropology Graduate Scholarship fund at Northern Arizona University, and half to the Havasupai Tribe.

We do not know why Robert Euler did not publish these tales in their entirety between Spier's death in 1961 until his own in early 2002, despite Spier asking him to do so. Perhaps Euler held back because Carma Lee Smithson, an anthropologist at the University of Utah, had already since 1958 been working on Havasupai mythology and religion. She also died in 1961. Euler then worked to publish her notes along with his brief field research, in the volume *Havasupai Legends*.[9] In comparison with the sometimes disjointed accounts in Smithson's collection of stories from 1958, the earlier Spier-Gunther stories of 1918–1921 seem both more comprehensive and more comprehensible. The earlier versions are far more detailed, and the story lines far more complete. This is probably because the earlier narrators grew up in a precontact time when memory was the only means of communicating cultural knowledge. Unfortunately the time gap between Spier's field collection and their current publication has resulted in at least one doctoral thesis based on the incomplete evidence of the Smithson and Euler (1964 and 1994) editions, which only contained brief references to what Morris (1974) called the Monster Slayer cycle, leading him to conclude, possibly erroneously, that this myth element came *from* Athabascan influences. In fact, it appears prominently in Havasupai myth as well, appears to predate the joint Yavapai–Apache San Carlos imprisonment, and probably predates Athabascan migration into the Southwest. Certainly the Monster Slayer cycle exists in similar forms in the myths of other Yuman-speaking peoples in southern Arizona, California, and northern Mexico. Hero twins who avenge their father and slay a large monstrous bird also appear in the Mayan *Popul Vuh*. It is possible that this part of the myth cycle was rather more likely to have been a cultural transmission from this group of Pai *to* their Athabascan relatives.[10] Or, if his brief discussion of Canadian Athabascan myths is correct, Morris's evidence could also possibly point to a pre–North American origin of the Monster Slayer cycle.[11] Speaking very generally, the Yuman/Pai myth style seems as different from the Athabascan myth style as each of them is from Hopi/Uto-Aztecan myth styles, but further comparative work needs to be done.[12] It is not surprising that the three main language groups in Arizona have produced different cultural and conceptual approaches to creation stories.

In January 2002 Robert C. Euler died in Prescott, Arizona. This left the editors with the problem of deciding in what manner and format the Spier manuscript should be published. In discussions several years before his death, Euler explained his ideas about how various anthropological theories might be applied to the study of myth. Those who knew Dr. Euler well would tell you that he considered such seminar-style discussions the essence of his teaching/research model. The editors of this work feel a deep obligation to honor the Boasian-Spier-Euler methodological approach. In a brief but remarkable paper, Gladys A. Reichard describes the position taken by Boas concerning anthropological theory. She notes, "Boas frequently said when students expressed the notion that they (or others) 'ought to be theoretical,' you don't just have theories, your materials furnish your theories."[13] This approach is echoed in his student Leslie Spier and, in turn, Spier's student Robert C. Euler.[14] In our view, this approach to theory is the fundamental reason Spier asked Euler to ensure the full publication of the Havasupai stories. They are the data, they are the cultural library, and Spier, Euler, and Tikalsky have been very protective of this manuscript for good reason. Although we have tried to refrain from superimposing our own theoretical interpretations of these cultural materials, we are fully aware that others will do so. That is what we expect in the scientific tradition.

Thus, what have we included in this work?

In Part I we have provided a multidisciplinary context for the stories, which appear in Part II. There is first Robert C. Euler's article on the overall cultural prehistory of the Grand Canyon, followed by Douglas Schwartz's more narrow focus on the cultural life of the Havasupai. Schwartz was asked to contribute to honor the scholarly discussions he and Euler had over the years. This is followed by an overview of Havasupai history, leadership, and language by Robert Euler's daughter, historian Catherine Euler. We end with a chapter introducing interested readers to the scientific thought on sacred story and mythology by psychologist Frank Tikalsky and psychiatrist John Nagel. The bibliography comprises all sources consulted by all the authors for these chapters, and we have included brief biographies of the contributors, including narrators Manakaja and Sinyella.

In Part II we have published Spier's brief introduction, and then the translated and transcribed stories in their entirety as told by the Havasupai elders and headmen Manakaja and Sinyella between 1918 and 1921. The stories themselves have not been changed since the moment they were spoken from oral memory, except to the degree that translation into a nonnative language changes meaning. We present the entire Spier manuscript as it was prepared for publication, sans editing save for correcting errors in punctuation, spelling, and grammar. Some stories appear to be repeated, because this repetition is common in oral cultures, and also because Spier wanted to hear the same story from two different men. Each was also asked for stories at different times. This is a scientific anthropological research method that seeks to achieve the greatest accuracy and cross-check possible during the collection of cultural data. Many stories have overlapping elements, but this is faithful to the way they were told by Sinyella and Manakaja. While we regret the potential petrification of a live oral tradition that accompanies its committal to paper, we and most current Havasupai elders think it is the best way to ensure its preservation in the modern world. Because a living indigenous culture still exists among the Havasupai, we know this publication by no means precludes the emergence of new versions, new stories, and new songs in the future.

Lastly, for those unfamiliar with the Yuman peoples in general and the Havasupai in particular, we suggest some reading. An excellent general introduction to Yuman peoples is Edward H. Spicer's "Yumans" in Chapter 10 of *Cycles of Conquest* (1962). John Martin's article, "The Prehistory and Ethnohistory of Havasupai-Hualapai Relations" (1985) and his "The Havasupai," in *Plateau* 56, no. 4 (1986), are excellent and scholarly introductions, as is Stephen Hirst's very important 1976 classic, *Life in a Narrow Place*, republished with modern additions in 2006 as *I Am the Grand Canyon: The Story of the Havasupai People*, told as much as possible from the tribal viewpoint. We also recommend the moving and elegant work by Hinton and Watahomigie, *Spirit Mountain* (1984); the factual and easily read volume by Dobyns and Euler, *The Havasupai People* (1971); as well as Laird's classic examination of another Colorado River culture, *The Chemehuevis* (1976). Useful comparisons can also be made between these stories and those published in Spier's *Yuman Tribes of the Gila River* (1933), and Kroeber's *Yuman Tribes of the Lower Colorado* (1920), which contain some similar myth elements and similar names for the twin hero-creators.

To those who are beginning their study of indigenous oral tradition, we trust this is a good introduction. To experts focusing on Yuman or Havasupai ethnology or linguistics, we hope the Spier materials provide some insight. To the Havasupai committed to preserving their cultural traditions and tribal integrity for those generations yet unborn, we hope this publication helps to do that, and we support future publication of an edition of the stories translated back into Havasupai. According to experts in American Indian language education programs, teaching native language oral traditional stories within the tribal school curriculum is critical to preservation efforts.[15]

In closing, we express our deepest thanks to our departed friend, scholar, and father, Robert Euler, who said of the sacred oral tradition of the Havasupai, "There is something important here—something that demands our attention and reflection."

Frank D. Tikalsky, Catherine A. Euler, and John Nagel
Editors

| NOTES |

1. Ong, 1982; Abram, 1996.
2. Shlain, 1998.
3. Hirst, 2006; Dobyns and Euler, 1971.
4. Manners, 1974. The contributions of Henry Dobyns, Robert C. Euler, and Robert A. Manners to the Indian Claims Commission are summarized in this work. The most thorough treatment of the tribe's history of land reassignment will be found in Steven Hirst's *I Am the Grand Canyon*, 2006.
5. Hirst, 2006: 198–200, 228–37; Jacoby, 2001: Ch. 7.
6. Basehart and Hill, 1965.
7. Perhaps one of the best examples of Spier's position is to be found in his paper, "Historical Interrelation of Culture Traits: Franz Boas' study of Tsimshian Mythology." (See S. A. Rice, ed., *Methods in Social Science*, pp. 449–57.)
8. This research, funded by the Doris Duke Foundation, supervised by Robert C. Euler, and collected by Elizabeth M. Euler, remains in the form of taped recordings in the archives of the Museum of Anthropology, University of Arizona, Tucson.
9. Smithson and Euler, 1964 (1994).
10. Clyde Morris, 1974: 12.
11. Morris, 1974: 71–72.
12. Frank Waters, 1963; Paul Zolbrod, 1984.
13. Gladys A. Reichard, 1943.
14. Franz Boas, Gladys Reichard, Leslie Spier, Pliny Goddard, Elsie Clews Parsons, Erna Gunther, Alfred Kroeber and Edward Sapir were all members of the famous 1920s Columbia University/Museum of Natural History Tuesday "lunchers" who met each week to discuss past and future fieldwork and publications ideas (Parezo, 1993: 223, quoting Goldfrank, 1978: 17).
15. Gloria Bock Muñiz, 2007.

ACKNOWLEDGMENTS

The editors and contributors to this volume sincerely thank all those whose efforts have made this publication possible:

We are grateful for the invaluable research and writings of all previous researchers in this field, including Stephen Hirst, Al Whiting, John Martin, Leanne Hinton, and Lucille J. Watahomigie.

Particular editorial thanks are also due to Basin Printing, Jane Kepp, June el-Piper, Stephen Hirst, Anne Scott, Ivan Strenski, Matthew Putesoy, and Rosemary Thompson.

For many manuscript revisions and other endless secretarial services, we are in Linda Tikalsky's debt.

And finally, we could not have finished this task without the encouragement and advice of George Gumerman, Wolf Gumerman, and Thomas Euler.

| PART I |

Contexts

Anthropology, History, and Myth Theory

Chapter 1

The Prehistory of the Grand Canyon

| ROBERT C. EULER |

NEVER UNDERESTIMATE THE IMPORTANCE OF AN ARTIFACT, even one made of so humble a parentage as the willow tree. If it were not for split-willow figurines found in the Grand Canyon in 1933, and later companion findings, we might not know that human beings visited the canyon floor some two thousand years before Christ was born. Though we don't know much more than that about these pre-historic American Indians—there's a limit to how much we can read from a willow twig wound around itself—we can say with reasonable certainty that they were familiar with the depths of the Grand Canyon almost four thousand years before John Wesley Powell floated the first scientific expedition down the Colorado River in 1869.

They were hunters and gatherers, these American Indians, and lived in what archaeologists call an Archaic period. This much we can safely surmise. They came from the Desert West. They deposited their artfully constructed split-willow animal figures in limestone caves, probably as a form of imitative magic ritually depicting the animals they wished to hunt. Recently archaeologists located an almost inac-cessible cave in the canyon that contained figurines surrounded by cairns of rock—probably a shrine.

A few years ago, in excavations at prehistoric sites along the Colorado River, archaeologist Anne Trinkle Jones of the National Park Service uncovered campsites of people who lived in the canyon somewhat later than those who made the figurines. The Archaic levels of these shelters date from between 1135 and 85 BC. These people probably lived in those shallow caves and hunted deer, bighorn sheep, and other animals with spears. At certain seasons they also gathered edible wild plants. Domestic crops were probably unknown to them, as were the bow and arrow.

Researchers also recently discovered an Archaic site apparently unique to the Grand Canyon. This is a series of pictographs—paintings on the rock wall of a cave—probably related to similar examples of a religious nature farther north, in Utah. While archaeologists have not precisely dated this site, the style of painting indicates it was done sometime between 2000 BC and AD 1.

These newly discovered Archaic sites, together with the split-twig figurines such as those found in Stanton's Cave in Marble Canyon and the earlier discovery of Archaic Pinto-style spear points on Red Butte, near the South Rim of the Grand Canyon, point to a widespread use of the gorge by American Indians before the time of Christ. It is not presently possible to use archaeological data to relate these people to any of the later occupants of the Grand Canyon, at least not with any degree of reliability. They disappeared into the mists of prehistory. Where they went and why, we do not know.

But all the same, these early people contributed immeasurably to our knowledge of the Grand Canyon. Because they left those small artifacts and paintings, we know they existed, and it makes a difference of some 2,500 years in our chronicling of human use of the canyon as a living environment. Before the figurines were found, archaeologists had dated the first habitation of the canyon to about AD 500 with the advent of the Anasazi or Pueblo Indians, a people much more culturally complex than their Archaic precursors.

The Anasazi, thought to be direct ancestors of the present-day Hopi of northern Arizona, probably began as a Desert Culture people in the Great Basin.[1] Sometime around the year AD 1 or slightly earlier, they moved into the northern portion of the Southwest. Archaeologists refer to this period in their culture as that of the "Basketmaker," for rather obvious reasons. Using rudimentary techniques, these hunters and gatherers added corn and squash to their agricultural capability and hunted deer, bighorn sheep, and rabbits.

The Basketmaker style of life changed in several ways around AD 500. They developed new varieties of corn and planted beans. By grouping circular pit houses they began village life. They manufactured fired pottery and supplemented spear-throwing with the use of bow and arrow to kill game.

This stable economic base, combining hunting and gathering with the beginnings of diversification of crops, allowed the Anasazi to intensify and expand their territory and cultural achievements. After learning to grow cotton, they added spinning and loom weaving to their repertoire, weaving fabric clothing and adding objects of personal adornment. They learned to make exquisite pottery. Thus, midway through the eleventh century AD, Pueblo culture flowered into its classical traditions. This period, continuing into historic times, saw the rise of great communal pueblos in the Southwest, up to five stories high. These high-rise apartment dwellings housed several hundred people, and community living must have become highly organized. Evidence indicates that authority centered on a theocratic hierarchy of priests.

The Anasazi of the Grand Canyon lived on the fringe of this great cultural florescence. Some evidence indicates that they made sporadic forays into the canyon beginning about AD 500 or slightly earlier. By the middle of the eleventh century, however, they apparently found climatic conditions there to their liking, and between about AD 1050 and 1150, hundreds of sites were occupied in myriad recesses of the canyon and on both the North and South rims.

These were mostly small, one- to ten-room surface masonry houses with associated storage rooms, agave roasting pits, and occasional subterranean religious structures—kivas—in front of the pueblo. While we know the Anasazi grew domestic crops near their dwellings, new evidence from a small village occupied between AD 1049 and 1064 in the Coconino Basin near the South Rim suggests that corn, beans, and squash were not all-important in the Anasazi diet. This village had burned catastrophically, and normally perishable foods had turned to charcoal and were preserved. The evidence from this site indicates that its inhabitants focused on the exploitation and use of piñon nuts and other wild seeds rather than on farming.

About the time the Anasazi were beginning to explore the Grand Canyon, the Cohonina, another group of American Indians from west-central Arizona, were settling along the South Rim and in Havasu Canyon. The Cohonina achieved a veneer of Pueblo culture by imitating the pottery of the Anasazi and attempting to build similar masonry houses. They farmed essentially the same crops and of course hunted the same game, though to a lesser extent. Their social and religious life probably differed considerably from that of the Anasazi.

Sometime about AD 1150 both the Anasazi and the Cohonina abandoned their masonry settlements in and around the Grand Canyon. Though the Cohonina disappeared from the archaeological record, the Anasazi consolidated their numbers along more reliable watercourses—the Little Colorado, Rio Grande, and (usually) infallible springs of the Hopi country. For more than a century and a half the canyon remained completely uninhabited by human beings.

Then, about AD 1300, the Cerbat people, direct ancestors of the Walapai and Havasupai, moved from the southern deserts near the lower Colorado River to the high plateaus that had been the Cohonina and Anasazi homeland south of the Grand Canyon. The Cerbat lived in rock shelters and impermanent brush wickiups. Though hunting and gathering were their economic mainstay, they were incipient farmers who planted their crops near permanent springs. Although their material culture was simple, they established a stable way of life until the 1880s, when the U.S. Army forcibly restricted them to their reservations.

At nearly the same time as the Cerbat, another seminomadic people approached the Grand Canyon from the northwest horizon. Ancestors of the Southern Paiute, they settled along the North Rim of the Canyon and carried on an existence not too different from their South Rim neighbors, the Cerbat. They, too, remained in this aboriginal territory until Anglo-Americans established reservations for them in the late nineteenth century.

It was these native peoples—the Pueblos, Cohoninas, Havasupai, Walapai, and the Southern Paiute—who form the indigenous history of the Grand Canyon. Present-day visitors to the Grand Canyon may wonder how these early people could have survived the harsh summer environment of the canyon depths—and why they chose to try in the first place. Spectacular though the canyon is, they did not live there for aesthetic reasons. The choice was a matter of survival, and they survived because they adapted their culture to fit their natural environment.

Pueblo occupation of the canyon was apparently in large part seasonal due to the varying nature of food supplies from the Inner Gorge to the rims and due to the warmer winter climate in the lower elevations. In the summer, many people moved to the rims to farm. Indeed, one of the most significant agricultural communities of the twelfth-century Anasazi was located on the plateau near the canyon's rim, where in addition to farming, deer hunting and an abundance of edible wild plants contributed to their well-balanced economy.

But below the rims, they also hunted bighorn sheep and rabbits. Below the rims they could feast on the fruits of cactus, the beans of the mesquite, and the tender crowns of the agave plant. More importantly, at three thousand feet below the rims, they found long, almost frost-free growing seasons for their gardens. Sufficient water supply made it possible for them to farm in the recesses of side canyons where they discovered many springs.

Throughout many of these tributary canyons as well as on the rims, especially in the eastern portion of the Grand Canyon, we find Pueblo masonry ruins in association with low, agricultural check dams—abundant evidence that these farmers practiced erosion control and other conservation methods. There is a strong correlation between location of prehistoric habitation sites and access routes into the Canyon where its sheer walls have broken down, clear indications that the inhabitants moved with relative ease from rim to rim and throughout the canyon. Archaeologists now know more than one hundred routes used by canyon dwellers to gain access.

Environmentally, then, the canyon provided excellent resources to sustain Pueblo life, and they apparently made intelligent use of those resources. So why did they and their Cohonina neighbors leave the canyon? Archeologists once believed that their disappearance coincided with the advent of the Cerbat on plateaus along the South Rim and the coming of the forerunners of the Southern Paiute to the high, forested lands near the North Rim. Now evidence indicates that, at least in the Grand Canyon, the pre-1150 and post-1300 residents missed each other by more than a century. Certainly nothing indicates that the Cerbat, the ancestors of the Pai (as the combined Walapai and Havasupai once termed themselves), or the Southern Paiute forced the Anasazi and Cohonina abandonment.

Recently, teams of scientists including archaeologists, botanists, and geologists have made detailed studies of past climates around the Grand Canyon. Early in the twelfth century, there were many years of increasingly severe drought. By AD 1150 most of the Cohonina and Anasazi farmers could no longer cope with these deteriorating environmental conditions in an agriculturally marginal area; thus, they abandoned the canyon for more favorable climes.

When conditions improved in the fourteenth century, the Pai spread over the southern plateau and penetrated much of the western and central part of the canyon. They soon reached their maximum range and occupied all of the southern portion of the Grand Canyon and its plateau east to the Little Colorado River. Here they hunted, gathered, and farmed near permanent streams and springs. The habitation sites discovered within the canyon consist of rock shelters having floors strewn with cultural debris including reddish-brown potsherds, flat-slab milling stones, and arrow points, all differing from those of the Cohonina or the Anasazi.

The Southern Paiute maintained a similar existence on the North Rim uplands and in their tributary canyons from the fourteenth century on. Their finger-incised brown pottery, milling stones, and arrow points differed somewhat from those of the Pai, but they also occupied rock shelters and roasted agave in stone-ringed pits. That they sometimes camped in abandoned Pueblo ruins is evident from discovery of their pottery mixed with that of the Anasazi around masonry structures.

Both the Pai and the Paiute cultures were stable and long-lived. From about 1300 until the latter part of the nineteenth century, they continued to use the natural resources of the Grand Canyon. Both groups maintained amicable trade relations with the Puebloans in the present Hopi country, as evidenced by fragments of Pueblo ceramics found on many Havasupai, Walapai, and Southern Paiute ruins in the Grand Canyon. This yellow pottery, exquisitely decorated with designs in brownish-black paint similar to the Hopi ceramics of today, was probably traded for deerskins, red paint, and agave. From 1300 to relatively recently, the Hopi seem to have periodically returned to ceremoniously collect salt from a natural deposit near the confluence of the Little Colorado and Colorado rivers.

Though archaeologists need to learn much more, our existing data suggest a fairly coherent history of canyon habitation for more than four thousand years. Because of the rich legacy of artifacts left us by the Anasazi and, to a lesser degree, by the Cohonina, Pai, and Paiute, we can deduce what they were like and can somewhat envision their lifestyles. The same is not true of the canyon's original inhabitants, the split-willow artists and other Archaic peoples who sat in those limestone caves so long ago.

But why be pessimistic? The willow-twig artifacts waited more than three thousand years to be discovered and then had to wait another decade before radiocarbon dating established their age. And some of these twig animals were found still standing upright in the dust of canyon caves.

Never underestimate the patience of an artifact![2]

| NOTES |

1. Ed.: Recent theorists have also begun to marshal evidence for a southern migration from Mexico. See, for example, R. G. Matson, "The Spread of Maize to the Colorado Plateau," *Archaeology Southwest* 13 (1999): 10–11.

2. This chapter has been adapted from Euler and Tikalsky, *Grand Canyon: Intimate Views* (1982). There is a small group of anthropologists (notably, T. J. Ferguson and E. Richard Hart—paid consultants to the Zuni) who claim that the Zuni regard the Grand Canyon as the Zuni location of origin. The foundation of their claim is presented in Ferguson and Hart, *A Zuni Atlas* (Norman: University of Oklahoma Press, 1985), 51. Robert C. Euler and most southwestern anthropologists familiar with the prehistory of the Grand Canyon reject this claim. See, for example, Robert C. Euler, "The Grand Canyon Anasazi, Their Descendants and Other Claimants," paper prepared for the Anasazi Cultural Affiliation Workshop, Fort Lewis College, Durango, CO, February 20–21, 1998; The National Research Council, *River Management in the Grand Canyon* (Washington, D.C.: National Academy Press, 1996), p. 157. Similarly, early southwestern anthropologists regarded as experts on Zuni make no reference to Zuni claims to a Grand Canyon origin. See Ruth Bunzel, "Zuni Origin Myths," *Forty-Seventh Annual Report of the Bureau of American Ethnology*, 1929–1930 (Washington, D.C.: GPO, 1932), 547; Frank Hamilton Cushing, "Myths," *Thirteenth Annual Report of the Bureau of Ethnology*, 1891–1892 (Washington, D.C.: GPO, 1896), 375.

Chapter 2

The Changing Life of the Havasupai

| DOUGLAS W. SCHWARTZ |

A DESERT OASIS IS GREEN, FERTILE, AND WELL WATERED.
This perfectly describes the astonishing village of the Havasupai
people who live hidden and isolated three thousand feet below the
Colorado Plateau, in a side valley of the Grand Canyon. To reach this
haven, one must travel off the main road and across a piñon-juniper
forest to the head of one of only two trails into Havasu Canyon. From
there, one goes by foot or horseback down a dry, rocky, treeless, pre-
cipitous, ancient route. After what can seem an endless passage, one
emerges into a ribbon of brilliant green fed by a clear, cool stream that
cuts through this narrow, red canyon home of the Havasupai.

The stream that creates this refuge emanates from springs that
bubble out of the ground above the village. It gives the Havasupai
their name, "people of the blue green water." The clear water feeds
banks of lush vegetation—huge cottonwoods and thick stands of
willows. Havasu Creek also feeds irrigation canals that water fields
of corn, beans, and squash, traditionally the essential crops of the
Havasupais' summer way of life.

The segment of Havasu Canyon where Supai, the Havasupai village, sits is three miles long and, in places, only a quarter of a mile
wide. Below Supai, Havasu Creek tumbles down a series of mag-
nificent falls as it knifes its way through the narrow lower Havasu
Canyon, beyond which its bluish waters, flowing through an even
narrower, steep-sided canyon, mix with those of the Colorado River.

Positioned far below the rim of the Colorado Plateau, the village was originally only the summer home of the Havasupai. In the winter they lived on the plateau in a territory of some ninety by seventy-five miles covered in stands of pine and grassy meadows. It was there, during the cooler months of the year, that the Havasupai hunted and gathered to supplement their fall agricultural harvests.

The Havasupai divided their traditional life between farming in the canyon during the summer and foraging widely over their plateau territory during the rest of the year. In the early spring, family groups, who had been scattered across the plateau during the winter, moved back into the canyon. They cleared the debris from the previous year's garden plots and prepared the two hundred or so acres suitable for planting. They repaired the irrigation ditches and constructed low dams of earth and brush to divert water from the creek onto the fields.

In mid-April they planted, using juniper digging sticks and other simple tools. In addition to corn, beans, and squash, the Havasupai grew domestic sunflowers, gourds, and cotton. After planting the first corn kernel of the season, a farmer chewed another and then blew it toward two white marks on the canyon wall that symbolized the ancestral ears of corn presented to the Havasupai by their legendary twin culture heroes (see stories 1–3). After planting, farmers irrigated the corn a few times while some people returned to the plateau to hunt game and collect fresh greens. Those who stayed in the canyon cared for the growing crops and protected them from rodents and birds by setting traps near the fields or tethering pet hawks or dogs nearby. The periodic watering and weeding of the fields continued, and as the canyon crops matured and water on the plateau became less available in the heat of summer, the Havasupai remained for longer times near their fields, living in dome-shaped brush huts or in rock shelters overlooking the valley.

Crops began maturing in June and could be harvested through the early fall, when all the crops and many of the wild plant foods were picked and dried for storage. Farmers stored seeds for the next growing season in rock and mud granaries built into the cliffs, out of reach of predators and the damaging floods that occasionally roared through the canyon during violent summer rainstorms. In August, the Havasupai invited neighboring Hopi people from the east and Walapai from the west to Havasu Canyon for one of their few community-wide ceremonies—the harvest festival, when they feasted, gambled, and traded. Following the feast, they held a Circle Dance in which everyone joined hands, faced the center of the circle, and moved in short, sideways steps, expressing and reinforcing their group solidarity.

By the middle of October, with agricultural work completed, families returned to the plateau and to their scattered, semipermanent camps, from which they would once again range across the plateau and into the canyon. During the late fall, they gathered piñon nuts and the seeds, nuts, and fruits of catclaw, amaranth, shepherd's purse, goosefoot, tansy mustard, barrel cactus, prickly pear and other cacti, wild sunflower, mescal, mesquite, and wild grape. The women, who did most of the gathering, knocked or pulled the seeds from the plants and put them in small collecting baskets, later transferring them to large, conical carrying baskets that they backpacked to their camps. The seeds not eaten immediately were dried, toasted, and perhaps ground for storage. People frequently baked food in pits dug into the ground, with a fire built on top. Before they were eaten, grains, grasses, cacti, and small game animals were also parched and boiled.

As winter approached, each family moved to its traditional camping area on the plateau and built conical huts covered with brush and earth. The men used bows and arrows for hunting, their primary means of obtaining food at this time of year. Their best bows were made of ash, backed with sinew to make them stronger. Arrows were crafted of serviceberry or another hardwood, tipped with small stone arrowheads, and feathered from specially raised birds, particularly ferruginous and rough-legged hawks. Hunters carried their arrows in skin quivers slung over their shoulders.

The Havasupai hunted pronghorn antelope, bighorn sheep, and mule deer, as well as smaller game such as rabbits, turkeys, bobcats, porcupines, quail, doves, and small rodents. Because they had few techniques for easily preserving meat (other than salting and drying), they usually ate their kill shortly after the hunt. Small parties went out frequently to keep the camps provided with fresh meat.

The basic Havasupai social group and economic unit was the family. After temporarily living near the wife's relatives, a young couple moved and lived near the husband's close relatives. The family group consisted of husband and wife, their unmarried children, and their married sons with their families. Polygamy was permissible. Women cared for the children, cooked, and heated the hut with wood they collected in the forest. Occasionally they made trips back to the canyon to retrieve stored food from the granaries. As the long, cold winter of the plateau ended, the yearly cycle began again, and the Havasupai moved back to the canyon to clear the fields in preparation for another season of planting.

Most of their clothing was made of skins. Men wore a shirt, a breechcloth, leggings, moccasins, and a headband. Women wore a short under-apron, a long buckskin dress, moccasins, and, during cold weather, a rabbit-skin blanket. All buckskin clothing was made by the men. The Havasupai wore no elaborate ornaments except, occasionally, necklaces, earrings, and face paint.

The Havasupai cycle of life primarily involved rituals at birth, menstruation, hunting, planting, and death. Infants' faces were often painted with red ochre, and at about two weeks of age they were tightly bound on a cradleboard, where they spent most of their first year. Young children, who played freely around the camps, gradually assumed responsibility for daily chores. Only girls underwent puberty ceremonies, when menstruation started; they received a special buckskin dress, stained red with powdered ocher. For four days the girl spent most of her time on a bed of sand spread over heated rocks. At sunrise, she would run toward the east to ensure that she would always perform her work quickly and untiringly.

Religion emphasized shamanic rites having to do with healing, weather, and hunting. Shamans inherited their powers from a former shaman. His spirit, which used the shaman as its medium, came to the new shaman in a dream, when he also learned the songs he would use in his rituals. The Havasupai believed that the language of shamanic spirits was unintelligible to all human beings except medicine men, babies, and dying people. After death, bodies were cremated, as was most personal property, including houses and all or part of the deceased's crops. The Havasupai shifted from cremation to burial in the late nineteenth century. People believed that the soul left the body during dreams, and at death it traveled to the land of the dead in the sky. Some souls, however, remained behind as ghosts and caused illness and death. Sweat baths were and still are popular, particularly among men. Curing songs, sung in the small, domed, wood-and-dirt sweat lodges, helped to solidify the bond between humans and the spiritual powers of the universe.

The Havasupai traded mainly with the Hopi and Walapai, exchanging buckskins, foodstuffs, and baskets for cotton goods, pottery, and jewelry. Beginning in the seventeenth century, the Havasupai obtained European trade goods through the Hopi. Foreign items gradually became more available with the expansion of the American frontier. The Havasupai were largely protected from the frontier wars by the isolation of their canyon village, and they were among the last southwestern Native American groups to be affected by the encroachment of Western culture. By the middle of the nineteenth century, however, cattlemen had begun seizing their plateau territory, which forced them to concentrate their activities more in the canyon. By the middle of the twentieth century, they were restricted to a five-hundred-acre reservation within the canyon. With the loss of a major part of their upland foraging grounds (some of which were later returned), the Havasupais' life changed radically. Many of their important campsites, such as those around Dripping Spring (below Hermit's Rest), where for centuries their ancestors had hunted and gathered, were now off limits. Much of their old way of life, like that of so many other Native Americans, was gone.

Although great changes have taken place among the Havasupai, they continue to see the positive elements in their life. There is still no automobile road to Supai, nor does the tribe—recognizing the value of its relative isolation from the outside world—ever want to have one. So horses and the ancient trails into the canyon remain extremely important to them, as horses have been since they were first introduced by the Spaniards. Horses and helicopters pack in the mail, supplies, and even some of the healthy flow of tourists who come to see the beauty of the canyon.

The Havasupai continue to hunt and gather in some of their old lands, mostly on weekends, although now they reach these places in pickup trucks that they park at the canyon trailheads. Hunting was made much more gainful in the late 1970s when the federal government agreed to expand the reservation by restoring free use of 251,000 acres of the Havasupais' original territory, including their lower canyon waterfalls and much of their traditional wintering grounds. This was the largest Native American land return in United States history.

Although much of the Havasupais' life has changed over the past few centuries, their isolation, the beauty of their canyon home, and their success in recovering rights to their original lands have allowed them better fortune than many other Native Americans. Yet for any group of people, the past is irretrievable. This is reflected in the Havasupai stories that make up this volume, expressing their feelings about their origin, their past, each other, and their traditional way of life. *Farewell Song*, for example, recorded by the linguist Leanne Hinton, evokes the feelings of an old man who has spent his life wandering over the plateau and canyon but is now too old to travel. Although the song was not intended as an anthem to a traditional way of living, it does carry a sense of the changes that have overtaken the Havasupai and their oasis near the bottom of the Grand Canyon.

Farewell Song

Dripping Spring
Land I used to roam,
That place,
Listen to what I say,
Don't mourn for me.
I thought I would be alive forever
I thought I would roam forever,
But here I am
I can't continue on,
Now I am too weak.

Chapter 3

History, Leadership, and Language

| CATHERINE A. EULER |

ALTHOUGH SPANISH EXPLORERS IN THE HOPI COUNTRY
probably heard about Indians living in the Grand Canyon as early as
1540 or perhaps 1665, it was not until 1776 that the first European
visited the Havasupai village and wrote about his experiences. In his
journal, Father Garces, a Spanish Franciscan priest, describes how
he went "trembling" down the wooden ladder that then formed part
of the trail.[1] Only a few Europeans visited the Havasupai down in
the canyon between then and when Leslie Spier arrived, just over a
hundred years later, in 1918, when he struggled to describe the leadership styles of his main sources of cultural information, the headmen Manakaja and Sinyella. They narrated these forty-eight stories
in Havasupai with interspersed songs, main characters, and words
similar to those known by Yuman-speaking peoples throughout the
Southwest.

The Yuman-speaking Havasupai and Walapai, aboriginally located in the northwestern quadrant of what was later known as
Arizona, are two of what were originally thirteen subtribes of what
have collectively been called the Pai or the Northeastern Pai. Together
with the completely separate but nearly colingual Yavapai tribe, these
two groups are sometimes called Upland Pai.[2] The first European state
to claim sovereignty over aboriginal Pai territory was Spain; then,
after independence, Mexico (1821–1848). Control then passed to the
United States after the signing of the Treaty of Guadalupe Hidalgo in

1848, but American settlement was limited until after the ending of the U.S. Civil War in 1865.

Between 1848 and 1880 contact between Havasupai and Europeans was quite limited. No written account exists of European presence in the village itself between 1776 and 1861. In the 1848–1878 period most of what contact there was between the two cultures took place up on the Colorado Plateau, far from the main Havasupai summer village in the canyon bottom. The explorer Francois Xavier Aubry reported that his mule had been shot by Pai arrows up on the plateau in 1853,[3] but Anglo reports during the 1850–1900 period confuse Upland Pai groups with Apaches, and are often unable to accurately distinguish between Havasupai, Walapai, or Yavapai. The U.S. explorer Captain Lorenzo Sitgreaves possibly sighted the Havasupai in 1851, and they were briefly described by the explorer Lieutenant Ives in his 1861 report,[4] though he himself did not venture down the ladder to the village.[5] In 1862 the Mormon missionary Jacob Hamblin and his party met Havasupai up on the plateau, but spent only one day in the canyon village proper. The Indians urged them not to reveal its location.[6]

Although the summer village now known as Supai was isolated, late nineteenth-century events affecting surrounding tribes began to impact the Havasupai, who spent winters hunting in the upper plateau region. Between 1858 and 1873 Anglo-American and Mexican-American miners, settlers, and ranchers repeatedly came into conflict with Pai bands in northwestern Arizona. This ongoing conflict between peoples was partly a result of competition over scarce desert resources, like water, or new sources of animal protein, like cattle, horses, and mules, which were also used for transportation.[7] Cattle grazing contributed to the destruction of the traditional Havasupai vegetable food base, particularly the much sought-after *sele*, a spinach-like plant, and ranchers began taking control of most of the regional water springs and tanks.[8]

In 1858 the U.S. Cavalry established a military post at Fort Mohave, on the Colorado, after a wagon party was attacked by some Mohave, a riverine Yuman group who traded with the Havasupai and spoke a similar language. U.S. armed forces were rather more preoccupied with the Civil War than with the Indian conflicts out west, however, until after that war ended in 1865. Then U.S. troops began moving primarily between Fort Mohave on the Colorado, across to Beale's Springs for water, and on to Fort Whipple, in Prescott, because this was a major supply and freight route. The new communities were dependent upon regular shipments of goods transported by steamboat up the Colorado River and thence by mule train to northern Arizona. Because of this, most *official* military battles against Pai peoples in northern Arizona in the 1850–1870 period took place between Fort Mohave and Prescott.[9] However, pioneer settlers, like King Woolsey and Sam Miller from Prescott, also formed unofficial civilian militias to kill Pai and Apache people, when and where they deemed fit, sometimes in response to the stealing of mules or the killing of miners.

It was the actions of one of these civilian militiamen that started a particularly intense period of conflict, known as the Hualapai Wars (1866–1869). One merchant along the Colorado, William Hardy, made a paper treaty with the important Pai Headman Wauba Yuma in order to help his freighting business avoid attack (July 1865).[10] When Wauba Yuma later approached the freighter Sam Miller at Beale's Springs, he may have shown him this treaty or he may have, as Miller claimed, demanded payment in food and mules for passing through, calling this demand part of the unofficial "treaty." Miller did not continue talking to him, but immediately shot Wauba Yuma in the chest with his rifle.[11] In response, the Pai cut off the route from Prescott to the Colorado River ports, and the Pai leader Cherum began organizing Pai warriors from different bands.

The Pai were fighting a vicious enemy; many of the cavalry troops were hardened Civil War veterans. A brief peace prevailed after a treaty at Beale's Springs, and then continuous but intermittent guerilla-type warfare ensued until late 1868 and into early 1869.[12] Lt. Col. William R. Price, commander of the Eighth Cavalry, reported on his attacks on several Upland Pai *rancherias* during the three main years of hostilities:

> On the morning of the 10th, shortly after daylight in the vicinity of Walker Spring in the Aquarius Range, with 15 dismounted men on a high and rocky mountain, I surprised a Rancheria containing about 20 Indians; killed 3 bucks whose bodies were found, and severely wounded others; captured 3 squaws and 3 children, and destroyed this rancheria. . . . On the morning of the 13th, surprised another Rancheria containing 5 wickiups,

and killed or captured the entire band, killed 8 Indians and captured 7 squaws and 7 children.[13]

The Pai headman, Cherum, organized the different bands into a cohesive resistance force. In their biography of this "patriot chief," Dobyns and Euler (1998) describe Cherum as a "brilliant . . . strategist and tactician." The only Pai chief known to have forced the U.S. Cavalry to retreat, he consistently got between the troops and sources of water. "On one occasion, he held off a cavalry detachment by digging a rifle-pit inside his wickiup and barricading it with stones. From behind this parapet he fired several rifles to stand off his assailants."[14]

His success at unifying warriors from many of the Upland Pai bands helped to keep the U.S. Cavalry at bay for almost three years—no mean feat considering that the indigenous guerillas had limited access to guns. Cherum managed to mobilize nearly every Pai male capable of bearing arms in the struggle against the U.S. conquest of their traditional lands, possibly including some Havasupai warriors. As the cavalry closed in, and as Pai peoples became increasingly affected by European diseases, Cherum was eventually forced to surrender. Many Pai were incarcerated at a reservation on the Colorado River, near La Paz, to stifle any further resistance. Many died there of disease and starvation.[15] In 1875 the Upland Pai who had been incarcerated at the La Paz reservation returned to their own territory near the present-day Walapai reservation. They never again took up arms.

After the Hualapai Wars ended, Lt. Col. Price was promoted to major, left Arizona, and continued fighting Indians in Texas and Kansas throughout the 1870s, though he came back to Arizona in 1881 to make a formal military visit to the Havasupai.[16]

All Pai were affected by the Hualapai Wars, but the Havasupai were the only group to remain in their aboriginal territory following removal and disruption of other bands and tribes. Havasupai participation in the struggle mainly involved hospitality to refugees who made their way to Cataract Canyon. Tribal oral tradition indicates some individual Havasupai warrior participation in the general Pai resistance to U.S. occupation, although Leslie Spier's sources told him none of the old men then living (1918–1921) had fought in the wars, and that, in general, Havasupai didn't go to war, they farmed.[17] Edward H. Spicer (1962) went so far as to say that the Havasupai never carried on hostilities with the U.S. Forces.[18] However, intermarriage with Walapai band members was common, so whether individuals from the Havasupai subtribe fought or not, and this is apparently unknowable from the written sources, all these families were affected by the U.S. military conquest of northwestern Arizona.

The first postwar documented contact between the United States and Havasupai occurred in 1878, when a government surveying party led by a Lt. Touey and a topographer named Riecker briefly visited Cataract Canyon for the purpose of determining its mineral wealth. The Havasupai were welcoming and gave them melons, peaches, green corn, squashes, and sunflower seed bread.[19]

In 1880 the U.S. government ordered that the Havasupai be confined to a twelve-by-five-mile reservation in the bottom of Cataract Canyon, three thousand feet below the rim, thus cutting off the traditional migration route to the plateau.[20] But it is quite apparent that the U.S. government's idea of "confinement" was not that of the Havasupai, who in practice continued using the upper plateau throughout the nineteenth and twentieth centuries, albeit at greater risk. One unnamed Havasupai ordered ranchers away from Black Tank, north of Ashfork, in 1888, and another, Supai Tom, complained in 1890 to the Indian agent that some white family had taken over his family's place at Rain Tank.[21] In 1914 Anglo cattlemen caught Supai Charley with a dead calf, probably his own, near his family's traditional plateau range. He was taken to jail in Flagstaff, where he was killed without trial.[22]

The late nineteenth-century canyon-dwellers were also visited by wandering miners from the main Grand Canyon, who established a lead mine below the village and waterfalls and apparently forced some of the Havasupai to work there.[23] In 1881 the Havasupai were briefly visited by the writer and translator Elliot Coues, who reported that "we reached the wonderful blue spring . . . and the wonderful *rancheria* of the Indians."[24]

In that same year, an official military party from Fort Whipple in Prescott visited Havasupai Chief Navajo. Lt. Col. Price, the old Pai antagonist quoted above, was in charge of telling him the new rules about the reservation. Price wrote,

Navajo, the Supai Captain, was at first nervous, excited, and very suspicious—fearful that an effort might be made to remove them to some other reservation. They subsequently regained confidence and said that all they wanted was to be allowed to retain the little land they cultivated; that they were self-sustaining, and that they would cause no expense or trouble to the government. I assured them that our intention was to locate and set aside for them all the arable land they had ever cultivated and to secure for them all the water they had ever used for irrigation from any encroachment of the whites.[25]

The following year, 1882, southwestern anthropologist Frank Hamilton Cushing published (in the present tense) a description of the people he visited in Havasu Canyon:

The hair of the men is banged even with the eyes, but worn full length behind, and usually done up in a neat knot, tied with fiber. The women's, worn shorter behind, is banged as low as the chin. The men decorate themselves variously. Often a comb of long splints, beautifully plaited together with colored threads, is thrust into the headband, to which two eagle plumes, either white or red, are attached by cords, so as to float about in the wind. Huge earrings of silver or beaded cactus thorns, plugs of colored wood or buttons are stuck into the ears, which are pierced one, two, three and four times. Necklaces of shell and beads of bone, from which seashells, rudely cut and etched, depend, are marks of property. A bow-guard of leather or rawhide, bangles, either silver or brass, and numerous finger-rings, of bright red cactus thorns, complete the list of ornaments, the later being worn in great numbers by the women, because easily procurable. The faces of both sexes are painted with thick red ochre, applied dry or with oil extracted from the sunflower seed, varied among the men, sometimes, with streaks of blue paint, prepared from the root of the wild indigo, and put on in streaks, with a little wooden spatula, under the lower eyelid, and from the underlip downward across the chin . . . the Havasupai produce immense quantities of datila, mescal, watertight basketwork, and arrows. Nomadic hunters in winter, throughout the choicest ranges of the Southwest, they have become justly famous for the quantity, fineness and quality of their buckskins, which are smooth, soft, white as snow yet thick and durable. These buckskins, manufactured into bags, pouches, coats, and leggings, or as raw material, are valued by other Indian tribes, even as far east as the Rio Grande, as are the silks of China or the shawls of Persia by ourselves.[26]

Photographer Ben Wittick visited Supai in 1885, carrying his equipment down a rope ladder to get there.[27] General Crook himself briefly visited Cataract Canyon in 1885 "to settle a little Indian trouble between the Havasupai and the Moqui [Hopi]."[28] In 1894 an Indian Bureau school was established in the canyon, headed by an Agent Bauer, who carried on a campaign against cremation and the associated "destruction of property."[29] Photographer Edward Curtis also visited the tribe in the late nineteenth century, publishing a slim volume of photographs in 1908 called *The Havasupai*. Some of these photos are reproduced in the center section of this book. A short-lived scheme by a private company to produce electricity from the waterfalls was abandoned around the turn of the century.[30]

The author George Wharton James visited Havasu Canyon several times between 1899 and 1912, the first time with William Wallace Bass as a guide, a man who already knew many of the Havasupai because he and his family lived at the Grand Canyon.[31] In 1900 James published *In and Around the Grand Canyon*, which included a chapter on the Havasupai, and included a photograph of one of this volume's storytellers, the headman Manakaja, with whom he conversed. "No people on earth have a more picturesque home," James wrote. "Rugged grandeur, combined with quiet beauty; flowing water with ponderous rocky walls; blue sky and blue water; green trees and red precipices."[32] Tourists began visiting Supai more after the publication of Wharton's book, though tourism didn't begin to really increase until the 1960s.

Also around 1900, Flora Gregg Iliff spent several months teaching at the Indian Bureau school in Supai. She found there a people whom she later described as "dominated by ritual," with constant religious references to Coyote. The men often said that Coyote "'tell us all he know. Coyote our father. People do like he say.'" Iliff said the way they spoke about him gave her the feeling that Coyote was a member of the tribe.[33]

War and disease severely reduced Pai populations between 1865 and the 1930s, when numbers began to rise again.[34] Estimated at over 350 people prior to conquest, only 106 Havasupai survived a series of epidemics from 1900 to 1906. By 1968 there were 428 members and in 2006 some 650.[35]

Multigenerational cultural trauma was caused by the entire experience of foreign invasion. The Havasupai lived for years with and near desert guerilla warfare. They experienced the removal and incarceration of interrelated Walapai families. They survived the prohibition against migration to traditional plateau hunting areas. They held onto their own culture as much as possible, even when the Indian Bureau brought in new ideas about how they should run their funerals, their family and private lives, and even new ideas about which gender should make the clothing.

Havasupai responses to these late nineteenth-century pressures included participation in new religious movements, such as the Ghost Dance and the Peyote cult. Sometime after 1860 they began to stop cremating, perhaps because the Ghost Dance was supposed to bring the bodies back to life,[36] or perhaps because the Indian Bureau objected to the practice, although Spier's informants said that neither of these was the case.[37] Yet the Havasupai were one of, if not the last, southwestern and U.S. tribe forced to change overall aboriginal life patterns. At the turn of the century they hung onto traditional ways despite the traumas and changes they had experienced, both cultural and individual.[38]

Besides those visitors discussed above, few other non-Indian people visited Supai between 1776 and 1918, leaving few written records.[39] It was in 1918 that the next major non-Indian visitor of note, Leslie Spier, started collecting the stories published in this book. This is not to claim that he found this people living in "pure" aboriginal cultural conditions, or in some ahistorical "ethnographic present."[40] As noted by Iliff twenty years previously, the Havasupai were already using machine-made clothing and cooking utensils, attending white schools, and learning white religion long before Spier got there—in fact, most Havasupai were wearing manufactured clothing by 1884.[41] Spier himself thought probably no Havasupai ceramics had been produced since about 1870. But Spier did his best to document the life of what was then and is still the most isolated tribal community in the continental United States.

Spier's *Havasupai Ethnography*, published in 1928, remains the most definitive description of the Havasupai as he encountered them, some forty years, or roughly two generations, after conquest. Between 1918 and 1921 Spier spent several weeks with the narrators of these stories, the headmen and elders Sinyella and Manakaja, both in their early seventies. He ate with them and came to know their families. Because of their extraordinarily isolated location, the Havasupai maintained more of their aboriginal language, storytelling, and singing culture than any other Yuman-speaking tribe at that time. Spier states that the elders he spoke to were thoroughly conversant with every aspect of their traditional culture.[42]

He visited Supai three times: the first in August 1918, during which he collected material ethnographic specimens for and was paid by the American Museum, known later as the American Museum of Natural History, based in New York. From August through November 1919, he returned as a William Bayard Cutting Traveling Fellow of Columbia University, also partly funded by the American Museum. He made a third trip in August and September 1921, funded in part by the Southwest Society of New York. His wife, Erna Gunther, also went to Havasupai in 1921, collecting tales and "incidental material."[43] Spier described the inspiration for his studies thus:

[The Havasupai] have remained so secluded in their inaccessible canyon home, that we know little of them today. There are brief descriptions resulting from the visits of Ives' party in 1858, Coues in 1881 and of James and Curtis' parties at various times. Cushing, who spent a few days with them in 1881, has described *The Nation of the Willows* at somewhat greater length. Their cultural position still remaining in doubt, I was sent by the American Museum in 1918 for a general ethnographic study.[44]

Leslie Spier's first visit was announced in the *Scientific American* in 1919 as a "unique experience of observing a truly primitive people living at this very time not in the heart of darkest Africa but right here within the boundaries of the United States, the little-known Havasupai Indians of Arizona. These Indians are still what may be called a savage tribe and in most particulars are not much further advanced than our remote ancestors of the Stone Age."[45] Apologies now, of course, for the subordinating language used then, but that time's characterizations somewhat contextualize Spier's fieldwork.

Spier reported an almost idyllic, paradisiacal situation, as some later authors have also described Supai. In the 1919 article he reported that "here great fields of corn, beans, squash and fruit including the fig are raised. Wild seeds and cactus are gathered on the surrounding mountains in which deer, antelope, mountain sheep and wild turkey abound." He said he enjoyed delicious meals of mashed green corn and squash blossoms. He also reported that the Havasupai usually had two or three sweat lodges going at any one time, enjoyed making music with drums and rattles, and that they gambled with dice and had dances.[46] He collected examples of Havasupai-made drums, rattles, bows, arrows, rabbit sticks and rabbit rope, several types of baskets, a Tizon Brownware pot, gaming pieces, and feather headdresses. The items he collected during these visits are still in the collections of the American Museum of Natural History in New York, and photos can be viewed online.[47]

With fellow Boasian anthropologist Elsie Clews Parsons, Spier published a chapter called *Havasupai Days* in 1922. It is a nonacademic piece, but scientifically informed by his ethnographic research. It is a beautiful and imaginative description of Havasupai life as he saw it then, including descriptions of Havasupai cultural traditions, like having children run in the morning:

> Lanso is a hedonist of seven. Day dawns late down in Cataract Canyon, but even spring nights in Arizona are chill, and one's own soft-woven bedding, cedar-bark mat and rabbit-skin blanket, suffuse a warmth one would not willingly forego. But, "Lanso," whispers grandfather Sinyella, "up and run toward the daylight. Run, that you grow straight and lusty. And heed me; take your torch and touch it to your elbows and your wrists that you may never be rheumatic as I, your relative. Oh yes, and as you turn back, fling the torch behind you, turn once again and snatch it up, that your memory may be strong too, that you may remember quickly a forgotten deer charm when you go to hunt."

In Spier's story, when Lanso gets back from running up the canyon, his aunt, Round-one, has food for him: "a stew of ground corn and big-horn meat, little loaves of corn meal tied in husks and baked in embers, sweet mescal juice, and salt from the cave far down the canyon."[48] *Havasupai Days* includes vignettes of hunting, the sweat lodge, dancing, singing, and telling stories:

> Moonlight spread across the clearing as they danced: the eastern cliffs stood sharply black against the sky. The song ended, and the group around the pole melted away. Sinyella rose in his place among the watching families. "My own land, hear me. Let all of us remain alive always. I want to live well always. Ground, hear me." He prayed to the rocks, the ground, the creek: he told the young men to work hard, to dance well, to not be quarrelsome, as chiefs always spoke in the lull between dances. . . . He had made himself a chief. True, his grandfather had been a chief, like his fathers before him. But his own father was never chief; no one would call him that; he was a good-for-nothing. "Now when I die," he thought, "my two oldest sons will share it, as they will my fields. I have taught them both to talk like chiefs." . . . Sinyella smiled drowsily at the firelit faces: yes, all his own people. At his side he heard Lanso, "Grandfather, tell us just one story. Don't refuse this time; the snakes will not bother now, it is winter." Sinyella sat back where the children were listening, lying in the darkness. "Wolf and Coyote lived far to the west close to the ocean. Wolf said to Coyote, 'This country holds no game, no deer, no antelope.'"[49]

When Spier visited, Sinyella and Manakaja were elders who remembered what life was like before white people came. This would have been unheard-of in 1918 for tribes farther east, west, or south where Spanish and American conquests had occurred between the sixteenth and mid-nineteenth centuries. Spier's storytellers, the ones whose voices are published in this collection, were adolescents in the canyon prior to the outbreak of the wars, born and raised before any major cultural disruption by white people. A man who was seventy in 1920 would have been born in 1850, and the Hualapai Wars did not break out until 1865. Sinyella's and Manakaja's words were translated by younger native speakers who had been educated in English and are presented in this collection exactly as Spier and Gunther transcribed them.

PAI CHIEFTAINSHIP:

)⁓ *The World of Sinyella and Manakaja*

Anthropological evidence indicates that in precontact times the Havasupai and Walapai were probably two of thirteen distinct sub-tribes, each composed of patrilineal bands living in a kinship-based camp. Intermarriage and other evidence indicates that the precontact Walapai and Havasupai probably saw themselves as separate but within a larger tribal grouping of what we can call collectively the Pai, whereas the Yavapai were a completely separate and enemy tribe. [50] Despite high levels of mutual linguistic intelligibility, similarities in ceramic, stone tool, and architectural styles, and similar mythological narratives,[51] many Yuman groups were traditional enemies: the Yavapai and the Havasupai/Walapai of upland Arizona; the Mohave and Quechan of the upper Colorado, and the Cocopah and Maricopa of the lower river. "Warfare," comments Laylander, "was deeply imprinted in the ceremonial behavior of the Colorado River groups."[52] Dobyns and Euler even refer to an amity/enmity "system" among Colorado River tribes, and Spicer describes lower Colorado River Yumans as particularly prone to battles with groups that were more or less colingual.[53] Other Yuman-speaking peoples were amicable trading partners, exchanging, for example, seeds, pine nuts, suede, and antlers.[54] Despite this enemy/friend system, all Upland Yumans shared variants of the same myths, in more or less the same language.[55] This curious antipathy between cultural groups as similar as the Yavapai and Havasupai has given rise to a lively debate in the anthropological literature regarding the very definition of a "tribe" or a "chief" and about what evidence can be used to analyze their structure and authority.[56]

Although Robert Euler and Henry Dobyns disagree with Timothy Braatz about the nature of Upland Pai chieftainship, both emphasize that landscape elements and natural resources such as springs formed a major part of the Upland Yuman self-concept and world view.[57] Competition for such resources probably contributed to the antagonisms between the Yavapai and the other Upland Pai, though the stories themselves give very interpersonal reasons for this traditional enemy relationship (see story 4, "The Separation of the Havasupai and Yavapai").

One of the traditional Pai subtribes was even named the "Yavapai Fighters" and existed in the borderlands between the two groups: that vast, mostly dry Black Forest of scrub juniper that stretches from near Paulden and Walnut Creek up to Ashfork. Other bands' names were distinctly regional: there were the *Ko'audva Kopaya* or Plateau People, the *Witoov M'uka Pa'a* or Middle Mountain People, the *Havesooa Pai* or People at the Blue Green Water, and the *Ha'Kasa Pa'a* or Pine-Clad Mountain People. The *Hualapai* (*Hwal Pa'a*) were the people of the Big (Ponderosa) Pines. All were Upland Yuman, culturally almost identical to the Yavapai farther to the south from whom they were distinguished primarily by mutual and deadly antagonism, as well as some dialect and accent differences.[58]

Subtribes were comprised of smaller, family-based bands, some of them enumerated and named by nineteenth-century military observers. The size of a Pai band varied, but consisted of a camp, or *rancheria*, of loosely related families. Key resources, rather than regions, inspired the band names. For example, the Middle Mountain subtribe had two named bands just prior to conquest; the Yavapai Fighter subtribe had four; and the Plateau People subtribe had six band names: Grass Springs, Clay Springs, Hackberry Springs, Milkweed Springs, Peach Springs, and Pine Springs.[59]

Braatz's research indicated that Pai aboriginal structure was less formal than Euler and Dobyns had implied in their ground-breaking study, *Wauba Yuma's People*.[60] Euler and Dobyns insisted on the existence of formal subtribes made up of family bands, whereas Braatz concluded that formalized structures and headmen with cross-band leadership emerged only as a response to conquest pressures. Braatz accused Euler and Dobyns of supporting a "coercive" understanding of Pai tribal authority, whereas they in their response say, "No non-Athapascan native leader in Arizona Territory possessed coercive powers. All led by example and persuasion."[61]

The argument bears upon the current collection of stories inasmuch as Sinyella and Manakaja, our narrators, were referred to as "chiefs" by Spier, who maintained that the title was more or less inherited. Yet Braatz rejects the idea of hereditary chieftainship, maintaining that leadership was instead based exclusively on speaking abilities combined with war skills: "Ethnographic evidence suggests that before 1875 Pai leaders emerged based on speaking and fighting ability, not on heredity."[62] He quotes non-Indian diaries as evidence for this, and much of his other Upland Pai evidence is based primarily on the ethnography of the Yavapai, who were more exposed to conquest pressures than the secluded Havasupai. Yet Braatz's generalization must be modified in the light of Spier's research, and in some ways both the Euler/Dobyns and the Braatz evidence is overstated. Neither appears to fully analyze Spier's early work on Pai headmen, which contains elements of both positions.

Manakaja and Sinyella were not the only headmen, or "chiefs," that Spier encountered. Although "chief" now sounds liked an overly Anglicized word, Spier used it frequently while struggling to describe the leadership style he observed. His *Ethnography* states that in the early twentieth century, six coextant Havasupai "chiefs" led a population of 177 individuals that were organized into 42 camps or family units. "Chieftainship," Spier writes, "is usually inherited in the male line, but there is more than one instance where the connecting relative was a woman. . . . Men do not suddenly become chiefs, Manakaja being an exception, but people gradually come to call them so, as they develop prominence. They emphatically do not acquire official positions."[63]

Spier clearly states that "chieftainship is hereditary among the Havasupai,"[64] citing numerous cases and including detailed and convincing genealogical charts dating to before 1875 as evidence that such an hereditary structure existed before conquest. However, he *also* states that "the principle is clearly that a man is recognized as a leader because of a combination of distinguishing characteristics, bravery, enterprise, and shrewdness. There is a tendency to transmit the social position he makes for himself by inheritance but the heir must have demonstrated his own ability before others will recognize that he has inherited the status."[65] In others words, inheritance was conditional upon the man proving himself, and not automatic. Spier gives several examples where sons did not inherit leadership, but the status went to another, more capable relative, or involved an inheritance pattern from maternal uncles instead of fathers.

In this matter of governance Spier has clearly come across something he does not fully understand, for he also says of the chieftainships: "[I]t is not clear what is inherited; on the whole it seems to be the right to be styled chief, provided one shows signs of leadership."[66] Chieftainship was not a position, but an embodiment of functions and its functions consisted "largely in giving advice and admonitions. . . . This is so largely true that it might be said not that a chief is one who talks, but that one who talks is a chief."[67] (Other

Yuman-speaking groups, like the Cocopah and Diegueño, also had advisory/admonishing chiefs.[68]) One function was related to community "law": for example, if there was ever any sort of serious dispute with someone Walapai, one of these chiefs would go and speak with all the parties concerned.[69]

Ninety years ago Spier spent a considerable amount of time observing our narrators, Manakaja and Sinyella, and the other chiefs, carry out their other functions. He concluded:

> Chiefs tell their people how to act, especially the young men and women. The former are admonished to work, farm, hunt, and make clothing and moccasins; the latter to gather seeds, cook, plant, and make baskets. They are told not to be lazy, to care properly for themselves and their families, their farms and their property. If a man refused to obey their advice, refusing to work, they would repeat their admonitions. "Do not be lazy, do not cause trouble. If you do not work or help others, you may get into trouble or you may starve and nobody will help you." . . . In an obstinate case, they paid no more attention to the delinquent, but let him go his way. . . . Chiefs address their remarks to the assemblages on appropriate occasions, such as dances, formal gatherings for the discussion of important topics, invitations, etc., during battle, at death ceremonies, or informally at sweatlodges. . . . No one chief was either war or dance leader. In battle any chief temporarily assumed a directive capacity; the warriors would give more attention to a big chief. It is not clear that there is any other function besides giving advice. After the flood in 1918 washed the lower irrigating system completely away, Manakaja went about setting stakes to re-locate the ditch. Possibly this is his function, but this ditch supplied his fields as well as those of his neighbors. During the dances all of the chiefs took some leading part in the feasting, racing, etc., but it did not appear they had any peculiar functions. It is quite clear that chiefs have neither power nor prerogatives; they are simply leaders. Men become chiefs by prestige and renown based on their prowess in war, their prominence in intertribal relations, and their wisdom displayed in council, or by reason of inheritance. Personal qualifications are an important factor in the latter

case too. A chief must be dignified, industrious, and even tempered; a son who does not display these qualities will have little chance of ever being called chief. Sinyella's father failed to inherit his father's status as big chief. . . . Captain Navajo instructed Manakaja and Captain Jim, his older brother's sons, in the ways of a chief; Manakaja in turn is instructing his own sons in the same informal way.[70]

The six chiefs of Spier's time were distinguishable. "The Havasupai are accustomed to speak of 'big chiefs' and 'little chiefs.' . . . Jess [Chikapanega] differentiated between them by *múlvák-êjá* and *pagámûlvåkåvatéha*, literally, little chief and big-chief-man."[71] Spier was also told that the big chief was called the shortened form, *gamolva*, and the whole group of chiefs was sometimes referred to as the *mulovajidjagata*. The Havasupai of that time also referred to the U.S. president as *gamolva*.[72] The big chief was the most prominent man of the village, but the others had equal functions. None of them knew who was second, third, fourth, etc. Manakaja and Sinyella told Spier that "admonitions of the other *gamolava* would have just the same force as the *gamolva*."[73]

The six chiefs Spier found in 1918–1921 were Manakaja, big chief, and five "lesser" chiefs—Captain Jim (Kwaiyoiya), Watahomidja (Watahomigie/Watahomudja), Panamida, Big Jim (Puut), and Sinyella. Sinyella's great-grandfather, Captain Navajo (different, they said, from Navajo), had been a big chief, concluding peace treaties with many Arizona tribes sometime in the nineteenth century. Manakaja and Sinyella told Spier he was "like George Washington," but was "killed by Apache in canyon." Panamida's and Supai Charley's father, Wasakwivama, had been big chief before Navajo, who was from a different family. Navajo earned his position through brave and sometimes violent actions, thus eclipsing the former family, and instructing both his nephews, Big Jim and brother Manakaja, in the ways of a chief.[74] Manakaja was also, however, Wasakwivama's paternal grandson. Both Wasakwivama and Navajo were headmen sharing power at the same time: when in the late nineteenth century the Havasupai concluded a formal peace agreement with the Yavapai at the Hopi village of Oraibi, *both* leaders participated.

"When Navajo died, the *mulovajidjagata* met together and chose Manakaja as successor. The choice was between Manakaja and

Captain Jim, but Mana[kaja] was instructed, had sense, and was older, so after a few days they told everybody they chose Mana[kaja]. The present *mulovagidjagata* were then in office."[75] Spier includes descriptions of each of these tribal leaders:

> Manakaja, the head chief, is a man of seventy, dignified, reserved, somewhat simple, and with quiet humor; a man who spends much time in a sedentary way at home, is usually "on show" but far from pompous. His brother Captain Jim, slightly younger, is energetic, active as an organizer of the young men, particularly in relations with the Walapai and Navaho, who usually send dance invitations, etc., intended for the tribe to him. He is not a fluent talker but commands respect. Watahomidja, a man of about the same age, is quiet, reserved, not especially dignified, and is the center of the conservative element. He is a fluid talker, but not emphatic, and, I suspect, somewhat cynical. Panamida is a little younger; he is phlegmatic, not especially dignified, fond of horse-racing and encourages the boys in that sport. Big Jim, fifty-nine, is energetic, aggressive, busy, a fluent and effective speech-maker, making free use of rapid and graphic gestures, and a potent influence in council. Sinyella, aged seventy-one, is quiet, kindly, far more industrious than average, shrewd, observant, and active in directing the dances.[76]

Our story narrator, Manakaja, was planning to instruct one of his sons, who at that time were named as Jasper (age thirty-one), Dudley (twenty-eight), Francis (twenty), and Crook (age unknown), but, he told Spier, "they are very young. . . . people don't know yet which is best . . . wait until we see which has the best sense and takes care of himself best."[77]

The Pai style of chieftainship evolved over centuries of adapting to a vast desert environment. At certain times of the year, different families migrated to different resource areas, and these groups of families, or bands, each had their own leader; when they lived together to farm the bottom of the canyon, all the leaders were present. Pai leadership was dignified, industrious, and not coercive; verbal prowess in repeating the stories and in encouraging, teaching, and admonishing the community was prized. Sometimes it was hereditary, sometimes not. Yet there was no formal position as such, which is perhaps why Flora Gregg Iliff also seemed culturally confused by Pai headmanship. She rarely described it as such, instead merely seeing and describing old men who "harangued people" about staying true to traditional ways.[78] A key aspect of Pai cultural leadership, however, confirmed by Spier and Cushing, is that it included the ability to retell the sacred stories from memory, thus merging secular and spiritual authority.

Environmental/Spiritual Context of the Stories

The Yuman sacred stories in this book deal with animals and plants familiar from the peoples' seasonal movements, a pattern of resource collection crucial to desert survival. Clyde Morris suggests, "Together the cycles tell of mythic events that explain the relationship between the Pai food resources and their migratory way of life."[79] It is difficult to understand the stories without some understanding of the region's flora and fauna, and how these relate to the migratory and spiritual patterns of the people from whom they originate. "Every plant, every hill, every spring was the actual site of some historic or spiritual event in a tale, and the harvesting of a plant or arrival at some location would recall the rich set of events depicted in the tales."[80]

Alfred Whiting maintained that the Havasupai seasonal migration was not as strictly divided as some accounts might suggest.

> It is apparent that the typical picture of the annual cycle of the Havasupai was not sharply divided into a winter period of hunting and gathering [on the plateau] and a spring and summer period of agriculture [in the canyon]. Rather the two economies were fused.[81]

This mixed-subsistence strategy meant that in summer they lived in the canyon and also ate venison and used fresh herbs from the plateau; in the winter, on the plateau, they also ate dried pumpkin and corn bread. They were farmers, hunters, and gatherers almost simultaneously. In Western European history, the usual narrative is one of "progress" from migratory Stone Age hunter/gatherer to village-settled Neolithic agriculturalist. Distinct, separate phases like these may not work for a human group living in a vast desert with hidden springs and creeks. It seems probable that the Pai fusion of two means of production, and indeed, two "phases" of civilization, was a brilliant adaptation to the relatively harsh environment of the Southwest.

Even in 2009 some elders remembered leaving their farms in the canyon every autumn to go live and hunt on the plateau, and this annual migration is strongly reflected in the stories, which have both hunting and agricultural elements. In 1882 the Havasupai explained their twice-yearly migrations between the canyon and the upper plateau thus:

> But, alas! the Coyote ate a part of the heart of the great caci-que; hence, only during summer do we live in the home of the Mother of the Waters, and plant as she told us; but in win-ter we have to follow the deer with our father, the Coyote, and live only as he does, in houses of grass and bark; for the Mother of the Waters grew sad when her people became so foolish, and, leaving only one of her sons to take care of them, she went away to her home among the white shells, in the great world of waters.[82]

In precontact times migration and planting times were known through association with certain astronomical, as well as botanical, events. All the evidence gathered by their two major ethnographers points to the fact that the Havasupai tracked the movement of the stars in part by associating certain star clusters with characters from their myths and tales, and they used this astronomical time-telling device to know when to move to the plateau and when to move to the can-yon bottom, when to plant domestic crops and when to harvest wild foods.[83] (This tradition may have been affected by confinement, since one can only see a small portion of the night sky from the canyon floor.) Gifford found that among Southeastern Yavapai, elders could tell what month it was by asking the young if a certain plant had appeared, which was said to be synchronous with the appearance of a certain star.[84] The Pai Pai had a story called Owl's Daughters, who were said to be very beautiful before they turned into the Pleiades.[85] Among the Maricopa, the Morning Star was said to be the old woman from their Flute Lure tale. Time-telling, migration, the characters in the stories, and astronomy are linked among many Yuman-speaking peoples.[86]

Among the Havasupai, Alfred Whiting noted an emphasis on win-ter rather than summer constellations, and wrote that the positions of the stars, the phases of the moon, and "the rising position of the sun are used to determine the seasonal activities."[87] The very telling of certain stories may have coincided with the rising of related winter constellations. Solstices were recognized; Spier reports that one of our narrators, Sinyella, had a particular location in which he stood in order to observe the dawning sun on both the longest and the shortest days of the year.[88]

At least two of their twelve months are named after constellations associated with figures appearing in the stories (our November and January). The arrival of February is known by the dawn appearance of a certain constellation[89] later identified as the man who fell over a cliff with his wife and baby (see stories 27 and 28).[90] The Havasupai perceived the constellation of Scorpio as Coyote carrying a pole of smaller stars (January). Bat and his three wives became another constellation (story 47). Another star cluster well known to other Yuman-speaking tribes (and identically named by them), were the antelope, deer, and mountain sheep, known by Europeans as the three stars in Orion's belt. "Every child knew the personalities associated with these stories, associated with specific stars."[91] In one story, Wolf Man helped produce a baby by stirring abalone shell into water; when the child grew up, he became a bighorn sheep, who, after a series of adventures, became the star (see story 17, "Wolf's Boy"). Abalone shell, obtained from Baja/Pacific Coast Yumans, was considered a cure for infertility.[92] Even the directions, East and West, had a strong association with personages in, for example, Story 9. Symbolic associations in Yuman myths are eloquently discussed by Miguel Aguilera (2005).

The sun and moon are important and powerful entities in these traditions. Sun used to be a man and lived over near the San Francisco Peaks. His house was a red crater, or hole. Sun killed a lot of Indians, and Pine Squirrel battled against him. Sun got angry at Pine Squirrel and burned the whole world and the people had to hide inside the ground near this crater, with the ant people, to escape the fire. Or, in the second version, the people go through a tunnel made by Prairie Dog to Sun's house and then later go down to live with the ants, who cook *sile'e* seeds for them. Then all the Indians come up out of the ground as Pine Squirrels. The sun, who was a wicked man, caught fire himself, and to this day has to go through the ground under his camp and come up again at daylight (see stories 35 and 36, "Sun Sets the World Afire").

One researcher divides all Pai oral literature into two basic classes: those that have power and those that do not. "Examples of genres that have power are medicine songs, myth-songs, prayers and myths. Those genres which do not have power are the entertaining animal stories told to children and historical war narratives."[93] According to tribal members who talked to Spier, Smithson, Euler, Whiting, Martin, and Hirst, Havasupai stories, songs, and dreams are interconnected, and may in and of themselves carry the power to heal or alter one's perceptions of reality.[94] As philosopher David Abram has noted, cultures whose language traditions are transmitted *only* via oral tradition may regard *language itself* as magical, as well as a powerful means to move between the animal and human worlds.[95] Animal characters that appear in this collection, like Blue Jay and Bat, and magical plants, like corn, tobacco, and agave, help to mediate the important relationships between those worlds.[96]

These oral narratives do seem to serve the function, as Abram has insisted, of bridging the human and nonhuman worlds. He observes that "the scale of a harvest or the size of a hunt are always negotiated between the tribal community and the natural world that it inhabits."[97] From his studies of preliterate Indonesian societies, he generalizes that "the traditional magician or medicine person functions primarily as an intermediary between human and non-human worlds, and only secondarily as a healer . . . [because of ethnocentric bias], countless anthropologists have managed to overlook the ecological dimensions of the shaman's craft."[98]

Certainly animals formed a unique and important part of the Pai conception of the universe and its deities. Animals and men move between their respective worlds in these stories, and sometimes animals become men and vice versa. Animals who were also men in the Havasupai myths include Eagle, Coyote, Wolf, Mountain Lion, Porcupine, Rabbit, Turkey, Mouse, Squirrel, Scorpion, Owl, Fox, Bighorn Sheep, Wren, and Bat. Animals who were never men included snakes other than Rattlesnake; Deer and Bear; and post-conquest animals such as Cow, Cat, Horse, and Dog.[99] Among other Yuman-speaking peoples, the mythological animals have their own speech, a distinctly human characteristic.[100]

Among Yuman speakers, animals and dreams seem strongly linked, and dreams were an important source of power.[101] One Quechan researcher states that "[m]ythology informs dreams and vice versa, and this interplay affects day-to-day decision-making and behavior."[102] Dreams would bring contact with elements or spirit animals.[103] Sometimes the animals in dreams helped to diagnose and cure illnesses. Curing shamans might sing over a sick person for four nights, using a gourd rattle. A graduate student once sincerely asked Robert Euler, what did the Pai peoples, makers of Tizon Brownware, do with their spare time, since they didn't build multistory pueblos, maintain fields year-round, or design elaborate pottery? He paused for a split second and then replied, "They liked to sit and dream."[104]

One became a shaman partly through the occurrence of certain dreams, and, as Schwartz points out in a previous chapter, Havasupai religion was largely shaman-based, with different kinds of specialist shamans, such as snake shamans, deer shamans, weather shamans, and healing shamans. Songs might come through dreaming; dreaming of deer might make one a deer shaman, and thus an excellent hunter. Shamanic powers, along with their associated political powers, although usually inherited, could also come from dreaming.[105] Sinyella told Spier that his maternal grandfather often dreamt that Wolfman came to see him, and then when he sang for the sick, wolf spirit would come, enter his body, and cure for him; when the cure was complete, Wolf would leave his body.[106] Spier observed, "In the final analysis, power comes through dreams. . . . Rock Jones . . . dreamed of lightning and thunder, saw the pouring rain and hail and dreamed that he sang to make it rain. Now he uses that song."[107] When Mark Hanna (one of the translators of this story collection) was in training to be a shaman, he always placed his gourd rattle at the head of his bed. "When he wakes he seizes it and tries the song he has dreamed."[108] Yuman-speaking peoples, especially along the lower Colorado, have actually been designated as "dream cultures,"[109] in which songs and spirit animals come to dreamers to assist in shamanic healing, and all power comes from dreams.[110]

Mike Burns, a Yavapai captured by the U.S. military in 1872, remembered many Yuman-language creation stories whose characters were identical to those in the Havasupai stories. In his 1920s memoir, Burns tried to explain how these creation stories and characters were integral to Pai spirituality:

The grandmother raised the boy and he came to [be] a great master of all beings: the same as we take as Christ was. He had the same spiritual power. He commanded the weather.

He can command the great sun to stand still: and can command the wind to blow hard or can blow just easy and change its course. This boy can also understand every living animals: talk to them. And anyone got hurt come to him and can be cured. . . . it is said that once a quail he shot and broken its leg and was just going to shoot again but the boy was surprised by this quail he wounded: [who] yelled at him: and addressing him as grandchild: as this old quail wanted the boy not to hurt her any more: and wishes him to fix her leg: and makes her have a whole leg again as she has a great story to tell this boy: So the boy went to the old quail he shot at with an arrow: and rubbed [it] on his breast and touched the wounded parts: with his hands: and sure enough the old quail she was running around fast having a whole leg: and could not notice see any wound: on the leg. [original Burns punctuation/grammar][111]

For many coastal and riverine Yuman peoples, telling stories was and is a spiritual act that invokes power. When Sinyella told Spier his version of the Yavapai origin tale, he added at the end that "the Yavapai man said one must not tell this story; if he did it would rain all the time" (see last paragraph of story 13, this collection).

All Pai groups state that myths are told on winter evenings, while the people sit around a campfire. Morris maintains that

the myths are so powerful that their telling requires special care to prevent injury. The Havasupai say that "a myth must be completed the same evening or the teller or his listeners might become crippled in some way." A similar crippling affliction is said to occur if Northeastern Yavapai listeners do not "get up before daybreak, run to the stream and wash their faces" the morning after listening to a myth. The Southeastern Yavapai state that after hearing the Dying God story "listeners would rise and shake themselves for good luck . . . it was thought that if myths are told during the summer, 'spiders, snakes and bears [would] hear the stories and bite people. In winter these creatures are dormant and do not hear."[112]

In precontact times, multiple cultural meanings might have been simultaneously transmitted when the stories were told, or when songs related to the stories were sung. Specific animal-spirit characters might be related to specific healing needs, to stars, or to specific migratory or agricultural times of the year. Shamanic power might be invoked through winter recitations.

The stories also imparted lessons for everyday life and behavior, including how to make arrows, as well as guidelines for specific familial relationships, including the taboo against sex between a father and daughter. The stories contain information about who could be traded with, and who was an enemy. Sacred associations with the natural landscape, such as the Pacific Ocean, the San Francisco Peaks, Red Butte, and other formations, are also present. Spier discusses the multiple interconnections between myth stories, dreams, songs, astronomy, shamanism, spirit plants and animals, and sacred landscape in his study of the Yuman tribes of the Gila River. These interconnections were integral to the desert-based cultures of all Yuman-speaking peoples.[113] Their myths are "intangible and spiritual artistic expressions, in opposition to the monumental material culture . . . of Mesoamerica."[114]

Certainly the telling of the stories was affected by the Anglo conquest, for after 1880 Havasupai were forbidden from living and hunting on the plateau in the winter, which is where the stories had traditionally been told.[115] By 1900 they knew they could be arrested if caught with a deer,[116] but deer, plants, the annual migration, the stories, and other cultural activities, like singing and dreaming, were closely linked. Being banned from their traditional storytelling/hunting areas may have had an impact on the memory of the stories, as well as on their potential for constructing Havasupai imagination, understanding, and self-concept.

The plateau was not freely available to them again until after 1975. As Stephen Hirst so eloquently writes, "By 1974 the grandparents were still reciting the tales of Coyote, but his trickery and occasional wisdom held little conviction within the chill confines of the canyon. No longer could listeners see from the lodge the endless spaces stretching away in which Coyote could work his feats, in which all things might be possible. . . . In winter. . . . the loss of the past bore down heavily indeed."[117]

This collection of forty-eight stories is the earliest, most complete, most accurate rendition we now have of the prehistoric cultural library that was carried for centuries in the minds of Havasupai headmen and elders. Every winter they passed the stories on to the young of each generation, thus adding to their chances of survival in one of the most challenging environments on earth.

Linguistic Context of the Stories

Before Spier and Gunther transcribed these stories in the early twentieth century, they were preserved by memory alone for unknown hundreds of generations. The Havasupai language has existed in written form for only thirty years.[118] By contrast, the European temporal/cultural distance from orality is one of about three thousand years; European/Western understanding of oral cultures is therefore circumscribed. Partly because of this, there are ongoing tensions between indigenous and European ways of knowing.[119]

In both living memory and current practice Havasupai oral tradition remains extraordinarily powerful. In precontact times those with strong memory skills were accorded higher social status—these stories were the only TV and radio that existed. Yet they were far more than entertainment—they were a living library of religious and cultural information. The nineteenth-century Havasupai headman Navajo told Cushing that "the only books our fathers gave us were our hearts and our mouths."[120]

The language that gave birth to, cradled, and preserved these stories, Yuman, is one of the oldest in North America, where some 600 languages evolved over the last 12,000 years or so. "Approximately 150 indigenous American languages are still spoken in the United States; however, it is estimated that by the year 2050 only twenty of them will remain."[121] Some Yuman languages and dialects are already extinct, and only a few hundred people speak those that remain. Yet language carries the oral/verbal/conceptual originality of the human group from which it evolves. When a language becomes extinct, evolutionarily unique conceptual nuances are lost. Indeed, a primary identifying element of human culture is lost.[122]

In Arizona there are three main indigenous language groups: Apachean (Athabascan or Na-Dene), Tepiman (Uto-Aztecan), and Yuman. Yuman languages are themselves a subgroup of a larger linguistic classification known as Hokan. These are unrelated language groups, each with several subgroups. North American linguistic families are approximately as different from each other as the difference between contemporary English and ancient Sanskrit multiplied by three.[123]

Apachean-speaking peoples in this region are the Navajo and Apache, northern migrants who arrived relatively late (1500s–1600s). Early inhabitants seem mostly to have been Tepiman speakers, including the Ute, Paiute, Hopi, Akimel O'odham (Pima), Tohono O'odham (Papago), as well as many of the indigenous peoples of Mexico all the way south to Durango. Tepiman speakers were mostly, though not exclusively, wattle, adobe, or masonry village-builders over the past 2,500 years or so. The Paiute and Chemehuevi are major exceptions to this.[124]

The Havasupai belong to the broad group of Yuman-speaking peoples of the Southwest; they usually built more temporary brush structures because they often have a migratory cultural pattern. In Arizona, Yuman is divided between the Upland Yuman speakers, the Yavapai, Havasupai, and Walapai; and the Riverine Yuman speakers, the Mohave, Yuma or Quechan, and the Maricopa.[125] While linguists tell us the Yuman languages are some of the oldest in North America, the related archaeological evidence seems to date Cerbat/Pai appearance in southern Arizona to around AD 700 and in northern Arizona to around AD 1300, or just after the great drought associated with puebloan depopulation.[126]

Maps of modern linguistic Yuman distribution point to its prevalence along both coasts of Baja California Norte, into the deserts of Southern California, up the delta of the Sea of Cortez, continuing up along the course of the Colorado River and its many tributaries: up and past Cataract Creek and Supai as far east as the Little Colorado; up the Gila and Salt tributaries of the Colorado, and up the tributaries of the Salt, including the Verde River all the way to its headwaters north of Prescott. Yuman languages are currently spoken by the Havasupai, Hualapai, Yavapai, Maricopa (Halchidoma), Cocopah, Southern Diegueño or Kumiai, Northern Diegueño or Ipai, Quechan (Yuma), Mohave, Pai Pai, and Kiliwa. One Yuman language, also called proto-Yuman, Cochimi, has no known speakers and is apparently extinct.[127] Most of these tribes are today located along the Colorado River and its tributaries, in Southern California, and in the northern half of the Baja Peninsula, in Mexico. Exact linguistic categories for some Yuman languages are still being debated in the academic literature.[128] Each year the Yuman Language Conference brings together representatives of these tribes to celebrate, promote, and preserve Yuman languages, each of which has only a few hundred fluent speakers.[129]

The high rate of mutual intelligibility of Yuman languages has been widely noted.[130] Yavapai elders, for example, report being able to understand many words spoken by the older Pai Pai of Northern Baja California, Mexico.[131] Some linguists have even suggested that the Pai Pai of Baja California Norte and the Upland Pai groups of Arizona speak the same language, with differences being merely dialectical.[132] Many Yuman myths have identical elements, such as the flood, the hero-twin-deities, or the coyote that steals the heart of the chieftain who is being cremated; the names of prominent sacred landscape features change.[133] We know that on both sides of the border, Yuman-speaking peoples interacted and traded with Uto-Aztecan speakers for several centuries. Mexican scholars point out that "these [Yuman] groups, in spite of possessing distinct languages, cultures and economies, share Uto-Aztecan mythological characters, such as coyote or the divine twins, who figure as creators of the universe."[134] Whether and how the oral culture of Yuman speakers influenced that of Uto-Aztecan speakers or vice versa is still a matter for scholarly research. Linguistic and archaeological evidence suggests that the Yuman stories evolved among some of the earliest peoples in North America who, over thousands of years, migrated down the California coast into Baja, and from thence through the deserts of Southern California up the Colorado into northern Arizona.

Although the publication of this complete oral tradition is unique, its serious limitations must be acknowledged. Most obviously, the stories are in English, whereas Spier first heard them told by men who mainly spoke Havasupai. The original narration was not recorded; it appears only the translations were written down. This is problematic, especially since 93.8 percent of tribal members in 2007 still spoke their native language—a percentage far higher than any other modern North American indigenous group.[135] The language problem could be partially rectified in the future if an edition of the stories is translated back into Havasupai for use in language preservation efforts. Two stories, "Wolf Boy" and "The Bungling Host," are presented in both Havasupai and English in Spier (1924).

Less obviously, these stories were originally interspersed with related songs.[136] Spier notes at the end of story 13—which to us is only a few pages long—that it took twenty-two hours over several

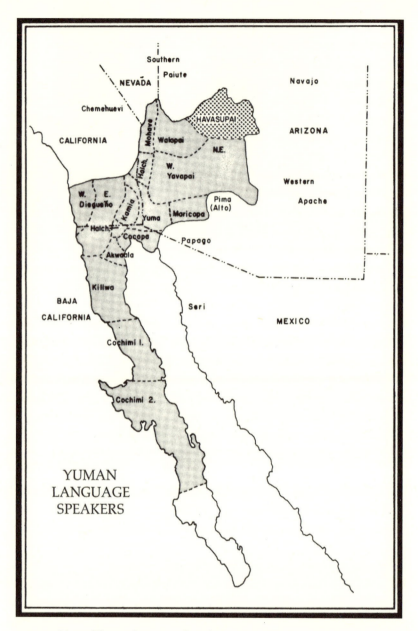

YUMAN
LANGUAGE
SPEAKERS

MAP 1: Map of Yuman language distribution in Arizona, California, and Northern Mexico. Reprinted with permission from Dobyns and Euler, *The Havasupai*, Flagstaff: Northland Press, 1971: 3.

consecutive days to tell. Modern Havasupai elders accounted for this by the missing songs. Gifford, the early ethnographer of the Northeastern and Western Yavapai, recorded that they felt it was "wrong to relate them without singing the songs."[137] Kroeber and others have pointed out that among Riverine Yumans, prose and song myth-cycle tellings were common.[138] An entire class of literature, Native American dream songs, is largely associated with Yuman myth retelling.[139] In his doctoral study of Yuman myth/song cycles, Clyde Morris remarks that "spoken words and sung words are two distinct, but complementary, forms of communication with important supernaturals."[140]

According to one modern Havasupai elder, some of the traditional stories printed in this volume were still being told from memory alone in 2006, mostly with songs, but also, though much more rarely, by themselves.[141] Another elder, in his eighties, said he regretted not having remembered more of what his grandparents tried to tell him about these stories. Although he remembered many stories, he said he couldn't remember all the songs that used to go along with them.[142]

Many efforts have been made to preserve Havasupai and other Yuman peoples' songs. Leanne Hinton's *Havasupai Songs: A Linguistic Perspective* (1984) is helpful for cultural preservation, as is the CD of traditional Havasupai songs recorded by Roland and Jeff Manakaja (2006). The 525-song cycle that recounts the creation and origin of the Yuman-speaking Mohave people has also been preserved, as have many songs and stories of the Californian Yumans, who have a similar story/dream/song framework.[143]

Questions arise about whether additional stories were known by people who had already died, or who chose not to speak to the anthropologists; or whether, as Halpern found among the Quechan, there were different men's and women's versions of the stories.[144] Modern informants seem to think the stories of the two were the same, but that the accompanying songs were most often sung by men.[145] The field research conducted by Carma Lee Smithson on Havasupai women (1959) was the source of some of the stories published in 1964, and these do seem, as a generalization, to have a slightly more feminine content (childbirth, marriage, and menstruation) than the Sinyella and Manakaja stories from 1918–1921. However, the Smithson stories are not as detailed and complete as the earlier ones.

As anthropologist Walter Taylor said, "[A]bsence of evidence is not evidence of absence."[146] We may never know what cultural treasures have been lost to the southwestern tribes; we do know that this most complete and earliest collection of Havasupai stories should rightfully take its place among those that have been found.

All those materials, whether cultural, genetic, or physical, which have been obtained from sovereign native peoples, should be dealt with carefully and with tribal consultation; we have tried to do so with this book.[147] This basic tenet of intercultural respect has not always been granted the Havasupai, who have always been a generous people. In respect for those who produced these stories, we have made an attempt to understand the wider archaeological, ethnographic, historic, and linguistic context of the Havasupai. Yet the stories themselves may contain more information than all our attempts at multidisciplinary contextualization. As anthropologist Ruth Benedict observed, "The advantage of mythological material over any other, for the characterization of tribal life, consists in the fact that here alone we have these things recorded wholly as they themselves figure them to themselves."[148]

| NOTES |

1. Coues, 1900.
2. Martin, 1985.
3. Dobyns and Euler, 1967: 49.
4. Indian Claims Commission, 1968: 226–29.
5. Ives, [1861] 1969.
6. Euler, 1979: 12–65.
7. Dobyns and Euler, 1967; Dever, 2000.
8. Dobyns and Euler, 1967: 42; Kroeber, 1935.
9. Michno, 2003: v. Later battles in the 1871–1890 period took place further east, primarily against the Yavapai and Apache, near the Verde and the Salt rivers.
10. U.S. Government Printing Office, Walapai Papers, 1936. A copy of Hardy's treaty-contract, attested by three Walapai chiefs, Wauba Yuma, Hitchie Hitchie, and Cherum, is on p. 35. It did not say the Indians had the right to a stock toll, rather that they would be paid one dollar for every head of livestock they recovered and returned to Hardy's company.
11. Thrapp, 1967: 40–52; Farish, Vol. 2, 1915: 257–62; Spicer, 1962.

12. Messersmith, 2002.

13. Dobyns and Euler, 1967: 46.

14. Dobyns and Euler, 1970: 15.

15. Dobyns and Euler, 1967. See also *We Are Hualapai*. Azcentral.com, 2007. http://www.azcentral.com/culturesaz/amindian/tribes/hualapai_amind. html

16. Sperry and Myers, 2001. An excellent overview of nineteenth-century U.S.-Pai warfare can be found in Peter Cozzens's (2001) *The Struggle for Apacheria: Eyewitnesses to the Indian Wars, 1865–1890*. It includes Lt. Col. Price's first-hand account of his 1881 visit to Chief Navajo, the uncle of Manakaja, who is one of the narrators of these stories.

17. Spier's unpublished field research notes (1918–1921), courtesy of the Division of Anthropology Archives, American Museum of Natural History.

18. Spicer, 1962: 275.

19. *The Arizona Miner* [Prescott], Sept. 15, 1878.

20. Dobyns and Euler, 1971: 21.

21. Dobyns and Euler, 1967: 45.

22. Hirst, 2006: 93.

23. Spicer, 1962; Dobyns and Euler, 1971; and modern Havasupai tribal member remembering her grandparents' stories about this mine.

24. Coues, 1900.

25. Cozzens, 2001: 229. Quoting from a report Lt. Col. William R. Price submitted to the Assistant Adjutant General, Department of Arizona, from Fort Whipple Barracks, Prescott, July 1, 1881. Of course, had this been true, then the Havasupai would still control Indian Gardens and Moencopi, aboriginal farms many miles east of Cataract Canyon (Dobyns and Euler, 1971). The government's reservation boundaries, by excluding the plateau, completely ignored Havasupai mixed-subsistence patterns.

26. Cushing, 1882: 551–53.

27. Broder, 1990.

28. Cozzens, 2001: 447, quoting from Henry W. Daly's recollections, 1933.

29. Spicer, 1962: 273.

30. Iliff, [1954] 1990.

31. William Wallace Bass came to the Grand Canyon in 1884 for health reasons. He spent more than forty years living there and during that time did some prospecting, worked an asbestos mine, got married and became the first person of European descent to raise a family at the Canyon.

32. James, 1900.

33. Iliff, [1954] 1990: 140.

34. Dobyns, 1989.

35. Jacobs, 1999; Roberts, 2006.

36. The Havasupai told Spier they started to inter rather than cremate the deceased about sixty years before his visit.

37. Spier, 1928: 292.

38. Dobyns and Euler, 1971: 14–21.

39. One might also mention in this context the big horn sheep hunter, Charles Sheldon, who hired Sinyella and Manakaja's son Jasper to go hunt sheep with him for a few days in the autumn of 1912. His brief account is so evidently racist that the historical or cultural importance of his visit is probably negligible. His photographs, however, are fascinating. Carmony and Brown, 1993.

40. Dobyns and Euler, 1998.

41. Dobyns and Euler, 1971: 27.

42. Spier's introduction to the stories, this volume.

43. Spier, 1928: 83.

44. Ibid.

45. *Scientific American*, 1919: 323–24.

46. *Scientific American*, 1919.

47. Some 157 photographs of these items have been digitized and are available for viewing online at: http://anthro.amnh.org. Search the "Collections Database" of the Anthropology Department of the American Museum of Natural History > North American Ethnographic Collection > Southwest > Havasupai.

48. Spier, 1922: 183.

49. Ibid.: 187.

50. Dobyns and Euler, 1970: 73; Martin, 1985.

51. Gifford, 1933: 348. After examining Spier's notes, Gifford wrote that Havasupai mythology "virtually duplicates" the Northeastern Yavapai mythology, not unexpected for colingual groups, but less expected for traditional enemy groups. Forbes, 1965, also has a section discussing the similarities of Yuman myth.

52. Laylander, 2006.

53. Dobyns and Euler, 1999a. See also Forbes, 1965; Spicer, 1962.

54. Wilken-Robertson, 1999.

55. Morris, 1974: 8.

56. Historians have debated similar themes of authority and structure in respect to the colingual, culturally similar but warring tribes of the Greek peninsula.

57. Dobyns and Euler, 1970; 1999b; Braatz, 1998; 1999a; 1999b.

58. Dobyns and Euler, 1970.

59. Ibid.

60. Braatz, 1998; 1999a; 1999b.

61. Dobyns and Euler, *Pai Cultural Change*, 1999b.

62. Braatz, 1999b: 138.

63. Spier, 1928: 237.

64. Ibid.: 254.

65. Ibid.: 242–43.

66. Ibid.: 237.

67. Ibid.: 235.

68. Spier, 1928.

69. Spier's unpublished field research notes (1918–1921), courtesy of the Division of Anthropology Archives, American Museum of Natural History.

70. Spier, 1928: 236.

71. Ibid.: 235. Jess Chickapanega was one of the native translators for Manakaja and Sinyella, helping Spier collect their stories, as well as a former pupil of Flora Gregg Iliff's (Iliff, [1954] 1990: 111).

72. Spier's unpublished field research notes (1918–1921), pp. 40–43, courtesy of the Division of Anthropology Archives, American Museum of Natural History.

73. Spier's unpublished field research notes (1918–1921), pp. 42–43, courtesy of the Division of Anthropology Archives, American Museum of Natural History.

74. Sinyella's son Dean married Panamida's daughter Fannie (Spier, 1928).

75. Spier's unpublished field research notes (1918–1921), pp. 42–43, courtesy of the Division of Anthropology Archives, American Museum of Natural History.

76. Spier, 1928: 237.

77. Spier's unpublished field research notes, p. 42, courtesy of the Division of Anthropology Archives, American Museum of Natural History.

78. Iliff, [1954] 1990: 18–19.

79. Morris, 1974: 61.

80. Hinton and Watahomigie, 1984: 6.

81. A. F. Whiting, undated mss., Ethnography, 161. NAU Special Collections.

82. Cushing, 1882.

83. Spier, 1928; Whiting, misc. unpublished manuscripts in NAU Special Collections.

84. Morris, 1974: 58.

85. Aguilera, 2005: 97.

86. Spier, 1933: 276 and elsewhere.

87. Whiting, "The Fixed Stars," n.d., 74, unpublished manuscript in NAU Special Collections.

88. Spier, 1928.

89. Spier, 1928.

90. Whiting, n.d., manuscript in NAU Special Collections.

91. Whiting, "Havasupai Indian astronomy and calendrical observations," n.d., 29–31, 117, unpublished manuscript in NAU Special Collections; Spier, 1928.

92. Spier, 1928: 287.

93. Morris, 1974: 4.

94. Smithson and Euler, 1994.

95. Abram, 1996.

96. Ibid.

97. Ibid.: 7–9.

98. Ibid.

99. Whiting, Ethnography, n.d., Tables 13.1 and 13.2. NAU Special Collections.

100. Langdon, 1978.

101. Smithson and Euler, 1994: 3–19. See Wallace, 1947, for the dream in Mohave life.

102. Cleland, 2005.

103. Spier, 1928; Smithson and Euler, 1964.

104. Author's personal recollection of a field lecture, 1991.

105. Spier, 1928.

106. Spier's unpublished field research notes, p. 5, courtesy of the Division of Anthropology Archives, American Museum of Natural History.

107. Spier, 1928: 278.

108. Ibid.

109. Kroeber, 1920; Bahr, 1996.

110. Underwood, 2002.

111. Mike Burns Manuscript. DB82, Item 2. Prescott: Sharlot Hall Museum Library, 123. Unpublished manuscript sent to Sharlot Hall by Mike Burns, ca. 1923.

112. Morris, 1974.

113. Spier, 1928.

114. Aguilera, 2005: 20. Translation by author.

115. Hirst, 2006.

116. Iliff, [1954] 1990.

117. Hirst, 2006: 21.

118. Havasupai Tribal Website, 2006; Hirst, 2006: 241.

119. Muñiz, 2007.

120. Cushing, 1882, quoted in Farish, 1918, Vol. 7, 115.

121. Muñiz, 2007, Abstract. This exceptional doctoral dissertation contains web-based policy and contact information for indigenous language education programs in all fifty U.S. states.

122. Ibid.

123. A. L. Kroeber, in Parsons, 1922: 8.

124. Shaul and Hill, 1998.

125. Gumerman, 1994: 187.

126. R. C. Euler, "The Prehistory of the Grand Canyon," Ch. 1, this volume. See also John F. Martin, 1985. Also McGuire, Adams, Nelson, and Spielmann, in Gumerman, 1994: 260.

127. Native Languages of the Americas, n.d. See also Kroeber, 1920.

128. Mixco, 1983; Aguilera, 2005; Garduño, 2003; Mithun, 2001.

129. Cook, 2003.

130. Biggs, 1957.

131. Author's personal conversation with Yavapai elder, Yavapai-Prescott Indian Tribe, Prescott, Arizona.

132. Kendall, 1983; Langdon, 1996; Campbell, 1997.

133. Erdoes and Ortiz, 1984: 77; Aguilera, 2005; Hinton and Watahomigie, 1984. See also all early Yuman ethnographers, Spier, Meigs, Kroeber, Gifford, Densmore, Waterman, etc.

134. Wilken-Robertson, 1993. Aguilera, Miguel. Las creencias indígenas y neo-indias en la frontera MEX/USA, Travaux et Reserches dans les Amériques du Centre (TRACE), Vol. 54, pp. 45–60. http://trace.revues.org/index468. html. There is no further discussion of which culture borrowed these elements from which culture, although, as in this citation, migratory peoples (Yumans) are usually assumed to have borrowed cultural elements from the supposedly more advanced settled peoples (Uto-Aztecans). In some cases, however, it is possible that the more migratory cultures are older in time, as the linguistic evidence indicates for Yuman.

135. Brenzinger, 2007.

136. Hinton and Watahomigie, 1984; confirmed in author's personal conversations with tribal elders in 2008.

137. Morris, 1974: 2, quoting Gifford, 1933: 348.

138. Bahr, 1996.

139. Bahr, 1994.

140. Morris, 1974: 2.

141. Informal discussion with Rex Tilousi, former tribal chairman, June 2006.

142. Informal discussion with Stanley Manakaja, former tribal chairman, February 2008.

143. Davia Nelson and Nikki Silva, *House of Night: The Lost Creation Songs of the Mohave People*, produced by The Kitchen Sisters, Davia Nelson and Nikki Silva with Jim McKee at Earwax Productions, Lost and Found Sound Project, 2000. Recordings collected around 1972 by Guy Tyler, of Mohave Creation Singer, and elder Emmet van Fleet. See also Herbert W. Luthin, ed., *Surviving Through the Days: Translations of Native California Stories and Songs* (University of California Press, 2002). See also, *Bird Songs of the Colorado River*, Quechan and Mohave songs recorded by Joe Guachino, J. R. Holmes, and Wally Antone in Needles, CA, 2005 (Indian House, Box 472, Taos, NM, 87571).

144. Halpern, 1980.

145. Alberta Manakaja, 2008. Personal conversation with author.

146. Author's personal recollection.

147. See United Nations Commission on Human Rights, Sub-Commission of Prevention of Discrimination and Protection of Minorities, Working Group on Indigenous Populations, 19–30, July 1993. First International Conference on the Cultural & Intellectual Property Rights of Indigenous Peoples, Whakatana, 12–18, June 1993, Aotearoa, New Zealand, The Mataatua Declaration on Cultural and Intellectual Property Rights of Indigenous Peoples. http://www.ankn.uaf.edu/IKS/mataatua.html. In the case of these stories, consultations about their publication with various tribal members, elders and the tribal council were conducted over a five-year period, ending when the tribal council gave formal permission for publication.

148. Benedict, 1924, quoted in Parezo, 1993.

Chapter 4

An Overture to the Scientific Study of Myth

| FRANK D. TIKALSKY AND JOHN NAGEL |

Science must begin with myths and with the criticism of
myths.

—Karl Popper (1957)

UNTIL THE LATE NINETEENTH CENTURY THE ANCIENT
phenomenon of myth was regarded as it had been since the Enlighten-
ment, as a primitive way of knowing, a phenomenon to be supplanted
by science. The growth of the social and behavioral sciences in the
early twentieth century led to the recognition of the vital role that
myth plays in the lives of people in most cultures. By the beginning
of the twenty-first century the study of myth included the application
of numerous psychological and anthropological theories. What does
that abundance of theory reflect? As one distinguished mathemati-
cian/physicist put it:

> The existence of a variety of theories about a given phenom-
> enon is a sign that it may be perceived in a variety of different
> ways. This may be a sign of scientific vitality; not weakness,
> especially if we are perceiving a marvelous phenomenon.[1]

Most people no longer use mythic explanations to account for
natural phenomena; and in fact it is now widely believed that this
never was the primary function of myth. Instead, the myth's *raison*

d'etre may be, to functionalists such as Bronislaw Malinowski, to enhance the functioning of social institutions. For Jungians the study of myth provides insight into the mind of man. This Jungian notion is evident, for example, in the popular writings of Joseph Campbell.

Although a variety of scientific theories have been applied to myth study, Segal emphasizes that no scientific theory deals exclusively with myth.[2] Instead theories of larger scope, most from psychology and anthropology, are applied to myth. In psychology, these theories exist in the theoretical categories of Freudian psychodynamics, neo-Freudian theory, and Jungian individual psychology. In anthropology, the social anthropological theories of structuralism and functionalism prevail. The obvious implication is that any introduction to the scientific study of myth must introduce these theories. And to appreciate these theories one must begin with the meaning of the scientific concepts *theory*, *fact*, and *hypothesis*.

As a hypothetical example of the scientific use of the terms *theory*, *fact*, and *hypothesis*, imagine a fourteenth-century sailor on a ship making observations of other ships in the distance. In those pre-Copernican days, it was almost universally believed that the earth was flat. Strange as it seems to us now, this belief was supported remarkably well by some astronomical observations. The important point for us to grasp is that this belief in the earth's flatness is a theory. Now the sailor is an astute observer because his observations (facts) of the ships are inconsistent with the flatness theory. The ships sailing away from him toward a distant horizon do not appear to diminish in size to a vanishing point, but instead, at a distance of some seven nautical miles, they appear to sink! His empirical observations are inconsistent with the assumption (theory) that the earth is flat. Now, he must modify the theory or develop a new one. The sailor does just that by assuming, "Perhaps the earth is round." A great step forward in scientific inquiry occurs when the sailor goes on to develop his hypothesis. A hypothesis may be defined as an "if, then" statement which can be tested. An example could be: "If I sail continually in one direction, then I should return to the point of origin." What can be learned from this example? We learn that there is an intimate relationship between theory, fact, and hypothesis, and that theories give the things we observe meaning. This is one of the most important understandings we should develop. But we should understand, in addition, that theories also define the observations we make, point to gaps in our knowledge, and predict facts. As this example shows, we do not experiment directly with theories; rather, we experiment with hypotheses deduced from theories.

In addition to knowing something about theories and their application, the person new to myth study needs some basic knowledge of myth. A brief, readable authoritative text is Robert A. Segal's, *Myth: A Very Short Introduction* (2004). This work will provide an understanding of the central topics addressed in myth study: origin, function, and subject matter. In conjunction with reading and study, taped interviews by Bill Moyers with Joseph Campbell may enhance appreciation of the phenomenon of myth.

To achieve a further understanding of how a social science theory may be applied to myth study, we have selected the theory of cultural evolution, which has played a vigorous role in anthropology and whose most famous advocate is Leslie A. White.[3] The analysis provided here is neither extensive nor definitive; however, it is generally accurate. In our example, we will focus on the Havasupai.

Cultural evolution theory holds that the way a society harnesses energy, and the means at its disposal for harnessing such energy (technology), determines how social affairs will be conducted (social organization), and that technology and social institutions are the ultimate determiners of the beliefs, values, and philosophies of any cultural group. For example, it is clear that a simple, food-gathering culture has different educational needs from western industrial societies. Therefore, to the cultural evolutionist, the way societies function results from technological and social factors, not primarily from the psychological nature of any individual or group.

What was Havasupai culture like when the myths in this volume were first recorded? In the preface to his classic work, *Havasupai Ethnography* (1928), Spier states that cultural changes in Havasupai culture were minimal between the time when the myths were first collected and the writing of the ethnography in 1925.

Spier maintained that "the Havasupai were largely agriculturists."[4] He goes on to assert that food gathering was minimal and done largely to provide food when crops were poor. The early pattern of the Havasupai was to farm during the summer months at the bottom of the Grand Canyon, and in the winter months live on the canyon rim. Thus, hunting deer and desert sheep was most important during the fall and winter. Spier describes the principal agricultural crops as a blend of various corn types, with some varieties being received from neighboring peoples, principally the Hopi. In addition, beans, squash, and watermelon were part of the Havasupai diet. The Havasupai were adroit basket weavers and fashioned clothes from deer hides and rabbit fur. Havasupai myths "The Culture Heroes" and "The Origin of Corn" suggest their skill at basket weaving and clothes making as well as showing how they lived the deeper meaning of the myths. There were significant culture changes as the result of the Havasupai forced abandonment of the canyon rim in the late nineteenth century and the assumption of year-round occupancy below the canyon rim. Nonetheless, they continued to be essentially an agricultural people.[5]

"Religious matters," according to Spier, "occupy but a minor place in Havasupai life and interest in the supernatural is neither extensive nor developed in any systematic form."[6] He then explores Havasupai spiritual concepts for several pages. So, a caveat is in order here. Whatever Spier, Euler, or any social scientist says about Havasupai spirituality, it should be viewed with the understanding that the Havasupai currently, and probably prehistorically, did not fully disclose many beliefs about this sacred oral tradition. In our recent consultations with the Havasupai, many have affirmed its importance.

Spier reported that "[s]hamans alone commonly see ghosts, or rather, their familiar spirits see them out at night and report their doings, and yet others may see them. . . . Ghosts are said always to be malignant."[7] While Spier indicated that the Havasupai believed that "[e]ach human has a soul in his heart" (see "The Origin of Corn"), Carma Lee Smithson and Robert Euler found that many believe soul and heart are synonymous.[8]

To summarize, there are many examples of Havasupai myths that are concerned with crop success, food gathering, and relationships with neighbors from whom agricultural skills were assimilated. Complex religious organization, formal institutionalized tribal practice, planned worship structures, priests, and ministers are not evident. Animistic, pantheistic beliefs along with shamanistic practices were common, and this is precisely what evolutionary theory would predict based on Havasupai technological development.

This, perhaps, is a good place to compare the nature of analysis used by culture evolutionists with some other theoretical approach, for example, Freudian psychology. Whereas evolutionary theory sees social variables as the critical determiners of myth development, the

Freudians see the mind as the primary determiner. Freudians explain the social in terms of the psychological, not the converse.

Freud was deeply concerned with the processes by which aggression and sexual drives are managed in any society, since not inhibiting these impulses, to some significant extent, could lead to social chaos. Havasupai sacred stories caution about sexual involvement "too young" as in "The Boy Who Killed Blue Hawk" and "Wolf's Boy." Analogously, stories such as "The Separation of the Havasupai and Yavapai" give direction for managing aggressive impulses. In other words, traditional myths and stories not only help the child master and redirect sexual and aggressive impulses, but also provide culture heroes and role models for getting through conflict and difficult times.

A question often posed by those studying myths is, "Why is it that some myths survive and some don't?" This question is particularly relevant to the Havasupai because apparently some of the myths published in this book are no longer completely retained in their cultural memory. It could be that some myths are so sacred, similar to the Trobriand Lili'u, that they simply will not talk about them to people external to their culture. It is also possible that some stories were not sacred or disappeared because they no longer had culture utility.

Functionalism, as an anthropological theory, exposed by Malinowski, argues that all social institutions, including myths, exist because they ultimately contribute to culture survival. Hence, some myths may fade or dissolve because they no longer contribute to the survival of important cultural features. Since agriculture no longer plays the critical role that it did when the myths in this volume were collected, perhaps some myths have been forgotten because they no longer provide culture survival value. In other words, the myths in any culture are seen to exist in a constantly changing process. Some persons have erroneously concluded that the disappearance of some myths from culture memory is a sign of the weakening of culture vitality. That assumption may not be true. Cultures are continually changing.

It should be noted here that the only systematic scientific study of Yuman myth, focusing exclusively on a Yuman people (the Havasupai are a Yuman people), was a dissertation by Clyde Patrick Morris (1974). The study was predicated on the work of Claude Levi-Strauss (1967) whose anthropologic theory is ordinarily referred to as structuralism.

We have assigned the title of "First Scientific Myth Theorist" to Sigmund Freud. Freud's theory of psychoanalysis has been enormously influential. In fact, for the first four decades of the twentieth century the theories of Freud and Jung almost monopolized psychology's scientific investigation of myth and contributed greatly to the development of a field known as "Culture and Personality." And while Freud's influence has diminished, it clearly continues in the twenty-first century.[9]

The psychoanalytic tradition suggests many theories about the functions and meanings of myth, applicable both to individual and to group behavior. Freud theorized that myth is rooted in the psychosexual development of children and the psychodynamics of family experience. In *Totem and Taboo* (1936), he explored his belief that the manifest content of both myths and folktales made explicit the unconscious experience of the developing child—for example, in the Oedipus complex. In his view, unconscious wishes and forbidden, repressed desires were manifested in the dreams of individuals as well as in the myths and tales of cultures.

No scientist has been more intensively involved in the study of myth theory than Carl Jung, whose analytic psychology has impacted several scholarly fields in profound ways. Nor has any myth theorist better summarized his position and the importance of myth for mankind generally as Jung when he wrote the following:

> The primitive mentality does not *invent* myths, it *experiences* them. Myths are original revelations of the preconscious psyche, involuntary statements about unconscious psychic happenings, and anything but allegories of physical processes. Such allegories would be an idle amusement for an unscientific intellect. Myths have a vital meaning. Not merely do they represent, they *are* the psychic life of the primitive tribe, which immediately falls to pieces and decays when it loses its mythological heritage, like a man who has lost his soul. A tribe's mythology is its living religion, whose loss is always and everywhere, even among the civilized, a moral catastrophe.[10]

Jung built his theory on his experience with his clients and his cross-cultural study of art and myth. Two of the many concepts formulated by Jung are central to understanding his views about the origins and function of myths: archetypes and the collective unconscious. It is impossible to overestimate the influence of these concepts in contemporary theorizing about myth. The work of Joseph Campbell is but one example. In *Archetypes of the Collective Unconscious* (1959) Jung expanded Freud's "structural theory" of the human psyche. Freud had posited three layers of human personality: conscious, preconscious, and unconscious. Jung included both a "personal unconscious" and a "collective unconscious."[11] He introduced the concept that certain symbolic "mythological motifs" are "archetypes" or "primordial images" that reappear in various cultures and historical periods. Hence the collective unconscious, as described by Jung, is a reservoir of latent memories inherited as "archaic remnants" from human prehistory. Thus, humans share a common meaning in a wide variety of symbols such as water, fire, and the circle. In *Symbols and the Interpretation of Dreams*, Jung observed that these "mythological motifs . . . vary a great deal without losing their basic pattern."[12] The individual's "inherited tendency is instinctive, like the specific impulse of nest building, migration, etc. in birds." He noted that these "representation collectives occur practically everywhere, and [are] characterized by the same or similar motifs. They cannot be assigned to any particular time or region or race. They are without known origin and they can reproduce themselves even when transmission through migration must be ruled out."[13] Jung speculated that myths represent the deepest level of psychic life "of whole nations and epochs," and so "can be interpreted as a sort of mental therapy for the sufferings of mankind such as hunger, war, disease, old age and death."[14]

A good summary of Jung's theory can be found in almost any textbook on theories of personality. An extensive examination of Jungian theory in its application to the study of myth is Segal's *Jung on Mythology* (1998). The reader who develops an interest in psychoanalytic views of myth, should begin by reading Freud's discussion of the Oedipus complex, which occurs in his book *Symbols and the Interpretation of Dreams* (1959). For Freud and Jung the dynamics of myths and dreams are closely related. Other theories pertaining to myth exist in the fields of folklore, linguistics, and communication theory.

It is critical to include in our essay a brief summary of Bronislaw Malinowski's extensive contributions to myth theory. After earning a Ph.D. in Philosophy and Physics at the University of Krakow (1906), Malinowski developed an interest in so-called primitive cultures that led him to formal study in anthropology under the British scholar Charles Seligman and to field study in New Guinea (1914–1918). In the field of culture and personality study, Malinowski is honored for his cross-cultural investigation of Freudian theory (Oedipus complex) focusing on the myths and stories of peoples in the Trobriand Islands.

"Myth as it exists in a savage community," Malinowski wrote, "that is, in its living primitive form, is not merely a story told but a reality lived."[15] "Myth is to the savage what, to a fully believing Christian, is the Biblical story of creation, of the Fall, of the Redemption by Christ's Sacrifice on the Cross."[16] Further, such belief performs specific functions. Malinowski asserts, "Myth fulfills in the primitive culture an indispensable function: it expresses, enhances and codifies belief; it safeguards and enforces reality; it vouches for efficiency of ritual and contains practical rules for the guidance of man."[17]

As these quotations suggest, Malinowski's ideas combined elements of psychodynamic and functionalist thinking. It is because of his enlightened and insightful functionalism that we include a discussion of his theoretical position as it pertains to myth.

Malinowski conceptualized culture as a living, integrated whole, whose parts are interrelated. In other words, parts of a culture, such as myths, can only be fully understood as elements in a whole, functioning system. The history of a culture is not of crucial importance to a functionalist; culture is to be investigated and studied on a single time plane. In the language of psychological theorizing, Malinowski's theorizing has a Gestalt flavor. Certainly, his background in physics acquainted him with the scientific concept of the *field*, and field theory is prominent in Gestalt theory. Malinowski's work has been wonderfully edited and introduced by Ivan Strenski (1992). A critical evaluation of Malinowski's theorizing about myth is found in Strenski's *Four Theories of Myth in Twentieth Century History* (1987).

Clyde Kluckhohn made one of the clearest statements of the functionalist position concerning myth.

- Myths and rituals are "cultural forms defining individual behavior which are adaptive of adjustive responses."
- Mythology may be understood as a "cultural storehouse of adjustive responses for individuals."
- Myths offer "cultural solutions to problems which all human beings face."[18]

This introduction to the scientific study of myth omits many critically important theorists. For further reading we have already recommended the wonderfully written works by Segal. Doty's (2000) *Mythography: The Study of Myths and Rituals* is another place to begin.

Finally, a few words should be said about communication theory, and how such theory may apply to the Havasupai. Myths should be regarded as special forms of communication, not to be confused with the oral transmission of ideas to which modern man has become accustomed.

Compare a classroom psychological experiment with a phenomenon often found in preliterate societies. In the classroom experiment fifteen or twenty students sit in a circle. A few lines are whispered to the first student, who is instructed to whisper that information to the student sitting to the right, and so on around the circle. The last student in the group reports the content of the orally communicated message. That message is then compared with the one that was initially communicated. Gross discrepancies are the rule. For example, the initial message could be, "The spirit is willing, but the flesh is weak." The last person in the group might report, "The vodka is acceptable but the meat is rotten."

Although this experiment is relevant to communication, it does not apply to the oral transmission of folktales and myths. Nor does it apply to long-standing oral traditions such as we are presenting in this volume. For example, we can see from Spier's *Havasupai Myths and Tales* manuscript that he had visited the Havasupai in the Grand Canyon on at least three occasions (1918, 1919, and 1921) with the primary objective of collecting ethnographic material—especially the traditional stories narrated by tribal elders. On occasion he would ask the same person to retell a story after an interval of months or years. These retellings are faithful and accurate to their first telling, an indication that these stories stand apart from everyday conversation and information sharing. This finding matches the conclusions reported by philologists and pioneer folklorists Jacob and Wilhelm Grimm in the preface to the second edition of the 1819 book *Kinder Und Haus Maerchen*. Here the Brothers Grimm celebrate the contribution of Frau Vichmann, a particularly gifted *maerchenbeitragerin*, or story keeper, who was able to recite stories "exactly, . . . eager for their correctness" even after a passage of time between tellings.[19]

Communications theorist Walter Ong offers an interesting comment on the discrepancy between the errors in transmission in a class experiment and the remarkable accuracy we often find in the transmission of myths. Discussing the work of Albert B. Lord, Ong observes that "illiterate singers in the widely literate culture of modern Yugoslavia admire literacy and believe that a literate person can do even better what they do, namely, recreate a lengthy song after hearing it only once. This is precisely what literates cannot do, or can do only with difficulty. As literates attribute literate kinds of achievement to oral performers, so oral performers attribute oral kinds of achievement to literates."[20]

Summary

In this essay we have attempted to provide a brief introduction to the scientific study of myth. At the outset, we acknowledged that there is an abundance of theory and we quoted a distinguished mathematician/physicist to suggest that this may be a sign of scientific strength.

Philosophers of science may cringe at our account of theory, fact, and hypothesis. Because myth study is replete with theory, we wanted the person attempting such study to know that theory is more than a mere guess.

We applied the theories of cultural evolution and Freudian psychology to Havasupai culture in order to give a "feeling" for theory application, not to provide a comprehensive study. We suggested readings for those new to myth study. We were careful to emphasize that many theories beyond the purview of this essay, particularly in folklore and linguistics, are major contributions to the study of myth.

Robert C. Euler and Robert A. Segal, the former well known for his archaeological and social anthropological investigations in the Grand Canyon and the latter well known for his myth theory scholarship, are excellent guides for introductory study of Havasupai myths. Both of these scholars have authored introductory texts: Dobyns and Euler (1971) and Segal (2004). And lastly, another starting point we favor is Carma Lee Smithson and Robert C. Euler's *Havasupai Religion and Mythology* (1994).

| NOTES |

1. Personal correspondence, Frank Tikalsky and Darryl Holm, Professor of Mathematics, Imperial College, London, June 20, 2009.
2. Robert Segal, 2004.
3. Leslie White, 1959.
4. Leslie Spier, 1928: 101.
5. Dobyns and Euler, 1971. In 1880 President Hayes seized three million acres of Havasupai homeland and restricted the tribe to 38,400 acres in a five-by-twelve-mile strip. Their winter homes on the canyon rim were burned, and the Havasupai people were officially confined to the bottom of the canyon.
6. Spier, 1928: 275.
7. Ibid.
8. Smithson and Euler, 1994: 3.
9. In spite of the ascendance of behavioral and cognitive psychology and the apparent diminishment of Freudian analysis, the work of Alan Dundes (folklore) and Northrup Frye (literary criticism) thrives.
10. Jung, 1959: 154. The words "civilized" and "primitive" were not used pejoratively by Jung and would not be employed by contemporary scholars.
11. Ibid.: 1–3.
12. Jung, 1938: 63.
13. Jung, Vol. 18, II, 1959: 228.
14. Ibid.: 238.
15. Malinowski, 1948: 78.
16. Ibid.
17. Ibid.: 79.
18. Kluckhohn, 1942: 64–66.
19. Grimm and Grimm, 1819: 3–4.
20. Lord, 1960: 28; Ong, 1982.

PLATE 1: Mooney Falls. Photo by Frank D. Tikalsky, 1974.

PLATE 2: Mooney Falls. Photo by Frank D. Tikalsky, 1974.

PLATE 3: Havasupai Creek. Photo by Frank D. Tikalsky, 1974.

PLATE 4: Early Havasupai structure built no later than the early 1900s. Note from Robert C. Euler. Photograph by Frank D. Tikalsky, 1970.

PLATE 5: Molly Mulgullo. Mother of Havasupai Tribal Chairman Lee Marshall.
It was Marshall who said to a congressional committee in the 1960s, "You talk
about the Grand Canyon: I am the Grand Canyon." Note from Robert C. Euler.
Photo by Robert C. Euler, 1956.

PLATE 6: Pachilawa, Walapai Chief. From Vol. II, *The North American Indian*, 1908. Photo by Edward S. Curtis. Original photo owned by Frank D. Tikalsky. During our interview with Lee Marshall in 1962, he said of this photo, "We are the same people."

PLATE 7: Tonovige, Havasupai Woman. From Vol. II, *The North American Indian*, 1908. Photo by Edward S. Curtis. Original photo owned by Frank D. Tikalsky. Of this photo Curtis wrote, "The Havasupai were encamped in the high country above their canyon home. As a snowstorm was raging at the time, Tonovige's hair became dotted with flakes as this picture reveals." Some say Tonovige was Walapai.

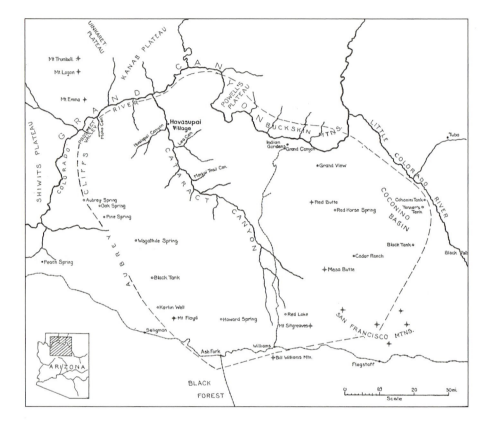

MAP 2: Map showing aboriginal Havasupai territory, as well as past and current reservation boundaries, with inset map of Arizona. Courtesy of the artist, Charles Sternberg.

| PART II |

The Sacred Oral Tradition of the Havasupai

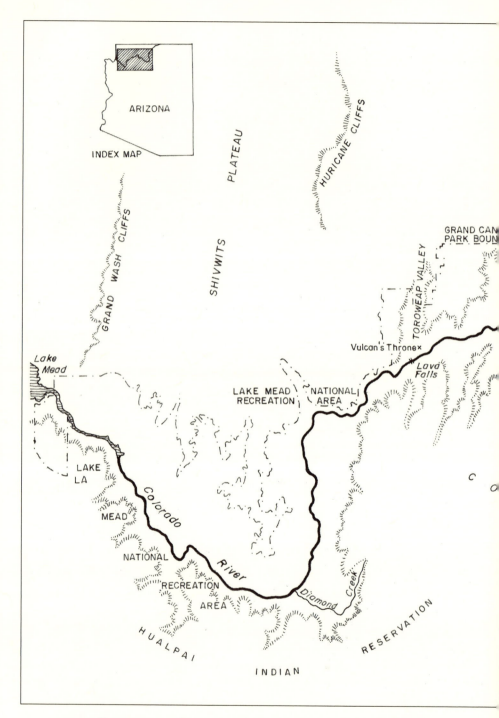

MAP 3: Havasupai Grand Canyon environs. Courtesy of the artist, Charles Sternberg.

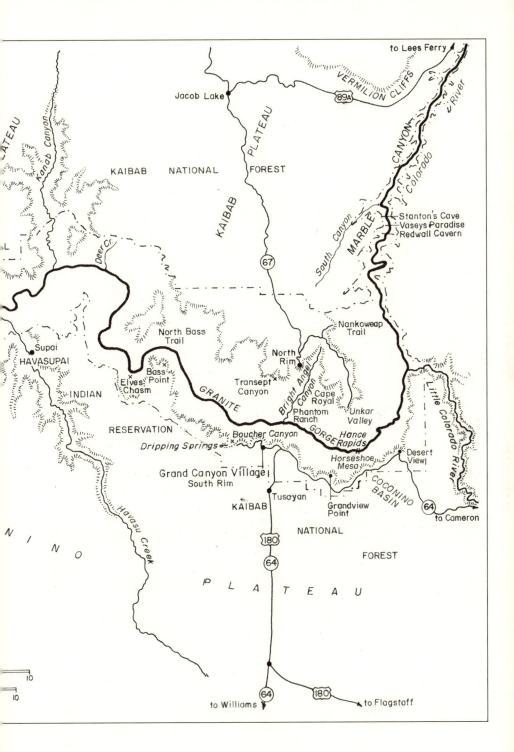

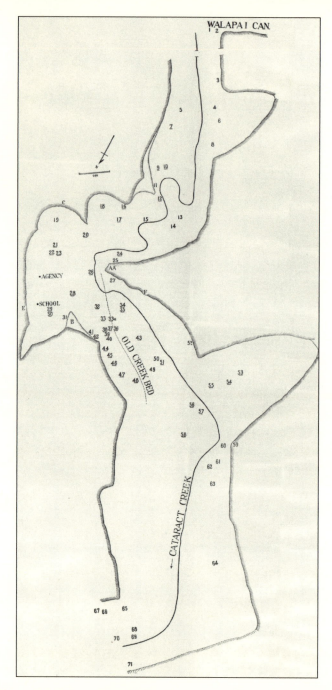

MAP 4: The original map of Supai Village and surrounding rock formations as hand-drawn by Leslie Spier for his *Havasupai Ethnography* (1928: 321). Letters in the collection of stories that refer to various rock formations can be found here: AA, C, E, and F. The numbers refer to the locations of particular family camps.

Introduction

| LESLIE SPIER |

THESE TALES OF THE HAVASUPAI OF NORTH-CENTRAL ARIZONA were collected in 1918, 1919, and 1921 by Leslie Spier, and in 1921 by Erna Gunther. The work of the former was subsidized by the American Museum of Natural History and the Southwest Society of New York, and carried on in part as Cutting Travelling Fellow of Columbia University. Other versions of a few of these tales obtained as texts have already been published (Leslie Spier, "Havasupai [Yuman] Texts," *International Journal of American Linguistics* 3: 109–16, 1924).

This collection comprises all the tales known to two old men, Sinyella and Manakadja, or this is at least true of the former. Both were men of about seventy, both chiefs, and thoroughly conversant with the simple culture of their people in all its phases. Character sketches of the two can be found in Leslie Spier, *Havasupai Ethnography* (Anthropological Papers, American Museum of Natural History 29(3): 237–41, 1928). Neither was a good raconteur, but Manakadja was the better of the two. Spier used Jess Chickapanega as interpreter with Sinyella and Mark Hanna with Manakadja; Gunther used Lillie Burro's services with the latter informant. These three were about thirty years old, had a moderate command of English, and were all relatively uncontaminated by white civilization. In some of the earlier tales collected by Gunther, Manakadja, or more probably the interpreter Lillie, may be suspected of toning down or avoiding obscene elements. The result of this is apparently so slight as not to affect the value of the tales. The tales recorded by Erna Gunther are so indicated.[1]

I have followed as nearly as possible the words of our interpreters, although it results in tedious and sometimes ungrammatical diction. It is my conviction that relatively little was lost in translation. This could be checked, at least in the case of Spier, by a slight knowledge of Havasupai, but better, by the fact that the interpreter's phrases were of the same duration as the narrator's. While many locutions and clichés characteristic of the tale-teller may have been lost, I feel in this case at least that these English versions do give much insight into literary style. This can be checked in the pages that follow by comparing the several versions of the same tale, told by the original informant through the same interpreter after a lapse of several years, where there will be found almost word-for-word repetition.

I have not attempted to divide this collection into myths and tales. The Havasupai make no such separation. These are all tales about the *itckiu'ga*, the men-animals of long ago. Our informants did not feel that there was any difference between a tale that we might feel was historic, such as "The Separation of the Havasupai and the Yavapai," and the obvious origin myths, nor between these myths and trivial tales, such as "Turkey's Revenge." On the other hand, stories of their own exploits, or those of their fathers or grandfathers, are not classed with the tales published here. Some of these incidents have been related in *Havasupai Ethnography*.

Leslie Spier
May 1929

| NOTES |

1. Erna Gunther also had an interpreter she simply named "West," whom we believe to have been West Sinyella, the son of Chief Sinyella's younger brother Baa Gjuda and brought up by Sinyella when Baa Gjuda died (Hirst, 2007, personal communication).

The Stories

1. THE CULTURE HEROES[1]

AT MATAWI'DI'TA [WEST OF WALAPAI CANYON] ALL KINDS OF
Indians lived. This is the first place they had before the water came.
When they were living there, the two brothers (called Hukama'ta and
Du'djipa) told everybody that there was a good place for the Havasupai.
"We will give them farms, crops, buckskin, and clothes." Then the two
brothers took the Hopi to their present country and gave them crops
and sheep. They told them how to make blankets, and how to bring
them to trade for buckskin. Then they did the same for the Zuñi. So
these three tribes alone have crops and such things; no other tribes
have them. They told the Walapai, "You will have no farms, no crops,
no clothes, and nothing to eat," and they left them right there. Then
they left the Mohave at the old place and gave them only corn with
small ears and other things. But they gave no clothes, just like the
Walapai. This is all I have heard them tell about these two brothers.[2]

These two brothers thought what they were going to make. The
younger brother finished thinking before the elder, and told what he
was going to make. The younger made the sun, the moon, the stars,
and everything on the earth. After this the younger brother was sick.
He told his relatives, "When I am dead do not take my body away; do
not move me. Put wood around my body, start a fire, level the ashes,
put water on this, and see how the crops grow." So they put wood over
his body, set fire to it, leveled the ashes, and threw water on them. In
a day or two, one corn plant came. When the corn grew up, it had
three ears. The first, the best, they gave to the Hopi; the second, they
gave to the Havasupai; the third, a little one, they gave to the Mohave.
To the Walapai they gave nothing. They said to them, "You will have
nothing, no corn; you will eat seeds," and they sent them away.

1. Told by Manakadja; interpreted by Mark Hanna, 1918.
2. Sinyella stated that facts relating to Matawi'di'ta, Hukama'ta, and Du'djipa belonged to Walapai, not Havasupai, tales.

2. The Origin of Corn[1]

A LONG TIME AGO THERE WERE TWO CHIEFS. ONE WAS SICK. Many Indians were there with their head chief. The chief said, "I am very sick; I want to lie down in the shadow." The Indians made him a flat-roofed shelter. The sick chief said, "No, I do not want that. I want another kind." They made one dome-shaped. But the chief said, "I do not like that. Make it conical." He wanted them to cut trees and set them in the ground to cast a shadow. He said to the Indians, "When I am dead, I want you to make a fire and put me in it. Take a stick and scatter my ashes when I am all burnt up." That is what he told them when he was sick.

He lay there sick. After a while he was dead. They made a big pile of wood. Coyote said that he would get fire, so he ran far away to the rocks to get flint to strike a fire. Coyote was gone for many hours. They had wood all ready for lighting, so they started it. Coyote ran as fast as he could. He turned around and saw the smoke of the fire they had started, so he came right back.

He came back to where the Indians had built the fire. The body was all burnt, except the heart. The Indians were all crying, standing around the heart. Coyote ran around in back of them, asking, "Where shall I stand to cry?" They would not let him in the circle, so he went behind a dwarf, jumped in, and got the heart. Coyote ran away with the heart. He ran fast and the Indians ran after him, but they could not catch him. They returned home and built a fire. They made the ground smooth where they had burned the man, and put water on it. That is what the chief had told the Indians to do when he was sick.

They came to the place every day to see what had happened. After some days green things came up. They put water on these; after a time they had corn. Ears grew on the corn and when they were ripe, they picked them. The chief who was left said that the Hopi should take the best corn and the Havasupai should take the little ear. Each should take one. The corn is the dead man's heart. That is, the small corn, because Coyote ran away with the big heart (?).

When Indians plant corn, they talk to it, saying, "You must grow and ripen quickly." It grows because it hears what they say.

Hopi, Havasupai, and Mohave have corn, but the Walapai have none. Walapai only travel around, camping and picking piñon seeds. The Mohave got the little ear of corn.

| NOTES |

1. Told by Manakadja; interpreted by Lillie Burro; recorded by E. G., 1921.

3. The Separation of the Tribes[1]

ALL THE INDIAN TRIBES WERE ENCAMPED AT WIGA'MA' [NEAR the Mohave country]. That is where they came out of the ground. They came to Matawidita and camped. Hokumata, the head chief, was sick; after a while he died. They made a fire to burn him. But Coyote seized his heart and ran away. They took water, which they sprinkled on the ashes, and corn grew there. After three years the Indians gathered it and gave the largest ears to the Hopi, the next in size to the Havasupai, and the smallest to the Mohave. They gave nothing to the Walapai. The Indians said, "You Walapai shall have nothing. You will roam about and eat what you may find." Coyote ran away with the heart to a camp where there were many coyotes. They have plenty of corn there because he stole the heart.

The little children were playing with a baby, who cried. The grandmother whipped the children, at which everyone got angry and fought among themselves. They made balls of soft sand to throw at each other, and they made small arrows. Then the Mohave ran away to Wiga'ma'. The Yavapai went to Wigwalko'lva, where they now live, and the Paiute to their country. The Havasupai and Hopi came here. The Hopi said to the Havasupai, "Camp here; do not go else-where. There is good water here and it is a good spot to grow things. You should keep this country." Then the Hopi hung the corn on the pinnacles[2] and left for the country in which they now live. Pagio'va[3] left corn, pumpkin, melon, and other seeds with them. "That is what you will plant," he said. Then they took half of the Havasupai east-ward with them to live on the Little Colorado. The Hopi lived there close to the Havasupai (who in fact lived like the Hopi). Pagio'va left the Walapai behind. "You shall have nothing to plant. You must simply roam under the trees. You shall gather wild seeds, but you will not plant anything." The Zuñi are brothers and sisters of the Havasupai.

All the Havasupai at the Little Colorado sickened and many died. A few ran away and came down here [in Cataract Canyon] to live with the other Havasupai.

| NOTES |

1. Told by Manakadja; interpreted by Lillie Burro; recorded by E. G., 1921.
2. I.e., a white mark high on the cliff above the village.
3. Pagio'va is the same as Du'djipa, according to this informant.

4. The Separation of the Havasupai and Yavapai[1]

LONG AGO WHEN THE HAVASUPAI WERE MEN-ANIMALS (itckayu'ga) they lived up on the point where the ruin is. Some of them also lived in the caves right above Manakadja's house. Some enemies lived on the talus slope at the point of the cliff opposite [A]. Their house may still be seen there [crude house ruins]. One of their women went down to the creek to fetch some water. A young man living on the ruin-point [B] saw her and ran right down. When she was at the water, the young man came up and seized her, carried her into the brush, and had his will of her. The woman went back home and told her husband. The woman's husband felt very angry. He went down and crossed to the other man. He caught him by the hair and punched him. (Perhaps he killed him, I do not know.) They fought with each other. Then the enemy went back to his point, and the Havasupai, in their home on the opposite side of the canyon, said, "Let us all go and climb up over there." So a great many went across, climbed right up to the enemies' house, and fought with them all with their fists. By and by they got their weapons and began to shoot; The Havasupai killed one of the enemies' men. Then the Havasupai went home and all the enemy crossed after them. The enemy stood up in a row on one side with the Havasupai similarly on the other. They shot back and forth. The enemy killed two or three Havasupai, then they went home.

The head chief of the Havasupai said, "Perhaps we will have to fight all the time now. I want one man to go down below Navajo Falls, where more Havasupai are living on the cliff on the west side, and tell them to come help fight." They called to those Havasupai from down in the canyon bottom, and when these had joined the others [at B], all went together to the enemies' place. They fought there until many of the enemy were killed. The enemy became afraid of the Havasupai so they all came down from the talus slope and fled up the canyon. The Havasupai pursued them. When they got just above Lee Canyon, where some more of the enemy were living, the latter joined those who were fleeing and all went off together. The Havasupai followed them closely, killing many men, all along the canyon. When they were far up, just below the Moki trail, they were joined by more enemies who lived there. They fled too; all going together. A great many Havasupai pursued them, pushing them on up the canyon and out onto the plateau. The enemy moved in a compact group with Havasupai spread out in an arc. They chased them on and on, traveling right across the plateau southward. They kept on going, fighting all the way until they were far beyond ᵃwiguvau'la, perhaps as far as Jerome. Then the Havasupai said, "Let them go. We will call you people living there, itcuhua' [Yavapai, or generically, 'enemy']." So they went on their way while the Havasupai returned to live here.

Before that, when the enemy were down here with the Havasupai they talked the same language to each other. After they were chased off to live in another country, their language changed a little bit. The words are just a little different. Maybe those Yavapai know about this and perhaps that is why they came down here to kill Havasupai all the time. They are not good men. They are wicked; they always like to kill someone.

| NOTES |

1. Told by Sinyella; interpreted by Jess Chickapanega, 1919.

5. The Sun and the Moon Are Made (first version)[1]

TWO MEN, WHO WERE ANIMALS, WERE WAY DOWN UNDER THE ground. They came up and emerged here. It was dark so they could not see far. One said, "We ought to have a sun. I wonder how we can make it, so that when it rises, there will be light and we can see far away." So he made a big disk of ice, chipping the edge smooth all around. While making the sun that way, this one thought he would carry it to the west and throw it down there. He said, "In the morning you are coming up to be the sun; then we can look all around." He did this, but when it was rising it did not look right; it looked like the moon. As they could not see very far, he saw that he had made a mistake. Then the other man said, "That is moonlight. We must call that the moon. I think I can make the sun. We will try to do it." The first man said, "I tried to make the sun, but I made a mistake. But it will be all right for you to try." Then the second man did as the first had done when he made the moon; he broke off the edges of a heavy, thick piece of ice. "You made a mistake carrying it to the west. This is the place for the sunrise." He carried it to the east. At first before the sun rose, there was to be a little light, and after it had risen he would be able to see a long way off.

One of these men had a daughter, whom they had left behind under the ground. She was angry at being left, so she thought what she would do to kill them. There was a little spring close to the house. She transformed herself into a frog and produced water which kept rising until it gushed up the hole in the earth [by which they had emerged]. The men heard the wind driven out of the hole and, looking down, saw the water nearly to the top. The men said, "Perhaps that woman we left behind is making this water. Perhaps we will be drowned."

But the water flowed out and rose up to the sky. The two men were drowned with all the others, save for a few.

When they saw the water coming out and knew they were to be drowned, they said, "We had better take a big log, cut a hole in the middle and place a girl in it, with meat and other food. Then we will cut a stick to plug the hole, and tying it in, put piñon pitch over it to make it watertight. When the water comes out of the hole, the log will be carried away and swirled around. After the water has risen nearly to the sky it will subside again. When you [the girl] feel it lying on the ground, knock on the log; if it sounds like this, the ground is not yet dry. But if it sounds like this, it is dry and you should come out. When you come out look around for San Francisco Mountain and go there." That is what the two men told the girl. So they placed her in the log, and the water carried it away. When she came down she went to the south side of San Francisco Mountain. The others were dead; she was the only living person. So she thought how she would make some boys. . . .[2]

The one who made the sun thought, "We made many men. We do not want them to live long. We want them to be old men, but we want them to get the sicknesses we created and die. You can watch me; when I get sick I will become thin and lie down, and pretty soon I will be dead. Then carry me a little way to where you have piled up sticks. Pile them over my body, then set fire to them and burn my body. The smoke going up to the sky is me, and when I am alive again [i.e., as a spirit] I will be Pagio'va, the reanimator."[3] So he went up there as he said he would, and now when a man dies and goes up there, this man, Pagio'va, makes him alive again.

| NOTES |

1. Told by Sinyella; interpreted by Jess Chickapanega, 1919.
2. The incidents related at this point were identical with those in the first version; unfortunately they were not recorded.
3. See *Havasupai Ethnography*, p. 276, where this individual is identified with God.

6. The Sun and the Moon Are Made (second version)[1]

A LONG TIME AGO THE SUN WAS NOT LIGHTED, BUT WAS DARK. There were two men, brothers. The younger said, "You must make the sun lighter in order to see rabbits and kill them." But the older man said it was light enough. The younger man said, "You do not know how to make the sun a little lighter, so I am going to be the older man." Then he got a pipe, put some tobacco in it and smoked. He just blew the smoke out and his hair turned gray. When his hair became gray he said, "Now I am the older man." The younger man said, "I will be the older man. I am going to make the sun a little lighter." He took a stick and pushed up the sky a little higher so that the sun shone with a bright light. When he was going to make the sun he got a big piece of ice to make a disk. Then he threw it where the sun comes up; then the sun appeared there very bright. The youngest man's name was Tudja'pa and the other one's was Hogumata. When they made the sun, they made the stars too. He put water in his mouth and blew it up to make the stars. (That is all of this story.)

That is the way he made it light so that people could see rabbits, deer, and antelope; so that people could see to go everywhere they wanted to. People are all happy in the sun's light. Now in the daylight they go everywhere they want to go.

Of the same two men, the older made the moon and tried to make the sun, but he just made the moon. He took a piece of ice to make the moon.

The same two men made the people hereabout. They made the various tribes: Havasupai, Mohave, Apache. They just cut arrows, about fifty or one hundred, and threw them where the sun comes up and they were people.

When they made the people they made the food for them. They made piñon, corn, beans, and peaches.

1. Told by Manakadja; interpreted by West; recorded by E. G., 1921.

7. The Early Migration[1]

Just above the junction of Haga0ei'la [Little Colorado River] and Hagatai'a [Colorado River] is Hagadjapa'ka, the place where a great many men climbed up from beneath the earth.[2] They came out and stayed there. The chief said to Crow [gasok, raven?], "I want you to fly about and look for a good place to raise plenty of corn. When you return and tell us, we will move there." When Crow came back he said, "There are red cliffs halfway up the Little Colorado; then the canyon opens out a little wider. That is a good place for us." They all moved to that tolerable place and camped there. They planted a little corn to see if it was promising. Then the corn came up. After a time it had ears, but the ground was not good; it was alkaline and this killed the corn. It did not grow well, the ears were small. The chief said, "We ought to have good ground. I want you to fly about and find another place. Come and tell us; then we will move again." The people kept traveling up the canyon bed. Crow flew off and returned: "I found a place that seems somewhat good to me." So the people moved there and tried the land for planting, making fields on both sides of the river. This was at Wiinya'gawaiawaia (a little black mountain just below Black Falls). This place was somewhat good, so they stayed a little longer there. The chief told Crow to go look again for the best land. "Our people are many, so search for a place where they can have big fields. I want you to find it for us." Crow found such a place, and returning, said, "I found the sort of land you want. It looks very good to me." Then the old people wanted to move again, but the youngest brother did not want to go. He wanted to go back. So he cried, cried all the time.

The oldest brother said, "We want all to go on with us." The younger brother said, "No, I do not want to go with you any longer. I want to go back home. I like the place we left better." The elder brother said, "All right, we will give you corn. We will give you but a single ear. I will just break those we have in two. I will give you part of the red and white corn (teyadjipa') and you can have half of the blue ear." He had two ears of corn. He broke each in two and, giving the halves to the younger brother, he said, "We will also give you our buckskin. We do not want to take any buckskin with us. We have some sheep; they will furnish skins for us." The younger brother wanted to go back alone, but the older brother told the old woman, their mother, to go back with him. So those two went back together. The older brother said, "Do not eat the pieces of corn I gave you. Save them. Go back home to the north side of the little mountain and plant a little in the open places there where the ground looks good. Test it; do not plant all. This is the place you can call your home, your country. There are plenty of deer there. They are yours, your own animals. Camp there. Then travel about looking for a place with many springs and where the ground looks right. Plant there. To the north of this mountain [Wigatuwi'sa, Red Butte] there are little caves [Kamwidiminyuwa', old woman's house?]. When they camped there they tried to plant corn in that ground. There was no water for irrigation. They needed water. So they traveled about to find a spring with which to irrigate, but they could not find any. So they came this way [westward] and found this canyon. They followed down it until they found Havasu' [Cataract Creek]. They found that the ground on both sides of the stream was pretty good. So they [*sic*] went back and told their mother, and then all moved down here [Cataract Canyon]. They planted down here. It was very good; so they said, "This is the sort of well-watered place we sought. Things look pretty good to us now." This place in the canyon was a little narrow. The water was good and there was plenty of good land on both sides of the creek. "This is the kind of place we sought," they said.

By and by more men were alive; men, women, and children. They were not plentiful, but just about as many as the Havasupai are now. The old woman said, "I am not going to stay here. I think I will go far off toward the west. Our children will stay here." Thus the old woman spoke to her son and her relatives. She asked the boy and another, younger brother, "What are you going to do? You should stay here." The boy said, "This place which I found is good, but I want to leave it. So when you go, I and my brother are going to be rocks. Then we will stand up together. The other people should stay here and be called

Havasuapa'. They will form only a small tribe. The canyon is small, so there will not be many, but they will number enough." They named all the good things they had. "They will have buckskin and many things to plant: corn and peaches. We would like to do many things for them before we leave," the two brothers said. They said, "We have two ears of corn. We will tie them together and hang them near you, so that you who remain may know how to plant corn and other seeds. These two ears hold your food. Do not lose them. If you keep them all the time, your crops will grow well.[3] We call you our people; you must not fight among yourselves. Do not be wicked, warlike. We say you must be good people. It is not right to fight.[4] That is what the two brothers said before they left. "We made only a few of you, a small tribe. Do not get sick; then if any other people come to fight, they will not be able to kill you all." That is what they said. "You should hunt on the plateau, and when you kill a deer you should tan its hide good. Then carry it to our older brothers living over there. We call them Sa'u'u (Zuñi).[5] They call you younger sibling (giniga); you should call them elder sibling (nyei'ga). The younger brother should kill a deer, tan its hide good, and go over there, carrying it to his elder brother to trade for his blanket. That is what we say." Thus they spoke and then they left a few children here. Today we are just as they said we would be; not many people, only a small tribe.

| NOTES |

1. Told by Sinyella; interpreted by Jess Chickapanega, 1919.
2. There is a big hole there now, half full of water: it is never dry. By walking noiselessly, a man can approach and look into the hole. He will see the water boiling up. The water does not like to have men look at it.
3. This refers to the marked rocks on the canyon wall resembling ears of corn; see *Havasupai Ethnography*, p. 102.
4. At the time (1918) the Havasupai were exercised over the possibility of having their young men drafted for war. They vaguely conjectured that my [LS's] visit was in connection with this. It is likely that this reference is a reaction for my benefit.
5. I [LS] do not doubt that he would have referred to the Hopi, had he not known that I had lately come from Zuñi.

8. The Culture Heroes Become Animals[1]

TWO BROTHERS LIVED TO THE EAST OF GRAND CANYON STATION
at Rain Tank. They went hunting and killed many deer for food. They
had no wives. They had no crops there; nothing but meat for food. I
do not know how long they stayed there. The [gray, plateau] squirrels
told the brothers how to live, how to hunt and farm. When they went
hunting every day they killed two deer apiece. When they killed a
deer, they skinned it, scraped the hair off, and tanned the hide. Then
they made clothes and moccasins, and gave them to the Havasupai.
When they were alive they told men all the arts. After they were dead,
they said, "We are going to be squirrels." They left everything at Rain
Tank for the Havasupai. Before they went away they told the Indians
to hunt deer between Williams and Rain Tank. "Kill the deer and
make clothing. We are not going to be men when we leave here: we
are going to be squirrels. We will leave everything here." That is what
they told the Havasupai. The two brothers then went away.

All sorts of animals lived near here before there were any men.
They did not want to work and did not want to be men. Coyote said,
"I do not want to be a man. I am going to be a coyote." Wolf was
lazy and said, "I do not want to be a man. I am going to be a wolf."
Badger was lazy and said, "I do not want to be a man. I am going to
be a badger." So did the birds, the eagles, and all sorts of animals.
That is all I know.

| NOTES |

1. Told by Sinyella; interpreted by Mark Hanna, 1918.

9. The Flood (first version)[1]

THE TWO BROTHERS HAD A PLACE IN A LITTLE CANYON. WHEN Coyote came down the canyon, he did not see what was on the road. One brother said, "I am going to fool him." Coyote said, "Why are you going to fool me?" "I am going to kill you." But he did not fool him and Coyote went back.[2]

Then Coyote looked in all the cracks of the rocks at the edge of the water. But only after he had looked around four or five times did he find a crack with a frog in it. He took out the frog, tore it to pieces, and threw them away.[3] Then he went off, saying, "Make the big flood come." In a few days it began to rain. It rained for about a year, day after day. After that it snowed for a whole winter, until I do not know how deep the snow was. In the spring and summer it rained again, and then in the fall the floods ran down the hills and down the canyons. Then people got logs. The two brothers told the people to take a log and cut a hole in it, making it hollow. Then they got the log, a soft log. They cut a hole in it as big as this house and put in it all kinds of seed, corn, peaches, dried deer meat, soapweed, and all kinds of dried meat and seeds. After the food was in, they put a little girl inside. They closed the hole with a round wooden plug and put pitch around it to make it tight. After a half day it floated away. Before they put the girl in there, they told her what she was to make. They told her how to make clay into pots, horses, men, cattle, burros, deer, mountain sheep, and all kinds of animals; to make all kinds of things. "After the log floats away and turns about in the water, it will finally come to rest. Then come out and look for San Francisco Mountain (Wihaganapa'dya), for that is our country. Then make all these things, and when you are ready go there to the mountain."

The log was swirled around in the water. When the water subsided the log came down on a hill on the other [eastern] side of the
Little Colorado River. The girl pushed the plug away and came out.
She stayed there. She took some mud and made pots. Then she made
a cottontail rabbit of mud and said, "When I make Indians and they
are alive, they are going to kill and eat this." Then it came to life and
ran off. So she made jackrabbits, deer, mountain sheep, and Indians
the same way.[4]

She stayed there until the ground was dry. Then she went to
San Francisco Mountain and in the night she heard the red-shanked
[-shafted?] flicker (kaku'u) call to her. When the flood covered the
earth, this bird stayed up against the sky. He has a pointed tail because
of the water lapping his tail feathers. The bird called "tciu, tciu" and
scared her. "Well, what is that! What is the matter with you! Nobody
is here; everybody is drowned. Why do you come here?"

When she came to stay beside San Francisco Mountain, she said,
"I do not know what I can make for company. I am lonesome." So she
tried to make a baby. She lay down under a little spring, where only
one drop came over, which fell into her. When the sun first shone on
the high hill, she lay down and the sun shone into her. She had connection in this way. She stayed there working for herself. She gathered
seeds and cooked them for herself. After a while, a month or two, she
had a baby boy. Not very long after that she had another baby boy by
having connection with water and sun again in the same way. Both
were of the same age.

She left them in bed in camp while she went for seeds. The babies
went out hunting and killed some birds, which they hung in front
of the door. Then they went back to bed. When she returned she
said, "Who killed those birds at my door?" So she threw them away,
at which the boys cried without stopping. When she went for seeds
again, the boys went hunting. They killed some birds, and hung these
at the door. When she came back she roasted the birds and they all
ate them. The boys did not cry any more. When the two boys were
older they went hunting. They took a rock in their hands and killed
a cottontail. Then they took a rock in their hands in the same way
and killed a jackrabbit. She ate those too. When they were big enough
they went hunting with curved throwing sticks, which their mother
made for them.[5] They hit the deer and mountain sheep with these,
but they could not kill them. They came back and told their mother,

"We struck those big animals with the sticks and stones but we could not kill them. What are they for?" The woman said, "Those are deer, mountain sheep, and antelope. People had bows and arrows with which to kill them."

The boys said, "Where are the bows? We want to get them so we can kill the animals and get their hides for you." "Well, the bows are too hard to get. They are over there in the Yavapai country and those enemies might kill you." When they were hunting again, one said, "Well, we will go to see if we can get bows. Mother said it was hard to get them." They went there, but they did not see anybody; so they cut down a willow tree. Then they came back and said, "Mother, you told us it was hard to get the bows. We did not see anybody, so we brought them back." "Well, mother, how are we going to use them to kill deer and mountain sheep?" So she made a willow arrow without feathers or point and when they shot it, it just bounced back from the deer's side. Some time after that the boys asked their mother, "Well, mother, where are the arrow reeds? We want to get them to shoot with. These arrows are no good; they bounce back." "Well, the arrow reeds are too hard to get. They are down this way, to the north, in Cataract Canyon. You cannot get them. If you got down there between the rocks, the sides might come together and kill you." Before they went to get the arrows, they asked their mother, "When we kill the deer and scrape the hair off the hide, what do we do with it?" "Well, boys, the hide is used to make moccasins and clothing." "Well, mother, we are going to get some arrows and kill some deer, so you can make clothes from the hide." "Well, boys, the arrow reeds are too hard to get. The rocks might close and kill you." One time they went hunting again without telling their mother. The elder said, "Well, brother, we will go get the arrow reeds." So they went to the canyon not far from their camp and, looking down, saw lots of arrow reeds. They took some logs, carrying them down into the canyon held cross-wise on their heads. Then the walls came together, but they were stopped by the log which propped them apart. They got plenty of arrow reeds and carried them back to camp. They said, "Well, mother, you told us it was hard to get arrow reeds, but we got them. We took logs, held them across our heads, and when the rocks closed, they held them apart. So we got these arrow reeds."

When she made them arrows, the boys went hunting again and shot deer, mountain sheep, and antelope. But the arrows bounced back, because they were merely pointed and had no stone heads. They went back and asked the woman, "Well, mother, where are we going to get arrowheads?" She said, "The arrowheads are too far away to get. I cannot show you how to make them." "Well, mother, where are they?" "They are over at Kwasugame'e [a place eight miles southwest of Howard Spring]. But they are hard to get, because the stone shoots out and kills everybody." Then the boys said, "Let us go and see about the arrowheads." So they went there and picked up the little arrowheads lying all around the outskirts of that place, but when they got near the center, the rock was ready to shoot. They took stone as big as their fists, hiding them under their clothes. Just when the rock was going to shoot, they threw the stones and broke it to pieces, nearly killing it, so that it could not shoot. They took the best arrowheads and returned home. The woman said, "Well, boys, how did you get the arrowheads? They are very hard to get." "Well, mother, when we got there, and the rock was about to shoot, we took some heavy stones and threw them at it and killed it. Then we took the best." So the mother fixed the arrowheads on the arrows for them. The boys said, "When the arrows are pointed they are too soft. We need hard sticks for the foreshafts. Where is the best place to get them?" "Well, boys there are a lot of such sticks at Kaθilkahale'va [south of Williams], but they are too hard to get. The Yavapai are over there and they might kill you." The boys went after the sticks there, but they did not see anybody. So they got them: some sort of willow. They brought them home and their mother fixed the arrows good for them, fastening the arrowheads on. "Well, mother, where do we get feathers to put on these?" "Well, boys, hawks' and eagles' feathers are very good for arrows." So they went looking around for young birds. They put them in a cage and when they grew up, they took their feathers for the arrows. Neither the eagles nor the hawks fought: they got them easily. When the arrows were nicely finished, they went hunting and killed a great many deer, perhaps two or four each day. They scraped the hair off and tanned the hides nicely; then made clothes and moccasins of them. When they had a lot of buckskin and buckskin articles, they stayed at home.

Then the woman made some flageolets (daldal).[6] When they came home from hunting every evening, they climbed on top of their house and played the flageolets. When they played, the sound was heard all over the world. After that two girls came to the place. (I do not know where they came from.) They said, "We heard fine, pleasing sounds. We came to see where they came from." One fellow answered, "That was someone hollering." "No, not that. That was a pleasing [pleasant?] sound." So they went on from place to place, until after two or four days they came to the boys' camp. The boys were away hunting and only their old mother was lying there. "Well, what do you girls come here for? I am only an old woman lying here. Nobody else is here." The girls only laughed and said nothing. So the woman got up and gave them some dried meat, because she wanted them to go home. When the boys came home in the evening and had supper, they climbed on the house top to play again. Then the girls said, "That is what we heard"; they were glad.

The girls stayed all night. The woman did not sleep in order to save her boys, because she thought the girls might go to her boys and she did not want this. When nearly daylight, one of the girls said, "Make that woman asleep." But the boys said, "We do not know how to make her sleep." When the woman slept, the girls went to the boys. The oldest girl went to the oldest boy and the younger girl to the younger boy. The boys would not let the girls into their beds, but after a little while the younger boy let the girl into his bed and had connection with her. When the girls went out, they sat down, and the older girl said, "Well, sister, we will urinate and see who is married." So they did and the older girl only urinated a little, but the younger's urine gushed out. So they knew the younger girl had been married. Then the older girl said, "Sister, you are married; stay here, I am going home alone." The younger said, "No, I do not want to stay alone." The older said, "No, you stay here; that older boy does not like me. I am not married; I am going home." But the younger said, "No, I am not going to stay alone." So they both went home.

The boys went hunting again. The older killed two deer, but the younger killed nothing. Because he had gotten married, he could not see anything. His mother was angry that the girl had married him. She did not like him to be with the girl. The boys said, "Well, mother, we will go see about the girls. When a man gets older he ought to get married." "You ought not do it. Those are Yavapai and they might kill you. It is too difficult to marry Yavapai. I do not want you to go." But they answered, "Well, we want to get married to those girls." When they were ready to go each took a long hair from his head and laid it on two poles crossing under the roof of their house. They tied a little piece of down to each end and said, "If the Yavapai kill us, these hairs will break and blood will flow from them. Then you will know we are dead." When the boys went over to the enemy and stayed at the girls' camp, the enemy at once killed them both. Then the hairs broke and blood flowed out of them. The old woman cried and began to mourn. The old woman tried to kill herself but she could not. When she threw herself off onto rocks, she was not killed. So she stayed at the camp and took care of the boys' belongings.

A boy was born to the younger girl who had married. He lived over there with her. The older sister told the little boy that his father had been killed. The little boy thought about his father being killed. He climbed to the house top and his tears flowed down the house post. His mother saw them and said, "Who told you your father was killed? Who told you of the trouble?" But the boy did not answer. When the Indians hunted for cottontails they used rabbit-sticks like the Hopi. The boy got a stick like this and went to where the men were. He said, "I want to hit that bush over there. I want you all to stand together over there; no one should stand any other place, because he might get hurt." So they all stood together and he threw the stick and killed everyone. He went back home and killed everybody, including his mother, and left only his mother's older sister alive. He asked her, "Where does my grandmother live?" She said, "She lives over there." Then he killed her too and was alone.

The little boy went to his grandmother's camp. The old woman was lying down. She got up and said, "Where do you come from, little fellow? I am too old; nobody comes here. What do you come for?" He said, "My mother's sister told me my father was killed over here [sic] and that my grandmother lives here. She told me to come over here to find her. I come here and find you. You are not related to me, so I will kill you." The old woman said, "I am related to you; you are my grandson." So they stayed together in that camp.

When the boy was a little older he went hunting and killed deer, antelope, and mountain sheep, and all kinds of animals, just like his father. The old woman thought, and said to the boy, "You take half your father's belongings and go to the east. I will take half to the west and we will leave our country. I made everything here, all the animals, and everything else. The Havasupai can have this country here." So the boy went to the east (hamankanyawe'va, boy—), and the woman went to the west (kamwid'imakanyawe'va, old woman—), and left the country for the Havasupai. When they were ready to go, she said to him, "When you are in the east you will not die; when I go into the west I will not die either. After I go to the west and get old, I will go into the water and wash; then I will be a little girl again. When you go into the east and get old, go into the water and wash; then you will be a little boy again. We do not need to die. I have made all the people and animals, as my parents told me, and now we can go away. So when you go to the east, stay there, behave yourself, and keep your property, and so will I, when I go to the west." Then the boy took horses and other things and went to the east, and the woman took only half as much and went to the west. When ready to go the woman said, "When you want to see me, come over there. I cannot go over there to see you; it is too hard to travel. You are a boy; get on a horse and come over to see me."[7] That is how the two brothers and the girl gave things to the Hopi and the Havasupai.

| NOTES |

1. Told by Manakadja; interpreted by Mark Hanna, 1918.
2. This incident was told in an abbreviated and confused manner.
3. See *Havasupai Ethnography*, p. 288.
4. This incident is recorded in an abbreviated version.
5. Rabbit sticks are not used by the Havasupai.
6. Not a Havasupai instrument. (This means Spier did not observe any flute-like instruments at the time of his visit. Ed.)
7. Sinyella added, "She said, 'I will make beads of seashells.'"

10. The Flood (second version)[1]

FROG FOUND A LITTLE STREAM OF WATER TO LIVE IN. COYOTE came by and Frog called to him. He came to look, so Frog went under a little rock. Coyote could not see him, so he went back. Then Frog ran under the rock. Again Coyote did not see Frog and he looked around. Then Coyote said, "Who is calling me? Come out, I want to see you." But Frog would not come out, so Coyote caught him and tore him to pieces and threw them away. When Coyote tore Frog all to pieces, it made rain and snow.

It snowed every night and every day. When the snow falls every night and every day for ten or twenty days, there is going to be rain. It rained every day and every night. Some people said the rain was going to kill all of the people. There was so much water that it was all over the world. Then the old man said he was going to get a big log and with a knife make a hole in it and a little door. Then he put in a little girl. When he put her in it he put some food in it. He shut the door and sealed it up. The people were all drowned.

The little girl stayed in the log, lying in the water. When the water had filled up the entire world, she was carried up in the air in the log. After the water had filled the world, it began to go lower and lower. Then the little girl in the log just sat still until the log settled down on the ground. Then she opened the door and came out. She saw every place. She saw the east side of San Francisco Mountain. Then she knew the mountain.

She took mud and made a water pot and cup. She made rabbits and some mountains, and antelope, and deer of mud, and threw them where the sun comes up. When she threw them away she said, "You are going to be deer, rabbits, and antelope. You are going to be in this land." She made a man of mud. She made ten or twenty men and threw them where the sun comes up, saying, "I want you to be people here."

While she made the men the ground was getting pretty dry. Then she moved to this side of San Francisco Mountain and lived there. When she moved from the other side of the mountain there were no people near her. She thought she would make a child. Then she raised two boys beside a spring. When they were old enough the two boys left the old woman and traveled somewhere to try to get married. When they got to a camp the people killed both of them.

One boy got a wife and she had a child. When he had been married quite a while, and the other had not yet found a woman, the people in the camp killed them both. When both were dead, the wife of one raised a boy.

When the boy was old enough, he went to see his grandmother. He stayed there for a long time. Then the old woman went to the west and the boy went to the east. The old woman said, "I shall go to the west; you go to the east and live there."

| NOTES |

1. Told by Manakadja; interpreted by West; recorded by E. G., 1921.

11. The Boy Who Killed Blue Hawk (first version)[1]

I DON'T KNOW WHERE THIS OLD WOMAN LIVED, WHETHER north or south, or east or west; just near this country.

There was only one woman, who saw no one else. She lived alone a long time. She thought, "What will I do to have a child?" She looked around to find something to father it, but could find nothing. By and by she found a little spring dripping a drop at a time. Then she said, "Perhaps I can have a child by this water," so she lay right under the dripping water to have connection.

After a little while she became pregnant and gave birth to a boy. She cleared a space on the ground, and rubbing up juniper bark into a soft bed, kept the baby on it. She made her breasts give milk and suckled the child. By and by he became larger; when he started to walk she told him to walk every morning to the daylight and come back. By and by he started to run a little; so he ran to the daylight and back. When he was a little older, about so high [a meter], she thought she would make another child. Again she lay under the dripping water. Soon she became pregnant again and gave birth to another boy.

(This is the way they used to tell the story. That is the way the old man told men when I was a little boy. Perhaps it is not right, but that is the way they said it, and so I tell it to you.)

By and by the boys were about so tall. They saw birds walking about close to the house, so they picked up pieces of stone and piled them by the house. Then holding them between their forefingers, they filliped them at the birds and killed a good many. Then the woman made bows and arrows for the boys. Each carried his bow and arrows and went a little way from the house to kill birds and small animals. She made them reed arrows. She put the arrowshaft straightener in the fire until it was hot and then straightened the arrows in its groove. So she made plenty for both boys. She fastened feathers on these with sinew and flaked stone arrow points which she tied to the arrows. When they were finished she gave them to the boys and said, "There are plenty of deer a little way off. Go and hunt them. Kill one and bring it home; then I will skin it." So the boys went, carrying their bows and arrows. They hunted until they found many deer grazing and walking about. The boys thought, "How can we get close to them in order to shoot?" They sat down and watched; finally they began to crawl toward them, until they were very close. The older boy shot and hit one just behind the left foreleg, killing it. They carried it home, where the old woman skinned and butchered it. Then they had plenty of meat. The woman showed the boys: "That is the way to straighten the arrow; that is the way to make a boy; that is the way to feather the arrow; that is the way to make arrow points. Thus I teach you," she said. By and by the boys knew how to make them for themselves, so they manufactured them. The boys asked their mother, "In which direction are plenty of deer?" The woman said, "There on the little mountain, up on the little mesa." The boys went out hunting now and every time they brought back many deer, so that they had plenty of buckskin all the time.

Now they were grown to be young men. After they returned from hunting, they would climb up on top of the house. There they played on a flageolet (da'lda'le) and the notes could be heard in a long way off in every direction. They did this each time they returned from the hunt. Soon after, two very fine looking women arrived at the house while the boys were out hunting. They came from the south. Only the old woman was home when they arrived. By and by the two boys came back with some deer, climbed up on the house, and played their flageolet. The two girls said to themselves, "Yes, that is what we heard; that is what we were looking for." The old woman said to the girls, "I am a pretty poor old woman. I stay here, but I do not want you two girls to stay here any longer. I want you to return home right away." The old woman knew that the two girls desired her boys.

The old woman said to her boys, "Those two girls are sitting just beside the door. Maybe those two girls want you, my boys. I am telling you so that you may know. You two boys are still too young; you are not yet old enough. It is not right for young boys to have connection. If you do that, you will be pretty weak; you will no longer be strong. I do not want you to make love to those girls. Just let them go back home. I want you to listen to what I say; leave them alone. If you do not attend to me and have intercourse with the girls, then when you wake in the morning and feel pretty sleepy and yawn, I will know that you have done it. I do not want you to. Also you won't be able to catch any big bucks when you go hunting. You will see no more; all you will be able to see will be their tracks, for they will scent [*sic*] you and run away so that you will see none. All you will be able to kill will be fawns; they won't understand about you." So the old woman talked to the boys, and then the sun set.

When it was a little dark, the woman talked to the girls. "I thought you two girls had gone back. I talked about a lot of things to my boys. My boys do not want you." The girls were sitting within the door, one on each side. The old woman lay down crosswise in front of them. The two boys slept in their bed in the center of the house. The old woman watched the two girls to prevent them from going to her boys' bed. The old woman sat awake nearly the whole night before she began to nod. Then the older girl said to the younger, "Younger sibling (gini'ga), you know how to make her go to sleep." Then both the girls went right to the boys' bed. The older girl went to the older boy; the younger girl went to the younger boy. Both girls tried to get into the boys' bed, but neither could get in. They tried without success for a long time. Finally the younger girl dug away the ground beside the spot where her choice lay and rolled him into the hole. Then she went right into his bed and had her way. When it was nearly daylight both girls left and went off a little way, and the older sister said, "Both of us will sit down and urinate, so we can see who has been married." They did so and that of the youngest gushed out quickly, but the older sister retained hers. Then the older sister said, "One boy did not like me. I am going home by myself. The other boy has already married you. You can stay here, but I will go home alone." The younger sister said, "Yes, I had connection, but I do not want to stay. We will both go back home; all I wanted was to have connection. I will go home with you."

The two boys took their bows and arrows early in the morning and went hunting. The older boy killed two big bucks and carried both right into the old woman's house. The youngest brother could see none at all, until, when the sun had nearly set, he found a very little fawn that had just been born, weak, and lying down. This he carried home. Then the old woman was angry at the younger boy. "Did those women do something to you? I warned you but you did not heed me. I know because all you saw was the little fawn." Again the boys went hunting early in the morning. Again the older brother killed two big bucks with big antlers; he brought them to his home first. The younger brother got only a fawn which was walking. This he carried home and threw down beside the house. The old woman was angry, so she would not touch it. After a while the old woman pointed her finger at the fawn and said, "I told you it would be like that when you went hunting, but you would not listen to what I said. I thought you had ears here," putting her finger in his ear, "to hear what I said. And just as I told you, because you are very young to have connection, you will not grow big; you will be very short. If you were older and were a man, and then got married, that would be all right. You are not properly grown now." Again they went hunting early in the morning. Again the older boy brought in two big bucks, which the old woman skinned and butchered. Again the younger brother tried to get a big buck, but could not see any. All he could get was a single year-old buck, with prong horns. A fourth time the boys went hunting, and again the older brother brought in two big bucks, while the younger brother again got a yearling buck with short horns. Four times they went hunting. Again they went out in the morning. Both boys saw many deer. The older brother killed a big buck, while the other killed a smaller one, with three prongs on each horn. Both brought their game to the house, and the old woman said to the younger boy, "I knew that when you went out you would get only fawns four times. Now that you have gone a fifth time and got a buck, I know you will do so in the future." They went out hunting all the time, and each time they brought back bucks of the same size. Then the old woman said, "You are all right now."

The boys went hunting. When they were some distance away, the older said, "Maybe we can go after those two girls who came to the house. We will go after them and bring them home." When they got home, they did not tell the old woman. By and by they talked to her about it. "We will go after both of those girls who were here. One girl alone was married to the younger brother, but we will go after both." The old woman began to cry, because she did not want the boys to go. She said, "I know where those two women are from, but the people there are wicked. They are pretty bad; they always kill strange men.

I do not want you to go." The boys said, "We might try it and see if we can get the two girls to bring back." The old woman said, "I think you will be killed if you go, and never reach home again. I am sure you will be killed over there." The boys said, "We are going. Certainly we can go." The old woman said, "All right, you go. I will prepare some provisions for you." The boys put on their good clothes. When they were ready to start, each pulled the longest hair from the top of his head. They tied them together, and tied this across under the roof of the house. Then the boys said, "You watch our hair, which we leave here. If we are not killed, it will not break; but if we are killed, it will break and blood will drip to the ground. Then you will know that we are dead."

The boys were now ready to start. (I do not know what the story says about which direction they took. Perhaps it was south, down where the Apache [Ahua'dja] are.) They went on and on, until they reached the border of the other people's country. When they reached their village, someone told them, "Your two girls have one house; they are living in that one right there." The boys went into the house where the two girls lived, as the sun was setting. In the morning the head chief of those people said, "I am thinking what we should do about those two men who came. I think the best way is to kill them."

Hawk (dju'da) had a house high up on a cliff. The chief said, "Hawk should kill those two boys." His place was out quite a distance, and the chief sent word to him: "Two men came. Our chief wanted me to tell you to fly high in the air, and then swoop down and hit them on the neck with your rabbit stick to kill them." Hawk said, "All right." So he flew up in the air and swooped down, hit both men, and knocked their heads off.[2] When the two men were killed, they dragged them away.

After a while those people took their brain cases and made them into plates to put food in. The younger of the two sisters who had been to the old woman's house had given birth to a boy. The boy grew big enough to walk and play about. He was given food from the skull-plates. They did this many times. The boy's maternal grandmother told him about the plates: "That is your father's skull you are eating your food from. Two of them came here and that man over there, Blue Hawk (Dju'digavahasu'wa) killed them both. Those people here called them Haθ'vodjga'viga [The Two Who Came Here (a Walapai word)]." The boy listened to all this and then climbed on top of the house, and lay there crying and crying without stopping. The boy's grandmother tried to make him stop but she failed. She told him to come down and get something to eat, but he would not come. The boy's mother also tried to coax him down to eat something, but the boy would not come; he kept on crying. By and by his tears ran down the house post. The boy sang,[3] "My grandmother told me things that made me lie down feeling very angry. I will think what I will do about Blue Hawk. I want you, grandmother, to point out in which direction Blue Hawk's house lies." The old woman told him, "He lives in a place that is pretty hard to reach. It is way up there on a cliff. Nobody can climb up there. That man is wicked. If any other man does not know him, he kills him just that way." The boy sang, "I want you to take me over just to show me where his place is." The old woman said, "All right," and she took the boy over there. She did not go close, but stopped a long way off and pointed, "You see that place very near the top of that high cliff; his house is right there." The boy said, "I will go see him."

When the boy wanted to go, he put tobacco and his pipe inside his shirt and was ready. He went to the foot of the cliff just below Hawk's house. He filled his pipe and smoked it. He blew one puff up along the cliff face, "Pfff . . . ," then another, "Pf f f . . . ," and then another, "Pf f f . . ." and again "P f f f. . . ." He did this four times and the cliff broke open; a narrow cleft running up right to the edge of that man's house. There were little stones and sand all along it, so that it was good for the boy to climb. He climbed up until his head was just above the ledge. He saw the man sitting in the warm sunshine a little way from his house, stretching buckskin [with his hands]. The man did not see him, so the boy climbed up on the ledge and walked toward him. The boy stopped near the house beyond which the man was seated, and blowing smoke at him, said, "You cannot turn around to look at me," and went on into the house. He hunted around the room for rabbit sticks, but he could not find them. The boy said, "I wonder where he put them." There were a great many things piled in one spot. The boy tore down the pile and found the sticks at the bottom. They were wrapped in a big buckskin. There were four of them. Two of them had no blood on them; the other two were very bloody. "All right, I know," he said, "I saw them." And then he rewrapped them and put them away again. He said, "Those are the things I wanted to see."

He went out and walked toward the man. When he was close to him, the man said, "Ha[n], that is a very small boy. How did you get up here?" The boy talked to the man, "I just wanted to see you, your belongings, and your house up here. This is a pretty good place in which you live. I can see a long way off. It is very nice." The man said, "All right. You can walk about and look at my things, both in the house and out here. You can play about." The boy did this. He just looked around at everything and asked the man questions about them. By and by the boy went into the house and got the rabbit sticks and carried them outside. He came close to the man and said, "What did you kill with these two sticks? They have fresh blood all over them." The man said, "Did you never hear about those two men who came from another country? It was difficult to kill them, so they sent for me. I used both those sticks in killing them." The boy said, "Oh, is that so? I had not heard about that. All right, I am going to put them away." But he did not, he continued to carry them about. He held one by the end and asked the man, "How do you throw the stick when you want to kill? Like that?" making a motion. The man turned his head and told him, "Yes, that is the way I do it." The boy said, "All right, go ahead and attend to your buckskin; I am going to put the rabbit stick away." The man turned away from the boy and busied himself stretching the skin. The boy felt very angry. He threw the stick and hit Hawk on the neck, knocking him over the edge whence he fell with a thundering crash to the foot of the cliff. The boy threw down all the man's property and then he climbed down again. When he got to the foot, he looked for the best things and carried them back home. When he was still a little way from his home, he left the things he was carrying. He told his grandmother, "You said that it was pretty hard to get to that man's place, but I went up there and I killed him, knocking him down to the foot of the cliff where he is now. I killed him." His grandmother said, "All the people here are relatives of that man. When these men find the dead body there, they may kill you."

The sun had set and it was a little dark when the head chief talked to all his people. "Coyote should take a little brand about daylight, carry it off a little way and build a fire. Wait there until all the boys and men come, then all go together to hunt rabbits, and gather them in one place, so we can roast them." Coyote did this. He took a little firebrand with him, and waited there until all the others had come, all except the little boy who stayed at the camp. The boy said to his grandmother, "I will go with them. I will go see how they kill rabbits. I do not remember how to throw a rabbit stick," so he went, carrying Blue Hawk's rabbit stick. He walked along until he came to the top of a little hill below which all the men were assembled. The boy spoke to them, saying, "My rabbit stick is somewhat bent. I do not know if I can throw it properly. I will try to throw it at that little object near you, so that I can see if it can be thrown straight. I want all you people to keep away from that thing which I am going to hit. All stand together in one place. If you are scattered, my rabbit stick is bent and when I throw, it may go this way or that, and perhaps one of you will be hit." All stood together in one place. The boy feinted at throwing his stick at the spot, but he turned around and struck all the men, killing everyone. Some had arms broken and some had legs broken, so they were only unconscious; these he clubbed until they were dead. After he killed the men, he came back to the village and killed all the women and children, everyone. He also killed his mother and everyone, except his grandmother. He stayed with her and asked her more questions; that is why he did not kill her too. He sang, "You are my grandmother. You told me things that made me very angry so that I killed everyone of them. That is what you wanted me to do. I want you to tell me in which direction my paternal grandmother lives. Tell me truthfully which is the direction; I want to know." (The little boy had killed a lot of men, a whole tribe, and now he wanted to go back to his paternal grandmother's house.)

Those first two boys, when they went back to their mother, each pulled out a hair, tied them together and fastened them across that woman's house. When the hair broke in two, the old woman saw it, and cried and cried. She wanted to kill herself; so she tied a cord around her neck and pulled it tight, but she did not succeed.

When the little boy asked his maternal grandmother in which direction his paternal grandmother lived, she said, "She lives over that way." The boy got ready to go and then he clubbed his maternal grandmother to death and set off. The boy went off to see his paternal grandmother. When he reached her house, he went close to the entrance and looked inside. There he saw an old woman lying close to the fire. He stood there, but said nothing for a time. Then he said to her, "I want to see you; that is why I came over here." The old woman said, "I am only a poor, very old woman who lives here." But the boy said, "My maternal grandmother told me about my father, who, with his brother, went over there, where Blue Hawk killed them. That is what my maternal grandmother told me. I felt angry so I killed a lot of men, and I also killed my maternal grandmother. Then I came over here." The old woman, his paternal grandmother, fell on him, weeping "Aua, aua, aua," and both began to cry. The boy said, "I want you, my paternal grandmother, to walk out and dig up yucca roots, mash them, and put them in water, so that I can wash my body all over. I have been in a great fight and killed a lot of men, so I am foul. I want to get clean." The old woman did this. She got soapweed roots and washed the boy's body all over and cleansed him well. Then he stayed with her.

The old woman said that she wanted the boy to go out to hunt. The boy killed a deer and brought it home. On another morning the boy again went out to hunt. Again he killed a big buck and carried it home. It was a pretty good camp at which to stay. The old woman said, "I think we will not stay at this house. This house is not good. We will not stay here. When I had two boys, little boys playing around here, this house was not good. I think we ought to leave. I think you ought to go toward the east. It will be called Monk^r edjaginyue'va (Where the Little Boy Lives)." And she said to herself, "I will go to the west where the sun sets. That will be called Komwidimaginyue'va (Where the Old Woman Lives)." The old woman said this and the little boy went toward the east. She said, "You, little boy, go to the east and stay there. You will not die; you will always be alive. I will too. I will go down toward the west; there I will always be alive. I am a very old woman; I like to be that way. If I remain the same, I will not die. You in the east and I in the west will hold up the sky."

| NOTES |

1. Told by Sinyella; interpreted by Jess Chickapanega, 1919.
2. The action is that of a falcon, not a hawk.
3. This and similar soliloquies of heroes are rendered in a chant.

12. The Boy Who Killed Blue Hawk (second version)[1]

THEY DID NOT TELL IN THIS STORY WHERE THAT OLD WOMAN first lived. She lived alone where there was a little spring at which she got water. The spring dripped drop by drop. She thought how, without a man, she could conceive a child. So she thought she would try the spring. She lay there, and let it drip into her. By and by she became pregnant and had a boy. Then she tried the same thing, and made another boy. Now she had two.

By and by when the two boys were larger, they asked their mother, "What do they use to make bows?" "Yes, I know the place where it grows. When I tell you, you can go out some, so that I can show you how they make bows," she said. The boys said, "What kind of wood do they use for arrows?" "Yes, I know a place where plenty grow." So she sent the boys to gather these two things for bows and arrows. They brought them to their mother. She made them for them. She made bows and straightened the arrow shafts. "That is what they do to make them," she told the children. "We have no deer sinew for bowstrings; we will make them of soapweed. We will tie on the feathers with this, too." And she did so. "What do they make arrowheads of to set on these shafts?" The old woman said, "Yes, I know the place where you can get something to make arrow points." She showed them in which direction it lay and the boys went to fetch the black obsidian. They brought lots of it and the old woman fashioned arrowpoints for them.

She made everything for them, and the boys got ready, and she said, "Now, both of you can go out to hunt. The deer are quite near here, all about. When you see deer, do not kill an old buck. When young boys like you kill, they kill only young deer with spike horns."

So the boys went. They found lots of deer, but they did not kill a big buck; only a spike horn deer, which they brought to their mother's house. Their mother told them, "Take out the sinew along the back; that is the kind to use in making moccasins and feathering arrows. The other kind of sinews in the deer leg are used to make bowstring." So the boys did as she told. She said, "The spike horns of the deer you caught are used as arrowhead flakers." The boys asked her, "What kind of feathers are used for arrows?" She said, "Yes, I know the feathers are those of the chicken hawk and eaglets." The boys found the birds. "Keep them until they are grown, with big wing feathers which you can use on the arrows." So the boys did it. Then they asked, "How do you prepare and put them on?" So she showed them one feather, split it; split another, and a third. "That is how they put them on the arrow," she said. She taught the boys. Now they have everything and know how to make them. Their mother told them, "When you are out, see if you can find a fawn lying somewhere. Catch and skin it, and give it to me to tan with the hair on, so I can teach you how to make quivers." So the boys went out again and did it. The boys' mother taught them how to make everything necessary for hunting. They made them and were ready.

They went out hunting every morning and each brought home two deer. They stayed there all the time doing this. The old woman scraped the hides and tanned some. Then she showed the boys: "That is the way they make moccasins, leggings, pants, and shirts," and made them for the boys to wear. So the two boys now knew how to make them. Now they were young men and stayed with their mother.

The old woman sang, "Each day at dawn run toward the daylight. If you do this, you will feel good. Run fast and throw out your arms toward the daylight, and run your fingers through your hair and fling them toward the daylight, so you will never have lice. If you do not run this way before the sun rises, you will feel drowsy all the time." So they did as she bade them.

The two boys went hunting again. While they were away, two fine-looking women came to the old woman's house. She said to the girls, "I do not have a very good living here. I am very old."

The girls said: "We saw a big lizard back on the road. When we arrived at his house, we asked him, 'We heard a musical sound from a far distant place. We would like to find out what it was.' He said, 'I did it.' We said, 'All right, do it now, so we can hear what it sounds like.' So the big lizard whistled on his thumb, but we said, 'No, it is not that; it is something else.' Then we came here." They asked the old woman just as they did the big lizard. She said, "I never heard anyone make a sound like that, either here or in the distance." After a while the two boys returned from hunting laden with deer. They threw off their loads and climbed up on top of their flat-roofed house. Then they made music with a flageolet. The two girls inside the house said, "Yes, that is what we heard."

The old woman told the girls, "I do not want you to stay here. I want you to go home." But the girls did not move till sunset. Then the old woman sang to the boys about what the girls would do. "After the sun had set and it is a little dark, they take black sand, intestines, and lice, mix the three together, and roll them in a tube of buckskin. Then they put on an arrowhead and shoot it toward the sunset. That is what a woman does," she told the boys. "These are no good. You should not feel attracted to these girls. I am warning you." Then the old woman sang to the boys, "Perhaps you want to possess them, but do not do it. When boys are too young, like you, they ought not do it. They do not feel good; they are pretty weak; they cannot do anything right, cannot run fast. Or when you are hunting, you will not catch any good bucks, or you will not grow any more."

Just after sunset, when it was a little dark the boys came down from the house-top and entered. Both lay down to sleep. The old woman sat right in the doorway. She said to the girls, "I want you to go back home. Hurry; go." But the girls did not leave; they were just outside on each side of the entrance. None of them slept. The old woman watched the girls because she did not want them to reach the boys. By and by, shortly after midnight, the older girl said to the younger, "Did you say you knew how to make her sleep quickly?" The younger said, "All right," and made the old woman fall over asleep. Then the girls jumped right over her and went to where the boys were. The older girl said, "I am going to try the older boy; you, who are younger, can take the younger boy." The boys were wrapped up tightly in the bedclothes, and they could not succeed. Finally, the younger girl had her way with the younger boy.

When day dawned both girls went out. "Maybe the boys do not like us; let us go back." So they went home. Then the boys went hunting again. The older brother got a deer and brought it home first, but the younger brother, who did not return until sundown, brought only a little fawn. The old woman said to the younger boy, "That is what I warned you. Whenever you go hunting now, you will not get a big buck." The older boy brought in a buck each time, but the younger brought only a young buck.

By and by the boys said to their mother, "We think we will go to search for those two girls who were here. We will follow their tracks to see where they are from." The old woman said, "I do not want you to go where they are. Where they come from there are enemies. You will be killed over there." The boys said to their mother several times that they wanted to go. Finally she said, "All right, you may go." When the boys were ready to go, the elder pulled the longest hair from his head and stretched it across the rafters of the house. "Watch that when I am gone. If I am killed over there, this hair will snap in two and blood will drop to the ground; then you will know I have been killed."

The boys went. I do not know how far they went, perhaps it was two or three sleeps before they found the people. Someone saw them approaching. The boys asked him, "We are looking for the two girls who returned here from our place. Show us where they stay." They went there. Then everybody saw them and wanted at once to kill them. So they sent some out to tell Blue Hawk, who lived on a high cliff, way up in the sky. He said, "All right," and picking out a good rabbit stick, flew up with it. Then he swooped down and struck both their heads off. When the boys were killed the hair which the elder had left at home snapped in two. The old woman cried; she wanted to kill herself by strangling, but she could not, nor by choking with sand. She tried throwing herself on a burning pyre, but the fire went out, and she was not killed. She tried jumping from a high cliff, but she was not killed. So she still lived there.

The younger girl had a baby boy. By and by he began to talk and walk. They had made a bowl of the skull cap of one of the boys. They gave the child his food in this. The little boy's grandmother told him, "That is your father's skull cap." When the boy heard this, he would eat and drink no more. He climbed up on the house top and cried day and night. He sang, "My grandmother told me that she served me food in my father's skull cap. I am very angry. She also told me that it was Blue Hawk who killed them both." The boy's mother said to him, "What are you angry about, that you neither eat nor talk?" The boy said, "My grandmother told me that my father was killed by Blue Hawk. That is why I am so angry." And the boy asked his mother where Blue Hawk lived. "Show me where it is. I would like to see him." The boy's mother said, "That is Blue Hawk on the high cliff wall. That is where he stays." The boy said, "I am going to see it." Then he went and found where Blue Hawk lived. He arrived at the base of the high cliff directly below. He looked about, wondering how he could climb up; the walls were very smooth. After a while he smoked tobacco and blew a puff up the cliff four times. Then a crevice opened all the way up to Blue Hawk's house, in which the boy climbed up.

When he arrived he saw Blue Hawk just a little way off, sitting at the edge of the ledge and tanning buckskin. After a while Blue Hawk looked around and saw the little boy standing there. The boy said, "I wanted to ask you for your rabbit stick." But Blue Hawk said, "What do you want to use it for?" The boy said, "I do not want it myself; it is someone else who wants it. They wanted me to come and ask it of you." Blue Hawk said, "You can look and find one for yourself. I have a great many in the house." Blue Hawk kept on tanning buckskin. The boy looked for the rabbit stick; there were a lot of them. He picked out a good one. Some of them were wrapped in a buckskin. He unwrapped and examined them; one was covered with blood. He asked Blue Hawk about this one: "What did you kill with this rabbit stick that it got so bloody?" Blue Hawk said, "Did you never hear about that, about me killing two men who came from another place? They asked me to, and I killed them with that stick." The boy took this stick. Blue Hawk, sitting off a little way, was gazing down below the cliff. So the boy struck Blue Hawk, knocking him off, to fall dead at the base of the cliff. The boy took another rabbit stick and descended. He went over to Blue Hawk's body, struck it all over, and then returned to his camp. His mother asked, "Did you see Blue Hawk?" The boy said, "I could not find him."

While the boy was away, all the men had left camp. He asked his mother where all the people had gone. She said, "They have all gone hunting cottontails and jackrabbits." The boy said, "Perhaps I will go see them hunting." His mother said, "All the people have gone in this direction." He said, "I am going to hunt too." So he followed the men's tracks. After a short distance he heard the people talking loud. All the men were in a group, waiting for more to join them; they had not yet built a fire. The boy stopped where he was, still a little way distant, and talked to them: "When I try to hit something with one of my rabbit sticks, it flies [illegible] I always miss. I think I will try it here. Do not scatter, but keep together in one spot off there a little way. If you scatter, perhaps my stick will fly on a tangent, and it might kill one of you." So all the men moved off and stood in a single group. The boy seized his stick and aimed carefully at something to one side, then he suddenly turned and threw it at the men, killing nearly everyone. Some had only legs or arms broken; he ran right over and clubbed everyone to death. Then the boy returned to the house and killed all the women and children. He killed his own mother too, and his maternal grandmother.

When he was left alone, he sang: "My grandmother told me Blue Hawk killed my father. That is why I wanted to kill all the people living here. My grandmother told me my father's mother is living off in this direction. I think I will see if I can find her." When the boy was ready to go, he did not know which direction to take. So he took a little piece of down and blew it away. He tried it in this direction and that, but it did not fly off, it just dropped to the ground. Finally, when he blew on it, it flew off. He followed it as it traveled along. He kept following on and on. After one or two sleeps the down arrived at the old woman's house.

The boy was standing right by the entrance. He saw just one old woman lying in the house. She heard the boy; someone was approaching. She said, "I am not a good woman living here. I am pretty old; my house does not look good. I do not feel as though I wanted to have any good-looking men or women come to see me." She felt quite mournful because her sons had been killed; that is why she did not want people to visit her. The boy said nothing. After a little while, he sang, "Two young men went from here to the place I came from. They went trying to marry those women. One was my father. That is what my maternal grandmother told me. She also told me that you lived here. I felt so angry that I killed all the men, women, and children at the place whence I came." The old woman said, "You are my son's child. You are here at last; it is all right," and she embraced him. The old woman felt happy that he had arrived. She said, "Yes, that was your father. My two boys and I lived here. I think all his belongings are still here in the house: his bow, arrow, quivers, buckskins, and all the things he used," and she showed them to the boy. Then she washed the boy, and cooked venison for him to eat. Then she told him, "You just go hunting and catch some deer, just as my boys formerly did. You will do exactly as they did."

The boy sang, "I am going to see if I can make my father alive again." So he sang, "My father, come to life, come back; we want you." So, soon he heard the two men coming, talking. They stopped a little way from the house; he could not see them. He sang that way four times, but they did not come; so he stopped. The boy said, "I cannot do it. Just I and you will stay here together. I will go out hunting." So he went hunting and got deer just as his father had done.

I do not know which one said this, the woman or the boy: "I am going toward the east, the place where the sun rises. There I am going to stay." The boy said, "You go to the west to the place where the sun sets; you can stay there the same way. The place where I am going to stay, they will call Hama'nk^{r}edjaginyuwe'va (The Little Boy's Home), and in the same way the west will be called Komwi'dimaginuwe'va (The Old Woman's Home)." Then the boy went to the east, and the old woman went to the west. "You, old woman, stay alive over there. You will never die. It will be the same with me. I will never be a man; I will always remain a little boy. Neither of us will ever die, just stay as we are." The boy said, "Any time I feel that I want to go to see you, I will cross high in the sky. As I go, it will be clouded all over; after I see you, I will return."

| NOTES |

1. Told by Sinyella; interpreted by Jess Chickapanega, 1919.

13. The Yavapai Origin Tale[1]

MANY PEOPLE LIVED DOWN UNDER THE EARTH. ONE MAN was named Hukama'ta. When he was asleep, he dreamed he was up on earth. "I was out there and looked around over that country. It is a better country up there. There is plenty of game; all kinds of deer, antelope, mountain sheep, cottontails, and jackrabbits. There are also things which grow: yucca fruit, goosefoot [sile'], and pigweed seeds. All such things that grow, I dreamed I saw."

Hukama'ta said, "We ought to go out after ten winters [tcu'dinya-vuwava]. I have a few grape seeds and a few spruce [kaθodovhe']² seeds. Prepare the ground and plant all the seeds together in one place." They planted them and after a while the plants came up. They poured water on them from time to time while the plants grew taller and taller. Hukama'ta wanted the grapevine to twine about the spruce as they grew together. "They should grow straight up until they reach the sky; then we can climb up," he said. They grew until they reached the sky. Then Hukama'ta said that he wanted his people to climb up there to the sky and dig a hole through.

Hukama'ta's daughter was a grown woman, but she was unmarried. She was very angry because she was not married; nobody liked her. She and her father lay on opposite sides of the fire to sleep. About midnight the woman went out to bring in a big armful of wood, which she put on the fire. When she had built a big fire she lay down with her feet toward the fire and her skirt drawn above her knees. Then her father saw her vulva, and he thought, "Maybe the girl is asleep. I think I will put my hand on it. When my daughter is married, and she sleeps with her husband, he will feel it. My daughter's vulva is pretty big." So he put his hand there, but the girl was not asleep; she was watching him from beneath her lowered lids. The girl said, "Nobody likes me; only my father thinks what he will do," and she cried, because she felt very angry. She thought, "What will I do to him? I can make him sick. I will make him sick the way men get sick and grow thin and die."

The man was not yet sick; he asked his people, "Have you finished making a hole in the sky so we can go out through it?" The people said, "Yes, we have finished the hole. We looked through, but there is no daylight. It is all dark and we could not see anything." Then he sent a few out again. "Take a slow match with you and make fires everywhere out there and look around at the country." When they came back they told him it was a very good country. Then he asked them again to prepare places to sleep on the grapevine. They made ten camping places. He said, "We are now ready to move; we can climb out on the other side of the sky. I do not feel good; my body aches all over." He was just a little sick, when they started up. They wanted Hukama'ta's girl to go too, but she was still very angry and refused. Her father talked to her and tried to take her with him, but she said, "I do not want to go; I intend to stay here." So he left her and went with the others. They traveled for ten sleeps before they emerged. The place they arrived at was so dark they could not see anything. They made many fires so that they could see to gather the things that grew up there. They stayed there some time.

Then Humaka'ta sent two boys to fetch his daughter. The boys knew where she lived, but when they arrived she was gone. They thought she had just gone off a little way, so they looked around and shouted, "Where are you? Where do you live?" Then the boys found her tracks and trailed her. They had followed but a short distance when they could no longer see any tracks; they ended abruptly. They looked all around but could find no more. Instead they found wild tobacco plants growing right where the tracks ended, handsome green plants. So the boys pulled out a few and took them with them. When they reached home they said, "We did not find her. We do not know where she went. The day we went down she was still at the camp: we saw her fresh tracks, which we followed. This tobacco grew at the end of her tracks, so we brought a few plants." Then the old people wanted to smoke the tobacco. They smoked it; "It is pretty fine tobacco," they all said.

Hukama'ta said he wanted to send boys down again. "Go down and look around there again. Perhaps you can find my daughter.

I want her to come right up as she should." So the boys went down to where they had found the tobacco. The tobacco was gone; they found none where they had seen it growing before. The woman's tracks led back from that spot to the place where she used to camp. There was a spring they always used at this place. The woman was sitting right at its edge. When the boys had nearly reached there, the girl stood up, and jumping into the spring, became a frog. When she jumped in the water rose, and the spring bubbled while the frog moved around in it. The water rose higher and higher. The boys said, "We do not know what is going to happen that the spring should gush so fast; things are going to change. We had better go back and tell them," so they came right up here. They told the old people, "When we were down the last time, the girl's tracks led to where the tobacco was; she had become the tobacco, so we brought a little. But now when we got there it was gone. We saw the girl. She was sitting close to the spring, and when we had nearly reached there, she jumped into the water and made the spring flow faster and rise high."

| |

Hukama'ta was the oldest brother; Tu'djipa was the younger. They were brothers by the same mother. Tu'djipa said, "You are older than I; I thought you would know what to plan, but what you say is worthless. You are like a big chief, but you do not talk to any purpose. You do not know much; I think I know many things. I think I will take your place as chief." Hukama'ta said, "How did you know then, that I am no good, that it is wrong for me to be big chief? Yes, I am chief; what I say is worthwhile. I am all right." Tu'djipa said, "All right, if you know everything, tell us; then we will make the sun so it will be light and we can see things a long way off. Then when our people are out hunting deer, they can catch them easier; and then the women can see when they are out gathering roots and seeds." Hukama'ta said, "Yes, I am older, so I know many things. You are very young; you do not know. You want to be big chief in my place, but you do not know how to advise, and all the things they might make would be wrong."

Then Tu'djipa asked him, "You are big chief, you say. Show me your possessions; all the things you yourself use. Show me what your moccasins look like." So Hukama'ta showed him new moccasins that he had never worn. Next he showed him new leggings that he had never worn. Next he showed him his buckskin shirt, a new one that he had just finished. Next he showed him his buckskin breeches, and next the headband. Tu'djipa said, "Yes, I can see you are older; that you are wise. I can see by your things that you are chief. You are all right. Show me some more things." So Hukama'ta showed him his cane, a new one he had never used. "Show me your bow, arrows, and quiver." He showed him the arrows that he had just made and never used; similarly the bow was just finished; the quiver of mountain lion hide was new, too. When the bow and arrows were in the quiver, the whole set was new. Tu'djipa said, "You showed me your belongings; I see they are all right. I want you to show me a lot more of your things. Show me your pipe." He showed it to him, a new one that he had never smoked. Next, "Show me your tobacco sack with the tobacco in it." The tobacco sack was made of new buckskin and the tobacco had never been used; the whole thing was new. "Show me your gaming poles [for the hoop-and-pole game]." Those he showed him were new; nobody had ever played with them. Next, he showed him the hoop: that was new too, it had never been used. "Next, show me the ball for the hiding game." It was a new one, and all sixteen counting sticks were new; no one had ever carried them, so they were not dirty.

Tu'djipa said, "I want to ask you to do more things." At that time the sky was not so high, just a little way up. "I want you to move the sky higher." Hukama'ta said, "All right, I can do that too. I am an old man; I know everything, so I say, 'All right, I can do that too.'" Then he drew something, a long pole, out of the ground and pushed it against the sky to raise it. So he pulled and pulled the pole up, pushing the sky higher and higher, until he got it way up; then he stopped.

Then Tu'djipa said, "All right, now make the sun. Make it so that when it comes out at daybreak, people can see a long way off; that will be pretty good." So Hukama'ta got a big, flat, thick disk of ice and broke off pieces around the edges to make it perfectly round. Then he carried the disk of ice to the east and threw it toward the east, and came right back home. Then Hukama'ta said, "I made the sun so that when it comes up, daylight will start close to the horizon; when the sun finally comes out, you can plainly see things round about." Then it dawned, and by and by the sun rose; but they could not see far, because he had made the moon. It came up across the sky and set. The men who were out hunting and the women who were out gathering plants could not see distinctly. The deer would hear them, become frightened, and run off, and the men would only hear the noise as they fled.

Then Hukama'ta got very sick and Tu'djipa said, "You are not an old man; what I said was true, you do not know anything. The things you think of cause trouble; that is why you are sick. If you could think wisely, you would be all right." Hukama'ta said, "Well, show me your things just as I did for you." So Tu'djipa said, "All right, I will show you my belongings. These are the sort of things that used to be worn by old men." First he showed moccasins, pretty old moccasins, all worn out; next, leggings, which were also pretty old and torn; then breeches with the fringes nearly all stripped from the sides, a very old pair. Next the buckskin shirt with the fringes under the arms and on the shoulders nearly all torn off, and buckskin patches everywhere, a pretty old shirt. Next was the hat; this was drawn down over the head, made of buckskin—an old one. It had some owl feathers tied in two bunches on the top and two eagle tail feathers. These were very old too; all that was left were the barbs at the tips. Hukama'ta said, "Show me your other things just as I did: your bow, arrows, and quiver." He showed his arrows, very old arrows, cracked, and crooked, with the feathers nearly all gone. His bow similarly was very old and cracked, and the string was knotted and old. His quiver was made of a foxskin, with the hair nearly all worn off and with big holes, which had been sewed up: a very old one. He showed him his cane; it was very old too, and his pipe was made of clay (like that we obtain from the creek): an old one. His tobacco sack was a squirrel skin with the hair all gone except on the tail and with little holes stopped with piñon pitch, and the tobacco in it was old. His pole and hoop, his hiding ball and counters were all old too.

Hukama'ta said, "You do as I did. If you think you can do it, push the sky higher." Tu'djipa said, "All right." He pulled up something from the ground and pushed against the sky, pulling and pushing to lift it higher and higher until he felt it stick, then he stopped. Then he made a disk of ice by breaking the edges off. He carried this to the east and threw it toward the east. Then he came back and told Hukama'ta, "I threw it toward the east; it will travel across the sky and then go down. Then it will travel under the earth to the east again. When the sun is underneath the earth it will be somewhat like daylight, and when it has nearly risen, it will still be a little dark, but you will be able to see a little way. By and by the sun will rise, so that you can see the first rays on the high mountains; soon it will shine right on you and make you feel warm." Then it came up as he said it would: Tu'djipa had made the sun.

Hukama'ta said, "You are an old man: you can be chief now." So Tu'djipa said, "I am going to make the stars too." So he blew all over the sky, "psss . . . ," and spread little and big stars over it. Then he said, "I am going to be a pretty old man," so he took his pipe, filled and lit it, and smoked. He puffed the smoke over his limbs and his face and trunk so that his skin looked like that of a very old man; his hair became gray, and his face was that of an old man. He said, "You, Hukama'ta, made the moon; we will call that the moon."

Now Hukama'ta was very sick; he was nearly dead, so he called to everybody to come to him. He told them to build a house. "When I am in it, I will tell you what I know." Everyone came and first they build [built] a shade [an open-sided house], but he said, "No, I do not like that sort; build another kind." So they built a house of poles set up in a cone like a hogan, and he said, "No, I want another kind." So they thought what kind he might mean. Then they pulled up big cottonwood trees, and set them up in holes. "Is that the kind you want?" they asked. He looked: "Yes, that is the sort I want. When the sun is rising, it will throw a long shadow; that is what I want, so I can lie in the shadow. At midday the shadow will be right at their base; then I will move inside, and when the sun is sinking, the shadow will extend this way, and I can move with it. That is the kind I call wai'aase'kaa'mdjiva (house shadow moves)."

"I know everything, because I am an old man. I do not think any of you know so much as I do, so I am going to tell you all I know before I die. When I was a boy I used to play with the hoop and poles; now you people can watch the constellation Ipe'ha rising at daylight.[3] The hoop is right there; you can see it too. When I was a boy I wore down tied on top of my hair. That constellation will come out too; you can call it Tci'ut. When I was a boy I wore the little horns and head skin of a young mountain sheep which I tanned good and wore for a hat. That constellation will appear too; you can call it Hane'kwa. Now that I am old I use a cane. You call them [those stars; another constellation] Nyiswto'tvidj. You will see them too."

"I want you, my people, to begin to count by months. Count how many months it will be until it gets warm in the spring. About that time the sile' is just coming out, pigweed, goosefoot, sunflower, mata'k; piñon trees are just budding; so is soapweed, prickly pears, and juniper berries. I want you people to look at all these things, so that you will remember the names I gave them. They will all start to grow and ripen at the same time. I made these things for you to use and eat so that you may live after I die. When you are hunting and kill bucks, tan their skins soft and make moccasins, leggings, breeches, and skirts for the women. Kill mountain sheep, antelope, jackrabbits, and cottontails, and eat their flesh. When you people have little boys, let them always run at daybreak, and let the young girls when they have their first menses run in the same way before daylight. They should do this four times, and after the period, they should wash their hair, and their bodies, and then they can eat meat. If the girl fails to wait until the flow is completed before tasting meat, she will become barren. When the boy has grown to manhood and is married and his wife menstruates, they should both do this. They should run four times at dawn; both should wash before sunrise; then they can eat meat. If they do this she will not become barren. When running before dawn young boys should carry a short slow match. They should run toward the dawn, stop over there and touch their wrists and elbows with the fire. This is done in order that when you are older you will not get sick in these joints. Do this: then run back toward the house and throw the slow match backward over your head. Run a little way, then turn back quickly, and run and pick it up again. If you do this, you can remember, on some occasion when you are going away, to go back quickly after you have gone but a little way and get anything you have forgotten."

Hukama'ta was very sick, nearly dead. He said, "My daughter, whom I left down there under the ground, is doing something wicked. I heard her. This ground rumbles." So he sent boys down. "Go down underground and see." They went down to see, but they did not get quite to the bottom of the vine. They found the water rising higher and higher. "We found the water was up to the third camp on our tree-and-grapevine route," they said when they returned. Then Hukama'ta said, "I think that is what I heard her doing. That water will rise until that place is full, and then it will come up through the hole and flood this country too, and we will all drown. That water will come up and kill us all. I know this. Cut down that hardwood tree and you, Bee-men, hollow it out for its whole length. At the top make a place to put meat; just below that put in provisions to fill the hollow, and get a little girl who has just been weaned to put inside. Do not put her in yet, but watch the water rise. When it is nearly through that hole by which we came, put the girl in the log. Make a plug to fit the hole in the log and make it watertight. Then the water will lift the log higher and higher, and carry it around up in the sky. After a while, the water will subside, so that the log will float lower and lower. Tell her not to open the plug when she thinks the water has gone down so that the log is stranded, but to stay inside, and pound on the log with something. If it is still in the water, it will sound dull. Tell her to pound again. Finally when the log is dry it will give a sharp sound; then she should open it. Let her look about to see where the log lies. Tell her to come right to this mountain [San Francisco Mountain]; this is our country."

Hukama'ta was now nearly dead. He said, "I am sick; I am causing myself to die. You people living here will get sick and die when you are still young; children, too, will get sick and die quickly. A man who does not fall sick will live to be a pretty old man, but then he will die. That is the sort of thing I create; I tell you so that you will know you are going to die. Watch me when I die. After I am dead I will never be alive again. Lay my body down, and tell everyone to come and see me, so that everyone will feel sorry and cry. Let everyone throw things—arrows, leggings, buckskin shirts, breeches, bows, buckskins, and such things—let them throw these on me. Dress me in good clothes. Do not bury me. Gather wood into a big pile and place my body on it and place things there too. I do not want Coyote to be with you when you burn me. Send him a long way off to a mountain called Wiao'o to fetch fire with which to burn me."

Then Hukama'ta died and they did as he had instructed them. They all came and cried. They dressed his body in good clothes and threw good things on it. They made a pile of wood and put the body up there. Then Tu'djipa sent Coyote away. "When you are going away, do not stop to look back; just keep on running." Then a little while after Coyote had gone, they got out a fire drill, made a fire, and burned the body. All the men stood around it in a circle. Each man had a long pole with which to poke the body,[4] so that it would burn faster. Coyote ran and ran toward the mountain. When he had nearly reached there, he stopped. Looking back, he saw the smoke, so he turned and ran back home. All the men there were crying and rapidly poking the fire. The body was nearly all consumed; the heart alone was left when Coyote arrived. He said, "Where will I stand to cry too?" The men were in a close circle with their hands clasped tight; they would not let Coyote in. So he walked around and around outside, crying, "Let me in." By and by he found a place where Badger stood—he was very short—so he jumped right over his head into the circle. He snatched up the heart and, jumping out at the same place, ran off with it. The men who were standing about crying ran after him to recover it. They could not catch him, he ran so fast. Even when the best runners chased him they could not recover it.

They chased him toward the south. When they had almost caught up with him, he ran over a low hill and transformed himself into a big dead tree. They could not find him. They hunted around and went off a little way. Then he ran off again. When they saw him again they took up the chase. Again when he was nearly caught, he made himself into a cactus. They could not find him, so they hunted around. When they were a little way off, he ran again. Then they chased him again, and when they had nearly caught him, he ran over a little hill and changed himself into some grass. They looked around but failed to find him, but when they had walked by, he sprang up again. He ran again until they were out of breath. Then he made himself very small and crawled into a little hole in a tree gall [?]. The wind blew hard and rolled this into a little canyon. It took him a long way off. Then he came out and went off, carrying the heart with him. He carried the heart off toward the south to the Yavapai or Enemy-Coyotes [Itcahuakaθot, said to be the name of the Yavapai near Jerome for people living further south]. This man's heart, when it grew, was corn. It has [illegible: ears, tears?] today. When the men who chased Coyote could not find him any more, they abandoned the search and came back home.

Tu'djipa said, "I want two or three of you boys to go down to look at the water." They went down and found the water nearly at the top of the tree. They came back and told Tu'djipa, who said, "Clean that place where Hukama'ta was burned after he died; then water it. Do this four times." By and by some little plants grew there. They did not know what they were. After a time the plants grew taller, and when they were fully grown, the people could tell it was corn. Then they hoed, weeded, and watered it. In a little while it bore ears. It had four ears. When they were ripe, Tu'djipa said, "I will give the longest ear to the Hopi; the second I will give to the Havasupai; the third I will give to the Zuñi, and the fourth ear, a short one, I will give to the Mohave."⁵ They gave them to the four tribes.

Then the water came out of the ground and flowed through the little canyons. People went up on the little hills to look at the water. They had the big log already stocked with provisions. When the water had nearly reached the log, they put the little girl in it. They told her all about it: "The water will carry you off in that big log." Then the water floated it away, higher and higher. The other people climbed up on a high mountain, but soon the water covered the mountain top and all were drowned. It rose until it reached the sky. Only the red-shafted flicker (gaku'u) flew up against the sky. The water nearly caught him too. His tail hung down in the water and it became black, as it is now. All living things were drowned.

Then the water began to go down. It carried the floating log around and around. The little girl inside felt it moving. Finally the water subsided entirely, and it seemed to her that the log was lying still. After a while she pounded on it, but it still sounded wet. "Perhaps it is still wet or perhaps it is lying in water." She repeated the pounding from time to time, and by and by it gave a sharp sound; it was dry. So she pushed out the plug and peered out: all the water was gone and the ground was dry. So she came out. She looked for San Francisco Mountain. Her log lay on the east side of the Little Colorado (Hagaθei'la) so that she would see the mountain easily. She felt glad to see it. She stayed close to the log and gathered some clay left by the flood, pounded and ground it, and kneaded it up with water to make a pot.

She stayed there quite a little while. Early in the morning the flicker that escaped the flood cried, "tcsss . . . tcsss. . . ." Then the girl said, "I wonder what sort of thing makes that noise up in the tree early in the morning. I thought everyone was drowned. I thought I was the only one alive. I wonder who you are." The bird said, "Yes I know that all the people were drowned except me and you. The water nearly caught me too. I was up against the sky too. The water soaked my tail, and then it went down. I know we two are the only ones left. I looked all around but could not find anyone else, just you here. We will be partners."

The girl still had some provisions left in the log. Then she thought that she would build a house of stone to live in. She made one and lived in it, and ate everything she had left in the log. That house she built is still in the canyon leading from Oraibi to the Little Colorado;

the pottery she made is there too. Then she moved when she had only a little provisions left to carry. She went across the river to San Francisco Mountain and along its north side. Then she got to Pokadespai'iva [Cedar Ranch: Hull Spring?, north of San Francisco Mountain]. She stayed a while at the spring and made little stone houses, like our storage houses. Then she moved to Hawaiᵃtenyu'da [a little west of a crater lying west of the mountain called Inyanyawa', Sun's House]. There she stayed drawing pictures on the rocks. Then she moved again to the head of Cataract Canyon on the north side of Bill Williams Mountain. There she stayed and built little rough stone houses [?]. Then she moved westward to Gaθi'lgisivko'va [on the mesa three or four miles east of Ash Fork] and she stood on the mesa and looked off to the west. Then she went on down the mesa southwestward to Djɯqaᵃwi', where there was a spring at which she stayed a while [eight or more miles southwest of Ash Fork, where there is a mountain; i.e., Black Forest?] and then she moved again. She said to herself, "I will look around to find a good place where I can stay so I will not have to move any more." So she went down toward the southeast [down the Chino Valley?] to the rim at the head of the Verde Valley. "This is a good place that I have found now." She built stone houses right on top of the red cliff there. The girl said, "I will call this stone house Wawi'legehwa'ta; then if anybody is ever alive in this country, they should not forget what I called it." She lived there a while and then she moved a short distance. She said to herself, "I have not yet reached the place I want," so she moved again. Then she said, "I am there now. The name of this place will be Aho'qodjoqo'oya [water, drop by drop, cave]."

She stayed a long time in that cave, while she gathered many things that grew, goosefoot and pigweed seeds, gota, and ie'la, for her food. After a time she had grown to be a young woman and she thought, "What will I do to have a child?" Then she thought of the dropping water; so she lay down and let the water impregnate her. Then at early dawn she lay down in the spot where the first rays of the sun struck, and these entered her, too. By and by she became pregnant and gave birth to a girl. She pinched and molded its face and head, straightened its limbs and hands, put it on a cradle bedded with rubbed cedar bark, and gave it nourishment.

By and by the child grew to be a big girl who walked about to help her mother gather things to bring home. "Now you are old enough to go out by yourself to gather growing plants, but do not go far away. It is dangerous for you to go a long way. I know all the places around here. It is all right so far, and over there. No evil things come into my grounds, and we can gather good things here in safety." The girl went gathering all the time, until eventually she became a young woman. Her mother told her, "There was no man with me; no one else. I conceived you by myself from this little spring. I think you can do that too." Now her daughter tried this; she lay down and watched the drops forming, but none fell. She tried several times without result. So she told her mother. When the girl had gone away the water resumed its dripping. So the mother said, "That spring made you; perhaps he thinks you are his daughter, so that he does not want to have connection with you. I think I can contrive so the water will drop right down on you." So the girl lay down in that spot and her mother lay on top of her. Then when the water dropped the mother jumped aside and the water entered the girl. The mother told her daughter, "I lay on the spot where the first sunshine strikes; you can do the same." So the girl did it, and after a short time she became pregnant. She gave birth to a boy. Her mother said "This is what people should do when any are alive," as she tied and cut the navel cord. Then she dug up soapweed roots and washed the baby, pinched and shaped it, and put it in the cradle.

The boy's maternal grandmother told him to run at daylight. He did this every day. Then his mother and grandmother went out gathering seeds, leaving the boy at home. Birds came close to the house. He filliped some pebbles at them and killed a great many. These he threw in a pile, which the women saw when they came home. His grandmother said, "I wonder what thing came here and killed so many birds and piled them by your house?" Every time the women went out the boy killed more birds. Finally he told them, "I did it." His grandmother said, "All right, that is a good thing to do. I am glad you do it." So she made him a bow and an arrow; she had no sinew, but used yucca fiber instead for the bowstring. The boy went off a little way to shoot.

His mother was now a full-grown woman. When she went out gathering food, her mother told her, "Do not go very far. It is dangerous; perhaps some animal will catch and kill you." But the daughter did not heed; she went way down to an open space where fine fruits grew. Then she heard something make a rumbling noise. "I do not know what that is," she said, looking around. Then the girl saw an eagle coming down, so she tried to run, but the eagle swooped and carried her away. The eagle killed her and carried her way up to his nest on a very high cliff.

His grandmother said to the boy, "You are a boy now, and I made a bow and arrow for you so that you could kill birds and small animals. I warn you that at some place near this country there are monsters. I tell you so that you will remember. I told your mother, but she did not heed. She went off a long way gathering; the eagle carried her off and killed her. There is another dangerous thing lying down in an open glade; I know of that one too. It is a bull (wakasi').[6] The place where he lies is called Mátyito'ta [ground, a sloping height], and a little way off is Matsile' [sandy or alkaline ground], where the antelope buck stays; he is dangerous too. Both those animals try to kill me. I know, so I tell you. Then there is the eagle who lives near the top of a very high cliff; that is where he came from to kill my daughter. Another one over that way a little distance is the bear; he will kill a man if he sees him. The owl over there killed men, too. Up in this direction a lot of people were living at I'ilgadjaka'va, and a man came down who stared at them, killing them with his eyes. He is wicked, too. Those are all the bad animals living near here. One man is called Itcahua'si'taθagaa'mdja [enemy, one, walks]; he is a man who walks around alone. He lives in that direction and perhaps if he sees you he will kill you. He has a face in back as well as one in front and can easily spy you. When you go a long way off to hunt deer, he may see and kill you."

So as the boy went hunting deer, he thought. He felt pretty angry that the eagle had killed his mother. He thought, "What am I going to do?" Then when he came back at night he asked his grandmother, "In which direction is the bull that is lying down? Point it out; I would like to go see him." His grandmother said, "No, you cannot go to see him. Perhaps he would kill you if he saw you. And the eagle flying way up there would see you and catch you, too." But the boy said, "I am determined. I want to go see him," so she showed him the way and he set out. He went along, hiding as he went, and lay down on a high hill. From there he saw the bull and he thought, "What will I do?" So he called together the badger, the prairie dog, the mole, and all the burrowing animals. When they came, he told them to tunnel under the bull so that there would be only a thin crust of earth under him. Then he made a spear of a long pole and put it in a handle [sic], and he said, "I want you, Badger, to dig first under the bull." But the badger failed; he dug only a short way and then he said the tunnel was finished. Then the boy told the prairie dog to try, but he did the same thing; he could not reach the bull. Next the rock squirrel tried, but he failed too. The fourth time Matmau'lig tried.[7] He dug the ground away right under the bull and dug a little hole through the crust right under its armpit. Then the boy said, "Yes, you made it properly. Dig a hole that I can jump into and hide after I do something to the bull, so that he cannot kill me." Now the boy could go through the tunnel with his spear heated red in the fire. He said, "Dig the hole deeper, pretty deep, so I can go right into it." The mole did this and the boy said, "All right." When everything was ready, the boy went back to where he left the other men-animals. "Everyone should gather wood and keep the fire burning all night to heat the spear red-hot. Then I can come in the morning and carry it there and stick it into the bull," he said.

Then he went home to his grandmother, but he did not tell her. "I want to see about that bull lying down; perhaps I can kill that one first." In the morning he went again to where the other people were. Then he heated the spear red in a big fire. Then he said to the others, "You watch the bull lying there while I go. I will stick the spear right through his heart. Then he will jump up suddenly, and turn to look around, wondering what thing struck him in the heart. When he knows, he will hook the ground. I do not know if the hole is deep enough, perhaps he can kill me. But the bull won't last long; after a little he will fall down dead. Then all you people race down to him; the best runner, he who gets there first, shall have the good soft hair to make a nest." Then the boy took the spear and went through the tunnel under the bull. He thrust it through his armpit and jumped down into his refuge, the deep hole. The bull jumped up and looked around but he could not find who had struck him. After a while he knew; he saw the hole. Then he hooked at the ground. He nearly killed the boy; he grazed his head and back with his horns. Finally the bull tottered about and fell dead. Then the other people on the hilltop raced down toward the carcass. The fastest runners were Rat and Mouse; the last to arrive were some little birds. So the boy said, "Now Rat and Mouse shall have the soft hair to make nests of"; that is why they make their nests of soft things today.

The boy said, "It is all right now. You people skin the bull; I want that hide. We have so many men here that we must divide the meat. All who can get it can have a piece. There will be four pieces of meat, so that when men are alive and butcher a deer, or the carcass of some other animal, it will always be divided into four parts. That is how I will cause it to be. When the hide is raw, like that one is now, make me a shirt of half of it. I want you also to make a wooden hoop about so big and stretch the other half of the hide over it with thongs. Then fill the small intestines with the bull's blood and tie up the ends with thongs. Then tie a lot of these around the circumference of the hoop. Fill some other intestines with the bull's brains and fasten these on in the same manner. I have several tanned buckskins with me; just cut them into strings and tie them to it in loops. Then when I set out to kill the eagle, he can grasp the loops and carry me up to his home. And also tie some loops underneath so that I can fasten them around my body. That is all I want you to do. I killed the bull first. I brought all you people together to help me. Now you should all go home, and any time I think that I need you, I will call you together again." Then all the other people went home and the boy carried the things they had made for him back to his grandmother's house. When he was nearly there he left them; when he got to the house he had nothing in his hands. Then he told his grandmother, "You said that the bull was pretty hard to kill. But I killed him easily. I left his hide and meat out there; you go fetch them." So she brought them into the house. The boy said, "Cook the meat so that we can eat it."

The boy stayed with his grandmother a while. Then he asked, "In which direction is the antelope? I want to see him." So she pointed out the way, and he set out. (I do not remember how the boy killed the antelope, but he did it.)

Then the boy said to his grandmother, "I want to kill all the wicked animals, and make this a safe country for people to live in. I do not want to miss any, to let one live. If I do, he will continue to kill people. I want to make it safe for humans when they are here. Tell me where there is a good hard wood of which to make arrow points. I want to get some. The wood here about is not good for arrow points; it is too soft and breaks easily." His grandmother said, "I know the place where many sticks from which to make arrow points grow, but Bear is there. He owns and uses them. When a man wants to get good sticks, Bear hears him breaking them. He rushes out to catch and eat him. He always does this; he is very wicked." The boy said, "I know that is what he does. I want to go and see whether I can get some or not." So the boy went to the thicket and broke some branches. Bear heard him and immediately ran up. The boy said, "Do not do that—run at me. My grandmother said she wanted to be your wife; I have been looking for you." So Bear stopped and said, "That is what I like, to have some person come to me. All right. Do you want some sticks to take with you?" "Yes, that is what I came to ask about, too." And Bear said, "I know where the good ones are. Come with me and gather them." They went into the middle of the thicket and broke off some good branches, then tied them in a bundle which Bear slung across his shoulders. Then he followed the boy.

When they were near the camp, the boy said, "You wait here with the sticks. I will tell my grandmother and she will come to you." So the boy told his grandmother, "It was all right; I did not see the bear. I just gathered some sticks and brought them with me. I left them out there. I want you to fetch them." So she went after the sticks. When she saw Bear, she was frightened and ran home and told the boy. She said, "Bear followed you. He is right where you left the sticks. I saw him and I am afraid, so I did not get them; I ran home." Then the boy said, "When Bear saw me, he was going to kill me, but I told him he could marry you and he said, 'All right.' So I got a lot of sticks and he came along with me." His grandmother said, "Are you sure that is so?" and the boy answered, "Yes." So the old woman washed her hair, painted her face, put on her good clothes, and went to where Bear was waiting. Then she brought the sticks in to the camp. Bear married the woman, and they all lived together in that house.

Then the boy asked his grandmother, "Where do the best kind of arrow reeds grow? I would like to get some to make arrows." She said, "It is a very dangerous place where they grow down there, I know. No man has been able to get any. It is that way," pointing toward Havasu [blue water; Cataract Creek]. "When you are in that canyon the cliffs will come together and crush you. It has killed many men that way." But the boy said, "All right, I will just go to examine it." He cut some long, strong poles and carried them over here to Cataract Canyon. He came down into the head of our canyon, but the walls did not move. He failed to find the arrow reeds, so he kept on down the canyon. He got to the head of the creek, when the cliffs started to close on him. So he held the long poles crosswise on his head, and when the walls tried to come together, the poles propped them apart. When the walls stopped they stayed there; he made this canyon as it is now. So he came right down here and gathered some arrow reeds. Then he heard someone coming. It was Owl, who owned the reeds. Owl came at him just as Bear had done. The boy said, "My grandmother wants you to come to marry her. She sent me down here to get you." Owl said, "All right. We will gather a lot of reeds. I will carry them for you. I know where the best are." So he gathered plenty for the boy and carried them.

When they approached the boy's grandmother's house, they did as before. The boy let Owl stay behind with the arrow reeds, while he went into camp. "Yes, I was in the canyon you spoke of, where the cliffs come together. I did not see any cliffs do that, although I was in there. I gathered many arrow reeds and carried them here. I left them over there; I want you to fetch them. I did not see Owl or anybody else; it was safe enough." So the old woman went out and saw Owl sitting close to the arrow reeds. She was frightened, so she hurried back and told the boy, "Owl followed you. He is right there where you left the arrow reeds. I was afraid and came back." The boy said, "Oh, no; he carried the reeds for me. I told him that he could marry you. Go fetch him." So the woman washed her hair, painted her face, put on good clothes, and went out, returning to camp with the arrow reeds and Owl. His grandmother was married to two men.

The boy said, "I do not know how to straighten the arrow reeds in the fire. You two men know how to straighten and feather them; prepare them for me." They did this for him, feathered and provided them with good hardwood foreshafts. Then the boy asked his grandmother, "I wonder where the good stone arrowheads are. Point out the direction so that I can go get them." "Yes, I know where they are, but it is difficult to approach and pick them up. They might kill you." "That is so, but I just want to go to look at them, to see whether I can get some," the boy said. So he went where a great many stone points were and picked them up, putting them in a sack. When he had gathered a great many, he thought he had enough. He did not see or hear anything to be afraid of. When he was ready to start home, he took a big stone and smashed the largest stone blade [?] which lay there. Then the blade began to burst and fly in every direction, striking the boy all over. Then all the big blades began to break and fly about, hitting him repeatedly. But he was wearing that bull-hide shirt and the stones only cut into the shirt. He was running off as fast as he could to get away from them, without heeding the direction, when he heard someone shout, "Just come over to me." So he turned toward that sound and went there. When he got there the stones had ceased bursting. The man he found there said, "These are my own stone points that are here. Why did you not come to me first to ask for them? Then I would have picked out the good ones for you, so that you would not have had to go yourself. They are very dangerous. Well, I will pick out the good ones for you." So he picked out the best and gave them to the boy. This man was Talkwo'm.[8] The boy carried them back to his grandmother's house.

Then the boy said that he wanted those two men, Bear and Owl, to prepare his arrowheads for him, because they knew how to do it. Bear and Owl said, "We have not the proper tool to make the arrowhead with." The boy's grandmother knew what they needed: the single prong of a young buck. The boy said, "I will go out and see if I can find one." He went out and killed a young buck with little prong horns and brought a prong back for them to make arrowheads. Bear and Owl prepared the heads for him. Then he went hunting and killed two big bucks which he carried home. Owl and Bear butchered them, and they all had plenty of meat to cook. "It is very pleasant," he said. Then his grandmother said to him, "Formerly when a young man killed a deer, he used to run at dawn toward the daylight. So you too must run four times around San Francisco Mountain and pull up one big spruce [kaθodovhe'] to fetch home with you." The boy did as he was told. The tree is right in that cave now.[9]

The boy said, "I do not know how to make arrowheads. I think I will learn so I will always know." He made one stone arrowhead; then he picked a coal out of the fire and fashioned it into another. He made many with coals. When Bear saw them he said, "Are you going to set those arrowheads on your arrows, and carry them to shoot deer or some other big animals? I think you will not be able to kill anything with those coals; they will not penetrate. They will not hurt." The boy said, "Don't you think so?" The Bear answered, "Yes, I think you cannot kill anything with them." The boy said, "I will put one on my arrow, and you stand off a little way, while I shoot at you. Let us see if it will kill you." He put all the coal heads in a pile close to the fire, while he hid the stone head to one side under some sand. The boy said, "All is ready." Then he took some deer sinew, wet it in his mouth, picked up a coal and showed it to Bear. "See that one; I will fasten that one on." He said, "I will put it in the fire to warm a little," but while he held it near the fire, he secretly dropped it and picked up the stone head. He tied this tightly to an arrow with the sinew. Bear stood just a few steps away. The boy said, "I cannot shoot that close. You go off a little farther; it is the distance at which I shoot deer." So Bear went off a little way and stood with all four feet together so that his side was exposed. When the boy stood ready to shoot, Bear lurched toward the boy several times. The boy waited to see if Bear would move or stand quiet. He kept pointing the drawn arrow at Bear. Then the boy picked up a coal and, laying it on his foot, said, "I am going to shoot at you now; stand still." He let the arrow fly and it went right through Bear's chest and out the other side. When Bear was hit he roared, "Grrr . . . ," and rushed at the boy. Then the boy kicked the coal off his foot and he said, "Right where that coal fell, you will fall down dead." Bear dropped dead at that spot. Then the boy pulled out the arrow and the blood ran out both sides on to the ground.

Then the boy told Owl, "Collect all of Bear's blood you can, and when it is dry mix it with sand and tie it in something. I do not want to waste it; I want to keep it for myself. Let the rest of the blood remain, so that at some time when people are living here they will know it as good medicine for a broken arm, a swelling, or a hurt. They can take it, rub it in water, and put it on the hurt place. I will call it sama'gainyadj [spirit, black]."

Owl did this, and when he had finished the boy told his grandmother, "Owl saw me kill Bear. I think Owl is pretty bad. I think that now that he knows, he is afraid that I will kill him, too. I think Owl moves his heart around in his body, on the tip of his finger, on top of his head, in his ear, or some other place in his body, trying to hide it. I want you, my grandmother, to feel where his heart is when you sleep with him. Then you must tell me, and I will shoot at his heart wherever it is. I want to kill him too." When his grandmother went to bed with Owl, she felt his chest but his heart was gone. Then she felt all over his body but she failed to find it. Then she told the boy, "I could not find it. I could not feel it any place." The boy said, "You just feel again; perhaps you will find it." So when Owl was asleep, she felt all over his body again and finally located it in the sole of his foot. The boy told his grandmother, "When Owl is asleep again, you feel his sole once more to make sure it is there. Then tell me and I will shoot right where his heart is." She did this; she felt Owl's heart still in his sole, so she told the boy. Then the boy shot right through the heart and killed Owl, too. Now he had killed four of the monsters.

Then the boy asked his grandmother, "Which monster is next? I want you to tell me so that I can go see him." "The next monster is a man who has a face on the back of his head as well as one in front. He is perpetually traveling around." The boy asked, "What does he carry about with him, an arrow or something else?" His grandmother said, "Yes, he has an arrow and a long knife. He carries just these two weapons all the time so he can kill men with them." "Point out the direction in which he is; then I will go to his place and look around for him," the boy said. So he took a long knife he had made, an arrow, and a parcel containing the blood of Bear, and his bow, and went to that wicked man's place. Then he went about feigning to hunt deer, but really looking for that man. Then he found him skinning a deer. The man had two faces, in front and in back of his head. So the boy hid and thought what he would do. Soon he came out of hiding, and instantly the man's rear face saw him. Siko'digaa'mdja (—Walking Around), the boy, went down to the man, Itcahua'sitaθagaa'mdja (Enemy Who Walks Alone), who was skinning the deer. The man said to the boy, "I killed a big buck here, but I have not finished skinning it. It is all right, I let you discover me. Come and help me skin it, and then we will broil some meat, and you can take some of it home with you." The boy said, "No, I do not want to help you. I have been hunting another deer myself, and soon I will catch it, so I am in a hurry." The man said, "No, you help me, and when we have finished we will broil some meat and eat. Then we will talk."

The boy said, "I heard that you are a bad man; when you find a man alone, as I am, you kill him. I think we will fight right now." Then the other said, "All right." The man had a long knife and the boy had another of the same size. The man said that he wanted to change places; he wanted to stand uphill. But the boy said, "No, I am the shorter and so I will stand here uphill while we fight." The other said, "All right." The boy went down close to him and held his knife up so he could stab down into the other's thorax. His opponent held his knife in the same way. Then both stabbed at the same moment and pulled their knives out again. The boy fell on his face down the hill and the other man fell on his face up the hill. The boy was badly wounded and blood flowed plentifully, but it could not run from the other man's wound at all. When all the boy's blood had run out, he came to life again. He took the blood collected from Bear, rubbed it on the cut in his throat, and soon it was entirely healed. But the other man did not return to life; the blood could not run out, so he grew bloated and died.

Then the boy went home and told his grandmother, "I killed Enemy Who Walks Alone, too." And she told him, "When a boy as old as you kills an enemy he must not be lazy. He should run toward the daylight every day at dawn. When you run toward the daylight you must not run on that road along the edge of the cliff. The man, who lies there all the time, lies across the road, and when any man comes along it, he kicks him over the cliff into the canyon. That is where he keeps them to eat. Other people down in the canyon kill strangers by staring at them." Then the boy said, "I want to go see him. You tell me all about him, so that I can go see the man who lies across the road." When he was ready to go he fetched his ax, his fox, his rattlesnake,[10] his gwematau'vgia'm,[11] his pipe and tobacco, put them in something to carry them, and then set off. He went along the road on which the man lay. When he reached the man, the boy said, "I want you to move out of the way, so I can pass." But the man said, "Just walk right by over me; that will be all right." The boy said, "No, I won't do that; maybe you lie, and will kick me off the cliff." The man said, "No, I will not do that." And the boy said, "Yes, I know you will. I will see if you are kindly disposed. I will try something else first to see what you will do." So he pulled out his fox and threw it down. The fox tried to jump over the man but he kicked the fox over the cliff, so that it fell to the bottom where many men were living. These men killed and ate it. The boy could hear them talking down there; they were glad. So he drew out his rattlesnake and threw it right on the man, who said, "That is what I am afraid of." He wanted to jump up, but he could not; he had grown roots right into the ground. He wriggled about to get away from the rattlesnake, until his roots began to be pulled out. Then the boy drew his ax, chopped them through, and kicked the man off the cliff to the others below. Then the boy said, "Nobody can lie on this road now; this is just an ordinary road."

Then he went by on the road. After a short distance it became impassable; there was a high cliff that he could not descend. So he filled his pipe and drew smoke. He blew it on the cliff four times. Then the cliff cracked open wide enough for him to climb down to the base. So he went where all the people were. When he was a little way off, one saw him and said, "Someone is coming." Some of them said, "Where is he?" "He is right over there," and as he came, everybody looked straight at him. When he arrived he took Bear's blood—he had a little with him—and made a cross with it on top of his foot. Everybody drew around to gaze at him, so that the boy became unconscious and nearly died, but the cross on his foot jerked him, so he was aroused. This happened four times.

Then the boy looked around for dead cedar trees and asked them, "Which one of you burns best? Sometimes sparks fly off when I burn good hard cedar wood." He gathered a lot of this sort and carried his load where the people were. Then he lit it, and the fire snapped and sent sparks flying about. When it was all burnt to coals, he took out the deer paunch and threw it into the fire. Then he said, "You people keep watching that thing all the time. If you think you want to eat it, just keep on gazing at it." Pretty soon the object in the fire began to swell until it nearly burst. There was one little boy, who could only crawl, sitting back a way. This one said, "It looks to me as if that thing in the fire is going to burst right in your faces." Then it burst and flew in their faces, blinding them. Then the boy took his ax and killed all those people down there except the little boy, whom he carried off with him. After he had killed them all, he looked about in their houses and gathered up the good articles. These he tied with a yucca rope and, slinging the bundle on his back, placed the baby on top and carried it up out of the canyon.

When the boy neared home he left the bundle he was carrying a little way from the house. He told his grandmother, "I brought some things and a little boy with me. I want you to fetch them." His grandmother went out, but found only the bundle there; the little boy was gone. She went a little way, following the tracks where the baby had crawled, and then turned back to tell her grandson. Then the boy followed the tracks as fast as he could run. He tracked the crawling baby until he saw him quite a distance ahead. It was on the far side of an open plain, about to crawl into a little cave at the base of a cliff. So he ran as fast as he could across the plain and got to the baby just as it was crawling in. Only one foot protruded and this the boy seized, but the baby pulled its foot out of the moccasin and crawled inside. The boy felt sorry that the baby had escaped, and he thought, "How will I get him out and kill him?" So he returned home. Then he thought he would take his rattlesnake with him and let it loose at the hole. He told it, "When the baby comes out, you strike to kill him." Then he hid and watched the hole. The baby came out and sat in the sunshine by the side of the hole. The boy crept up under cover and when he got near, thinking the baby did not see him, he ran up to catch him. But when he got close the baby sprang back into the hole. His own rattlesnake was lying asleep right by the hole and failed to hear the baby as it came out quietly. The baby came out this way four times. The snake lay close to the hole but it did not strike at all, so the boy caught it up and threw it away. Then he gathered a lot of dry wood and stuffed it into the hole together with some green leaves. Then he took his fire-drill and set fire to it. He made the smoke go right into that hole, so the baby would die of suffocation. He plugged up the mouth of the hole with stones and sand, and then he went back home.

By and by he came back to see how the baby was faring. The rocks were still there with dirt packed in the crevices, just as he had left it. He thought that the baby was dead; that all was well. Then he looked around and found the baby's tracks quite a way off, where he had crawled out by another hole. He followed the tracks a little way, when he saw that the baby had stood up and walked. He followed those tracks a short time, until he reached a place where the baby had burnt cedar wood, stone blades, cactus, and yucca together. These had burst into fragments which became men; the boy saw their tracks. He followed the baby's tracks but a short way when he came up to the baby with all those men. They were all lined up on one side and when the boy reached them they began to shoot at him, and he at them. He fought until he had killed all the men the baby had created: only the baby was left; he was difficult to kill. So the boy let him go and returned to his grandmother's home. Again the baby burned cedar, stone blades, cactus, soapweed, and narrow leaf yucca, and again they burst into fragments which were men. The boy [grandson] called all his men together, all the animals who used to be men. They followed the baby and his men. They caught up with them after a long journey and began to fight. The baby was a young man now, and he killed a lot of the grandson's men. They fought until all the men on both sides were killed; only the two leaders were left. So the boy let the baby go and went back home.

Then the boy called together all the [other?] men-animals (itckayu'ga) until there were a great many, and then all followed the baby's tracks. The baby had built another fire of cactus, stone blades, yucca, cedar, and of another kind of wood that snaps as it burns, and these burst in fragments which became men. Their tracks were very wide, there were so many, as wide as this canyon. The boy caught up with them again a long way off, and again the parties fought. The baby had created more men than the grandson had. They stopped at a pretty good place. The baby thought he would make something else to fight with; he knew all such things. So he created a lot of horses, so that they could ride and chase the boy's men, seize them by the shoulder and pull them across the horse to club them on the head. They killed all the grandson's men, but not many of the baby's men were killed. It was very difficult to kill the baby; he knew how to make so many things. So the boy let him go. His people are now many. They have plenty of houses. They are enemies of the Yavapai.[12]

The boy, Siko'takaa'mdjiga, asked his grandmother, "Where does that eagle live who killed my mother as you told me? I want to go and kill him too. How many are up there, do you know?" "Yes, that cliff is particularly high. His nest is very near the top, and his little ones are in it. It is very dangerous to go over there; he might kill you. If he catches you he will carry you up there and you will not know how to get down. You will have to stay up there." His grandmother said, "When you get there make a signal fire for the eagle to see; then he will come and perhaps take you right up." The boy said, "Some people made a hoop with the bull hide fastened to it for me." He carried it off with him. When he got to the place his grandmother had spoken of, he lit a fire with his slow match. Then he sat down and, covering himself with the bull hide, tied himself to it. He stayed there until he should hear Eagle. He waited a long time but Eagle did not come. Then he came out from under the shield and, carrying it with him, continued his journey. Again he made a signal fire, covered himself and fastened the hide, waiting and listening. He waited a long time but he did not hear Eagle come. Then the boy said to himself, "What can be the matter that he does not come?" So he got up, went on further, and made another fire. This time he heard Eagle making a big noise high in the sky; so high he could not see him. Then he crawled under his bull hide and tied it tight to himself and waited. He had arranged loops on top so that Eagle could seize it. He heard Eagle coming closer and closer. When Eagle had nearly reached him, he felt so frightened that he pulled all the loops down. Then Eagle swooped but found nothing to catch his talons into, so he flew off without it. Eagle did not return again.

A fourth time he made a fire. He had but started it and it still smoldered when he heard Eagle coming. So he crawled under the hide and tied it on, thinking, "Well, this time I will go," so he left the loops loose. Then he heard Eagle swoop, and pick him up. Eagle flew around with him, higher and higher, way up in the sky, and, carrying him a little higher than the nest, sailed down to it. When he got there he threw the hide right into the nest where his little ones were. Then Eagle went off a few steps to sit on a point at the edge of the cliff to plume himself. While he sat there, the eaglets wanted to eat what he had brought, so all four came close. Then the boy said, "Sss . . . ," and all the eaglets ran back. By and by they tried again and just as they were about to eat, he said, "Sss . . ." again. In a little while they tried again and just as they were about to eat, he said, "Sss. . . ." Then one of the eaglets said to Eagle, "We tried to eat what you killed, but it says 'Sss . . . ,' so we will not touch it at all. Perhaps it is still alive." Eagle said, "No, I killed that early in the morning; we have had it a long time. It is the holes that I made with my talons that make that noise. It is not alive." So a fourth time they tried to eat it, but again the boy said, "Sss. . . ." One eaglet cried, "Oh, it says 'Sss . . .' all the time," and then Eagle came quickly and pounced on it again and again. The little intestines filled with blood and brains broke open so that the contents were smeared all over. The blood and brains had kept so long that now they stank. "That is what I do. You see it is not alive; it is dead," said Eagle, and he went back to sit in the same place. After a little while he flew away again.

Then the boy came out and talked to the eaglets. "I do not think eagles should kill men, merely cottontails, jackrabbits, and other little animals. I do not think it is right for them to kill men." Then he asked the oldest eaglet, "How many eagles are up here?" The eaglet said, "There are four of them; the one who brought you up here and three others who have not come yet." The boy said, "The eagles go about hunting men near here and are gone all day. Do they come back one at a time to see you? Tell me what they do." The eaglets told the boy, "If one comes who failed to kill a man or anything else he goes over to that point to arrange his plumage and then he flies off again. They do this one at a time by turns. If one kills a man or something else, he comes up here where we are, and leaves his kill with us, and then goes over to the point, just as you saw the one who brought you." The boy said, "Do they do anything else, or is that all?" The eaglets said, "Yes, we have told you all they do." The boy said, "That is all right. I am going to hide here, and when an eagle comes with something he has killed, do not tell that I am here. If you do not heed me and tell, I will throw you off the cliff and kill you. Be quiet and do not tell." The eaglets said, "We will not tell; that is good."

The boy heard an eagle coming, making a great noise. One of the eagles, who had killed a woman, came and threw her to the eaglets, and then went over to the point on the cliff edge to plume itself. It had its head down under its wing, preening its feathers, when the boy came out of hiding with his rabbit stick. He struck the eagle, knocking it off the cliff to fall fluttering and screaming to the bottom, where it died. Then the boy asked the eaglets, "How many are left?" They said, "There are three left. You killed one, so there are three now." The boy went back to his hiding place, saying to the eaglets, "Perhaps the three others heard that eagle fall and will come quickly to ask you little ones what made so much noise, but you must not tell." So he hid. After a little he heard the noise of another eagle coming. It came into the nest and asked the eaglets, "What made so much noise? I thought one of you fell down. That is why I came back so soon." The eaglets said, "No, none of us fell; we are all up here in safety. We did not hear anything make the noise you heard." The eagle said, "Has anyone come home yet?" The eaglets said, "No, no one has come yet. You are the first to arrive. The three others have not yet returned." The eagle said, "All right," and went over to the point, where he sat preening himself. Then the boy came out of hiding while the eagle's head was buried in its feathers, and hit it with his rabbit stick, knocking if off the cliff whence it fell down dead. Thus he killed two of them. Then the boy told the eaglets, "Do not tell, as I warned you before." They said, "All right, we will not tell." The boy asked, "Are there just two more?"

He heard another eagle coming. The eagle came in and asked the eaglets, "What was it that twice made so much noise? Twice we heard a big noise. I thought one of you had fallen. Have any of the three other eagles brought in anything they killed?" The eaglets said, "No, none of the three have come yet. You are the only one who has come." "What was it that twice made so much noise right here?" asked the eagle. "Did you locate those two sounds that were made near here?" "No, we did not hear any noise at all." Then the eagle said, "Do not go near the edge of the cliff. Stay back in the nest all the time; perhaps one of you might fall over the edge. Twice I heard a noise up here, so I hurried home. I am going out to hunt again." Then it went over to the point and preened its wings. The boy crept out and knocked this eagle off the cliff, just as he had served the others. Then the boy asked the eaglets, "There is only one more left, is that not so?" And the eaglets replied, "Yes, there is only one left."

Then the boy heard the last eagle coming. It came into the nest; it had not killed anything. It asked, "What was it that made so much noise three times? I heard a noise as though something had fallen down right here. I thought that one of you had fallen. Have any of the other three returned yet?" The eaglets said, "No, no one has come except yourself." "That is all right. I am going out to hunt. You stay back there in the nest. Do not go near the edge; one of you might fall over." The eagle said, "Wait for the others; if they have killed anything they will come soon. I am going out to hunt too." He went over to the point of rock to preen himself. The boy crept out of hiding with another rabbit stick and knocked this eagle over the edge, too. Then he asked the eaglets, "Is that all?" and they replied, "Yes, that is all; there are no more now." Then the boy said, "I think that eagles should not eat man the way they did. They should just eat cottontail or jackrabbits, and sometimes little antelope or deer. They can kill those kinds of animals to eat. It is wrong to kill man. I am going to kill all you little ones, too." So he picked them up one after the other and threw them over the cliff.

Then he thought, "How can I get down? I knew when I came up here that it would be difficult to descend." Then he filled his pipe, smoked a little while, and puffed it four times on the ledge where he stood. Then he blew on his hands and pushed the ledge lower and lower until it became hard to push. Then he puffed more smoke on it and pressed it down again lower and lower, until it was as high as that little cliff over there. There it stuck, and would not go any further. He tried more smoke, but it would not go. The rock was so hard that it could not be compressed any more. Then he thought, "How can I get down?" By and by he was starved, for he had no provisions with him. Then he thought he ought to have food. The eagles had not eaten any cottontails, jackrabbits, antelope, or deer; the only thing they had fed on was man. There were only the bones and skulls of men up there, but the boy could not eat those.

He stayed up there a long time. He wanted to see somebody going by the base of the cliff. After a time he saw a man passing down there. This man was Gila Monster (pa'nyamu'lta). The boy said, "I am related to you, my father's older brother. You are the man who knows about rocks. When a cliff is like this, you know what to do, you said. Climb up here and get me down." Gila Monster said, "How did you get up there that you cannot get down alone but want me to come up to fetch you? Nobody has ever climbed up to that place." That is all he said to the boy. Then Gila Monster went home to fetch his pipe and tobacco. When he returned to the base of the cliff he smoked and puffed four times up the face of the cliff, so that the wall cracked open right up to where the boy stood. Gila Monster climbed up through the crevice, but it got narrower as he went up. When he was nearly to the boy it became so narrow that when he had nearly reached there he was wedged so tight that he could not move, and there he died.

Then the boy looked down to find another man. He saw a man named Bat and said, "My maternal grandfather, I want you to come up and take me down." "How did you ever climb up there, that you cannot get down but want me to come after you?" Then he went home and got his burden basket and his tobacco. When he came back, he flew about. He flew up and down and around, getting higher and higher all the time, until he reached the ledge where the boy was. Bat sat down on the cliff edge and smoked. The boy said, "I am glad you got up here; it is all right now. I have not had a thing to eat for a very long time so I have nearly starved to death. I do not know what I can give you for taking me down. I think the best that I could give would be my eagle tail feathers." Bat said nothing. "I do not know what you would like best to have," the boy said. "I think that perhaps you would like me to give you the feathers of both wings." Bat said nothing. He kept on smoking and did not look at the boy. "I do not know what you would like. If you will tell me, I will give it to you," the boy said, but Bat said nothing. "Maybe you want the good down from under the tail feathers." But Bat said nothing. The boy said again, "Maybe you want the feathers taken from all over the body." Bat said nothing. Then the boy said, "Perhaps you want the pin feathers from his breast," and Bat said, "Hi," meaning "yes." So Bat got the little pin feathers. Then Bat said, "I will put you in the burden basket so that I can carry you." The boy lay down in the burden basket. Bat said to him, "You had better shut your eyes tight. Do not open them until I reach the foot of the cliff; then when I call to you, it will be safe to open your eyes. If you do not heed me, and you open your eyes while I am still flying, then something will happen." And the boy agreed, "All right, I will do that." Then he lay in the basket. Bat flew off, carrying him. He flew down and up and about. The boy lay there with his eyes shut; "I have felt and I have heard him fly a pretty long time." He wanted to open his eyes; he was very tired of holding them shut. "I do not know where he is going." Then the boy thought, "What will he do if I open my eyes? I will try and see what he does." When he opened them, Bat shrieked, "Yiii . . . ," and falling, dashed to pieces on a little height. Then the boy plastered Bat together with his own cuticle (ma'tinya, black dirt) so that Bat was alive, as whole as before.

The boy said, "Those eagles, who killed a great many men, are the last enemy. I have destroyed them all. This is the good long down from under their tail feathers. Tie this around the edge of the burden basket." And Bat did it. Then the boy said, "Now the last monster, Eagle, is killed. We will tell all men, everywhere, and call them together to have a dance. That is why I killed the seventh bad enemy, who killed men all the time. Tie the down on your burden basket and carry it along. Think of a song to sing at the dance, and try it right here, where I can watch you." So Bat slung the burden basket on his back and danced around singing. Then the boy said, "That is all I have to do to the enemy. I killed all except a little boy who escaped in that direction [south]. He was too difficult to kill; I let him go. He will always be an enemy (gweitchuai'a, some enemy), always kill many men. That is the one I chased off to another country. That is all I can do now. You fetched me down and I am glad. Now, I am going back home to my grandmother. That was a fine-looking dance you did here. You go home and stay there a little while; meanwhile I will think and then come and see you again." So he carried all the eagles' feathers back home.

When he was near his grandmother's house, he put down the things he was carrying and entered empty-handed. His grandmother was at home, and the boy told her, "I am still alive; I was not killed. Yes, what you told me about the eagles, that they killed men and women, was true. They tried to do that to me. They caught me and flew far up to a nest where the eaglets were. When I was there, I hid, and as they came in one by one, I killed them all. Then I thought how

I would get down, but I could not get down. So I stayed there, feeling sad. Then my grandfather Bat went flying by the base of the cliff. I called him, so he flew up and carried me down, and then I came home. I got all the eagles' feathers; I left them right out there. I want you to fetch them." So she went out and brought them in. The boy said, "I am very hungry. I did not have any provisions with me and I have not eaten in a long time. Hurry with something to eat."

Then he said to her, "I am going out to call together all the men everywhere. I want to have a big dance because our enemies are dead. I want them to dance." Then he set out inviting all the people living everywhere to come, all the animals and birds. They all came together at his camp. Then the boy told Coyote, "Clear the ground for a dance. Then gather wood and pile it over there so we can have a fire to dance by." Coyote cleared the ground and piled up wood. Then the boy asked, "Which man knows how to sing for the dance?" They said, "No one here knows how to sing for the dance. The only man who knows how is named Paqa'qankanyo'dja (Crow)." He was not there with the others; he had stayed home. The boy said, "One of you go ask him to come right away." So [some]one went to fetch Crow. Coyote built a fire at the dance ground and waited there, howling for the others to come. The boy said to them, "I have plenty of down from the eagle's tail feathers, so all you people can tie it on the top of your heads, and then we will dance. Some enemies who killed men were in this country. That was pretty bad. But they are all slain now; there are no more enemies. When any of you go hunting alone you need not fear enemies. You can go and hunt; women can go about gathering seeds; and children can go as far as they like to play. Now a man can safely travel alone on the road to visit other tribes. That is why I thought I would kill all those monsters." Before the boy had finished talking, Coyote became impatient waiting for the people to come to the dance ground, so he began to dance and sing by himself. Then Crow, who, with the other people saw Coyote and heard him, thought, "Coyote knows how to sing for you. I do not have to sing. I am going home—qoq," and away he flew.

Then the boy said that he wanted all to go over to the spot Coyote had prepared to dance. All the men stood in a circle with women in between, just as we do. One man sang and the boy said, "That is not a dance song. The song you sing now is intended to cure a broken leg or a hurt or swelling. There is another one, the dancing song."

Then they sang another song, but again the boy said, "That is not a dance song; that is used in the sweatlodge. That one is not the proper song." So they tried another and the boy said, "That is the song used by a shaman when he shakes his rattle to cure the sick. I do not like that one." Then they tried another song about going out to hunt deer, but he said, "That is not the right sort of song for a dance. It is still another kind." They tried again, but he said, "That is a song to sing to cure a man whose wound, caused by the enemy, has swollen. I do not like that, for it is not a dance song." Then they sang another, but he said, "No, that is the song to cure the infant's stomach trouble. I do not like that for a dance song." At last the people said, "We do not know what sort of song you want for the dance. That is all we know to sing and dance by. If you know what kind of song is best for us to dance, you should show us by dancing alone and then we will know." Then the boy said, "Crow alone knows many good songs. I know he is the only man who knows. He was here, but when Coyote started to sing his own song, Crow saw him and said, 'You know the song; you people sing by yourselves. I will not sing. I am going home,' and off he went." Then Sako'tagaa'mdja, the boy, said, "All right, I am going to invent a song to be used when some of you go out to fight, to kill a lot of enemies. You can dance to the song I am going to sing. Never forget it. If at some time men are alive in this country, they should not forget this song, but dance to it every time they return from a successful raid. That is the kind of song I am going to sing. I am not going to sing much. I am just going to sing four songs for you." Then they all sang and everybody danced. "That is the sort of song I spoke of," the boy said.

They had danced but a short time when one young man's wife went right in between several young bachelors. Her husband was angered, and dragging those men out of the dance, beat them. Then the woman cried, and Sako'tagaa'mdja said, "I do not want you to do that. After I made this country safe by killing all the monsters who lived here, you do wrong to fight. I do not like it. You are doing wrong. After I told you how to do things that are good, you insist on being bad. I think I will not stay here. As soon as the sun rises in the morning, I am going toward the east." When the sun rose in the morning he set off. After he had gone a little way, one man talked to him: "How soon are you coming back, or are you never coming back again? Tell us and then go. What are we people here to do to live without you? Tell us all you know and then go." Sako'tagaa'mdja stopped and listened. Then he answered briefly, "I told you people many things, but you would not listen. You keep fighting. You are angry with each other. You think you want to behave that way all the time. Half of you are like enemies toward the other half. If you want, you can continue to live that way. So I will it, and I go." Then he went on toward the east, saying to himself, "My grandmother told me that my father is the sun. She told me his home is in the east. I would like to go and see him."

So he continued eastward. (Maybe he got there quickly or maybe after many sleeps; I do not know.) He reached the house of his father, Sun. Sun had a wife at his home: both were sitting outside the house. The wife was delousing her husband, whose head lay in her lap, so she saw the boy coming first. She said to her husband, "You say you never have anything to do with other women when you travel across the sky. You lied to me, for here is your son coming." Then the man sat upright, and looked at the approaching boy. Sun said, "I am going to test the boy and see if he is my son or some other's." He walked into his house and got a long knife. When the boy stood in front of him, he struck him on top of the head and cut him in halves. The two halves lay flat on the ground, but after a little they gradually moved together and formed a perfect live boy again. Then Sun said, "Yes, that is my son."

Then Sun said, "I am going to make a sweatlodge." He made a big pile of firewood and fetched a lot of stones. When the boy first set out to see his father, he had thought of this and provided himself with a thick disk of ice and a big black fly which he hid under his shirt. Then when Sun had completed the sweatlodge, he said to his son, "I want you to go in first, far inside. I am an old man; I will sit close to the door." But the boy said, "No, I did not make that lodge. The man who made it should go in first. You go in first; I will sit by the door." Sun repeated his request several times. After a while the boy said, "All right, I will go in first." His father sat close to the door. The boy sat inside right where his clothes were lying outside. Before he went in he put the ice and the fly under the edge of the lodge cover. The boy went in first and Sun followed. Sun had filled the hole with plenty of hot stones. They stayed in a very long time until the stones were somewhat cooled. Then the boy said, "Those stones are cool. I want you to go out and bring more inside." So Sun went out and brought a great many more. It was pretty hot when they were in there, so the boy nearly died. "Where is my piece of thick ice?" he said, as he felt about. When he found it he held it against his chest. The fly flew about all over his body to cool him by fanning with its wings, so he did not get hot. The third time Sun brought hot stones in, the boy said, "Put a lot more in." Then they remained there again, but the boy did not get hot; he stayed cool. By and by Sun was so overheated that he complained he was nearly dead. "Put more hot stones in," the boy said. So Sun went out and a fourth time put hot stones in the hole. "Put a lot in; put a lot in," the boy kept repeating. Sun did so and went in again. They sat there but a short time when Sun got so hot he died. The boy had beaten his father; his father was dead. Then Sun's wife quickly dragged him outside and left him lying there. He was not dead, only unconscious. In a little while he began to move, and soon he was fully conscious again. Then Sun said, "Yes, I know you now; you are my son. I did not conceive you alone; the clouds did it too. We two conceived you; I made half your body, the other half, the clouds, the water, made. It is well; now I know you."

"Various kinds of horses I have made are right there. I made good saddles, blankets, bridles, ropes, and quirts. On each saddle is a blanket, a bridle, a rope, and a quirt; one set especially for each kind of horse. The horse I first made is white. I made it in the summer when it was raining, when the clouds were billowy. I made that horse of those very white clouds." The boy said nothing; he faced away and did not look at Sun. "The next one," Sun said, "is a red horse. I made that one after it had rained hard and suddenly stopped, and the sun shining on the clouds colored them all red. I made him of those clouds. Perhaps you want that one," he said to his son. But the boy said nothing. Sun said, "The third is a black horse. That I made when the clouds were very black; I made him of those clouds. Perhaps you want that one." But the boy said nothing; he looked away. Sun said, "The fourth horse I made when the rain had suddenly stopped, and the sun, having nearly set, colored the clouds yellow. I made a yellow horse of those clouds." But the boy said nothing and continued to look away. Then Sun said, "The fifth horse I made of clouds that were both red and white; of them I made a roan horse. Maybe you want that one." The boy said nothing; he looked to one side and did not turn his head. "The sixth horse I made of clouds that were white and only a little red; of them, I made a sorrel horse. Perhaps you want that one." But the boy said nothing; he faced away all the time. "The seventh horse I made when the clouds were gray; I made him of them. Maybe that is the one you want," but the boy gave no sign of hearing. "The eighth horse I made after it had rained for a long time, and finally, when it cleared off, there were no more clouds. Then I made that blue horse to ride myself. I am a pretty old man, and as I used him all the time, I think he is a very old horse. He is not good for you. I do not know which you will want for your horse. I put the saddle, blanket, bridle, rope, and quirt on him, and he is standing tied back there. Perhaps that is the one you want." Then the boy turned around and, peering at the blue horse, said, "That is a good horse you keep tied back there. That is the man I want. When a man has a son, he lets the boy have all his own belongings. You do not do that. You want to give me another horse, but that horse is yours, and as you are my father, you ought to give me that one." Then Sun said "All right; I do not care. You are my son and so you can have my blue horse," and he gave it to him with all its trappings. Then Sun said, "Go get the horse I tied there and lead him here, while I get the white horse for myself. That white horse I made by mixing lightning with the white clouds." Sun saddled the horse, tied on a rope, and let both horses stand side by side. Then Sun said, "We will move together. First I will put a foot in the stirrup and hold the bridle on the saddle horn; you do exactly as I do." So the boy did this. Then the old man said, "We are ready," and both mounting at the same instant, the two horses ran up into the air just like the lightning. They went up in the zenith and out through the sky on to the other side. They rode along to the west a little way, when they came to a big cottonwood tree. They thought it was a cottonwood, but it really was a wild tobacco plant as big as a tree.

(This is as far as the Yavapai man told me that story. He said there was still more to it. The Yavapai man said one must not tell this story; if he did it would rain all the time. That Yavapai started to tell this story soon after sunset and stopped at sunrise, but he said there was more yet. It was a night in November or December when nights are very long.)

1. Told by Sinyella; interpreted by Jess Chickapanega, 1919. The telling consumed twenty-two hours on several consecutive days. This tale was told to Sinyella by a Yavapai acquaintance forty-five (?) years before, during a long winter night. The original narrator then said that it was incomplete (see the note at the end of the tale).
2. Not derived from kaθoda, coyote, and ha', tail.
3. Said to represent Coyote carrying a pole, with his hoop nearby (*Havasupai Ethnography*, p. 167).
4. This is not a Havasupai custom. (This means Spier did not observe this at the time of his visit, which was after the Havasupai had begun to inter, rather than cremate. Ed.)
5. The ears of what the Havasupai call Mohave corn are diminutive.
6. Spanish vaca.
7. Ground antelope, so called because he has a yellow back and white belly: mole? See below.
8. A large bug found on the plateau.
9. Possibly referring to a petrified tree.
10. aluwi'nyahotova, literally, 'fox, his domestic [tame] animal.'
11. Literally, 'snake, his domestic [tame] animal.'
12. The narrator thought that these were the Yuma.

14. The People Become Rocks (first version)[1]

THE TWO BROTHERS MADE CATARACT CANYON. THEY TOLD
the two people [the pinnacles AA′][2] and the married man [C] to be the
Havasupai and to stay here. They gave them crops, and told them
to farm, and they made caves for them as places to live in. Cataract
Canyon was not wide enough to build houses in, so they built the
caves in the walls of the canyon. The brothers said, "Here is the corn
[F], hang it up there [on the canyon wall]. When you want it, go get
it and plant it." The two people [AA′] had a house nearby. The outer
pinnacle [A] is the wife of the inner one [A′], who has down tied to his
hair. The married man [C] lived in a cave above Billy Burro's house
[near B]. The man and his wife [AA′] lived on the opposite point. They
told the Havasupai that they were living in a house like those of the
Hopi and Zuni,[3] and that they did not want to go up on the plateau
for the winter. They said that they did not know how to build a winter
house, and that other man [C] did not know how.

In the fall there was no wood down here and people were going
to the plateau where they would have sufficient wood for the winter.
All the men were going away for the winter. The man [C], his wife
[D], and his wife's mother [E] lived in the cave above Billy's house. In
the fall they wanted to go up on the plateau for the winter. When they
were ready they went up the trail in the canyon near their house. The
man [C] went first, his wife followed, and after her came her mother.
The wife did not want to go up on the plateau, she wanted to stay
behind, so she remained there like a rock. And when the man looked
around at his wife he too became a rock. Her mother also wanted
to stay and so she became a rock too. When that man was ready to
go he called over to the other man [A′], "I am ready." Then that one

and his wife stood up on the point to see them; they were ready to go, too. When they saw the man and the others were rock, they too became rock.

| NOTES |

1. Told by Manakadja; interpreted by Mark Hanna, 1918.
2. These points are indicated on the map of Cataract Canyon accompanying *Havasupai Ethnography*.
3. There is an inaccessible pile of stones nearby which, as the natives contend, may be part of a house ruin.

15. THE PEOPLE BECOME ROCKS (SECOND VERSION)[1]

THE FIRST PINNACLE [C] WAS A MAN IN THE DAYS OF MEN-
animals; the second was his wife [D]. (I do not know where that pair
lived: perhaps on the point above Austin's house [B], perhaps down
below on the west side of the canyon above Navajo Falls.) The man
said, "I am going out of the canyon up onto the plateau." He walked
along, wanting to go out. He had his bedding and belongings in a big
bundle which he carried on his back. He also carried his baby there.
The baby sat on top of the bundle. He walked along the sandstone
bench. The man stood right up there and turned his head to look for
the woman, but he did not see her. The woman was far behind, sitting
down, defecating. So she became a rock [D], and the man became a
rock too [C]. The man said, "I am a Havasupai man, but I am going
to become a rock-man, and stand upright here." The woman said
the same.

| NOTES |

1. Told by Sinyella; interpreted by Jess Chickapanega, 1919.

16. Wolf's Boy (first version)[1]

WOLF AND COYOTE LIVED AT ᵃWIHAWA'Lᵃ [HUALAPAI PEAK, near Kingman]. Wolf lived there, hunting all the time and killing plenty of deer for food. He had no wife, so he went off to other people's camps to try to get one. But women and girls did not like him. He tried again and again without success. Then he thought, "How will I make a boy for myself? If I make one I will attract the girls with him; perhaps they will like him." He took an abalone shell (holgato'pa) and put it in a hole in a rock half filled with water. There he let it remain, going from time to time to look [at] and stir it. By and by a boy's face, which moved a little, showed in the water; soon a boy appeared. The boy remained in the water until he was older and felt somewhat stronger. Then Wolf took him out and carried him to his house, where Coyote washed him, just as a woman washes a baby. They cooked food and gave it to the boy. After a time he walked. Wolf said, "I want you, my boy, to walk off at daylight and return, and with another daylight you should walk further and come back. Do this each day until you are older, then run far away, anywhere you like, and return home about daylight. If you do this, I will make a good runner of you. Then I will send you to the place where the people we see all around here have their footraces. I am going to enter you in them."

Every day at daylight the boy ran around. Finally Wolf said, "Do you see that mountain over there [San Francisco Mountain] with snow on it? You must run four times around it, and break off a branch from each of four different kinds of trees, pine, fir, cottonwood, and juniper (?), and tie them in your belt." So he ran there and got them. When he ran home, he threw them down before Wolf, who said, "All right."

The Wolf named the boy Gau'me'. He told him, "You are old enough now. I think you are now ready for me to send you after the girls. I know a far distant place where there are fine-looking girls. I wanted them, but they did not like me, so I could not get one. We have no women to stay here to cook for us. I have to cook for myself all the time.[2] Perhaps you can get one of those girls to come and cook for us, so that after we have been out hunting all day, we can come back and find our meal ready." He told him that they would make good moccasins, leggings, shirt, and headband for him. They made everything for him to wear. They said, "You will find those people over there very wicked. The first thing they will do is to tell you that they are going to play the hoop-and-pole game, the hiding game, shinny, and the cup-and-pin game. You do not know how to play those games. They will win your whole body from you, then they will knock you down, and cook and eat you. That is how those people will act."

Wolf made all the clothing for him, wrapped it up, and told him, "You carry it back of that hill and put them on. Come right down that hill, so that Coyote and I can see if you look good and whether the girls will like you. If the clothes look well, I will tell you to go. If they do not appear good, you must not go; just stay here and lie down." The boy put them on and came over the hill. He was a rather nice looking man and appeared properly clad to go. Coyote said (holding his hand over his mouth, as women do), "If I were a girl, I would love you. You look very good to me. I think that when those girls over there see you coming, they will catch you at once and it will be all right." Wolf said, "You are ready now; that is why I made you. You are old enough to start. We need women to stay here to cook, so that when we return at sunset, the food will be ready and we can eat it. Now you can go." They said, "Take the biggest buckskins with you. When you are over there, you can gamble with them. Tie them up in a bundle with some food."

But the boy did not like to go after the girls; he hung his head and thought and cried. He cried a while, then he wiped his eyes, took up the bundle, and started off. He went a little way and began to sing, "Maybe Wolf, my father does not want me to stay at his home. Perhaps he lied to me. Perhaps he is sending me away among other people who are wicked and kill men. Perhaps he sends me there to have me killed so that I cannot come back. I am not old enough to like girls. I am not old enough to want them. Perhaps he only made that an excuse to make me go." He traveled along, feeling sad, and he cried. Then he said, "I am not old and I do not know how to play those games. I am going very far, so I will try to find out how to play them. First I will try the hoop-and-pole game." He rolled the hoop and threw the pole after it. The ring ran alongside of the pole and fell in the notch.[3] He did this four times and then he said, "I am all right, I have good luck (aha'nig'iu)."

Then he tried the hiding game four times as he traveled along. Each time he covered a ball and left it, going on a little way to hide another. So he left them by the roadside. The boy came to where the first ball was hidden and said, "I will try now to see if I can discover it at once. If I do not find it at the first trial, I will go right home. My father told me to do this." The first time he tried he picked it out at once and threw it down. He went on to the next hiding place and discovered the ball the same way. He left it there. He found all four the same way, never missing once. Then he went on, saying, "I am just a little bit good." He traveled along.

His father had told him, "Beyond the place where you play the four hiding games is an open glade where men play shinny." He took out his shinny stick and ball, set the latter on the ground, and struck it. The ball flew off; before it could reach the ground, the boy hit it again, and so kept running along. He went quite across the glade. Then he said, "I am all right." He went back to get his things to carry along with him.

His father had told him, "There is a big circular field, nearly half as broad as the world, which is the footrace ground. Nobody can run across it; I have tried. When you get there, leave your things at the border and run across." The boy found the field, left his belongings at its edge, and took off all his clothes. He made a hard lump of wool and piñon pitch, placed it on the ground, and started to kick it before him as he ran.[4] He ran across and stopped to look back from the other side. Then he sang, "I do not run [hardly] at all, only a little bit. Perhaps this is the place or perhaps it is another." So he went back to the other side and took up the things he had left. Then he stopped a while to eat until his belly was extended. Then he went on. He said, "I am all right. I can play the hoop-and-pole game, the hiding game, and shinny. I think I can go on." So he journeyed on.

"My father told me there is a high hill where men stop to sit and smoke. Perhaps that is the hill, which I see a long way off." He stopped on the hilltop. He had a little tobacco which he put into his pipe and smoked. He drew a few puffs and blew the smoke to the north, to the east, to the west, and to the south. "My father told me, 'If you do this, perhaps the odor of women will come from one of these directions right into your nose. If the odor does not come, you must come home. If it does, you must go in that direction.'" The boy did as he had been told, and the odor came from the south into his nostrils so very strong that he had to cover his nose with his hand.

The boy's father had told him, "You do these four things: play the hoop-and-pole game, the hiding game, and shinny, and stop to smoke on the high hill. You do not have to do anything else; just keep traveling. A little way further on you will come at last to the men's camp. The road is quite straight; at the end various men have houses along the roadside. The girl I like lives in the last house. The first house is Owl's. He has some daughters, but their eyes are no good, they are too large. I do not like that kind of girl. The next is Hawk's. He has daughters, but their hands are not good; they have big sharp claws and that is not good. The next one is Buzzard's. His daughters are all right, but their heads are no good; they are too red. The next is Eagle's. He has daughters, but they are no good; they fight all the time. The next is Sin𝑦i'da [a large bird]. He has daughters, but they are no good, because they fight among themselves to get at the meat. All the animals have houses along this road, but their daughters are no good, except Piñon Bird's (sasavasco');[5] but they did not like me. We want you to get one of them."

The boy approached the house where Piñon Bird's daughters were. That man's house was located high, so that he saw the boy coming when he was still far distant. He told his daughters, "I see a man coming. He looks like a pretty good man." The girls said, "We know that it is Wolf who is coming. If you speak of him when you tell us of a good man, he is no good. We know Wolf is coming again." The old man said, "No, it is not Wolf; it is another. I know. I am sure it is another man, a pretty fine-looking man. I know." The girls said, "No, that is Wolf." The old man said, "I know when Wolf comes. I know his walk and what he carries. I know this is not Wolf." But the girls laughed and said, "No, that is Wolf." The man said to them, "You will not laugh when the man comes. You will catch at him pretty quick and let him have his will of you all immediately."

Piñon Bird told them, "The man is at our spring now. One of you, who is fine looking, should get her burden basket, put some gourds [water bottles] in it, and go down to the spring for water." The man was at the spring and heard someone coming. At that time the women wore jinglers at the side of the belt.[6] The man heard these. He thought, "How will I hide myself?" There was a place where the women always set down their burden baskets. He carried a flat rock there and set it down, and being very small, he hid under it. The woman came and set her burden basket down right where he lay, while she filled the gourds and put them in the basket. She sat down in front of the basket to place the strap on her forehead. Then she tried to rise, but the man behind her held down the edge of the basket so that she could not stand up. She tried several times, and then felt angry. "I thought my basket was setting right. I wonder what it is that holds it down." As she said this, she saw the basket move a little. "I guess that is why I could not lift it." Then the man showed himself. He was a fine-looking man, so she let him embrace her. She said, "I wonder how I can take him into the house. There are so many men and girls. I do not want everybody to see me take you into the house. I will empty a gourd and put you in it and place it down in the bottom of the basket with the others over it." The man agreed, "All right." She carried him into her father's house where he came out of the gourd.

She said to the girls, "We will go play shinny. We will hit the shinny ball in through the door." They did so, and the man put his foot on it and sat down holding it like that. "One of you piñon bird girls, one of you who is good looking, go in there," said a coyote man. The ball was under the man's foot; the girl did not see the man. She wanted to get the ball, so she pulled at it, but he trod on it hard. By and by the girl looked up along his leg and saw him there. He was fine looking, so she embraced him. Then Coyote sent another girl to get the ball. She did just the same as the first. Then he sent the third after them, and the same thing happened to her. None of the girls came out, so Coyote went and looked in, and then he hollered. But the three girls were already married. They had a pretty good-looking husband now.

Piñon Bird, who was the chief of these people, said, "Our Coyote should carry some brands a short way off so we can start a big fire tonight. At first you must play the hiding game to see how that man plays it." Coyote did as he was told. That night they played the hiding game. Coyote had the ball; he hid it in the ground. The man tried to find the ball but he missed again and again, until he lost all the property he had, everything he could wager, except one white eagle feather he wore in his hair. By this time it was the middle of the night. Then he wagered the feather and won back all his belongings by sunrise.

When the sun came up they played another game, the hoop-and-pole game. The same thing happened; he lost all his clothes, moccasins, leggings, shirt, and beads. He said, "I have nothing left. I cannot play any more. You beat me, so we will not play any more." All he had left was the eagle feather tied to his hair. He sang, "I have just one thing left, this feather. I will wager this feather against all my belongings which you won from me." The others said, "All right," so they played. The others threw the hoop and the wolf boy threw his pole. The hoop ran alongside it and it fell in the notch. With just one throw he won all his things back again.

Then the chief, Piñon Bird, said, "That man is pretty smart. I thought my own people were knowing and would win his property. Try another game; try shinny. All our people should play shinny against him." Coyote got the ball and took it to the shinny field. He dug a hole and buried the ball in it. Then everybody gathered there to wait until the man came. They commenced to play. The boy could not hit the ball. Every time he struck he missed it, but his opponents played well and again he lost all his clothes to them, except his eagle feather. The boy sang, "I have nothing more; that is all I have. Divide it among your people." Coyote said, "No, that is not enough. We are many men and we want more things. Think of what else you want to wager and tell us; then we will play." Again he wagered the feather on his hair against all his belongings. Again they played and he hit the ball at the first stroke so that it flew a long way. Then he ran after it while the others ran following him. He ran up beside the ball and struck it again and again until it went over the goal line, so that he won all his belongings back.

The chief, Piñon Bird, talked again. "Our people should pick up some firebrands and carry them off a short distance to the place where we sit. The men who are good runners should go there a few at a time. When all are there they should start together toward the north." So they went off. The wolf boy stayed at the house when the others left. They said they wanted him to race with those other men; they wanted to test him. His wives said, "We do not want that boy to go. We want him to stay home," so they held him. The men who went ahead had been gone a long time. The boy wanted to go and said, "Let me go, I want to go." The girls were crying and holding him by his limbs: "The others have been gone a long time; you would be a long way behind. The others will be coming back and get here first, and when they win they will kill you and eat all your flesh. That is the way they have done many times. That is what they want to do to you. You have not lost to those people yet. Some one of them may be a good runner, and beating you, win your body." The man wanted to go, and finally the girls tired and let him free. The man said, "I will go and try. Perhaps I can catch the men. Perhaps they have only run halfway; if they have not yet turned back I can pass them. If you see one man coming back alone, that is I. Then gather all my possessions, which I will leave here, and get ready to leave for my home."

The chief, Piñon Bird, was up on top of his high house. He sang, "My daughters' husband is only a little way, while my relatives are already down to the mountain which they have now circled nearly four times. I would like to have my daughters' husband beaten by my relatives. I would like them to kill him, so that I can eat his brains." The boy had not yet started to race. He threw the kicking-stick he carried on the ground. He began to kick it, running very fast. He ran around the mountain four times and started back toward the house. Halfway back the boy ran past Piñon Bird's relatives. The boy slowed alongside the people and sang, "I never saw any footraces like that. I have seen women and children moving camp just like that. The way I race is the way to run footraces. I am going to run right home. Some of you men look hungry and thirsty. I will run ahead and tell the women to get some food ready."

The boy ran back to the house, took the girls, and started immediately for his home, Wolf's house. The other women said, "We like that boy," and every one of the women and children followed after them. The boy said, "You must not do this. It is not right. You all should return home, stay in your houses and live there." The women did not heed what he said, but still followed. By and by the men reached home from the footrace. They ate, and taking their bows and arrows, followed him. After a little way they caught up with their own women and children and killed them. A little further on they tried to kill the boy but they failed. Instead he killed many of them and again went on his way. They kept on fighting intermittently through the whole day until the sun went down, and it was dark so that they could no longer see him. So he hid himself. Then the people began to fight among themselves [in confusion] until they were all killed. As he hid, he heard them fighting until finally he heard no more; all was quiet. In the morning he saw that they had all been killed. So he went home to Wolf's house. There they all lived together. Wolf said, "This is the kind of girl I like; that is why I sent you. Now it is all right, we have some women to do the cooking."

That is the way Wolf sent his boy off to fight people and get women. That is the way Wolf taught men to be wicked and fight. When I was a little boy that is the way people acted.

| NOTES |

1. Told by Sinyella; interpreted by Jess Chickapanega, 1919.
2. This motive may have been dictated by a similar condition in Sinyella's own household. This was his constant complaint.
3. A winning score.
4. The Havasupai do not have the kicking-stick. (Spier did not observe one at the time of his visit. Ed.)
5. A bird resembling the piñon jay but slightly smaller; all blue, except for a somewhat yellowish breast.
6. This is not the present custom of the Havasupai, but was formerly.

17. WOLF'S BOY (SECOND VERSION)[1]

WOLF AND COYOTE CAMPED SOMEWHERE ALL ALONE. EVERY morning they went to hunt deer. Wolf wanted to get married, so he went to a place where the Indians camped. He wanted some girl to marry him, but the girls did not like him. So Wolf came back to his own camp and said to Coyote, "I want to marry a woman so she can cook for us when we come back from hunting. But the girls do not like me." Then Wolf said, "My nephew, I want you to cook something to eat and I will start to go hunting again. We have no ground seeds, only meat, because that is easy to cook."

The next morning Wolf went away, but he did not hunt, he just went to a little water hole. He sat down by the water and when the sun was low he came back to his camp. The next morning he went off again, but he did not hunt. He went to the water and sat there. He had put something into the water. When the sun was down he pounded his moccasins and wore off his arrow points on the rocks and then he came back to camp. He said, "My nephew, I thought you would heed what I tell you. I went around all day and hunted fast, so that my moccasins are worn out and my arrow points are all gone." In the daylight Wolf talked again to Coyote, "I want you to make me moccasins and fix my arrow points." Then he started off to hunt again. He went to the waterhole. When he was gone a little while, Coyote went to watch him. Wolf went to the place where he had put something into the water and found a tiny baby there. He took it out, wrapped it in a skin, and put it in a hole in the rocks. He covered the opening with stones. Then he went hunting. Coyote had hidden a little way off and saw what Wolf did with the baby. He said, "Oh, what has he been doing there?" After Wolf had gone away Coyote went over and looked at the baby. He took the baby out and ran back to camp with it.

Wolf came back from hunting with two deer on his back. They cut off some meat, cooked it and ate it. When it was dark Coyote said, "Listen, my uncle, there is a mouse somewhere. She is gnawing on our buckskins." Coyote had put the baby on the buckskins and told him to make that noise. Wolf did not think that Coyote had found that baby. Coyote said all the time that he heard something, and Wolf answered, "I think you have gone over there and taken what I put in the rocks. That is what I think." Then after a while Coyote got up and went after the baby. He brought it out and showed it to Wolf. He said, "This is my little boy." But Wolf answered, "You have no wife. That baby is your brother. That is my little boy. I put abalone shell (halgato'pa) in the water and made the baby that way. I shall call him Kᴿavasu'halgato'pa (Blue Abalone)." Wolf made the baby that way because the girls would not marry him. "I want to see if the girls will not like my boy," Wolf said.

In the morning Wolf started to hunt deer again and brought home two bucks. Wolf always brought two deer. Coyote stayed at the camp and took care of the little baby. He cooked something and fed him. The child grew. Wolf said to Coyote: "Coyote, you run races with him, so that he will become a good runner. Do this in the daylight, not in the morning." The little boy got big, and he had such long hair that it hung to the ground. Wolf said, "Coyote, you go and get soapweed and wash him with that, then paint him." The boy looked very fine and Wolf said, "You look fine; we have a pretty boy. Maybe the girls will take him away from me." The boy sat down on a blanket. Wolf said to Coyote, "I have pretty moccasins hidden over there. You get them and put them on my boy," and Coyote put them on him. Wolf said, "I made pants for him and hid them over there." Coyote got them and put them on the boy. And Wolf said, "I have a shirt hidden over there for him. I want you to get that and put it on him." When they dressed him up he looked a very fine boy. Coyote said, "Oh, I would like to be a girl; he looks so fine." Wolf brought a little sack made of wildcat skin, filled it with arrows, and taking a bow, gave it to the boy. He tied up the boy's hair, cut it in front and braided it in the back. He was the finest boy they had ever seen. Then Wolf said, "I have some very soft white eagle down." He put this on the boy's head. Wolf said, "I stole some fine white beads; I will make earrings for him. I have the beads hidden over there. String them with abalone. Put them around his neck; we will see how fine he appears." Coyote said, "Oh, I wish I could be a girl and marry you. Oh my brother, you look very fine." And Wolf said, "I stole some buckskin leggings, yellow ones. You get them and put them on him." Then he was all dressed; yet there was still another thing, a wildcat skin for a blanket to wrap around him. Then they went to bed.

In the daylight Wolf woke his boy and said, "I want you to wake up and run very fast to Flagstaff [San Francisco Mountain]. You go around the mountain there and come back here. I want to see how fast you can run." The boy ran as fast as he could. When he got to Flagstaff he broke off a branch of a pine tree and tied it on his back to show Wolf that he had been there. He came back the next morning just as the sun came out. The morning after, Wolf sent his boy away to go after the girls. Wolf ground corn for him and said, "I saw pretty girls over that way, but they did not like me. I want you to go over and see if they like you. If they like you, I want you to get three girls." Wolf told his boy to go to Piñon Bird's camp because he had very pretty daughters. Those girls did not like Wolf because he always ate greasy things. These were the girls the boy should get. But the boy said nothing, he just lay down. Wolf said the same thing all the time. The boy was afraid to go over there; he did not want to go. Wolf talked to his boy again, "When you go along this road I will tell you where the water is, and when you come to a certain place, I want you to race over that ground." But the boy said nothing to his father; he just lay there. A short way from the Indian camp there were two wild bears who killed Indians. Wolf told the boy to give the bears meat and they would let him pass. But the boy said nothing to his father.

Wolf always talked to his boy about going. After a long time the boy said, "All right, I will go." So he set out. He said to himself, "I do not know anything about this road, but my father sent me away. I do not know where the water is, but I may never get anywhere. My father and my brother sent me away. I might die somewhere. I ate his food; that is why he sent me away. I do not know the road and I do not know where the water is. I may die somewhere. I am not a big boy and I do not want to marry. He just sent me away." He went along the road and saw a big race course. He took off his clothes, and carrying them under his arm, he began to run as fast as he could. He stopped at the other end and looking back, said, "This looks like the place where my father told me to run, but it seems that I ran only a little way." He started to walk on and sat down where the Indians always stopped. He smoked tobacco, so that the girls could smell it. Then he went on and came to a place where the road was full of spines but he went over them. Next, he saw a house in the rocks and a waterhole. Then he went on and came to the wild bear. The bear was coming after the boy, but he suddenly fawned on the boy and licked his hands. The boy said, "Why did my father tell me a lie?" But the bear liked the boy so the boy did not give him the meat. He just went along.

Then Piñon Bird saw the boy coming and said to his daughters, "Oh, what a fine boy is coming here. I want you to cook something for him. He looks very pretty. It is not Wolf; it is some Indian." But the girls said, "Wolf is the only one around here. We think he is coming." The girls' father said, "It is a very fine looking Indian that is coming. I want you to cook something." The girls said, "There are no Indians over here. You tell us a lie. We will not heed what you say. When Wolf comes we will make him work, fetching wood and water." Then Piñon Bird said, "All right, when you like him I will laugh at you. He is a very fine Indian. I know Wolf's walk; he walks slowly. This Indian runs very fast and looks fine." The boy went past the Indians' camp. They saw him going along as they stood by their doors and offered him food, but he took no notice of them; he just went on. The girls' father said, "Oh, such a fine Indian is coming. I want you to cook something for him." But Piñon Bird's daughters and Coyote girl went to play shinny.

After a while they stopped. Then Coyote girl put plenty of gourds in a basket and ran to fetch water. The boy went down to the water where he heard the jingling of the girl's belt. So he made himself small and crawled under the rocks. Coyote [girl] put down her basket where the boy was hiding. She filled the gourds with water and put them back into the basket. She wanted to cook something for the fine Indian who was coming, so she worked fast. When she was through filling the gourds, she put the strap over her head, but she could not lift the basket. The boy held onto it from below. She got up, fixed the strap, and tried to lift it again, but the boy held it and she could not get up. "What is the matter with my basket? I am in a hurry. I must have the water at once. Someone must be holding my basket," she said to herself. Then the boy came out and stood there, looking handsome. Coyote [girl] said, "I do not want you to go away. I will put you in my basket." So she threw away some of the water and put him in the bottom of the basket. Then she went over to her camp. There were a great many girls playing shinny and they were thirsty, so they tried to get Coyote's water bottles but she ran off to her house. When she was inside, she took the boy out.

Coyote [girl] went out and said to the girls, "Come, we will play shinny again." She wanted to get the ball into the house. When it rolled into the house, the boy stepped on it. Coyote [girl] said to Piñon Bird's eldest daughter, "You go into the house and get the ball." She went in and when she wanted to pick up the ball the boy stepped on it. She saw his feet and then she saw all of him. She picked up the boy and sat down with him. Coyote [girl] said, "The girl I sent to get the ball must be drinking all the water that I put in my house." So she sent Piñon Bird's second daughter. She started to pick up the ball, but the boy stepped on it. She saw the boy and she embraced him and sat down with him. Then Coyote sent the youngest sister after the ball. Again the boy stepped on the ball. The girl saw the boy, jumped over him and stayed with him. Now the three girls were there in the house with the boy. They all liked him very much. Coyote [girl] said, "Oh, my, I have water in there; they will drink it all." She ran into the house and saw all the girls holding the boy. She called to the girls' father and said, "All your daughters have gotten married and they are all pregnant already." This was not true, but she said it. She came away. The girls' father said nothing, he just lay down.

Then Piñon Bird came and stood by the door. He put a buffalo horn on the ground and he said to the boy, "I want you to break this to pieces." He had a knife ready to kill the boy if he should fail. The boy said, "Do you always do that when an Indian comes here? I thought you would give me something to eat and drink." The girls said to him, "We do not want you to try to break the horn because he will kill you. He always does that; he kills all the men." The girls whispered this because their father was standing by the door. The boy said to the girls, "I want you to stop holding me," but the girls would not let him go. Then he stood up and stepped on the horn, broke it all to pieces and piled them together. The girls still held onto him because they liked him so very much. Then Piñon Bird said to his family, "I gave him my horn and he broke it all to pieces. I do not know where such strong Indians come from. I want you to play the hoop-and-pole game with him."

All the Indians went to the racecourse to see the game, but the girls held the boy fast and would not let him go. They told him that when the Indians play they always win from the others, winning their clothes, and then kill them. So they did not want to let him go. The boy said, "I want you to let me go to see the Indians playing." The girls would not give him up. He said, "Did you do that when the Indians came over here to see you? I want you to let me go." The girls all cried, "When they beat you, they are going to eat you." He tried to rise to go, but the girls held on to him and went along with him. He stood where the Indians played. They said, "All right, we want you to play with us, for we want to beat you." Then the boy said to the girls, "I want you to get away from me. I want to play with the Indians." So the girls sat on his blanket. Piñon Bird said to Coyote, "My nephew, I want you to play good and beat the boy." The girls now let the boy play. They played the hoop-and-pole game with many Indians on one side and the boy alone on the other. The Indians beat the boy and won all he had. This made the girls cry very hard. Then he played again and the Indians beat him once more. At last the boy said, "That is all I have; that is all you can win from me." Coyote answered, "No, I will not stop now; I want more of you." Coyote had taken all the clothes the boy wore. The girls were crying hard because the boy had been beaten. But the boy still had one white feather left. He said, "I have nothing left to give you; you must kill me now." Coyote said, "No, you have a feather." "But I will not give you that," answered the boy. So they played again. Before this the boy had not played hard. The girls were still crying. The Indians wanted the feather very badly and they played as hard as they could. Now the boy really played his best and he won back what he had lost. Then he said, "You took everything away from me but now I have it all back." The girls were very glad and cried no more. They just laughed from joy. He had beaten the Indians and won things from them. He won all they had, even their houses. Then they said, "We have nothing more to give you."

When night came they played the hiding game. The Indians hid the ball and called the boy. The girls went out with him. The Indians beat the boy and won his things until there remained only the one white feather. "That is all I have," said the boy. The Indians replied, "We want the feather on your head; we want that. When we have that we will kill you and eat you." The boy said, "All right, you try." Then the boy hid the ball and the Indians could not find it. And he won the Indians' possessions, their women and children, everything. Piñon Bird climbed on his roof and lay down, and the Indians said to him, "The boy has beaten us all. He looks very strong."

"In the morning," said Piñon Bird, "you run a kicking-stick race with him." The Indians went about half a mile; then they stopped there and made a fire. They said to the boy, "All right, we are ready to go." But the girls held the boy and would not let him go. The Indians were ready to start the race. The boy went over to the racecourse. He just walked while the others ran. They went over Moon Mountain. Piñon Bird sat on his roof to watch the race. "My daughters, your husband cannot run. He is just walking along and steps on the kicking-stick. I want him to come back so I can eat his brains." When they had gone around Moon Mountain and were coming back to the camp, the boy walked far behind them. After he had gone around the mountain four times, he began running. He ran as fast as he could, keeping the stick on his foot, never letting it touch the ground once. He ran close to the Indians. Piñon Bird said to his daughters, "Your husband is a nywi'laga [one who first loses and then wins]. He is beating my Indians. First he just walked along; now he is going faster." The boy caught up to the Indians now and ran along beside them. Then he ran past the Indians and said to Coyote, "You cannot run fast. You look as though you were moving along with a heavy pack. See how I run. I will get to the camp and tell the women to bring some water for you." Piñon Bird said, "I never saw anyone run as fast as that. It looks as though my family were not running at all, just walking along. Your husband is running as fast as he can. He is always nywi'laga."

When the boy came back to camp, where the girls were still sitting on his blanket, he took his blanket and started home to where his father lived. The girls went with him. The boy had beaten the Indians so he could take the three girls. All the women said, "Oh, we would like to go with him." So they all went with him because they liked him so very much. Piñon Bird's wife wanted to go with the boy too, so she picked up her things to put in a sack and go away. But Piñon Bird heard her moving around in the house, and he said, "I hear you move around. I think you want to go away too." "Oh, no," she said, "I want to go, but I am too old." But she picked up her things and went too.

There was nobody left in the Indian camp. The men were still at the racecourse and thought their wives were at home. Only Piñon Bird knew they had gone, and he told the Indians that the women and children had all followed the boy. He told them to get something to eat and then go after the women and kill them all. Piñon Bird said to the Indians, "I want you to kill my wife first and pull off her hair. I will want to put it on my hat. Then kill every one of them." "All right," said the Indians, "We will do it."

They started after the women. They saw an old woman walking with a stick, so they killed her and then killed all the other women. The boy had hidden the three girls, so the Indians wanted to kill the boy. They shot at him with their arrows but they could not hit him. The Indians killed one of the three girls. Then the boy made the other girls small and put one of them under each armpit. Now it looked as though only one person were walking along. The Indians wanted to shoot them with their arrows.

His father, Wolf, was at home. He said, "I wonder what they are doing to my boy; he is always crying. I do not know what is the matter with him. My nephew, I want you to go over and see what they have been doing." "All right, I will go and see my brother," Coyote said. Coyote saw his brother coming along with the Indians following him, shooting their arrows. Still they could not hit the boy. Wolf dreamed that Piñon Bird came into his house, and he killed him,[2] and threw him away. When Coyote saw the Indians coming after the boy, he started to come right back to his camp to tell his uncle. Then he stood and thought, "I do not want to go back and tell my uncle. He can do nothing to those Indians. I will go back and kill those Indians." Coyote said this to himself. He went on a while and said, "I wish nobody could kill me." Then he went on to his brother. The boy said, "Oh, why do you come here? The Indians are no good; they nearly ate me up. They are shooting with arrows, and my hand is all sore and my hair is worn out from the arrows. I walk slowly and turn away from the arrows, but you cannot do that. The Indians might kill you." Coyote said, "I do not mind what you say. I know everything they did. You do not know how to kill men. I know everything." The boy said, "All right, you shoot with arrows for me. I am very tired. I am nearly dead." Then Coyote tried to shoot with arrows, but the Indians shot at Coyote and he fell to the ground. The Indians went over to him and hit him with a stick, killing him.

Then Wolf sent Crow: "I want you to go down and see my boy. I dreamed that he was crying. Coyote has not come home to tell me." Crow started out. He went along and saw many Indians around the boy, ready to kill him. Crow said, "I will run back and tell Wolf." He ran back a short way, and he talked to himself: "Oh, what can Wolf do with those Indians? He just lies around all the time. I will go back and kill those Indians." Crow went back to the place where the Indians were. He made himself smaller, and flying high, went over to the boy. The boy scolded him and said, "I am very angry. Why do you come here? My brother Coyote came here and the Indians killed him. I am very angry on account of that. I do not want you killed. You go back." Crow said, "I am a man; you are a boy. I always kill enemies. Maybe I can kill them all." The boy said, "All right, you kill them. I will rest awhile." Crow flew up high and tried to shoot them, but the Indians shot him and he fell down dead.

Wolf always dreamed of his boy and he sent another man, Owl. He said to him, "Go see my boy." Owl started to go. Owl was always smoking and he used up all his tobacco right away, so he came back to the camp. He put plenty of tobacco in his sack and started out again. And in a few miles he used up all that tobacco, so he came back after more. He packed plenty into two sacks, put them on his back, and started to go again. He went along and had almost used it up when he saw the Indians coming along after the boy. When he saw that, he went back a little way and stood still, thinking. "I do not think I will go back to tell him. I will go down and kill the Indians." Owl stood still a while. Then he went back to the Indians and made himself smaller as he flew up in the air. He said, "Nobody can kill me now." The boy said to Owl, "Why did you come here? My brother and my uncle both came and they were killed. I am very angry. I do not think you can kill one, but they will kill you." Owl said to the boy, "I always kill Indians. I am going to do it now. I do not want you to make me afraid. I am going to kill them." Then the boy said, "All right, you shoot the Indians." Owl tried to shoot the Indians with his arrows but he just flew up and down. The Indians shot at Owl till his feathers were all worn out. He took his belt, tore it to pieces, and made it night so that the Indians could not see the boy. Then the boy ran away from the Indians. They could not find him and they shot at each other. The boy took the two girls out from under his armpits and they walked along with him. Then these three, together with Owl, ran up a big mountain and stayed there. The Indians could not see what they were doing, and they killed each other, until they were all dead. And the boy, the two girls, and Owl came down from the mountain and saw Coyote and Crow dead. The boy made them wake up. Then they all went along together to Wolf's camp.

During all this time it was dark. They waited for the sun to come out, but it did not rise. It was always night. Wolf's people said to him, "We want you to make it light." Wolf replied, "All right, I will try." He took four arrows and made them red. He threw one where the sun comes up. Then he threw one where the sun goes down. He threw one to the north and the last one he threw to the south. After a while daylight came. Then it was morning. Then Wolf saw the boy with his two wives, and he said to Coyote, "My nephew, I want you to get some soap root and wash them all clean. Wash the girls and the boy." Coyote washed them, made them clean, and dressed them with beads, moccasins, and blankets. They camped there. Every morning the boy went hunting and brought home two deer.

After a long time Wolf said to the boy, "I want you to give me one of your wives. I want the big one." The boy said nothing, he just went away hunting. After a while Wolf said the same thing to his son, but the boy would not talk. When he was out hunting the boy thought of what Wolf had said and he became very angry. He brought home two deer and lay down, but would not talk to Wolf. He went hunting all the time. Then he got some mountain sheep horns and took that along, but he did not hunt deer that day. His wives waited for him, but he did not come home that night. The next day he did not come, and for four days he did not come to his camp. Wolf said, "Maybe he was killed; maybe he fell from a hill or from the cliff."

Wolf followed the boy's tracks. Meanwhile the boy made himself into a mountain sheep and lay down where the mountain sheep were. He had mountain sheep horns on his head. He had hung his arrows and clothes on a tree. He scratched himself to make the hair come out. He took his hair and twisted it around his fingers to make mountain sheep horns. He made himself just like a mountain sheep. Then he walked about and looked for mountain sheep girls. He saw them down in a valley. So he went down there. Now Wolf came along and saw his tracks. He saw the boy's things hanging on the tree and saw the tracks of his bare feet, but after these there were only mountain sheep tracks. Wolf could not find the boy. He looked around and he saw plenty of mountain sheep in the valley, plenty of ewes and only one buck. Wolf thought that this might be his boy. So Wolf tried to make himself into a mountain sheep. He made himself into a mountain sheep girl and set out. The boy came after Wolf. He wanted to see him in this guise. He climbed on his father's back. Then Wolf pulled off the boy's horns and tore off his skin. He made him a boy again and took him back to his camp.

Next morning the boy went to hunt deer again, and for two days he brought home two deer. The third morning he started out again but he did not come home. He made himself into a mountain sheep again and stayed away for four days. But Wolf knew what the boy had done and after four days he went along his tracks. The boy had found his mountain sheep girls, and after he had hung his coat and moccasins and arrows in the tree, he went with them. Wolf saw the tracks and found the clothes hanging on the tree. He followed the mountain sheep but when he came near them, they ran away. But Wolf ran after them to catch the boy. He tried to catch him, but the boy ran away with the mountain sheep girls. Wolf followed the mountain sheep all the time. They went toward the west. At last they came to the ocean. The boy jumped in and went under the water. Wolf went after him, under the water, too. The boy came out of the water and went into the sky to become a constellation.[3] Wolf followed him and became a constellation, too. He is called amu'gatciama [mountain sheep's relative?].

| NOTES |

1. Told by Manakadja; interpreted by Lillie Burro; recorded by E. G., 1921.
2. That is, in his dream Wolf killed Piñon Bird.
3. Called amu, Mountain Sheep, probably Orion's Belt.

18. The Stolen Wife (first version)[1]

AN OLD WOMAN LIVED ALONE. SHE BROUGHT FORTH A BOY. She went out to gather seeds for food, leaving the little boy at home. While she was gone, the boy picked up stones and, throwing them at birds sitting close to the house, killed some. When the woman returned she found them piled on both sides of the doorway. The woman said, "What man was here, who killed so many birds and piled them on both sides of the entrance? I think I will throw them away." The boy heard what she said and cried all the time. Every morning she went out to gather pigweed seed, piñon nuts, or yucca fruit. When she came home at sunset, she found birds piled by the door, which she carried off and threw away. This happened several times; then she knew her own boy had killed the birds. Then when she returned again she cooked and ate them. The boy was glad and stopped crying.

By and by he grew up, and the old woman made him a bow and arrows. The boy carried these about, shooting and killing cottontails and jackrabbits. He brought them home for the old woman to cook, and they ate them. After a time he was a young man and killed many deer. When he was a man, he knew how to make arrows and bows. He hunted all the time, killing many deer. The old woman said to him, "Did you ever see anybody's tracks or his house when you were out hunting? Did you ever see anything like that? I told you, when you were a little boy, that there were no men living near here. I told you that I live here alone." The boy said, "No, I never saw anybody's tracks or houses."

When the boy was hunting on a mountain, he saw another country far distant where the smoke of a fire was to be seen. He saw this many times but did not ask his mother about it. He said nothing at all. The boy was now as old as that one [about twenty-five or thirty]. The boy asked the old woman about people: "Tell me where there are many people, men and women, living. Tell me about them. I want to know about them. Then when you tell me, I will not stay here. I want to go get a woman; that is what I want. When I was out hunting on a high hill, I saw another country where there was smoke. I think there are many women there, for I had an erection. I saw much smoke in that direction [south] beyond the mountains, and I saw smoke on the other side of the Colorado River." The boy asked the woman what kind of people lived to the south and what kind to the north. "Tell me. I saw the smoke," he said. The old woman said to the boy, "Well, I will tell you. What you think is smoke over the mountain is not smoke; it is fog. When it rains, it comes right down to the ground. It looks like smoke. It is the same off to the north. I am sure nobody is living close to us. Of course, I would tell you."

The boy went hunting again. He went near the place where he had seen the fire. He climbed to the top of a high hill and looked for the fire. He did the same thing off to the north. He went close to both fires, and he was sure somebody was living in the south and in the north. The boy returned to his mother's house and asked again, "I went over close to see and I am sure that was fire. I saw somebody's tracks," he lied a little. "Tell me. I am sure I want to go to see them; I want to get a woman for a wife. That is what I want, but you do not tell me." The old woman said, "Yes, the people living over there in the south are not good men. They are wicked. If a stranger comes to their country, they catch and kill him immediately. I know those people. They call them *itcahua'* [enemies, Yavapai]. Those to the north are of the same sort. They are *paiyu'dja* [Paiute]." The old woman said, "I do not want you to go away. I would like you to stay here alone with me. I want you to hunt. That is the only thing you do, and you do it well. I do not want you to go. If you go, they will kill you at once."

Then she said, "All right; you will have to go to the north. I know that man, Redwing Blackbird (*djaqɯ'ha*) has two wives. Those two women are pretty; steal both from him." The old woman feared to have her boy go; she cried. But she ground some corn and mixed it up with ground piñon nuts as provisions for him. She also roasted meat and pounded it up for him. He said, "There is clothing already made for me: headband, shirt, leggings, and moccasins. I will go over there a little way while you wait until I return. If I look good, you tell me and then I will go. If I do not look good, I will not go." The woman saw the boy coming wearing his good clothes. She said, "You look quite good. Those women will come to you very quickly." The boy said, "I am ready; I am going now." His hair was rolled up at the back of his head. He let it down, and pulled out the longest hair. He tied this across the house under the roof above the place where the old woman usually sat. He said, "You watch that while I am gone. If I am killed after I get to that people's country, my hair will snap in two and a little blood will drop to the ground. When you see it you will know that I am dead and will not return." After he did this he set forth.

The old woman knew the country where the boy was going and told him of the various places and things that were there. Going on his way, the boy said, "Just as my mother told me, cottontails and jackrabbits are plentiful here. She told me the truth. I will kill some. I do not want to cook and eat them; I will throw them away." He went to the next place where there were only mountain sheep. He did the same as with the rabbits. He just shot them, but he did not skin or eat them. There were so many he just shot them. At another place there were only antelope, and another only deer. There were a great many. He killed, but did not eat them. The boy said, "I am in a great hurry. I do not want to stop to eat them. I want to see the women right away." (We ought to have all that meat over here so we could eat it.)

The woman had told him about the Colorado River. "When you reach that river, take off all your clothes, bundles them in something, place it on top of your head, and walk right into the water. At the edge it is only up to your knee; when you are a quarter way across it will be up to your belly; right at the middle it will be up to your neck. Keep walking across. On the other side put on your clothes again." He got out on the other side, put on his clothes, and traveled on until he reached those people's country.[2]

He was nearly there when he found some women gathering food in an open plain. It was about midday. The boy kept in hiding and crept to where there were some thick bushes. He sat down there watching the women gathering fruit. Most of the women started to return to their homes. All went back, except two women who kept coming toward the man sitting in the bushes. They were looking about for the best of the things growing on the bushes. They came nearer, until they saw him sitting there; then they both quickly sat down beside him. The man said, "This is the kind of woman I am looking for. It is well that they came to me. All right." He said, "Tell me if you are both married or unmarried women. If you both say you are married, I will do as I intend. Show me where the big chief lives. I will go in his house and talk to him. I will tell him something and he will talk to me, too. If you tell me you are not married, I will not go to your relatives' house. I will just return and you will go with me at once." The two women did not answer. They hung their heads and did not look at him. After a while one said to the other, "We are not married, *ma'*."³ The man said, "It is a very hot day. I am thirsty. Have you any water with you?" The other woman carried a burden basket with a little water basket in it containing a little water. She handed it to him to drink from. Then he felt pretty good.

Then he started back, taking the women with him. They walked fast. They reached the Colorado, crossed it, and camped on the other shore just as the sun set. They slept there and then the man dreamed of Redwing Blackbird. He woke when it was nearly dawn and told the women, "You lied to me. You are not unmarried women; you are married to Blackbird. He came here and wanted to fight me, so I fought. That is what I dreamed," he said. Just as the day dawned, Blackbird arrived to get his wives. Blackbird said to the women, "I want you to give me my own thing." The women talked to each other and after a while, one turned away and pulled something from her parts and gave it to Blackbird, her husband. Blackbird cried, "Hai, good," and flew off home with it.

After the two women had given this to Blackbird, and he had gone home, they set off. When they had gone halfway, one woman fell dead. The man threw her away and took the other to the old woman's house. The boy said to his mother, "I got two women who were both married to Blackbird. While we camped halfway home, he came at daylight, saying he wanted his own thing. One of them gave it to him and then she died, so I have only one." The old woman felt sorry for the woman who had died, and cried a little. The man said, "Go out early in the morning and dig some yucca roots, put them in water, and then wash her body and wash me too." So the old woman did this for them both.⁴

Then the man said, "You know where the things which you gather grow. I want this woman to go with you so that you can gather them. My woman must not go even a little way from you when you get over there; you must stay close together. Watch the woman closely," he said. The old woman agreed and went off with the other. They reached the place where such things as they wanted grew and began to gather them. After a little, as they were gathering, the old woman turned her back. When she turned again, the other woman was gone. So the old woman cried. She wept all the way home; then she told her boy.

The boy said nothing. He just lay down. He felt angry. Early next morning he talked to his mother, "That is what I thought would happen. I knew you should watch her closely." The boy fetched his own down feather, from under the eagle's tail plume, and said, "Show me the place where you lost her." The old woman went ahead to the spot. "We were sitting here; she sat behind me. I turned away to gather something and when I turned back, she was gone. I do not know where she went." The man looked around for somebody's tracks, but he saw none. Then he stood exactly in the spot where the woman had been seated. He blew the eagle feather toward the north, but it did not fly off. It fell right down. He picked it up and blew it toward the south. It fell again. Then he blew it toward the east, but again it failed to fly. Then he tried directly toward the nadir, but it did not travel. Then he thought, "I will try up toward the center of the sky." So he blew it toward the zenith, *pθθ*, and the little white feather went up.

The man made himself into a tiny object within the white feather and traveled with it. The down continued going until it came to the middle of the blue sky, where there was a little hole. It went right through this hole. When it was up on the other side of the sky, the man looked about for woman tracks. He found them there and followed. After a little he came to where an old woman had her house out in front of the others. He said to her, "I lost a woman. She was headed this way. Did you see her?" The old woman said, "Yes, I saw her, a pretty fine looking woman, going by just a short time ago. Wind (*matahai'adj*) had her when he was traveling past."

The man went on to Wind's house, which was full of stolen women. Wind lay across the doorway. The man stood by the entrance. The woman he had lost was sitting in the middle of the house. "I lost you. I have been hunting for you. I want to leave here with you at once. We will go right home," the man said. The woman started to go out, but Wind, lying on his back, kicked her in the chest and threw her back to the middle of the house. Wind said, "You must run a footrace with me. The man who wins can have that woman." The other man said, "All right." They started to race. After a little the man drew ahead; then Wind became the wind again. The wind blew hard and went right past the man. Then Wind said, "I won the woman." The other said, "Why were you not the same as I? It is not fair when the wind blows hard." Wind said, "We will run it over again. This time I will be like you." They tried again. The man had a curved rabbit stick in the side of his belt. "If Wind does the same thing again, I will knock him down," he thought. They ran in the same fashion. After a little, Wind became the wind again. Wind transformed himself into a whirlwind and ran ahead. The man drew his rabbit stick and struck him on the neck, knocking his head off. After he killed Wind he took his own wife and, killing all the other men [animals and birds], returned home to the old woman, his mother. They told her all about it.

He said, "This is very dangerous for us. I want you to build a house of hard stone, not soft stone. Build one encircling wall, then another, then another, and then another, until it is four walls in thickness. Make little holes in the walls through which I can shoot; make such little holes all around the house." The old woman built the house just as he instructed her. All three stayed in it. The men he had killed on the other side of the sky came to life soon after. They all felt angry and came down. They arrived at the man's house with the intention of killing him, but the walls were too thick and there were only little holes by way of entrance. The man inside shot through the apertures at them until they were all killed one by one. That one man alone inside the house killed all those outside. Then more men came, and he killed them too. Again more came, but he killed these. That night when the sun went down there were no more enemies left.

Then he took his little white feather and blew it again toward the sky. He bundled up his back hair and placed his wife and mother in it. Thus they went up to the sky and went through the hole made by those men when they came down to fight. He stayed up there on the other side of the sky and became Pagio'ga [man-leader].[5] Sometimes he looks through the blue sky and, seeing good looking women or fine looking boys whom he desires, he makes them sick, and then when they die, he takes them away up there.

| NOTES |

1. Told by Sinyella; interpreted by Jess Chickapanega, 1919.
2. The incident is, of course, impossible, the Colorado being too deep and swift. (Spiers's impression. Ed.)
3. An affirmative exclamation, even to a negative question.
4. Probably the actual custom, although I was not explicitly told so.
5. See *Havasupai Ethnography*, p. 276.

19. THE STOLEN WIFE (SECOND VERSION)[1]

ONE TIME A WOMAN CAMPED ALONE WITH HER LITTLE BOY.
The woman went picking wild seeds which she put in a basket. When
she had plenty she came home. Her baby boy killed birds and hung
them up where they camped. When the woman came home she threw
them away. This happened every day and the woman always threw
the birds away. The woman did not think that her baby had killed the
birds. When the baby cried all the time, she took a bird and roasted it.
Then the baby stopped crying. When the baby boy grew a little bigger,
he always killed rabbits and jackrabbits while the woman went after
seeds. When the boy grew up he always hunted. Once he saw some
Indian tracks. He found a track with some things near it. He came
back and asked his mother, "Did you ever see any Indians around
here? Why do you not stay with the Indians?" "I am very sorry. There
are no Indians around here; just we two live here," the woman said. "I
just stayed here alone and after a while I made you. For a long time I
have seen no Indians around here." The boy hunted every day, killing
deer. His mother took the hides and tanned them.

One day he saw some Indian camps. He saw their tracks and the
horn and bones of deer. When he came back he asked his mother
again, "I want you to tell me something about the Indians. I saw their
tracks and what they do around the country. I want you to tell me
about them." But his mother said, "There is nobody around here. I
have seen no Indians around here. We are all alone." The boy said,
"What made you make me? Who is my father? If there is nobody
around here, how did you make me?" She said, "I tried to do it. I
walked around and saw the trees and the weeds. That is how I made
you. There is nobody around here."

Then he said nothing more to his mother, but went hunting every day and got many deer and antelope. He saw many Indian tracks, but he did not ask his mother because she would not tell him anything. His mother tanned the skins and made moccasins, pants,[2] and shirts for her boy. She dressed him up; he wore them. Then he hunted game, climbing up big mountains and looking around. He saw the Indian tracks and their ashes.

Then while up on the mountain he saw smoke a long way off. When he came home he did not tell his mother, but the next morning he went again and saw the smoke. Then he said to his mother again, "How did you make yourself if you are all alone here? How did you make me? I saw some smoke." "That is a long way off," she told him. "I have never seen any Indians around here." The boy said, "I am a big boy now; I do not want to stay around here any longer. I want a girl to marry. I have plenty of buckskins. I wonder where the Indians live that have girls. You tell me, for I want to go after them." His mother said, "No Indian around here has a daughter. There are no girls around here. You saw the smoke a long way off; that was made by no Indian. That one always kills good Indians like you."

The boy did not hunt again; he just thought about the girls. He made some clothes for himself. Then he said to his mother, "I want to get married. You are too old to cook and get seeds. That is why I want to get married and have my wife cook for you. Now you just lie down." His mother said, "I know I am old, but I do not want you to do that. There are no girls around here and you will get killed over there. I know I am old, but I do not want you to get married." She was very old now and could not stand. "You are too old to carry water and cook things to eat. I want to get a young girl to do it for us."

Then he ran away to the big mountain where he saw the smoke again. When he came home he said, "I do not like to stay here and be an old man. I am rich; I have plenty of things. A girl would look nice in my buckskins." The woman said, "I know that, but there is no girl around here. I do not want you to get married. That smoke a long way off is not that of a good Indian. He will kill you." The boy said, "I will not mind you. I am just going to see." Then the woman said, "I am not from around here. I came from where the smoke is and just camped here. There are plenty of girls there and plenty of Indians. If you want to get married, I will let you go over there. Blackbird has two wives who are sisters, and they are the only good girls. You steal them. They are pretty and always want to work. And when you leave me here, maybe I will die; I am old and cannot walk. When you go along you will see women and girls picking seeds. Go to where the big mountains are and when you see a girl there, talk to her. Maybe she will like you and will come with you. If she says 'no,' do not take her. I do not want you to go to the Indians' camp. They might kill you. I stayed with them a long time. They always do that. When you go along the road you will see big trees and plenty of deer there. Then you will see many antelope. You will cross at Gitcigwa' [the head of Cataract Canyon]. You will come to Wigatawisa where you will see many wildcats. There is a mountain there. Then you will see plenty of pine trees and that is deer country with many deer. Then you will come to Giu'ta [near Navajo camp in Coconino Basin] and there will be plenty of mountain sheep. Then you will see the Little Colorado, which is not deep. You will then come to some red hills and you will go between them. Beyond you will come to deeper water, up to your waist. Then you will come to water that is still deeper, up to your neck. Then you will come to the Indians' camp. But the women do not stay at the camp; they pick seeds all day. Only two of the girls are pretty, Blackbird's wives."

The boy started out. He saw the deer and antelope, and he said, "That is what my mother told me. She told me the truth." Then he saw the wildcats where his mother had told him. "My mother told me right; I see just what she told me I would." He walked along and said, "I might kill the deer, but I will just walk along." Then he came to Giu'ta, where he saw many mountain sheep. "I should like to kill some, but I do not want to carry them. I shall just go along." He went down the hill and crossed the water, which was ankle deep. "My mother told me right; I will always do what she tells me." He went along and crossed water again; it came to his knee. The next water he crossed came to his waist. Then he came to running water. He took off all his clothes and put them on his head, for the water came up to his neck. When he got out he said, "My mother told me the truth; she told no lie." Then he saw women's tracks. "That is what my mother told me. I guess they get their seeds here."

In the morning he climbed up a little mountain where he watched the women coming after seeds. Many women came by to pick them. Three women came close to where the boy was sitting. Two were together and one was further away. He saw the women and thought they were Blackbird's wives. He went over to see them. The women just picked seeds and did not look around. After a while they saw the boy. They sat down on the ground, stopping work. The boy looked very fine. They looked at him once and then hung their heads. The boy said, "I am traveling around and I do not know the road. I do not know where the waterhole is; I am very thirsty. I want you to tell me where you camp. I will go there and get a drink of water." The girls said, "Nobody camps here. This is a very long way off." "Have you any water with you? I want to drink." So they gave him water.

There were many women around, but they did not see the boy; they kept working. But the girls sat down. The boy said, "I was looking for girls; I am glad to see you girls. Tell me quickly whether you are married." The girls laughed and said, "No boys bother us. We are not married; we are just girls [virgins]." The boy said, "All right, I like that kind of girl. I came a long way after a girl. Would you like me?" "Yes, we like you, but we are not married; we are just girls." The boy said, "All right, you like me. We will just start to go. I do not want to go to the Indians' camp. I have an old woman where I came from. Maybe she has no fire, no water, and maybe she is dead over there. I want to go right back."

He started to go. One Indian woman stopped working; she saw the girls go with the boy and told the Indians. The boy and the girls ran along. When the sun went down they made a fire and slept. In the daylight the boy woke and said, "I thought you told me the truth, but you did not. You girls wake up. We will go to the old woman. You told me you were just girls, but I dreamed that you are married to Blackbird and that he is coming after me. You told me a lie. Blackbird is coming after me. I dreamed that Blackbird brought a hand drum (? *sigɷuva*) and played on it." When he said that, Blackbird came and stood there. Blackbird said to the girls, "I want you to give me my things." He did not want the girls to return. He said this again. The boy said to the girls, "You had better give him back what things you have. Hurry up and give them back." But the girls said, "We have nothing of his." Blackbird said, "I want you to give me back my things." Then the boy said, "You give him back what you have. When a man gets married, he dresses girls up. You take the things off and give them to him." But Blackbird had not given them anything, because he was very poor. Then the older sister tore off her *wagwa* [part of her vulva] and gave it to Blackbird. When she did that Blackbird ran back and said, "All right, that is what I wanted."

The boy and the girls went on, but after a little while the older girl died. So the boy had only one girl with him. When the girl died, the boy made a fire and burned her. Then they went along very quickly because the old woman might die. When he came home he saw his mother lying in ashes pretty nearly dead. It was very cold. He got wood and made a fire. In the daylight he said to his mother, "I want you to get some Indian soap and wash her. I have a girl." The old woman got the soap and washed the girl, and painted her when she was dry.[3]

The three camped there, and the women gathered seeds every day. The wife was all dressed up. The boy said to his mother, "When you go after *masala'* seeds, stay together and cut them. I do not want you to let her go away from you. Stay together. If you let her go somewhere, she might get lost." They went to gather seeds and came back. The boy went hunting deer.

One morning they saw plenty of seeds and the girl picked at one place. The old woman turned to pick at some others and when she turned back the girl was gone. She hunted around, but she did not see her and could not find any tracks. She cried. She walked around and came back home. When the boy came home she told him, saying, "I did not send her anywhere. I just went with her and we stayed together. I merely looked away and I lost her. What is the matter with her? I did not see her tracks." The boy grew angry at the woman and said, "I thought you would do what I told you. I told you to stay together. I do not know what we will do. Take me to where you stood."

They went to where they had started picking seeds, and she showed the boy where she had lost her. The boy could not find any tracks. He looked all around. Then he blew some eagle down in each of the four directions but it always fell to the ground. Then he blew it up. It went up, and he followed it up in the air. He went up to the sky. There was a road, and he found tracks. He followed them until he saw Indians camping. He saw a woman and asked her, "I lost my wife. I am looking around, for I saw her tracks coming along here. Did you see her?" "Yes," said the woman, "I saw her coming along with the Wind. He lives in the Indian camp. He always steals women from the Indians. He has many women in that camp. He steals pretty women." "I want to see my wife. That is what I came for," said the boy. "Maybe he took her into his house," the woman said. "I will see," said the boy.

He went on until he saw Wind's camp. He stood by the door and saw his wife sitting in the house. "I want you to come out and go home." The girl started toward the door. She was almost out of the door when Wind pulled her back. The girl lay on the ground. The boy said again, "I want you to come out." But Wind would not let her go. Wind sat by the door so that the girls could not come out, and when this girl tried, Wind threw her back.

Wind threw her back four times. The boy stood by the door and saw it. "That is why I look for her around here, for I lost her, and I want her back," said the boy. Wind said, "We will both urinate and who does it farthest can have the girl." "I do not want to do that. That is my wife and I want to take her with me." "No, you cannot do that. You can only have her if you beat me." The boy stood by the door and said, "All right, come out and we will try it." They went a way. Wind said, "You do it first." But the boy said, "No, you proposed it; you do it first." Wind said, "All right, I will do it first." But Wind could not beat the boy, for the boy threw it way off. Then the boy went after the girl. The boy said, "I beat you; I will get the girl and go home." Wind said, "No, I cannot let you go. We will try to defecate." The boy said, "Why do you fool me? I want my girl. You are teasing me." Wind said, "All right, we will try again." They started to defecate and the boy beat Wind. When the boy beat Wind, he said, "I beat you; I will take my girl and go home." Wind said, "No, you did not beat me. We shall try another test and if you beat me you may take the girl. I will run a footrace with you. If you beat me, you may take the girl." The boy said, "All right, I will run a footrace with you and if you beat me you may have my girl while I will go back alone."

They started to run a race and the boy beat Wind. Wind made himself wind, not an Indian. Wind went right by, saying, "I beat you." But the boy said, "Oh, no, you were not the same as I; you made yourself the wind. I can have the girl." Then they tried another footrace. The boy ran fast and beat Wind, but Wind made himself the wind again and went over the boy's head. "I beat you," said Wind. "No, you were not the same as an Indian; you made yourself the wind," said the boy. They tried again and Wind said, "I will not make myself the wind." The boy, as he went along, thought, "I do not know what they are going to do with me; they are just playing with me like this. I think I will kill Wind." He started to run fast and when Wind came by he hit him on the head. When Wind fell to the ground, he hit him again and killed him.

Then he went back to the house where the Indians were and killed them all. He took his wife and went back very fast, because he had left his mother alone. "My mother might get cold and die." When they reached home, they found the old woman in the ashes. He told her what he had done up there. He said, "I made a great deal of trouble up there because Wind took my wife. I killed them all. I want you to make a good house." The old woman said, "All right, I will do that." Then she made a house. When the boy saw it, he said, "That is not good. Make another house." She made one with a big domed roof and put sand all over it. The boy said, "That is not strong enough; make one of shiny stone (*halgadja'i*) because the Indians will come after me and will want to kill me. Make little holes like windows in it so that I can shoot out arrows." The woman tried to do it. It was made with two rooms. He said, "I will go in the upper part and shoot arrows from there. Clouds, wind, and snow will come first. Then Indians will come who will try to kill me." The woman made a strong house, big, and with windows. When she finished she said, "I want you to go see it." When he saw the house it looked fine. He said, "It looks fine and all shiny. You live down here and my wife and I will live up there, where I can look through the windows and kill them." He went in the upper part with his wife.

When the clouds and rain came he went inside. "The Indians might come this night," he said. The Indians came and stood all around the house. They tried to break his house, but they could not. The boy lay on his bed. He woke up and started to shoot with bow and arrow. The boy killed some of the Indians. They tried to kill him, but they could not. Rain and Thunder tried to break the house, but they could not. The house was well built and they could not hurt it. In the morning the Indians went back. They came every night and went away when daylight came.

(That is all I know of this story. The man did not tell me any more.)

| NOTES |

1. Told by Manakadja; interpreted by Lillie Burro; recorded by E. G., 1921.
2. Leggings?
3. This is the regular procedure on marriage.

20. The Water-Elk (first version)[1]

WOLF AND COYOTE LIVED FAR TO THE WEST, CLOSE TO THE ocean. Wolf said to Coyote, "This country contains no game, no deer, no antelope, no big game. All we eat is rats. That is all we kill and we eat their flesh all the time. I think I want you to go down into the water to its bottom." Many elk (*akwa'gata*) lived under the water. Coyote tried. He went close to the water and put his head down, but he felt afraid to go under. He said to Wolf, "I am afraid to go down. I want you to go." Wolf said, "All right. I will go down in the water to hunt. I will hunt a big elk and chase it out. I will come out again after four sleeps."

Wolf told Coyote that he would leave two full quivers with him; one had hard willow arrows, the others were the reed arrows used by boys. "When I go down, for a little while the water will continue to boil. While it does this, you must not shoot in the water; you must save the arrows," Wolf said, and then he went. After four sleeps, the water began to boil, and although the elk did not come, Coyote began to shoot arrows into it. But the elk failed to appear. He shot away all the arrows except one, the fire drill shaft. Then an elk came out. The elk walked a little way from the water to a nice sandy place where he lay down, rolled and shook himself, in order to dry his hair. He did this four times. Then Wolf lay on his back across the elk's horns. Wolf said, "The hair is dry now; it is pretty good. Coyote, you shoot him now." Coyote had no more arrows, only the fire drill. So he shot this, but it rebounded from the elk's side. The elk walked along with Coyote at his side, shooting. After a short distance he began to trot and then to run. Coyote could not kill him, as he ran beside the elk. Wolf lay on the elk's horns. The elk was running toward the east with Coyote running by his side, shooting at him. But he could not kill him. Finally Coyote became tired and turned back home, while the elk kept on.

He continued to run until he crossed the Colorado River at Needles [Wmka'vinyuwa, Mohave house]. Wolf said to himself, "I know this river. I have been here." The elk went running on until he came to Huwa'l [a mountain close to Kingman]. Wolf said, "I call that mountain Huwa'l. I know that mountain." The elk continued until he came to Bill Williams Mountain (Wgavau'la). Wolf said, "I know this mountain. I have been near this place before. I thought you were going to stop here," for the elk did not stop; he kept on running. "I do not know what place you want to go to," Wolf said to the elk. The latter ran on, going to the north of Sitgreaves Mountain (Wiga'akwaθa). Between Sitgreaves Mountain and Kendrick Mountain (Wiodji'a) the elk began to defecate as he ran. Wolf said, "Droppings, become elk and live around this place." The elk ran by the north side of Kendrick Mountain and by the north side of San Francisco Mountain (Wihagnapa'dja) until he crossed the Little Colorado River [Hagaθei'la, salty water]. He continued to run on toward the east while Wolf lay on his horns. Wolf cried and thought, "I wonder what place he wants to go to." He went on north of Gad'ia [a little black mountain south of Walpi]. He ran on and on into a country where we do not know the place-names. Wolf said, "I know this place, these small mountains, and the big ones." They kept on going through a country where there is no timber, only grassy plains. They went on over these, running toward the east. I do not know what Wolf said about the country there.

Finally they neared the eastern ocean. The only man who had women lived close to the water. Wolf said, "I am related to that man. Maternal grandfather, look at me. The elk carried me away. I am afraid he will carry me into the water. I want you to shoot the elk for me as we go by." The elk kept on running. The man heard him and saw them coming, while he was cohabiting with his wives. The elk came alongside his house. The man jumped up and took his arrows from the house, spit on his hands, drew his bow, and shot the elk just back of the ribs. The elk fell dead right at the water's edge.

The man sharpened his knife, and skinned and butchered the elk. Wolf carried the meat to the house, where they cooked some food. Wolf ate some but he could not retain it, for it passed right through his body. This was because he had not eaten in such a long time, lying there on the elk's horns, that his anus had become so enlarged that he could not retain what he ate. The man who lived at the water's edge thought about what he could put on Wolf's buttocks to hold the food. So he cut off a piece of meat and made a little hole in it. He put this over Wolf's buttocks and it prevented the food from coming through. They fed Wolf until he was fat again. The man said, "That is all right. You are just like me now." Wolf stayed a long time with the man in his house, eating all the time, until he felt quite strong. He stayed about four months.

Then Wolf said, "I think I will go back home. Prepare plenty of provisions for me and I will carry them as I travel home." They prepared food for him. They ground cornmeal and prepared all sorts of things. They did not eat all the elk meat, but dried some of it for him. They wrapped the elk meat in the elk skin, enclosing all the other things. Wolf took the bundle on his back and started home. When he reached his house, he took the things off his back and laid them down. He walked softly toward his house. There he saw Coyote inside lying close to a little fire. Then Coyote saw Wolf. Wolf said, "Is there any more of our corn left? I am pretty hungry. Cook some, so that I can eat." "I ate everything we had here. We have no more food. I am starving," Coyote said. Wolf said, "That elk who carried me toward the east, where the ocean is like that one here, was killed for me by that man. A great many elk live at that place. Perhaps I can get them to flourish here. You let the elk run off way over there in the east."

| NOTES |

1. Told by Sinyella; interpreted by Jess Chickapanega, 1919.

21. The Water-Elk (second version)[1]

WOLF AND HIS NEPHEW, COYOTE, WERE ON THIS SIDE OF A big water [the ocean] staying with many Indians. Wolf said, "We are tired of staying here with the Indians. We should like to go a long way to get things to make moccasins. We use the back of jackrabbits for strings for moccasins now. We want buckskin and we want plenty to eat. We will move in four days." Wolf said, "My nephew Coyote, you take the beads (apu'k) and play with them. Maybe the Indians will take [win] your things away." Then Coyote took the beads and went to play with the Indians. They beat him. He came back and said, "We are going to go now." Wolf said, "No, not yet. I did not mean four days; I meant four years. In four years we will start to go." "Now, four years are past and we are ready to go," said Wolf. Then he started to get his things, to tie them up and put them on his back.

Wolf said, "Now, my nephew, I want you to go and get a mouse to eat; then we will camp somewhere." They slept there and in the morning they went on again. They wanted something to eat. Wolf said, "Well, my nephew, tonight we want something to eat." Wolf saw a rabbit running. He whistled and the rabbit dropped dead. Then Wolf said to Coyote, "We do not want to eat it all. We do not want the blood and the entrails. We will bury them here where we camp."

In the morning they started again. When they started to go they saw jackrabbits running. Wolf whistled again and a jackrabbit dropped dead. They did the same again; they buried the entrails. Wolf said, "Coyote, remind me not to eat those things because we want to catch things by whistling."

In the morning they started on again. They saw another jackrabbit. Wolf whistled and caught the jackrabbit. They started to go.

Wolf said to Coyote, "We must go somewhere where we can get big buckskin and plenty to eat. That is why we are traveling." They went along and killed another jackrabbit. They roasted and ate it, but again they buried the entrails where they had slept. They moved again and caught another jackrabbit by whistling. They roasted and ate it, and again they buried the entrails.

In the morning they started to go again. Wolf went ahead of Coyote. Coyote thought of the buried entrails in the camp; he ran back and ate them. Then Coyote ran on as fast as he could. They saw a jackrabbit again and Wolf whistled, but he could not catch him this time. Wolf became hungry and could not get anything to eat. In the night Wolf became angry. At daylight he said to Coyote, "I thought you would heed me when I talked to you. I think you took what we buried at the camp. Now we shall get no more to eat."

They moved again and saw a jackrabbit. Wolf whistled but could not get him. They became hungry. They slept at a camp and then moved along again. Wolf said, "Now when we find a good place, we shall stay there and camp." They camped at the Colorado River, but they had nothing to eat.

Wolf said, "Coyote, I want you to make a fire and I shall try to get something under the water, some fish, to roast." Wolf went into the water and the fish stuck to him all over. He took them off and roasted them. They ate them, for they were very hungry. They went along the big river, fishing. They went to [toward?] Hua'lagasia'va [Powell Plateau]. Wolf fished again at their camp and they roasted the fish and ate them. Wolf called to the fish. They went along the river.

When the sun went down Wolf made a big fire and said, "Coyote, I want you to go into the water and get some fish for supper tonight." Coyote went in and tried to get fish. He took off his breechclout. The fish smelled him and all went away; he did not catch any.

They became hungry again; they slept. Wolf said nothing to Coyote, but in the daylight he talked to Coyote, saying, "I want you to heed me when I tell you two or three or four times. Now we are hungry and maybe we will die, for now we may get nothing to eat." They started out again and they had nothing to eat. They traveled along the river and camped. Wolf made a big fire and tried going into the water again, but he could not get them, so he came out again. They were very hungry and they just slept.

In the morning they started to move again. As they went along they saw many mountain sheep lying around. Coyote said to Wolf, "My uncle, I want mountain sheep. I am so hungry that I want to kill them." But Wolf said, "No, I do not want them." Wolf was angry at Coyote and Wolf was hungry too. Coyote was always mean. He said to Wolf, "I want to taste that mountain sheep. I want it." "No, I do not like that; it is not good to taste," said Wolf. Wolf liked them but he was angry and he did not want them because Coyote did.

They started to go again. They got where they wanted to be and there they camped. Wolf said, "This is a good place. I want to stay here." In the morning Wolf said to his nephew, "This is a good place, with many deer. We want to get deer. I want you to make me arrows, many arrows. Put them in two sacks [quivers?]."

Then Wolf said, "Coyote, I want you to go under the water and get a big deer. When you get the deer, eat it and then we can get many deer." Coyote said to Wolf, "No, I do not like the water. I am afraid of the water. I want you to go in." Wolf said, "I want you to go in and get a big deer to eat. Then we shall have lots of meat and a big buckskin. There are lots of deer around here." Wolf said again, "All right, I will go into the water and get a big deer. I will get inside its horn [between the horns?] and when I come out I will boil them.[2] Do not throw [shoot?] arrows into the water when I am in the water. Pretty soon it will come out. Then it will shake itself on the ground to get dry. Then you take an arrow and throw it at the big deer. I do not want you to throw arrows into the water." Wolf said, "I will go into the water in the morning. I will sleep down there and tomorrow morning when the sun comes up maybe I will come. You watch the water boil; when you see the water boiling, I do not want you to throw arrows into the water."

In the morning nearly at noon, the water boiled and Coyote held his arrow close to the water. He saw the water boil and he threw his arrow in. The water carried the arrow away. When he had thrown all of his arrows into the water, he waited a while. Then the deer horn came up out of the water and Wolf lay inside of the horn. The big deer lay on the ground. He got up and shook himself. Coyote sat there and watched him. He shook himself dry. Wolf from in [between] the horn[s] said to Coyote, "Well, my nephew, I want you to shoot my big buck and kill him. He might take me away." Coyote said, "No, my uncle, I have no arrows to shoot the deer." Wolf said, "Well, my nephew, I told you to keep those arrows. I want you to kill him right away. We want to eat him." But Coyote said, "I have no arrows. I used them all in the water." "Come and shoot the deer," Wolf said to Coyote.

When the deer had dried its hide, it started to run. Then Coyote tried to shoot it with the fire drill but he could not kill it. Coyote was always mean. The deer ran very fast. Coyote said, "My uncle, I want you to hang onto a tree." Wolf said, "Oh no, I cannot do that. He would kill me with his horns. I told you to kill the deer and we would eat it, but you did not do it. He will run away with me on his head and maybe I will be carried away."

The deer ran along. Coyote ran along with him a while, but Coyote became tired and went back. The deer went around Red Butte (Awikatawi'sa) and went down to the San Francisco Peaks [Wihaganapa'dja, "rocks snow"]. He ran around over all the big mountains as fast as he could. He went to Bill Williams Mountain (Wigavau'la). Wolf said, "I know where we have been. I have always run around this place and I know every spot. I know the place where you are taking me. Wi'gavau'la is the place where you are taking me." They came to Wegagaga.[3]

The deer ran fast. Wolf lay down inside of [between] the horns. He had nothing to eat. It ran to where the Walapai live. It ran as fast as the train and the automobile. Wolf said, "I know where you are going. You are going to take me where many Indians live; where Coyote and I used to stay; where the Indians play shinny. You want to take me into the big water there and kill me." The deer still ran fast and Wolf said, "I know you are going to go into the great big water [the ocean]. I know that is where you want to go in. All right; I do not care. You can go in all right." They came near to the big water and said, "My grandfather, watch me; I am going in." (He spoke to Tokʳepo'dʳa near the ocean.)[4]

The deer became tired and could not walk fast any more, but just walked along. The Indian children played around. They saw the deer coming and ran to tell their fathers. "Look at the big thing coming!" They had never seen that kind of thing before. The Indians said, "Watch him; we are busy. We have not finished yet." The children said, "He is running over this way." But the Indians did not get up. "Papa, papa, here he is coming, just walking, not running." When the deer walked by them, Tokʳepo'dʳa saw him. He took his old arrow and shot him. The deer fell dead by the water. The children said, "Oh, papa, it looks as though some Indian fell over there." When the deer fell, Wolf fell on the other side of the water.

Wolf was pretty weak and could not walk. The children said, "I saw him come out of the horn. The deer wanted to kill Indians, but you killed the deer." Wolf could not wake up, but just lay there, very thin from eating nothing. Tok^{r}epo'd^{r}a carried Wolf to his house. After he took Wolf to his camp, he took a knife to butcher the big deer. When he finished butchering he took all of the meat over to the camp and cooked it. Tok^{r}epo'd^{r}a's wife gave Wolf some meat, but Wolf could not keep it in his stomach. Wolf felt pretty badly. He took buckskin and made himself a new stomach and felt well again. Wolf ate the meat; he was well again. They dried the meat and piled it up. Wolf took plenty of it. He took the skin, put the meat in it, and carried it on his back to where he started.

He went along, sleeping somewhere, and in the morning he started on again. He came to where Coyote stayed. When he came near to Coyote's home he took off his pack and put it down. He went slowly toward the house without saying anything. Coyote lay in the sunshine. The flies sat on his mouth and Coyote snapped at them. He talked to the flies, saying, "I cannot get any meat for my supper." Wolf stood there and heard that, but Coyote did not see Wolf yet. He just talked to the flies. Wolf went to Coyote and stood there. After a while he sat down by him and said, "My nephew, I want you to cook me something to eat. I am hungry." Coyote said, "Oh, my uncle, I am very poor now and I am very hungry. I have nothing to cook now. I have nothing, just like you." Wolf said, "Have you some wild seeds under the sand?" Coyote said, "I ate them all up." Wolf said, "Where we made a fire, I left a little corn. Did you take that?" "No," said Coyote, "I did not take that." "Well, you take the corn and grind it and make mush for dinner." Coyote took the corn and made mush.

Wolf said to Coyote, "I want you to go over there and get what I put there. I want you to get it." This was what Wolf had carried on his back. Coyote went to where Wolf had left the pack, but Coyote could not lift it. Finally he lifted it and brought it over. Coyote was glad that Wolf came home. He jumped around, for he was glad to get meat.

Wolf and Coyote stayed there all winter. There was much snow. Wolf said, "I want you to go get big logs and make a fire to last all night." Coyote went after the wood, carried it on his shoulders and came close to the house. Wolf said, "Well, my nephew, I do not want you to come into my house any more." Coyote came near and said, "Well, my uncle, maybe I will hit you." Coyote went west and took the wood along. Wolf was angry because Coyote would never listen to him. Coyote went up to the sky and made himself into a constellation. He has wood on his shoulders now. Wolf got angry and that is why he made a constellation of Coyote.[5]

| NOTES |

1. Told by Manakadja; interpreted by Lillie Burro; recorded by E. G., 1921.
2. Probably a mistranslation; see below. As in the first version, Wolf says the water will boil as the elk comes out of it.
3. Possibly Mount Floyd.
4. A mythical (?) insect, like a spider, living near the water.
5. Another tale accounting for this constellation is as follows: Mountain Lion came to Coyote's camp and ate his food. Coyote was angry. They told him to get a long pole and build a fire. He did not want to burn his pole, so they told him to go to the west and come back from the east (*Havasupai Ethnography*, p. 167).

22. Bear and Mountain Lion (first version)[1]

BEAR AND HIS WIFE HAD CHILDREN BORN TO THEM. BEAR used to leave camp and spend all his time hunting. He hunted deer but could not kill any; all he could catch were badgers. Whenever he killed one, he did not bring it home. He roasted it in the ground, right where he killed it. He ate all the meat by himself, leaving only the bones. These he tied together and carried home. Bear's wife mashed them on her grinding stone. They always did this. Whenever the woman mashed the bones, she thought she was not being properly treated. She felt very angry. Bear's wife knew that another man, Mountain Lion, killed deer. She thought she would like to be married to him. So she went over to his house and married him. The woman said, "This is the sort of man I like. You are a pretty good man. You have plenty of deer meat." So she married Mountain Lion and stayed with him. She was glad, because they had plenty of meat.

Bear went off hunting again. While he was gone, that women went to Mountain Lion's house. When Bear came home, his wife was gone; she was not at home. He asked his children, "Where did the woman go?" They said, "We just saw her going that way," pointing. Bear tracked her, following until he got to Mountain Lion's house. Bear asked Mountain Lion, "My woman ran away from me." "I did not see any woman," Mountain Lion said. Bear asked several times, but Mountain Lion said each time, "I did not see any woman." Bear said, "Yes, her track led right in your house." Mountain Lion said, "Yes, she is in here." The woman spoke to Bear; she said, "He whom I married is a good man. He has lots of things I like. I do not want to go back to your place any more." She said this many times to Bear; finally Bear became angry.

Bear talked angrily: "I want to fight," he said. Mountain Lion said, "All right." Bear was standing just outside the door of Mountain Lion's house. "Hurry up," he said, "Come out and we will fight." Mountain Lion said, "Wait, I am not ready. I am going to wear a hard rock all over my body. I am ready now. I am coming out." "Are you ready?" he asked after he came out. As soon as Mountain Lion came out of the door, Bear rushed at him, tore him to pieces, and threw them away. Then Bear stood right beside the door. Meanwhile his wife was way down inside Mountain Lion's house. He called to her, "Come right out. We will go home."

Mountain Lion was broken to pieces and these lay scattered around. He died, but he came to life again. He walked quietly up behind Bear. Mountain Lion jumped right on Bear, and did just what Bear had done to him. He tore him to pieces and threw them away. Bear died. Then Mountain Lion went right into his house.

By and by Bear came to life again, stood at the door, and called Mountain Lion. As Mountain Lion came out, Bear did the same thing to him again, killing him. Then Bear wanted the woman to come out and go home with him. The woman said, "No, this is a good man I have married. I do not want to go back to your house. The man I married has lots of good things. I wear them. Look at me; I will show you what I wear," and she showed him her dress, her moccasins, and other things.

As Bear talked to the woman, Mountain Lion came to life again and came up quietly. Again he rushed, seized on Bear, and, tearing him to pieces, threw them away. Bear died. Then Mountain Lion went into his house. Bear came to life and again he stood by the door. Mountain Lion said, "How many times will you come to life after I kill you?" Bear said, "I will come to life four times. How many times will you come to life?" Mountain Lion said, "I will come to life eight times." Then Mountain Lion came out, and again Bear did the same thing, and scattered parts of Mountain Lion's body all about.

Mountain Lion came to life again and again he tore up the Bear and threw him away. After he did this, he went into the house. Again Bear came to life, and came and stood by the door. Then Mountain Lion came out, and again Bear destroyed and killed him. Mountain Lion came to life and again he did the same to Bear; tore him to pieces and threw them away.

But he did not return to his house; he just sat down. As he sat he thought, "What am I going to do so that Bear will not come to life again?" Soon he knew. He brought plenty of dry wood, dug a deep hole in the ground, and threw the wood into the hole. Then he gathered quartz stones and put them on top of the wood, and set fire to the pile. It burned until the rocks were red hot. He took Bear's heart and pared it around and around into a thin slice. One of the rocks was intensely hot. He spread the heart down beside it, and rolled the stone in the flesh. Then he threw this into the hole. He piled the big hot rocks on top of this. He covered this up with dirt and stamped it down tight. Then he stamped on it four times. "Now you will not come to life again," he said. Then Mountain Lion went into his house. So Mountain Lion, having beaten Bear, kept his wife.

| NOTES |

1. Told by Sinyella; interpreted by Jess Chickapanega, 1919.

23. Bear and Mountain Lion (second version)[1]

MOUNTAIN LION, COYOTE, WILDCAT, AND WOLF CAMPED BY the Little Colorado. Many Indians camped there by the water.

Bear had a wife and four daughters, with whom he lived two or three miles away. He went hunting every morning and slept out where he hunted. He killed a badger and roasted it. He ate it all, taking home merely the bones to his wife. She pounded them on a rock [metate?] and made some of the ground bone fly away. He hunted again, killed another badger, and roasted it. He brought it [the bones?] home to his wife and she ground the bones. Bear tanned the badger skin and made an apron for his wife.

In the morning Bear went hunting again. His wife stayed home. She became angry because she had no dress, only an apron. "I thought I would get all dressed, but I have only an apron. I will run away."

She ran over to the Indians' camp. She wanted to marry Mountain Lion because he was a good hunter and had much meat and many buckskins.

Bear came back next morning and saw the camp with nobody there, for his wife had taken all her daughters. He looked around for tracks to see where they had gone. He followed the tracks and came to the Indians' camp. He saw the tracks go into the Indians' house and saw his daughters all married to Indians. His wife had married Mountain Lion. The Indians had one house.

Bear stood at the door of Mountain Lion's house and said, "My wife, I want you to come out and go home." He said this three times. His wife said, "No, I cannot go back again. I am married here. I am all dressed up. I have a pretty dress and much meat, and I have plenty of everything." Then Bear said again to his wife, "I want you to come out and go home." "No, I cannot leave here. I am married here and I have plenty to eat. When I married you I had nothing to eat, no meat, and no dress." "Oh, no. You had meat and plenty of grease in your basket." His wife said, "I got married here and I have a shawl and a dress. I have good Indians to stay with. I ran away from you and I cannot go back." Bear said, "I have things for you just like those of Mountain Lion. I have them in my camp for you; just as good as Mountain Lion's." Bear grew angry, and talked badly and swore, and Bear's wife did likewise.

Bear said to Mountain Lion, "My cross-cousin, bring my wife out; I want to take her home." Mountain Lion said, "No. I will not let you have the woman." Bear said, "I want you to bring that woman to me." Mountain Lion said, "No. I am glad to have this woman. I will not let you have her back."

Then Bear said, "I want you to come out and fight with me. I will tear your skin to pieces and throw it away." Mountain Lion said, "When we were little boys we used to play, not fight, and now you are going to kill me." Bear was standing by the door. There were many Indians in the house. Bear said, "I want you to come out and fight with me, and if you kill me you can take my wife to marry." Mountain Lion said, "You cannot kill me, but I can kill you. How many times have you been dead?" "I have been dead four times and that is enough," said Bear. Bear asked Mountain Lion how many times he had been dead. Mountain Lion said, "I have been dead eight times; you, only four times." Bear said, "I want you to come out. I will throw you down, and tear your skin off and throw it away. I have been dead four times; that is longer than you."

Then Mountain Lion said, "All right. I will get ready now." He put on two shirts made of rocks. "When I finish putting on my shirt I will come and fight with you." Mountain Lion started to come to fight. Bear's claws wore out on the rocks of Mountain Lion's shirt. But Mountain Lion tore Bear all to pieces and threw him on the ground. When he had killed Bear, Mountain Lion went back into his house.

After a while Bear got up and went to the door and said he wanted Mountain Lion to fight with him again. Then Mountain Lion said, "All right. I will be there in a minute. I just have to fix my shirt with rocks again, then I will fight you again." But Mountain Lion did not do it; he just came out without his shirt. They started to fight and Bear tore Mountain Lion to pieces. Mountain Lion was dead. When

Bear killed Mountain Lion, he tried to go into the house to get his wife and go home.

When he got to the door Mountain Lion jumped up and pulled Bear away from the house. Mountain Lion had not fought hard; that is why Bear could kill him. Then Mountain Lion killed Bear again and tore him all to pieces and threw them away. Bear had been killed twice.

Mountain Lion went into the house and sat there. Bear woke up again and stood by the door. He said, "Come out and we will fight again." They fought again and Bear killed Mountain Lion this time. Bear tried to go into the house and get his wife, but Mountain Lion woke up and began to fight again. Mountain Lion killed Bear and threw him away.

Then Mountain Lion went into the house and said to Bear's wife, "My wife, make a fire, and the next time I kill Bear, I will take his heart and put it on the hot rocks."

Then Bear woke up and they started to fight. Bear killed Mountain Lion. Bear tried again to go in and take his wife and go home, but Mountain Lion woke up quickly. He started to fight with Bear again. He tore his skin and tore out his heart. Mountain Lion cut the heart open and wrapped the hot rocks in it. He put this in a hole in the ground and stamped on it. "I do not want you to come back here again." Then Bear did not wake up again. His wife and daughters all were married to the Indians and stayed there.

Mountain Lion gave Bear's wife to his nephew, Coyote, while he married one of the daughters of Bear. The Indians hunted, and killed deer and mountain sheep, and lived there. Coyote had two or three daughters.

Wolf spoke to the Indians. He said that he wanted to go to kill mountain sheep. He said, "My nephew, I want you to go down by the creek and shout. I will sit over on the rock where the mountain sheep go past.

Mountain Lion, Wolf, and Wildcat all went over to the rocks, but Coyote still stayed home. Many other Indians went there and camped. Coyote stayed in his house and made moccasins. When nearly noon he started to go; he crossed the water. Then he said, "I forgot my knife and my bag." He called to his children and his wife, "I forgot my knife and bag. I left it where I was sitting. Middle daughter (? *itcogaya' djagana'ga*), you bring them to me." He stood across the water. His daughter said, "I will throw them to you, my father." Coyote said, "No. I have my fire drill in that bag and it might break. Do not throw it. I want you to bring it to me."

Coyote's daughter went into the water, picking up her dress to her knees. Coyote said, "It is deep here." She pulled her dress up above her waist and Coyote saw how white she was. When the little girl came out of the water Coyote threw her on the ground and had his will of her. She cried. Then Coyote went away and left her crying. The girl's blood ran out into the water.

She lay there crying. After a while she went home and told her mother, and her mother cried with her. They cried all day, for they felt very badly. The mother and her girls were home alone. The mother said to her children during the night, "I thought I was married to Coyote, but he has made trouble for me. I am very sorry." The mother became very angry. She called all her children together and talked to them. "I am very sorry that my husband did wrong. I do not want to stay here and cook for the Indians. I feel very badly and I do not know what I am going to do with myself. We must all run away and not stay here. That is what Coyote wants." "All right, we will do as you do," the children said.

Their mother said, "All right, we do not want to stay here. We will go away all alone, while the Indians were [are] away. We will make ourselves look different—change ourselves so that Coyote and the Indians will not know us. I should like to make myself a piñon bird." She stayed there to see how the children looked when they were piñon birds. She said, "That is not good. Coyote and the Indians might kill you easily. Make yourselves something else. Make yourselves mice." But again the mother said, "That is not good. They might easily kill you." Then she made them rats (*ama'laja*). They made houses [burrows], but the mother said, "That is not good; stop that. Make yourselves rabbits. I will stay to see you. If you do not look right, they might kill us." Then they made themselves jackrabbits, but jackrabbits were not good, so they made themselves buffalo. She said, "That looks pretty good. You look fine. We will make ourselves buffalo."

Then she said, "We do not want to leave anything in the house. We will take all our belongings. We will take the water bottles to make our heads; and we will take metates (*api'*) for our tongues, and the mano stones for *toempu'va*."[2] They took sticks of the house for ribs (*'gioa'aω*) and the covering of the house to make their hides. She took the ashes and made blood for them. When they were all ready and had used everything they had, they waited near the camp. The woman called, "woi, woi, woi."

Coyote started to go where the Indians were. He killed a little mountain sheep and came to the Indian camp. The Indians all cooked the meat. Coyote stayed where the smoke was, but he ate nothing, and cried, "Smoke, stay away from me." He felt very badly, and cried. He would not eat. Then Wolf talked to him in the morning, saying, "My nephew, when I left you I thought you did something wrong over there. You did something wrong over there. I dreamed of the women we left over there."

In the morning the Indians tied up their meat and started to go home because Wolf had dreamed of trouble at home. Then the Indians saw that the camp did not look the same. They saw some big things where they had camped. They threw down their packs, ran after the big things, and tried to kill them. They threw [shot?] arrows after them, but the arrows fell down from their hides. They could not hurt them. The buffalo just walked along to where the sun comes up. Then they started to run. "My nephew, I want you to kill a buffalo. I want to put the skin on the sweat lodge," Wolf said.

Coyote's daughter already had a little boy, and the child sat on the horns of the buffalo. The child saw the Indians coming. Wolf, Coyote, and the other Indians ran after the buffalo to kill them, but they could not kill them with arrows. There were big rocks, but the buffalo made a pass through the rocks and ran right through. They could not kill one. Wolf made ice, but they cut through that and ran on. However, the woman stepped on the ice and fell, breaking her leg. It was at the Ute camp where she fell down. They killed her by hitting her with something. Where they killed her, they have buffalo there now.

They came back home, but they could not find their camp because the woman had taken everything to make the buffalo.

| NOTES |

1. Told by Manakadja; interpreted by Lillie Burro; recorded by E. G., 1921.
2. Not translated.

24. The Wronged Daughter[1]

I DO NOT KNOW WHERE WOLF'S AND COYOTE'S HOME WAS. Wolf said, "It is about time for the mountain sheep to raise their young. They are now in little flocks. I want you, Coyote, to go down in the canyon and chase them; scare them. I know where the sheep trail is narrow. I will wait there until you drive them past me. Then we will shoot and kill them, and so we will have some meat." Mountain Lion and Wolf each had four or five sons. Mountain Lion and Wolf and their sons went out first. They told Coyote, "You stay in the house until we have gone a long way. After a little while go down into the canyon." So they went.

Coyote crossed the creek close to his house. Then he hallooed, calling, "I forgot my knife. I want you, my youngest daughter (she was a good-looking girl) to find my knife and bring it over." Coyote waited and the girl brought the knife. They stood on opposite banks of the creek. The girl said, "I will stand at the edge of the creek and throw it over; perhaps you will get it." Coyote said, "No, walk part way across and hand it to me. If you throw it, it will break in two." So the girl started to cross the creek. When she was halfway across Coyote said, "A little further over in the creek it is quite deep; pull your dress well up on your body." The girl held up her dress as he told her. But the creek was not deep; Coyote only wanted to see her parts. So the girl crossed, and Coyote, his passion aroused, threw her down and had his will. At that time every woman's parts were white, but Coyote did wrong and spoiled them, so that they have since been black.

Coyote went off and chased the mountain sheep past the spot where Wolf and Mountain Lion were waiting. These two killed plenty of sheep. Each man skinned two, three, four, or five. They camped there two or three nights. Wolf dreamed. Coyote asked what he had dreamed. Wolf said, "Coyote, it is not right for me to tell you. You know what the dream is." So he did not relate it. He had dreamed of his women at home, that something was chasing them around among the houses.

Coyote's girl went home crying. Her mother asked her why she cried. She answered, "My father wronged me." Her mother was angry and thought, "We do not want to stay here. Perhaps we will become animals. I do not know what kind, though." She thought again and mentioned the first animal. "I am going to be a deer." But that was not good. Then she thought, "I am going to be an antelope. I will try that and see if it looks good." Next she tried being a mountain sheep. The old woman said, "That is not good. I do not know what kind of animal will be good. When I decide, we will run away. I do not want to stay here. Perhaps we will try to be bears," but this was not good either. Then she said, "Let us try being elk," but this was also a failure. Then, "We will try being [a larger deer]," but this too was not good. They tried being all sorts of animals. When only one, buffalo, was left, she said, "I think that kind will be all right." So they tried being buffalo and found that they looked very nice. She said, "This is good. Let us get ready as buffalo." They all became buffalo. She said, "When Coyote, Wolf, and Mountain Lion return, they will attempt to shoot us, but they cannot kill us because our hair is long and thick and hangs all over our bodies."

The men were coming home, but when they were still a long way off, the buffalo got wind of them. They ran off a little way, but then trotted back beside the house. When the buffalo saw the men coming, they grew afraid and ran away. Wolf and Mountain Lion said, "That is the kind of . . . [*page 177 of original manuscript is missing*]

| NOTES |

1. Told by Sinyella; interpreted by Jess Chickapanega, 1919.

25. Rock Squirrel's Grandson (first version)[1]

COYOTE AND ROCK SQUIRREL LIVED IN ONE HOUSE. ROCK Squirrel had a daughter. Coyote and Rock Squirrel killed a little mountain sheep and brought it home. There they skinned it, cut the body open along the belly, and broke back the ribs. The young girl was sitting close to where those two were butchering. Coyote dipped a finger in the blood and filliped it against the inside of the girl's thighs. Coyote said, "You are not right [clean]. When women are like that they cannot eat meat at all. All the blood will flow out in four days. Then after they wash clean they can eat meat." Then the girl was angry at Coyote because he lied; the blood was not flowing from her. The girl thought, "I am not old enough for this to happen. Perhaps Coyote dislikes me, since he does this. Perhaps he wants me to go away."

It was not long before she left. Her dog followed as she went toward the west. The dog kept following her. The girl said, "Go back home," but he did not obey. The girl said, "I am going to visit someone. I am only going because I am angry. Perhaps I will become thirsty and starve, and then die." But the dog would not return. So she tore off part of her labia minora and rubbed it on the tip of the dog's nose. That is why a dog's nose is black. The dog felt glad and went off home.

She traveled along but could not find any water. She thrust a gaming die (*sa'a'k*) deep into the wash in the bottom of the little canyon. When she withdrew it quickly, water gushed out. This she drank. She made this spring to drink from; then she went on. When she became thirsty again she did the same thing with another die, making another spring. The first spring she made she named Hagogo'θpa and the people were not to forget the name. The second spring she named Hagadjaha'dova. She went on. When she was thirsty again she used a third die. When she pulled it out, the water ran out. She stood and watched it run a while, thinking, "What name shall I call it?" She stood thinking for a time; then she called it Hagasik^uwa'lva. She traveled on and she became thirsty again. She made another spring with her last die. "This spring is the last I will make, so I will call it Hanyame'gaθavadi.'"

She went a little way and found many people in their houses. She stayed there in the house of an old woman. A man saw her and told all the other men, "I wonder where that girl is from. She is a good-looking girl. Perhaps she comes alone from another country and would like to be married. I think we might try to marry her. Everybody must come to that place, and each man in turn can go to see the girl. Perhaps she would like to take one of you men for a husband." They said they would try that plan. The first man went close to the girl, but she did not like him, so he returned. Then another went. All the birds and animals tried and were refused, until only Quail was left. Quail rubbed charcoal on a rock and smeared it around the margins of his face with his finger. He also added some white and set off to try his fortune with the girl. The girl looked at his face and said, "That is a fine-looking man. Now I will take this one," and grasping his hand announced him as her husband.

After a short time the girl was pregnant and gave birth to a boy from the hollow at the back of her wrist. His mother told the boy to rise early in the morning and run toward the place where the skylight begins. "If you do this, you will learn to run fast and win races." So the boy did as he was bid. By and by he had grown large. The girl told him, "I do not belong to these people here. I am a girl from another country. I left your maternal grandfather over there at our home. I want you to go over to see him." The boy made himself some arrows, placed them in a quiver, and started back in the direction from which his mother had come.

When he was halfway back, he found a number of women, but no men were camping with them. They were gathering piñon nuts and yucca. The women said to the boy, "We lost a boy; are you he?" The boy answered, "No, I am not a boy; I am a man," and he stayed at the women's camp. The women ground piñon nuts and boiled yucca, and gave them to the boy. He laughed and said, "Is that piñon nut gruel used to grease moccasins?" and he put it on his moccasins to grease them. He asked, "Is this boiled soapweed used to wash hair?" and he rubbed it in his hair. The boy carried provisions with him. He said, "I do not understand if these things are intended for food; I have cornmeal with me." He gave each woman a handful of his cornmeal. The women said, "That is not good to eat. People use that only to mark their faces. We do not like it," and they threw it away. The boy was angered at them, but they were not afraid of him because he was so small. They made sport of him and laughed. The boy said, "I am too small; you are not afraid of me. But I am going to kill all you women." So he killed them all with his club. He skinned them, and butchered them, making mountain sheep meat of them, which he heaped in a pile.

He carried a little along with him and found a group of men. He told these coyote men, "I killed a lot of mountain sheep back a way and piled it all in one place." So the coyote men went right after the meat and brought it on their backs to their homes. Every man tasted it. Buzzard said, "The kind of meat I find out in this country tastes good. This does not taste right. I think it tastes like man-meat. Maybe he killed our women. I dreamed that boy killed our women." He continued, "We want some boy or man to run right away to see if our women were killed." Then one ran over to where the women had been, but they were all gone. So he came back and told the men that they had been killed. The men wanted to kill the boy. Each got his bow and went close to where the boy was sitting. As the first man shot, the boy moved a little so that the arrow flew by. He did the same as each one shot, so that they could not kill him. The boy said, "You are not going to kill me. I will jump up and run away. You cannot catch me." He jumped a short distance off and ran into the woods. The men ran after him, but he ran fast so that they could not catch him, so they abandoned the pursuit. The boy escaped and went on to his grandfather's home, where he stayed. His grandfather did not go out to hunt, but remained at home with the boy. So he lived there working for his grandfather, and the two were squirrels.

| NOTE |

1. Told by Sinyella; interpreted by Jess Chickapanega, 1919.

26. Rock Squirrel's Grandson (second version)[1]

ROCK SQUIRREL AND COYOTE, HIS NEPHEW, CAMPED SOME-where near Williams. Rock Squirrel always hunted deer and brought them to camp. Rock Squirrel had a baby girl, but there was no woman there. Perhaps they were dead or had run away. Coyote took care of the child while Rock Squirrel went hunting. Rock Squirrel had a white dog who stayed home with the baby.

Coyote cut up the deer Rock Squirrel brought home. Rock Squirrel's child grew up and helped Coyote. Coyote took some blood in his hand and threw it on the girl's thighs. "Oh, my sister, you are ill," Coyote said to the little girl. She got angry at Coyote and just lay down. Coyote said, "My sister, I want you to get up and do work around here." She became angry.

In the morning she went away, the dog with her. When she got tired, she lay down in the shadow of some trees. She sent the dog back. She said, "I think my brother Coyote does not like me. I am not a big girl to be ill, I eat meat up; that is why he sent me away." She started to walk along and the dog went with her. It would not go home. She always sent the dog back, but he would not leave her. "My brother does not like me. I will not go back to our camp again." She started on again and pretty soon the sun went down. She said, "My dog, I want you to go home; I do not want to go home. My brother does not like me. You go back home." She had nothing to eat; she was very hungry. She went on and said, "My dog, I want you to go back. I do not know the road and I do not know where a water hole is. I may die here myself. I want you to go back." She went on further and then she stopped and said to the dog, "I am going to die somewhere. But I will give you something." Then she cut off her vulva and rubbed it on the dog's nose. The dog ran back. The sun went down and she slept somewhere.

The next morning she went on, but her mouth was dry. She had nothing to eat or to drink. In the afternoon she lay down under the trees. She had a tibia of a wildcat (*sa'a'k*, dice?) hanging on her belt. She stuck it into the ground. After a while the water came out and she drank it. After she drank the water she started to go on. She said, "I name this spring 'Water That Laughs' (Ahaga'djiha'diva)."

She went on and slept somewhere; the next day she went until the sun went down. She slept and the next morning, after she had gone a long way, she got water again. But all this while she had nothing to eat. She called this water 'Water That Talks' (Aha'jadjigaθo'va), and she drank that water. She went on until she saw water somewhere. She drank that and did not have to make water. She went where the sun goes down. She saw many Indians camped there far off. She went over there and came to the first camp. The Indians saw the girl and said, "Some girl has run away from her husband."

They made fire a little way off, and they all came over to see her. They all wanted to marry her, but she did not like them, and so they did not get her. Quail was the only one who had not come. Toward morning the Indians said, "She does not like any of us; you try her." "Maybe she will not like me. You are good Indians and she does not like you. She will not like me." But he painted himself and went over to where the girl sat. She sat with her head down, but was not asleep. He slipped down near her, and she jumped up and caught him. She married Quail. They camped a way off, and she had a baby boy.

The child grew very fast. His mother said, "I am not from here. I came a long way. I want you to go see your grandfather." But the boy pretended not to listen; he just played around with the children. Then he came back and lay on his rabbit skin blanket. In the morning he put sticks under his blanket so that it looked as though he were under it, and he went off to see his grandfather. In the morning his mother took a stick and said, "I told you to go to see your grandfather but you do not mind me." She hit the blanket with the stick. Then she saw that he was gone and she said, "Oh, where has he gone?"

He started to go. He said, "I want to beat my arrow." He shot his arrow and ran after it. The arrow stuck in the ground and the boy beat it. He shot another and beat that. Every one he shot he beat running. And he left all of the arrows where he had shot them. He had one arrow left with feathers of *mannii'n*.² "I will run with this one," the boy said. Then he shot the arrow and started to run. This time the arrow beat the boy. "You are the best one I have," he said.

The boy became very thirsty as he went along. He looked for water and found some. When he tried to drink it the water cried, "*Aha'gudjigaθo'va*." Every time he tried to drink the water, it cried out. "I should like to drink water, but you are not water; you are the same as an Indian," he said. Four times he started to drink, and each time the water cried out. Then he took a rock and threw it into the water's mouth and it cried out no more. Then he drank the water and went on. After two days he wanted to drink again. He saw water which he tried to drink. The water began to laugh. He did not drink it; he sat back and looked at it. He tried again to drink it and it laughed again. It laughed that way four times, and again he took a stone and threw it into the mouth. It stopped laughing and he drank the water.

He started to go again. He went along and found the road, and again he had no water. He saw tracks that looked like women's tracks. Then he saw a fire burning where someone camped. He stood still and saw four women camping there. They saw the boy. They said, "Oh, the little boy has run away. Maybe he will die." They ran after the boy and brought him to their camp. They were picking piñon nuts and were roasting them in the fire. After a while when the sun went down they cooked the dried seeds of soapweed and gave it to him to eat. They gave him some piñon nuts, but he rubbed them on his moccasins. He took the mush and poured it over his head, saying, "We do not eat that; we wash our heads with it." When he did this the girls laughed. They said, "What are you going to eat? You will get hungry." He took some corn and ground it. He gave the girls some and they said, "That is not to eat; that is to paint our faces." They laughed all the time.

When the sun went down, the girls all slept together. The boy stayed by the fire and slept there. The girls said they had come a long way to camp there to get piñon nuts. In the daylight the boy woke and listened to the girls sleeping. He went over and tied their hair together. He came back and lay down on his bed again. He slept and woke up again. He sat up and talked to the girls. "Wake up. I thought you had to get piñon nuts. You sleep too long. When it gets hot piñon pitch is soft and you will get dirty. In the morning it is very hard. Get up. You sleep too long." Then they tried to get up, but their hair was tied together, and they tried to pull apart. They laughed and said, "That little boy played with us."

They always laughed. The little boy got angry at the girls because they always laughed. He said, "I will kill you because you always laugh." He went over with a stick, hit them all on the head, and killed them. He cut their heads off and hid them in the trees. Then he cut them open and took out their internal organs, packed them on his back, and went to the camp where the girls had come from. He saw the Indians' camp. He went to the place where Coyote lived. He roasted his things there in the fire and ate them, giving some to the Indians. The boy said, "I killed mountain sheep over there. I put their meat up a tree and brought only the fat." Coyote said, "I am going after the meat." Asa'³ said, "That tastes like Indian meat to me. You go see what he killed. That is not mountain sheep."

Coyote ran as fast as he could after the meat. "My uncle killed some mountain sheep. But Asa' said that it was Indian meat." Coyote found the meat and carried it on his back. He said to himself, "I should like to see the horns." He put down his pack and hunted around for them. He could not find them, but he saw many little ants going up a tree. He followed them and found the girls' heads up in the tree. When he saw them he ran back and vomited when he thought of eating Indian meat. He ran back as fast as he could and he called the Indians. "Asa, Asa, *sagwala gasa'k*. He killed all your daughters." He ran through the camp calling this. "He killed them when they were picking piñon nuts."

The Indians tried to kill the little boy. They threw stones and sticks, but he jumped away, and they could not hit him. Coyote ran after him with a stick, saying, "I will kill him pretty quick." Coyote tried to kill him, but he jumped away. After a while the boy said, "Why do you Indians play with me? I will jump away from you." He jumped up in the air and landed out beyond the camp. He ran as fast as he could. The Indians ran after him and almost caught him. He made himself a soft ball (*gogo'da*) so that the wind carried him along. Then he appeared as a boy again and ran until he came close to his grandfather's camp.

He saw a man chasing deer. He stood behind a tree and listened. His grandfather ran after the deer and the dog was with him. He said to the dog, "Go on, my dog (*nyaaht'a bahu'*)." The boy saw the deer coming by so he shot and killed it. The dog ran over to him and the boy killed the dog. Rock Squirrel came running over to the deer and looked around, but he saw nobody because the little boy had hidden himself. "Who killed my dog? I wonder who did that? I should like to see the one who did that." Rock Squirrel got angry and said, "I will try to make the ground crack and you will fall in dead." He did not see the Indian; he just said this to himself. The boy came out of hiding. He stood there and spoke. "I came over here. I do not know you, but my mother sent me over here to see my grandfather who lives where the sun comes up. I do not know what kind of an Indian he is." Rock Squirrel said, "Oh my *akʷ'*," and embraced him.

Then the boy and his grandfather butchered the deer. Rock Squirrel took a small piece of meat and gave it to the little boy, saying, "You hold the meat and stand there. I will make the dog wake up." He kicked the dog three times in different directions, and the fourth time the dog jumped up. He got angry and tried to kill the boy. It ran after him and the boy threw the meat to the dog. When the dog ate the meat, he grew glad to see the boy and licked him. They took the meat and went back to where Rock Squirrel camped. They took the meat over to Coyote. Rock Squirrel said, "I did not kill the deer but my grandchild did." Coyote was very glad to cook it.

Rock Squirrel started to hunt again the next morning. He said, "My grandchild, you and the dog stay home. I want to take Coyote with me to hunt deer. Coyote has good eyes; he can see deer. My eyes are not good." Then he went away, saying to Coyote, "You look for deer with big horns. I will kill them." Coyote looked around and said, "There are great big deer lying on the ground." Rock Squirrel said, "Those are not deer; those are mountain sheep. When you see deer you show them to me and I will kill them. Deer have great big horns." When Coyote saw mountain sheep, he always said, "There is deer." But Rock Squirrel would not kill them and they went along. The Rock Squirrel saw a deer. He showed it to Coyote, saying, "That is what I call deer." Coyote said, "Yes, I see that; it has many horns." Rock Squirrel said, "You sit here and watch me. I will go pretty close and then shoot my arrow."

Rock Squirrel went after a deer and shot it. It was dead after a while. Coyote walked all around the deer and was very glad. Rock Squirrel sat down and put on his moccasins. "My nephew," he said, "I want you to hurry and cut him up, and take off the skin." "What is that white thing hanging on him?" Coyote [asked]. "That is what you eat when I bring it home," Rock Squirrel said. "And what is this?" he asked. Rock Squirrel said, "Stop your talking. You might cut it out. That is what you pound, and you eat it." Coyote said, "What is that?" pointing to the hoof. "You know that," Rock Squirrel said. But Coyote did not cut; he just stood and talked. "What is that?" Coyote said, pointing to the eyes. "You know that; you eat it," said Rock Squirrel. Then Coyote pointed to the ears and said, "What is that?" Then Rock Squirrel got up and took the knife and started to cut. Coyote said, "It might get up and run away from us."

Rock Squirrel went on cutting. Suddenly the deer got up and ran away because Coyote talked too much. Coyote and Rock Squirrel ran after it. Rock Squirrel said, "You did that." They ran and ran after the deer. The deer ran as fast as he could, and Rock Squirrel ran close to the deer, but when Coyote got tired, he went back. The deer ran into a big Indian camp where the Indians killed it. Rock Squirrel ran by them and tried to shoot with his arrow again. The arrow hit the deer on the breast and bounced off. It did not kill it.

Then Rock Squirrel ran back and the Indians shot at him. The Indians said to the man who shot at Rock Squirrel, "Why did you not get close and kill him?" They shouted, "Enemy (*itcahua'*)," to Rock Squirrel. They tried to kill him, but Rock Squirrel stood and shot with his arrows at the Indians. He killed some. "You stand there, and we will kill you and paint ourselves with your blood," they called to Rock Squirrel. The Indians called to Rock Squirrel, "Wigateai'a."

Rock Squirrel said, "My grandchild will come and kill you." After a while his grandchild came with the dog. Then Rock Squirrel was very glad to see him and said, "They nearly killed me and ate me up." But his grandchild and the dog killed the Indians. The dog bit their legs and when they ran away from the dog, the boy hit them with a stick. They killed all the Indians. Then Rock Squirrel, the boy, and the dog went back to their own camp and sat down. The boy never went back to see his mother, but stayed with his grandfather.

| NOTES |

1. Told by Manakadja; interpreted by Lillie Burro; recorded by E. G., 1921.
2. Not translated.
3. Bird, eagle?

27. The Man on the Ledge (first version)[1]

A NUMBER OF PEOPLE WERE GATHERING WILD *SILE'E* SEEDS on the plateau. One man said, "The eagle's nest is halfway down the white cliff, but the cliff is smooth and there is no way down. Get yucca leaves, mash them, and tie them together to form a long rope. Tie the rope around me and lower me so I can get an eaglet. We can keep it up here, and when it is big, we can take feathers from its wings for our arrows." They tied the rope around his body and let him down. When he reached the eagle's nest, the people above asked him, "Did you reach there?" He answered, "Yes, I got down here all right." Then those above threw the rope down. The man stayed right there and sang to himself, "What is the matter, that they leave me down here? I was going to get an eaglet, and then they were to pull me up again. Perhaps they do not like me. Now I will have to stay here all the time and perhaps I will die. I did not say anything to those people up there to make them angry. I do not know why they are angry that they should drop the rope. I will have to stay here. I have nothing to eat and no water to drink; only my adult eagles give me something to eat. My feces are white (from eating the same food as the eagles)," he sang. So he sang, "I have two wives. One could grind *sile'e*, or she could fill a little water basket and lower it. She does not do this. I am watching, but no one does this. I did not do anything to them. I thought all was right between us. I think they do not like me and will not help me."

The man stayed there perhaps for a year or a winter. He just lay there all the time. He was sitting on the edge of the ledge and looking directly down at the bottom; there he saw Gila Monster walking along. He sang to him, "I have been here a very long time. I am nearly dead. You are my mother's brother. Look at me up here. I am in a pretty bad way. You know how to get around on this rock. You tell me what to do. I want you to climb up and fetch me down." Gila Monster looked up and said, "How did you get up there? There is no good way up. How did you get there?" That is all he said and then he went home. There he got out his own big pipe and filled it with some tobacco. Then he returned with it, directly below the man on the ledge. The white cliff was smooth. He drew in a big puff and blew it out against the rock. He did this three times but the rock did not crack at all. The fourth time a crack appeared in the wall leading straight to the ledge. Then Gila Monster started to climb up the crack. When he was nearly to the man the crack was so narrow that he got wedged in tight and died.

The man up there waited for the Gila Monster, thinking he would arrive, but he did not come. The man continued to sit in one place on the edge of the ledge. He was seated there when he saw another man walking along down at the base of the cliff. He knew that man; he was related to him. He sang, "My mother's father, Bat, I am talking to you. I want you to come and fetch me down. I have been up here a very long time." Bat said to him, "How did you get up there, where you are talking to me? It is a very high steep wall. How did you get up there? Nobody else can climb up there; how did you climb?" Then he went home to get his pipe and tobacco and his burden basket. Then he returned directly below the man. He flew around, going off this way and returning, flying way up and then down again, but all the time rising higher and higher. After a long time he reached the ledge where the man was sitting right on the edge.

The man said to Bat, "That is what I wanted you to do. I am glad you came up here. I have nothing to give you if you take me down. All I have are my eagle feathers. I pulled all the good plumes from one wing and tied them in a bundle. I will give that to you if you will carry me down." Bat said nothing. The man said, "I will give you more from the other wing." Bat said nothing. He just kept smoking and looking down, not toward the man. The man said, "I do not know which feathers you like. Perhaps if I tie the good tail feathers into a bundle, you will like that." Bat said nothing, but continued smoking. The man said, "Perhaps you want the down from under the eagle's tail feathers. I will just tie the down in one bundle. You can have that." Bat said nothing; he just kept smoking. The man up there began to sing, "I thought you would like either the wing or tail feathers, or the down, and then carry me down below. I have nothing beside these; that is all I have. I thought you would take the down of which I spoke and stick it in the center of your hair." Bat looked as though he did not hear. He sat turned away and went on smoking. The man said, "I have nothing more to say. My eagle has only pin feathers left. Maybe you would like these. See if you like them. That is all I have left." Bat turned around to look at them and said, "He'he, that looks pretty good. That is what I want. They are pretty good for me." Then he put them all over his body. He has those all over his body now.

Bat said, "It is all right now. I am ready to take you down. If you have any belongings, bring them here, and we will put them in the bottom of my burden basket." The man had feathers, one bundle of each kind. He gave them to Bat, who put them in the bottom of the basket. Then the man lay in the basket. Bat said, "I will fly with you. I will fly down slowly." Bat told the man that he should keep his eyes tightly shut when he lay in the basket. He did not want him to open them to see how he was flying. "I think that if you tire of keeping your eyes shut and open them, something will happen," Bat said. "You close your eyes while I am flying and when we get to the bottom I will say 'All right' and then you can open them." The man said, "All right," and lay down in the basket. Then Bat flew off. Bat flew about; he did not go straight down, but flew from side to side, down and then up again, every which way, flying high and coming down; a long way this way and that. The man kept his eyes closed as he lay there, until after a long time he tired of it. Bat kept getting lower little by little, until he was nearly to the bottom. The man lying in the basket was tired. He thought, "I wonder where Bat is going. I am going to try opening my eyes so that I can see where he is going." So he opened his eyes, and then Bat and he fell tumbling over and over. Bat was broken to pieces, and was nearly killed. He was unconscious (*k^redjimpi'g*, a little dead). The man mended him, putting the broken parts together and plastering them with scarf skin (*martinya'a*) from his own body. Then they went off together to Bat's house.

The man stayed at Bat's house for a long time, about a winter. He ate Bat's food until he was in good condition, fat and strong, and he had been before. Then he said, "Prepare provisions for me so that I can carry them with me." They prepared the food and the man set out. He went to the place where his people's camp had been. The houses were all very old, rotted, and tumbled down. When he got there, he sang, "I wonder where they all went." He had some little soft feathers from the eagle with him. He sang, "I will blow them away and they will go in the direction those people went; then I will follow them." So he tried blowing the down toward the north, but it did not go. It merely dropped to the ground. He picked it up and blew it off again to the west, but it did not go. It just dropped the same way. He picked it up and blew it away again to the south, but the same thing happened. He picked it up again and blew it off toward the east. Now the down kept on going, moving off a little south of east. The man said, "You [the chief of those people] are my male cross cousin, *itcawahogagana'ma* [enemy—?, and insect; the walking stick?]. I know the men who let me down to my eagle's place feel glad. They talked and went away. I will just keep following wherever they went." The down could tell whatever the people were doing. At one place they had had a dance with a pole set in the middle. The down could tell what they had been doing there. It circled all around this place, and then it returned to the place where he stopped to camp, and told the man. The down found the camps where the people had been using light flat stones for pillows. The down felt glad for the man. When the chief of those people was lying down, he put his head on a rock set on edge and when he nodded the rock toppled so that he woke up. So he did not get to sleep until morning. Every time he woke he thought, "Maybe that man who was down in the eagle's nest got out and is coming to kill us."

The man, Hod'iyu', followed the people a long way. It took one winter, and then the tracks and camps became more distinct. By and by the tracks showed that it was only a month or two since the people had left. The man said to himself, "I will be glad to get to those people," and he continued to follow. "Their tracks are fresh now," he said, "I know my two wives' tracks. They are traveling along behind the other people." He followed until he got up to where their campfires were still burning. "They moved on only a little while ago," he said. "I will catch up with them today." He kept on and then he saw his two wives a short distance away. One was carrying a baby boy in her burden basket. The boy was looking back and saw the men coming. The boy said, "*ta'ta* (father)," and the women said to the boy, "*manyamitau'a* (that is your father) *asanyawa'vil* (eagle's nest) *gu'da* (long ago) *θel* (the place) *pim* (where he died) *vokowa'vig'iu* (we are traveling along)." The boy kept on saying, "*ta'ta'ta, ta'ta'ta*." By and by he began to jounce the edge of the burden basket, laughing at his father. But the two women did not look back; they kept on going. The boy continued talking and laughing until one of the women stopped and looked back to where the man was following close behind. One of the women said, "Yes, his father is coming," so they stopped for the man to reach them.

The man asked them, "Are there many people ahead of you? How far are they going before they will camp and wait for you to come in?" The women said, "It is not a long way, just a little way, until they will stop and camp. As they travel the young men are scattered killing rabbits, traveling ahead of the people. They kill a great many and take them where they are going to camp, and wait until the old people, old women and children come. When nearly sunset a couple of men dig a big hole and put plenty of wood in it. On this they pile stones, then they burn it to roast their rabbits, keeping it going all night. When it is nearly daylight, the head chief calls to all the women to go and dig out the roasted rabbits. Some men go along with them. The men wait at that place when the women come to dig away the dirt, trying to get what they want. Then the men pull them away by the shoulder, or by their belts, which break, so that the women cannot get any rabbits. If a woman's belt is strong it does not break, and she can get plenty of them. They always act this way about daylight. We do not get any rabbits at all." The man said, "All right." The man had some deer back-tendons. He blew on them to moisten them, and rolled them on his thigh into big ropes. He gave these to the women to wear for belts. Then he said, "All right, go on to where the others have made a camp. Do not make your camp too close, just a little way from the others. I will stay here until sunset. Then, when it is a little dark, I will come to where you camp." Then the women went on, while the man stayed there. When the sun went down the man went to the place where the two women had made camp. Then he slept with the women.

About daylight the head chief called to the people as he always did. All the women came together to get some rabbits. The men again tried to tear away their belts and throw them away, but this time they could not break them. So both women got plenty of rabbits and brought them to their camp. Some of the women whose dresses could not be torn open got all the rabbits and carried them away. The men who tried to break the belts of the two women said, "We wonder why we did not tear those women's dresses off. Perhaps Hod'iyu' is here.

We want one of the boys to run over to those two women's camp to see if that man is there." So a boy ran over to look at the camp. The man was still lying in bed, with a big white blanket, made of soft eagle down, over him. The boy ran back to the old people and told them, "Yes, Hod'iyu' is there."

Then the head chief said, "I want all the men, the young men, the old men, and the boys, to go out and hunt more rabbits. Coyote should take a brand and build a small fire a little way off. Then men should go there a few at a time until they are all there, and then all should go to hunt rabbits." So Coyote said, "All right." He got a little brand and carried it to where he was going to build a fire. Then he waited until all came. Everyone went, except Hod'iyu', who stayed at his camp. He said to himself, "I will go with them to hunt rabbits, too." So he went. He was the last man to arrive. All the old people were where Coyote had built the fire. Hod'iyu' came to the top of a little hill. Then he talked down to them, looking along his rabbit stick. "My rabbit stick is somewhat bent. I want to try throwing it just a little way from you people. Perhaps I can hit the spot," he said. "I do not want you men over there to be afraid. If you are afraid, I might hit one of you. I want all of you to move far away from the spot at which I want to throw my rabbit stick. Just stand altogether in one place," he said. All the men did this. They all stood together in one place. The man feinted at throwing at the spot he spoke of. Then he turned and threw it at the men, knocking them all down. Some had arms and legs broken; these were still alive. So he went around, hitting them on the head, and killed them all.

After he killed all the men, he went back to the camp, and killed all the women. He was so angry, he killed everyone. He said, "I am so angry that I killed all the people. I want both of my women to drag one of those dead women over to my camp and butcher her, and cook the meat so that I can eat it." The man ate a lot of it, and then told his wives to fetch more, so he ate a lot of them, until by and by his belly grew very big, filled up very tight. Finally, he said, "That will be enough. I feel as though I were going to defecate. I want one of my wives to walk on my right side and the other on my left, and lift me over to the edge of the cliff. I want to sit down there and defecate over the edge." So the women tried to do this, but he was too heavy. They could not pull him along very fast. So the man said that his boy would have to help the women, saying, "Let my boy push my back."

So the boy pushed him and they got to the edge of the cliff. When the man was near the edge, he said, "I want to be right at the very edge." The women were standing on each side of him at the edge, when he fell over and pulled both women and the boy along with him. All were killed by the fall. Then the man said, "I will be a star-man. I killed a lot of men, then I fell off the cliff. Now I will go up in the sky and be a star. If people are ever alive again, when I am a star and come out they will call me Hod'iyu'."

| NOTES |

1. Told by Sinyella; interpreted by Jess Chickapanega, 1919.

28. The Man on the Ledge (second version)[1]

MANY INDIANS CAMPED SOMEWHERE. THEY ALWAYS HUNTED rabbit and jackrabbit. One man was the only one who killed some every day. The Indians did not like him. "He is no good," they said. "He gets everything." The other Indians could catch nothing at all. "What shall we do with Hod'iyu'? He kills every day when we get nothing. We would like to kill him."

Hod'iyu' had an eagle up on the rocks. The Indians let Hod'iyu' down to the nest to get feathers. They said, "This man is no good. We do not want to pull him back up here. We will just leave him down there with his eagle." Hod'iyu' wanted the Indians to pull him up but they did not want to. A little snake bit the rope through so that Hod'iyu' fell down into the eagle's nest. The Indians went home and told Hod'iyu''s wives, "We are very sorry for him. The rope broke and he fell into the nest."

Hod'iyu' lay down near the eagle's nest. The Indians were afraid that he would come up so they moved away. Hod'iyu''s wives went with the Indians. Hod'iyu' stayed with the eagle a long time, perhaps two years. Hod'iyu' lay down near the nest while the eagle went away hunting for rabbits and jackrabbits. When the eagle came home he fed the little eagles. Hod'iyu' took some meat and ate it. Hod'iyu' was always hungry and he was very sick.

Bat and Maθu'l[2] camped somewhere away from the Indians, where they hunted rabbits. As Bat flew around he heard Hod'iyu' in the eagle's nest. Hod'iyu' saw Maθu'l and Bat walking down below. He said, "My grandfather, I want you to get me out of this eagle's nest. I do not know why the Indians were angry with me and left me here with the eagle. I want you to get me out." When Bat and Maθu'l arrived at their camp, Bat said, "I do not know what kind of man is there in the eagle's nest. He called me 'grandfather.' He wants me to take him out. He is your younger brother's son. We must help him." Then Maθu'l said, "All right, we will go." He saw the man up in the nest. He made a fire by the rocks. Hod'iyu' saw them below and said, "I want you to take me down." He was not related to them; he just wanted to be taken down. Then they said, "All right, we will fetch you down."

Bat said to Maθu'l, "You try to go up to get him first, and if you cannot, I will try." Then Maθu'l started to go. He filled his pipe and smoked it, standing by the rocks. He blew the smoke up along the rock. The rock cracked all the way up to where Hod'iyu' lay. Maθu'l had made a road with the smoke in which he started to climb. He came close to where Hod'iyu' was, where there was only a little crack, through which Maθu'l could not climb. He tried several times but he could not do it, so he came down again. Then Hod'iyu' said, "I want you to take me down." He was very thin, for he had no water to drink, just the meat that the eagle had brought.

When Maθu'l came back, Bat said he would try if he could get the man. Hod'iyu' said, "I want you to take me down. You are an old relative of mine." Bat started. He smoked tobacco the way Maθu'l had. Bat took a whole basket of tobacco. He started to climb up. He flew from rock to rock instead of going along the road he [Maθu'l] had made, and climbed very easily to where Hod'iyu' lay. Bat was very tired and he breathed hard. He sat down by Hod'iyu'. Hod'iyu' was so sick he could not get up but just lay there. He said, "I do not know how you can get me down. I cannot stand. I am very sick; that is why I wanted you to come and get me." Bat said, "All right, I am here to take you down. I will put you in my basket." Hod'iyu' had many different kinds of eagle feathers which he put in the basket first. Bat tried to put Hod'iyu' in the basket, but Hod'iyu' said, "It might break. I am afraid." So Bat put some big rocks in his basket and jumped around with them. Hod'iyu' saw that they did not break the basket. Then Bat put Hod'iyu' in the basket and said, "When I put you in the basket, I will carry you on my back. I do not want you to open eyes. Shut them just as if you were asleep. If you open them, it will be very bad."

Bat put Hod'iyu' on his back and started to go down. He flew from rock to rock. Hod'iyu' shut his eyes, lying in the basket. He became frightened: "Maybe he will harm me." He wanted to see, so he opened his eyes when they were just a short distance from the ground, and they fell down. Bat broke his wing a little. Hod'iyu' lay on his feathers in the basket and was not hurt. When they fell down Maθu'l came to see them. Bat said, "I told him to keep his eyes shut, and he minded me until we were near the ground. Then he opened his eyes, and I fell down and broke my wing. You sing for me; cure me (*djewi'ga*)." So Maθu'l rubbed Bat's wing and made it well.

They brought Hod'iyu' over to the fire. He said, "I do not know what to give you. I have nothing to give but my eagle fathers. You may have them." He had different kinds of little feathers. He gave them to Bat, but Bat did not want them; he wanted the best ones. Hod'iyu' offered Bat some other feathers, but Bat did not take them. Hod'iyu' said, "I do not know what you want. I have nothing but the feathers to give you." Then he gave him some other feathers. He gave him some down. Bat liked these. Hod'iyu' gave Maθu'l and Bat each half of his feathers.

Maθu'l carried Hod'iyu' over to his own camp. Maθu'l carried him now because Bat had brought him down from the rocks. Maθu'l cooked meat for Hod'iyu', but Hod'iyu' could not keep food in his stomach. Bat fixed him up and made him well. Hod'iyu' looked well again. Bat and Maθu'l went hunting every morning. Hod'iyu' went hunting and killed deer and rabbits. He got a great many just as when the Indians tried to kill him. Bat and his wife said to Hod'iyu', "The Indians that left you in the eagle's nest all moved away and your wives went too." Hod'iyu' did not talk to them; he just stayed there. Bat and Maθu'l tanned buckskin for Hod'iyu'. Then Hod'iyu' made himself clothes, everything that he needed. When he had made his clothes, he said, "I would like to go to my camp to see if my wives are still living. I want to go and see the Indians." Bat and Maθu'l said, "All right, you may go, but there is no one at your camp now. They all moved away." Hod'iyu' said, "When I go to the camp and see they are gone, I will follow until I find them. I will not come back here again."

He went to look at his camp but it was not there. He looked around but did not see his house. He did not see the tracks, so he decided to go where he thought they had gone. He slept in his old camp. He went along in the morning hunting rabbits and roasting them at night where he slept. He killed rabbits with his rabbit stick (*baloava*). He had arrows but did not use them. He went along for a few days and slept late until the sun was up in the sky. The next day he went on and found a nice place to sleep. He said, "I do not want to leave here." The next morning he went on and saw some new tracks and a new house. The twigs were all green and not yet dry, and the fires were fresh. He slept there. The next morning he went on and found the Indians' tracks. He put his hand on the ashes and found them warm. "They left here just this morning," he said. "I want to see the Indians." But he did not go; he slept there. Next morning when he started to go he thought, "I do not want to sleep now; I just want to keep on." He saw where they had camped and found the fire still burning. "I will keep on and see where they are trying to go," he said to himself. He ran along until the sun began going down. Now he saw the Indians. There were two women walking along. Hod'iyu' walked behind the trees. "Whose women are those?" he said to himself. "Why, they look like my wives!"

He walked fast. When he came close to them, he walked slowly and saw that one had a baby in her basket. The baby said, "Da, da." The woman said, "Your father is not here; your father is dead." But the baby said, "Da, da; da, da." "No, your father is not here. Your father was thrown down to the eagle. He is dead," the woman said. But the little baby always said "Papa." Its mother said, "Your father is dead. That is why we left our camp." Then his mother turned around and saw the man coming. She said to the other woman, "Oh, here he is coming. That is why the baby says 'papa' all the time." The other woman turned around and saw him too.

They both sat down, and Hod'iyu' sat with them. He asked them, "Where are you going? You go a long way. I wonder where you Indians are going. Why are you Indians moving such a long distance?" But the women said nothing. Then Hod'iyu' asked again. "They are afraid. That is why they run away." Hod'iyu' said, "Who are they afraid of? Nobody here did anything to the Indians. I have come a long way and I am very tired. Are they afraid of me because they put me in the eagle's nest?" "Maybe they are afraid of you," the women said. Then Hod'iyu' asked again, "What are you going to do? Where are you going? What are you going to eat, and where do you sleep?" The women told him, "The Indians told us to make our fire as we go along. They do not go along the road, but hunt and kill many rabbits and jackrabbits, and find much mescal." Hod'iyu' said, "Do they give you something to eat?" The women said, "I went over to get some and put it in my basket. When I got up they took it away because my belt was

torn and I could not get up. They gave me nothing to eat." Hod'iyu'
said, "Oh, I thought they gave you something to eat. I will fix up an
apron for you. Why did they get angry with you and treat you so?"

Hod'iyu' camped away from the women, who went along with the
Indians. He told them to camp a short way from the Indians and said
he would come to them after dark. When the sun was going down,
Hod'iyu' heard the Indians making much noise. When it was dark he
went to his wives' camp and lay down. He said, "In the morning I
want you to go over and get something to eat where they are roasting
things. I do not think they can tear your belt again." Hod'iyu' asked
if the Indians came to them, but the women said, "No, we stay here
all alone. We have stayed alone all the way along."

In the daytime the women went over to where they were roasting and put a rabbit and a jackrabbit in her basket. The women tried
to break her belt but they could not do it this time. She took plenty,
and the Indian women said, "Oh, what makes her belt so strong? We
cannot break it." Then the Indian women sent for the Indian boys
and said, "Maybe Hod'iyu' has come and fixed her belt. That is why
she takes the meat." The boys ran over to the women's camp and saw
Hod'iyu' lying on his bed. They ran back and told their people. They
all heard the news. They did not talk again until their big chief said,
"Well, Hod'iyu' has come now. We will not move, but will camp here.
You go and hunt rabbits and jackrabbits, and do just what you always
do." The Indians went about a half mile and made a fire.

The boys came to Hod'iyu''s camp and said, "The Indians are
going to hunt rabbits, and they want you to hunt with them." "All
right, I will go along," said Hod'iyu'. All of the Indians were over
where the fire was, but Hod'iyu' remained in his camp. He asked the
women of the Indians, "The men are all gone?" "Yes," they said.
Hod'iyu' said, "All right, I will go over there too." The women saw the
buckskin Hod'iyu' wore. He looked fine, so they all said, "M-m-m, he
looks fine." As he went along he tried his rabbit stick, breaking trees
and things to pieces with it. "That might kill something," he said.

Hod'iyu' was very angry with the Indians. He saw the fire of the
Indians. He talked to them, saying, "I want to try my rabbit stick.
You all stand together so that I will not hit you. I have not hunted for
a long time. Just lie down." Then he threw his stick, threw right at
them, and hit every one of them. Some of them were not yet dead, so
he ran over and hit them again. Every one of them died. "I am angry

with you Indians; that is why I cut you down," he said to himself. He went back to the camp and killed all of the women there. Some ran away, but he went after them, and killed every woman and all of the children. He left only his own wives and the baby.

Then he went back to his wives' camp and said, "I do not know why they left me down in the eagle's nest. I was very angry with the Indians and killed every one because they did that. When Indians kill deer, they eat the meat; so now I have killed the Indians, you cook them for me, and I will eat their meat." The women said, "Why did you do that? We will not eat that meat." Hod'iyu' said, "Do not talk to me. You cook the meat for me." The woman was afraid Hod'iyu' would kill her, so she got the meat and cooked it in a big pot. Hod'iyu' cut it. He ate the meat until he was full and the woman told him to stop. The man said, "You cut the meat small and put it in my mouth with a stick." The woman was afraid but she did it.

He became so full that it came out of his mouth. He lay down and said, "My wife, take me to the top of the rocks so that I can defecate. If I do it here it will smell bad." The women were afraid of him, so they carried him along. One woman carried his head and one his feet, and the little baby walked under his back. "Take me to the top and hang me down. When I am through, lift me back," Hod'iyu' said. They put him on the edge. He said, "I want you to let me hang far down." When he was on the edge, he fell down and pulled his whole family down with him. They were all dead. They became stars. When these stars come out, it becomes very cold and everything freezes. The stars are Cold Star (*hamasigadidi'*).[3]

| NOTES |

1. Told by Manakadja; interpreted by Lillie Burro; recorded by E. G., 1921.
2. "Larger than a lizard"; probably the gila monster.
3. See *Havasupai Ethnography*, p. 167.

29. The Jealous Indians[1]

MANY INDIANS WERE CAMPING SOMEWHERE WHILE AN OLD woman camped a short way from them. She had two boys. The little one went hunting, but the older boy lay around. When the Indians were off hunting, he painted himself and walked around where the women were. The women all liked him. His mother called him Patcikadiwe (Lazy Man) because he was not rich and he had no skins. The little boy hunted for jackrabbits with the Indians. The Indians were angry at the little boy because he always killed so many rabbits. He always got them first. The Indians did not like him. The older boy stayed at home, like a woman. The Indians went away about a mile and made a fire. There were not enough Indians there so they called others to the place where they made the fire. The little boy had not gone when they made the fire, but he started, and on the way caught jackrabbits. The Indians were angry with him. "I do not know what we are going to do with him; he catches all the rabbits and we get none." They wanted to kill him. They put a snake under the bushes and one said to the boy, "I see a pretty thing there; when I take him out he sticks to my hand and washes it." The boy let the snake crawl over his hand and it bit him. He died at once. They killed him because he was so very rich.

When they had killed him, they went hunting. When the sun went down they came back to camp. The woman thought her boy would come home, but he failed to return. Then the woman asked, "Where is my little boy?" "We saw him go along with us but we do not know where he went," they told her. The woman said again, "That is the only boy I have. He, Chicken Hawk (Sogu'ita), is the only one who killed things for me. His big brother is no boy. He is bad; the girls like him. He does nothing for me. I have only one boy who brings me meat." She inquired every day when they came home from hunting, but they did not tell her that he was dead. She went about crying, always asking for him. "I want you to tell me. I am an old woman. I never did anything to you. I want you to tell me truly. I want to know what you Indians did to my boy. He is the only boy I have. I want you to tell me; I am a very old woman." The Indians did not tell her, so she asked Coyote, her brother's son. Coyote said, "All right, my aunt, I will tell you. The Indians started to go hunting. They made a fire. They put a snake under a bush and told that boy to put his finger on it. Then the snake bit and killed him." The woman said, "All right, that is what I wanted to know. Now I have nothing to eat. I have one boy here, but he sleeps too much and he always wants the women. He never goes hunting." The woman said, "Now I want you to tell me truly, who told my boy to pick up the snake?" Coyote told her it was Pagia'mgitcima'dj. She cried and lay down. The Indians moved away from the woman's camp. The woman lay there crying. The big boy did not stay with her, but went with the Indians.

The Indians remained away from the woman for three or four years. Than the woman made herself a dress and robe and started to go after them. She wanted to see them. She slept each night at the place where the Indians had camped and in the daytime she traveled after them. She said to herself, "I am not a man. Why are they afraid and run away from me? I am going to see the Indians. I cannot do anything to them; I am too old." She found old fires of the Indians still burning. She saw them camping ahead, so she went back a little and hid there. She washed herself all over with Indian soap. She dressed up and painted herself. Then she looked like a young girl. She looked very fine. When the sun went down she started for the Indians' camp. When it was getting dark she came to the first camp. The Indians saw the woman and said, "Some woman ran away from her husband and has come here. Oh, she looks pretty fine. I would like to marry her." They all said this. They all came over to see her. When they had gone back to their camp, one Indian, who liked her very much, went to her. He stood there but she would not even look at his feet. He stamped, but she refused to look. She did not like him. Others came, but she did not like any of them. The Indians said, "That girl came here, and we want to marry her, but she does not like us." Pagiamgitcimadj was the chief. He stayed in his camp. They told him to see if the girl liked him. The chief said, "I am not good. You are good and yet she does not like you. Perhaps she will not like me." Daylight came and the Indians said, "You try. Perhaps she will like you." "All right," said the chief. "I will try; perhaps she will." He went where the girl was sitting and stamped on the ground near her. She immediately jumped up and embraced him. The chief took her to his house and lay with her. Then he fell asleep. The girl took out a knife, which she had on a string around her neck, and cut the chief's throat. Then she ran away. The Indians heard a noise and said, "What is the matter? The big chief has a pretty wife." When the woman killed the chief she sang, "That is why I came here, to kill the Indian. I will call him Θiugamodi', just as he called that snake." Then she went back to her own camp and sang, "Θiugamodi' wima, Θiugamodi' wima."

The Indians did not go after her, so she got back to her camp.

| NOTES |

1. Told by Manakadja; interpreted by Lillie Burro; recorded by E. G., 1921.

30. Turkey's Revenge (first version)[1]

TURKEY HAD A WIFE WHO WAS GRINDING GOOSEFOOT SEEDS.
She ground a lot and piled it on the edge of the metate. Turkey felt
very hungry and took a pinch to eat. He did it again and the woman
struck his hand away. "Let it alone," she said. Turkey said, "When
I do this when you are grinding, you always push my hand aside."
Turkey struck the woman, and she cried. She said, "When you were
a little boy, your parents were killed by people of another tribe, the
enemy. You were not killed. You just beat me all the time." (She told
him this because she was angry with him.) Her husband lay down and
thought. He said nothing. By and by the woman finished grinding and
cooking. When everything was ready, she called her husband to eat.
Turkey did not go; he just lay there and thought. He thought, "Maybe
I can go and be an enemy by myself." He thought he would make moccasins, leggings, and shirt to wear. When everything was finished, he
called to the woman, "Barren woman (pik ͬi'giθaai'adj), make provisions for me so that I can go." So she ground some seeds and made
provisions for him. She felt sorry and cried. Turkey said to her, "I will
take everything that I am going to carry and wear back of that hill.
Then I will run back here. I will come back acting as an enemy does.
You look at me. If I look good you say 'all right' and I will go, but if
I do not look good, you say so and I won't go." The man did this and
the woman said, "That is pretty fine; now you can go."

The man set off. He said to himself, "Maybe the place where I
was a little boy is right here. I do not know much about it; maybe this
is the place. Maybe this is where a lot of enemies killed my parents.
I do not know which way they went after they killed so many people
here. The houses here are old and rotted. They are nearly hidden by

weeds. I wonder which way they went back." He had some down with him, so he blew it away toward the north. But it did not fly off; it just dropped down. He blew it toward the west. But it did not fly; it just dropped down. He tried to the south and the down went off, so the man followed it. It kept going and he following, until it came to a very old camp. The head chief of those enemies was Itcahuwa'gagana'ma [enemy?, an insect with long legs: the "walking stick"?); when he was in camp, he pillowed his head on a rock. The down found every camp by means of these rocks. Every time the sun set, Turkey camped with a rock for a pillow too, and he sang, "My cousin, Insect, you went away a very long time ago, but I will not miss you. I will follow right after you. I will keep on your trail, until finally I find you." He sang, "My woman felt angry and told me that my parents were killed by the enemy. She said their names to me,[2] so I feel very angry. She liked to do that. So now I am following the enemy. My down can show me Insect's camp, where he used those stones. He can show me where Insect defecated. So I can sleep on the same stones and defecate in the same places. You, enemy, can go off to another country. You, enemy, can think I cannot find you. But I know every place; wherever you go, I can find you."

Next morning when he wanted to go, he blew his down, and the down followed the direction the enemy had taken. Turkey said, "Insect, you are head chief of many people; you keep going, but I keep following. At the place where you camp you make a dance ground and set up a post. There are a few traces of it which I can see. I keep following to the south." Every morning he sang, "I keep following you, enemy. Pretty soon I will find you, and I am going to kill every one of you. You have not much longer to live." The enemies' tracks began to appear a little plainer. The next morning he went on again and sang. The down went ahead and he followed. He did not see fresh tracks yet. The down went on and after a little way, when it was late afternoon, the down dropped to the ground. Turkey came up to it and saw fresh tracks there. Turkey stopped and looked around cautiously. He traveled on, hiding as he went and looking about him. After a little distance, he saw them and said, "There they are now." He kept into hiding in the bushes until the sun had set.

When it was a little dark Insect stood up to talk, saying, "It is now dark. Everybody, every woman, should come to the dance ground. We are going to dance all night. We do not [?] dance all the time. I thought perhaps that a boy belonging to those people, so many of whom I killed over younger, was grown to manhood and would hunt about for us, and perhaps reach here. All of our people feel glad because we killed so many people; that is why we dance every night." Turkey went close to them and heard all the chief said. The enemy danced that night. Turkey had a long net he carried with him. (I do not know what it was made of.)[3] He carried it four times around the place where they were dancing, enclosing it as in a corral. When it was finished, he sat down to wait for the dawn. Then he went right in where the enemy were. Turkey said, "My cousin, Insect, I am going to kill you first. You are not going to live any longer." Just about daybreak he went straight into their midst, hollering. He killed Insect first. The others ran and scattered, but Turkey had fenced them in, so they could not get away, but went milling around inside. The fence was pretty high; no one could jump out. So Turkey knocked each one down and slew them all. After he had killed all the enemy, Turkey took Insect's belongings and carried them back home where he had left his wife. "That is what you thought you wanted me to do, so I did it. I killed a lot of people," he said.

| NOTES |

1. Told by Sinyella; interpreted by Jess Chickapanega, 1919.
2. ni'djisimai'iga, to hear the name of a dead relative spoken.
3. The Havasupai do not make use of nets.

31. Turkey's Revenge (second version)[1]

A GIRL NAMED IKAΘUAI[a] MARRIED AN INDIAN. THEY CAMPED somewhere. She found some seeds and ground them. Her husband just lay down near the metate and ate the seeds as she ground them. The girl got angry and knocked the boy's hand away. She said, "You have no father and no mother to cook for you, but I feed you every day. The enemy killed your father and mother."

The boy did not answer. He went out and hunted some rabbit and jackrabbits. While he was away the girl cooked something for her husband, but he did not eat it He just lay down and in the morning he went away again. The girl always cooked but her husband would not eat it. For four days this happened. She always threw the food away because it spoiled. Then the boy said, "I thought you used to cook something for me and I ate that. But then you just talked back at me, and told me my father and mother were killed, and I felt very bad. That is why I did not eat your cooking. Now I will go over to the enemy, and see where they camp. You told me I did not kill them." He made pants, shirt, and moccasins, and a net (*saf'koba*).

He started to go to see where the enemy camped. He went by and saw many Indians there. He went away and lay down. When daylight came he went out and set a big net all around the enemy camp. He stood by the door and when they came out he hit them on the head with a stick. The enemy tried to run away by climbing over the fence, but they could not do it. He killed all those Indians when they came out. When he had killed them all, he went back. He thought, "I do not want to sleep here. I will go over to my wife's camp in one day and not sleep on the way."

He started to run as fast as he could. He hit his wife's house with his stick. His wife flew right out and fell down somewhere. He was very angry. Then he saw his wife lying over there. When she woke up, he said, "Did you hear what I did? That is what you wanted me to do. I want to kill you, but I will not. I just woke you up. You talk bad to me."

| NOTES |

1. Told by Manakadja; interpreted by Lillie Burro; recorded by E. G., 1921.

32. Snake's Exploits[1]

THERE WERE MANY INDIANS CAMPING TOGETHER. THEY WENT to fight their enemy. Snake, who wanted to go with the Indians, said to Coyote, "My nephew, I want you to carry me on your back and I will kill a head chief. Then you will be glad and dance." Coyote said, "You cannot walk. I do not think you can kill anything." Snake said, "I want you to carry me in your basket. I will go and kill the Indians." Coyote said, "No, you cannot kill anyone. You stay here, you cannot walk along with us." Snake said, "I know how to kill the Indians. I will go along; you must heed what I tell you. I always kill the enemy, the Yavapai. I know. I tell you I want you to carry me in your basket." Coyote then said, "You are not so big that I have to carry you in the basket; I will put you around my neck." He put Snake around his neck and went off.

They went along and saw an antelope. The Indians said, "If someone could get close and kill him, we could have meat. Which one of you Indians can shoot an arrow straight? Someone should crawl close to him." Snake said to Coyote, "My nephew, I want you to put me down on the ground and I will kill the antelope." Coyote said, "You have no arrow to shoot with. These Indians have arrows. You have no arrow to kill anything." Then the Indians said, "You put Snake down. Maybe he will kill him." Then Coyote put him on the ground. The Snake said to the Indians, "I want you to stay here and watch how I kill the antelope. I will bite him and he may run a little way, but he will die very shortly." Snake crawled along the ground and bit the antelope. The antelope ran a little way and fell to the ground dead. The Indians went over to cut him up. Snake said, "I do not want you to eat the blood. Do not eat too much, just a little. If you eat [too] much you will feel lazy and the enemy will kill you." The Indians started again and saw some water where they stopped to eat. They merely ground corn and ate it, but they did not make mush. Snake said, "I want you to make mush in my mouth." "No," said Coyote, "we do not want to cook it in your mouth."

Snake said again, "I told you I was going to kill the big chief. I want you to take me over to where the big chief lives and I will stay there. You can go back, but I will stay there. I do not run fast. You Indians had better go where some enemies camp. Do not go into the camp, but stay close to it." Then the Indians ran and saw the enemy. They ran back and told Snake. Snake said, "Do not eat much because you cannot run fast then. Do not drink with your mouths, but drink through the hole in the arrowshaft. Do not drink much." The Indians saw the enemies' camp. "We saw the enemy camp. You say you are going to kill them. How will you do it?" Snake said, "We will start in the night and we will stop very close to the Indians' camp. You put me down near the camp, and I will look around for the big chief when he stands up to talk. I will sit there and when the big chief comes to talk to his family, I will bite him. He will talk at dawn; then you surround the camp in order to kill them. When I bite him he will cry out. Then you should rush at the Indians. The big chief of the enemy will talk to his family, saying, 'I want you women to gather wild seeds.' Then he will cry, 'Something bit me.' Then you run in and fight with the Indians."

Coyote took Snake from his neck and put him on the ground. He started to go to the place where the big chief talked, when he saw a little hill. He said, "Perhaps this is where the big chief stands," so he sat down there. After a while the big chief came out of his house and stood there, saying, "The Indians must wake up and get wood to make fires to cook things to eat." Snake bit him. The chief cried, "Oh, something bit me; something is killing me." The Indians from Snake's camp rushed in, striking the enemy with clubs, killing them all. Snake said, "I am not going with you now. You leave me here. You Indians all go back."

Where the Yavapai [enemy] live, there are a great many snakes. They left Snake there. Because they left Snake there long ago there are so many there now.

| NOTES |

1. Told by Manakadja; interpreted by Lillie Burro; recorded by E. G., 1921.

33. The Roc (first version)[1]

I DO NOT KNOW WHERE FOX LIVED. HE AND HIS YOUNGER brother lived alone; they had no women. They thought how to catch game, and then made a trap. First they caught a mouse. It was about daylight when the elder brother woke and sang to his younger brother, "Get up. Run and see what is in the trap. I heard a noise there which kept me awake." The younger brother rose and ran to the trap. There was a rat in it. He caught it, brought it home, and roasted it in the ashes. When it was done, they tore it in two, and each ate his portion. Again at dawn, the older brother sang, "Get up. Hurry; see what is caught in the trap. I heard so great a noise it kept me awake." The younger brother ran there and found a chipmunk[2] in the trap. Again he took this home, roasted it, tore it in two, and each ate his portion. At dawn, Fox sang again to his younger brother, "Hurry; get up. Run see what is caught in the trap." He found a chipmunk,[3] brought it home, cooked it, and tore it in two the same way, and each ate half. Just at dawn, Fox sang to his younger brother, "Get up. Run to see what is in it again. There was so much noise it kept me awake." He found a rock squirrel in it. He brought it home, roasted, tore it in two as before, and each ate his half. (They set the trap every night in this story, not in the daytime.) Fox told his younger brother, "Get up and run to the trap to see what is caught. I heard a great noise; I heard the weight fall." The younger brother ran to look; the trap held a rabbit. Again he took it home, roasted it in the ashes, and each had half to eat. They caught all sorts of animals; at first little ones, then larger and larger. Again at daylight, Fox sang, "Younger brother, wake up. Run and see what is caught. I heard the trap fall." The younger brother ran over to it and found a jackrabbit with long ears in it. He took it home; this one he boiled, and they ate it. This was the biggest animal they had caught. Just at dawn, the older brother heard a great noise in the trap. "Younger brother, get up. Run [and] see what is in the trap." He ran there and found an antelope in it. He left it in the trap and returned to tell his older brother to come help him carry in home. They skinned it. Then they had plenty of meat to cook and eat. They sliced it in order to dry it. Again at dawn he sang, "Run and see what is caught. I heard a great noise which kept me awake." The younger brother ran to the trap, which held a big mountain sheep ram. He carried it home, skinned it as they did the antelope. They had plenty of meat, which they sliced and dried. Just at dawn, he said, "Run over and see what is in the trap. I heard much noise." The other ran there and found a big buck in it. When he saw this, he ran back to tell his older brother. Both went to fetch it home, skinned it, and had plenty of meat then.

Again at dawn, Fox told his younger brother, "Go look at the trap, to see if another animal had [has] been caught. I heard a noise which kept me awake." The younger brother ran there and found that the trap had caught an immense bird, larger than an eagle. His wings were very long (as long as an airplane). It was still alive as it lay there. Both brothers shot at it with arrows, but they could not kill it. So one ran home and got a heavy, stone-headed club. But he could not kill it with this: the heavy stone head just smashed to bits.

The bird was not killed. After a while he took the two foxes, put them on his back, and flew up. (This story does not say in which direction they were taken.) As he flew along, he gathered up more people to carry on his back. He flew on and on, straight to the middle of the ocean where there was an island. He alighted on this and took them from his back. He had been bringing people to this island for a long time, so that there were many there. The bird flew off again. It was four sleeps before he returned. Just as before he brought more people: men, women, and children. The big bird always gathered people to place on the island, killing one to eat as he wanted. He flew off again and fetched more children, men, and women. That is the way he used to gather them.

The older Fox sang to the people, "The big bird always flies off in this way to search for more people to bring here. If he catches everyone and eats them all, then no one will be left alive. This is what I have been thinking about. I will tell you people what we must do about the big bird. By and by we will all be killed and there will be no one alive in the world. Everyone should listen to what I think should be done."

The big bird flew off to hunt for more people. Fox sang, "Let us kill an orphan; then take stones to make arrowheads and fashion large and small flakes from them. Make plenty, mix them with the blood, and put the mass in the dead orphan's mouth." They did this. They dug a pit, built a fire in it, and roasted the body in it. Then they took it out and gave it to the big bird's wife. "When the big bird returns feeling very hungry, you give him the roasted body and see if he eats it," Fox said to her.

Fox sang first to Badger, "I want you to dig a hole quickly, a tunnel as long as you can make, make little diverging galleries along each side of it. We have a great many men, women, and children to hide in there." When Badger had dug the tunnel a little while, he said, "Well, I have finished." Then Fox went in to inspect it. It went quite straight down, but not very far. Fox said, "That is not right."

Fox sang to Rock Squirrel, "You next should see how you can dig the tunnel. Make it such that I can say 'Good,' so that it will be ready for use. When the big bird returns and his wife feeds him the roast, the sharp flints will cut his throat all around. Perhaps he will be nearly killed, and when he falls on the ground, he will spread his wings, and bringing them together catch us all between them and crush us to death. That is why we want the tunnel, so that we can take refuge in it when we think he is going to die, so that none of our people will be crushed and killed." Rock Squirrel dug the ground. In a short time he came out and said to Fox, "I have finished." He had dug only a little way straight down, with only a few side galleries. Fox went in to see and said, "No, that is no good."

Then he sang to [a burrowing] Rat, "You go quickly to dig the hole," and the Rat did so. After a short time he came out and said to Fox, "I have finished." Fox entered and walked along. "Your work is just a little good, but you do not dig deep. The earth covering the tunnel is too thin."

Fox sang to Prairie Dog, "I want you to try." So he dug. He did not come out for a very long time. When he emerged he told Fox, "Now, I have finished. Go in and look at what I have done." Fox entered and looked about. He said, "Good. That is what I wanted. Everyone should come close to this place."[4] So they all gathered near the tunnel as he told them. Fox said, "The big bird will soon return."

When the tunnel was completed the big bird returned. He was carrying many people on his back again. He alighted and took them off. He went directly to his wife and said, "I am quite hungry. Have you anything cooked, some meat?" She said, "Yes, I have the whole body of a boy roasted. I have the whole carcass. Here," and she gave it to him. The big bird ate it, for he was hungry. He ate half of it, a good deal. He began to feel his throat hurting. So he said, "There is something which does not feel good in my throat." So he coughed. After a while he ate the whole carcass. The others were all at the tunnel, watching him, until it seemed that he would die. Then Fox said, "You women and children go into the tunnel." Fox alone stayed at the entrance to watch the bird. As the bird was dying, he clawed himself all over and clawed at the ground. Then he opened his huge wings wide, first toward the north, and brought them together, rubbing them against each other to crush any men he might catch. But he caught no one. Then he turned to the west and did the same, but he found nothing. Then he did the same to the south, but found no one. Then he turned to the east, and did as before, but again he found nothing. Then he spread his wings, making a feeble fifth attempt, when with a cry, "maaa," he fell dead.

Fox was in the hole, too, where he stayed for one sleep. Then he let out plenty of flies. "Fly into the bird's nostrils, or any other opening, to feel if it moves." The flies went into the bird's nose, mouth, eyes, and ears, and anus, everywhere, but he did not move. Then Fox let out the bees, [saying] "Do as the flies did. Go, sting the bird all over. See if he is dead." They flew there, stung his body everywhere, but he did not move. They returned. "Yes, he is dead." Then fox let out the mice. "Look at the big dead bird. Nibble off his pin feathers. Make your nests everywhere on him." They bit him everywhere, on the nose and mouth, but he did not move. They reentered the tunnel and told Fox, "Yes, the big bird is dead. He is beginning to decay; he is somewhat bloated." Then Fox said, "Let several of us go out to see." So they went out and saw that the bird had begun decaying. Now they were sure he was dead. One of them returned to tell the others they could now come out.

When they were all out, they stayed near that place, building camps everywhere. Fox thought what they should do. He thought they ought to cut off the bird's second longest wing feather. After several sleeps, Fox sang to the people, "Ducks, you know how to go way down into the water to get some good axes. Bring them out so that we can cut the feather off. Then we can try setting it on end at the water's edge, lower it for a bridge, and see if we can walk across." The ducks dove and fetched the axes. They cut off the shorter feather, stood it upright like a tree, and toppled it into place. It reached nearly to the other side; there was just a little clear water beyond. Then they tried another; they cut off the longest feather. This too they stood upright and toppled into place. This feather reached all the way to the shore; there was no open water. Then Fox said, "That is what we wanted to do. Now it is all right. Walk right over to the other side. When we are all there, I will tell you what I think. Then you can do as I say." They walked along a groove in the shaft of the feather, just like that in an eagle's.

Fox then told them his thoughts: "That big bird used to gather us and kill us one at a time, until he would have killed everyone. But I knew how to kill him. I am glad we all escaped. All the tribes are mingled here; you yourselves know which you are. Each shall stay in a different locality." They did as he instructed, for he said, "You should go in the direction in which you think you properly belong." They dispersed to the north, west, south, and east, everywhere. So they scattered, only the two fox brothers being left there.

The older brother said to the younger, "I think I will not go back whence I came. I think I will not be a man any longer. I am going to be a fox here." Then he became a fox, scampered up a tree trunk and down again, and then ran up the cliff, crying "kau, kau," as a fox does.

| NOTES |

1. Told by Sinyella; interpreted by Jess Chickapanega, 1919.
2. The variety with stripes and a curled tail.
3. That with indistinct stripes and a straight tail.
4. These are probably the actual burrowing characteristics of these animals.

34. THE ROC (SECOND VERSION)[1]

WILDCAT AND HIS BROTHER STAYED WHERE THERE WAS A wide river. Then both moved away. When the sun went down he told his brother to make a trap and get something to eat. The brother went away. When daylight came Wildcat told his brother, "My brother, you run over and look into our traps." They caught a little mouse and tore it up and ate it. Then they moved elsewhere and slept there then they set the trap again. He sent his brother again to look into the trap. He found a little larger mouse. Wildcat gave his brother some of it; they ate the mouse. Then they moved on again. When the sun went down they stayed some place and set the trap again. "That is all we have to eat," Wildcat said. In the morning he sent the little brother to the trap again. He found a rabbit, which they ate. After they had eaten the rabbit they moved again and got something to eat, so they went along. When they stopped they set the trap again. He sent his brother to the trap. He found a jackrabbit. They roasted and ate it. They moved on again, and when the sun went down, they camped and set the trap again. In the morning they found a mountain sheep in the trap, and they roasted it for breakfast. When they were through eating they moved again and where they stopped they set the trap. In the morning his brother found an antelope in the trap. He brought this to Wildcat and they roasted and ate it. They moved on again and when the sun went down they camped and set the trap. The next morning Wildcat sent his brother to the trap, where he found a deer. He brought it to camp and they ate it. When they had eaten that they started on again. When the sun went down they stopped and set the trap. They always did that.

Finally Wildcat said, "I do not know what we have in our trap. You make a noise like thunder so that I did not sleep all night." The little brother went to the trap to see what was in it. There was something big in the trap. The boy hit it with rocks and sticks because it was not dead. He came back and told his brother. Both went to see the trap. They hit the thing in it with rocks and sticks, and they shot an arrow at it. Wildcat chopped it about the head with a hatchet, but it was not dead; it just lay there. "He looks as though he were going to catch me," Wildcat said. "I am afraid to kill him." In the trap was an eagle. The eagle took them on his back and flew away with them. He flew around and around up high. Then he set Wildcat and his brother down in a dry place [an island] surrounded by water.

There were many Indians where Eagle left them. All of those Indians had been brought there by Eagle. The Indians played games and shinny all the time, but Wildcat lay down to think. Wildcat said, "Eagle eats the Indians; that is why he brought us here." Wildcat said to the Indians who were playing, "You do not know anything about it. Big Eagle is going to eat up all Indians. I knew it when he came home, for he said, 'I am hungry; I eat Indian meat.'" That is what Wildcat told the Indians.

The Indians stopped playing and Wildcat said, "We will try to kill Eagle. We will kill a little baby, put something in it, and roast it so that Eagle will want to eat it. That will kill him." Wildcat said, "Then we will cut his throat and he will soon be dead." When the Eagle came home he always said, "I want to eat my Indian meat." And the woman said, "I have already cooked it for you and put it here." Every day they brought two or three Indians down to eat because they did nothing but play games.

The Indians killed a baby and put him in a hole. Eagle found it there in the hole and ate it. His eyes rolled and his wings rubbed against each other; he appeared to be dead. When he rubbed his wings together he always killed Indians.

When the Eagle was dead two or three days, Wildcat said, "Flies, go see if Eagle is dead. Maybe he is not dead." The flies went and got into his mouth, eyes, and wings. The flies said to Wildcat, "He is dead." Wildcat said, "Maybe he is not dead, but wants to get all the Indians and catch me too." So he sent the bees to see if Eagle was dead. The bees came back and told Wildcat that Eagle was dead. "We stung him and found he was dead." Wildcat did not believe the bees, so he sent the mouse, saying, "You go eat his feathers and see if he is dead." The mouse came back and told Wildcat, "I bit him all over and he did not wake up. He is dead." Wildcat did not heed him. He sent a larger mouse to see if Eagle was dead. Wildcat said, "You go and make houses in his feathers and see if he is dead. He might wake up and catch all of the Indians." The mouse came back and said, "I bit his feathers and built a house in them. He looked as though he were dead. He is rotting. I am telling the truth; he is dead." When the mouse said that, the Indians said, "Eagle is dead. We shall go out." Wildcat said, "All right, we shall go out and see big Eagle." The Indians all went to see dead Eagle. Wildcat said, "This is the one who killed everybody. Now we are glad we killed him." They were all glad and wanted to go home.

Wildcat wanted to cut off Eagle's wings and put them across the water so that they could go home. Wildcat sent the duck to get a hatchet from under the water, to chop off the wings. Then Wildcat cut off the wings, put them on the water, and pushed them off. The water carried them across. They reached the sand on the other side; they were glad to get there. All day they ferried across and at last all had reached the other side. There they camped. Wildcat said, "Now all of the Indians are over here. We are very glad that we killed Eagle. Now let us all go back to where we came from." Then the Indians went home. Wildcat and his brother were the only ones to stay at the camp. They ran around making a noise. "I am always to be a wild-cat," he said.

| NOTES |

1. Told by Manakadja; interpreted by Lillie Burro; recorded by E. G., 1921.

35. Sun Sets the World Afire (First Version)[1]

LONG AGO THE SUN WAS A MAN. HIS HOUSE WAS JUST THIS side [northwest] of San Francisco Mountain. His house, a little mountain [*inyanuwa'ha*, sun's house] was burned so that now it is a round red hole.[2] The sun was not a good man. He said he would like to have men come from other countries. He called to them to come and play games: the hiding game, the hoop-and-pole, the cup-and-pin game, and run footraces. His own relatives who lived there played with those who came, and always won from them. Then they killed the strangers, butchered, and ate them. This is what they always did. Sun was chief of his relatives. Pine Squirrel[3] was also a smart man. "Let us see who is the best. Let us play for people as stakes," they both said. Sun said, "If I win your relatives, I will cut their bellies open," and Pine Squirrel said he would do the same. Pine Squirrel's name was Amagwiθita. They began to boast to each other. Sun said, "I have a good young runner, the antelope. What have you?" Squirrel said, "I have a young doe." "Well, start that one first; we will see who can win. If my antelope beats your doe, I will kill you." So these two started first to the north, then far around to the west, halfway around the earth, before they turned back. At first the antelope ran ahead, until they started to turn back, when the doe ran ahead and reached home before the antelope. So Sun said, "Your doe has beaten my great runner, the antelope, so you can kill me now." Squirrel carried a long knife in his hand, but when he was about to do it, Sun cried, "Wait, we will try something else."

Sun had many daughters, so he said, "I want your relatives to have my daughter. See if you can find out how my daughter's privates feel." The squirrel people said, "All right, we are going to do it." Squirrel warned them, "Don't heed him, my relatives. I think this is very hard to do. I am the chief and I will try first. I will test her with some object, and if it is all soft like my hand then you can have your way." So he got a very hard bone as big around as his neck, and fastened it secretly in place of his penis. He thrust it in a little way. The vagina was toothed and began to chew it until there was only a stump left. By this time the teeth were all broken off. Then Squirrel said, "Now I have fixed it good. Go ahead and have your will."

Sun said, "You beat me twice. You are pretty smart, so you have won. I do not know any more tests." Then Squirrel spoke to his own relatives. Mountain Lion, Wolf, and other animals were his relatives. "Everybody should pounce on Sun, cut him open, break back his ribs, and cut his heart out.⁴ Everybody should take a bit, but do not drop any blood on the ground. If you do not do as I say something will happen to frighten you," said Squirrel. So Squirrel's relatives sprang upon Sun, cut him open and broke back his ribs, but they became frightened and left him without cutting out his heart.

Sun was not killed. After a while he got up and said, 'Where is my fire drill?" He found it hanging under the roof of his house. He took it down and rubbed it between his cheek and hand. So he set fire to his house and let the flames spread to the trees and grass, until it spread all over the world. "I do not want anybody to be left alive," he thought. Squirrel knew what Sun was thinking, so he became frightened and ran away, with his relatives following. The squirrel chief said, "Soon we will no longer be alive. We did not cut his breast [heart] off. We will all be burnt up. I wanted you to cut the heart off and devour it. I knew what had best be done. I told you, but you did not do it. Now you will be killed. You had better go do it. Walk back to the house and look for it." So they walked back some distance, then one of his relatives went ahead and looked toward the house. When he returned he said, "The house is burned down and the fire is following us." The squirrel chief saw some water on the road as they were traveling. So he asked the water, "Do you burn?" It said, "Yes, I am used for boiling. Men use me to make things soft. I burn." Then the chief asked the ground. The ground said, "Men make a hole to roast food, and burn wood in it. I burn." Then he asked a tree. The tree said, "I am wooden, and wood burns until it's all consumed." Then he asked a rock. The rock said, "Yes, I can be heated very hot. Things burn quickly near me." Then he asked the red ant. "No, I do not burn. Men do not like me and try to destroy me and my house by fire. If I can go way down under the earth when they try, I am safe. Then I come out and go to some other place. Men cannot burn me." So squirrel said, "That is the place we want. The fire is coming, so I and my relatives want to go down into that hole." The ant said, "All right." Then they all ran on until they came to the hole and all went down into it. But the fire was close behind while two or three were still outside. The cottontail was among these, and when the fire had nearly reached the hole, he asked the brush at the edge of the hole if it was inflammable. "No, we do not burn, except the top which is somewhat dry. You can hide under here." So the rabbit crouched down under it. The fire came, burned the tips of the bushes, and scorched the back of the rabbit's neck yellow.

Those people who had gone far down under the ground stayed there until the earth had cooled off. Then they came out. The chief of the squirrels said, "Some of you people know in which direction your home is. So you might as well go home and thus be scattered over the world." So they all scattered. "I and my brother are going to be pine squirrels," the chief said. When he was an old man he said, "Gwa,' gwa' gwaa'," and sprang into a pine tree and ran from one tree to another. The squirrel chief beat Sun, so Sun, burning his house with his fire drill, took [caught] fire himself. He was a wicked man who always killed and ate people. When he was burned, he went down through the ground under his camp. He came up when it was daylight and went down again at dusk, and so he goes today.

| NOTES |

1. Told by Sinyella; interpreted by Jess Chickapanega, 1919.
2. This hole was identified with a crater in the side of a volcanic peak near San Francisco Mountain.
3. A variety living on the plateau.
4. This procedure was also recorded as the method of destroying a malignant shaman, practiced on at least one occasion historically (*Havasupai Ethnography*, p. 239).

36. Sun Sets the World Afire (second version)[1]

MOUNTAIN LION CAME FROM POWELL PLATEAU. HE CARRIED everything on his back across the Colorado. He went to Wigahawa'dja. There were many Indians over there. When he got there he saw houses and tracks of the Indians, but he saw no Indians. He looked around but saw nobody. Then he saw Coyote there. Mountain Lion said, "My nephew, where are all the Indians? Have they moved somewhere? I want to see the Indians. I came a long way to see my relations. That is why I came here." Coyote said, "There are no Indians around here. I am the only one. Stay here; live here." Mountain Lion said to Coyote, "You have houses here, many houses, and different tracks. I want you to tell me the truth. Where are the Indians all gone? I want to see the big chief and smoke tobacco with him, and see my relations. That is why I came. I came a long way from Powell Plateau." Coyote said, "There are no Indians around here. I am the only one here. I made the houses; I always change around." Mountain Lion said, "You may be the only one that stayed here, but I see women's tracks and babies' tracks, and seeds that women picked. I do not think you do that." "I am the only one around here. I make myself into an old woman to gather seeds and I make myself into a baby to walk around. I always do those things," said Coyote.

Mountain Lion did not come into the house, but just stood by the door and talked to Coyote. He said, "All right, you do everything around here. You cook seeds for me and I will come into the house. It is too hot here outside. It is midday. You put tobacco there, Coyote, and I will come in."

Mountain Lion became angry at Coyote and talked angrily to him. "You tell me straight; you tell me the truth. You are making fun of me.

I am a big chief, not a little boy. You tell me where Indians are; tell me where they are, or if something has killed them all. Tell me right away. The sun is on my head and my head burns. Now tell me. Do not lie to me." Coyote said, "All right, my uncle, I will tell you. There were lots of Indians around here, but the sun killed them all and ate them." "Why did you not tell me that right?" Mountain Lion said to Coyote.

"When he killed them all I was very hungry here," said Coyote. When Mountain Lion came he had a pack on his back which he had put down a short way from Coyote's house. Now Mountain Lion went into Coyote's house. He lay down and slept, saying nothing. When he woke, he said, "You say, Coyote, that you are very hungry. Go out there. I left my pack, a little pack. Go and get it." When Coyote brought the pack they cooked some meat and ate it. In the morning he asked Coyote again, "What was the trouble that the sun killed all of the Indians and ate them?" Coyote said, "They went up to sun's house and played games. Sun beat them and ate them. The sun beat them all and won everything. That is why he killed them."

"I am thinking about that; I do not know what to do. I should like to make Indians," said Mountain Lion. He sent Coyote away to get some rocks of various kinds: red, shiny ones. "We will make Indians of those," he said. "We will grind the rocks like corn and make Indians." Coyote brought many rocks on his back. He laid a buckskin on the ground, put *hawe'gasa²* on this, and used a deerhorn prong to cut the rocks. Then he put the powder in a buckskin, laid it down, and slept.

When daylight came Coyote went where the sun rises. Mountain Lion had told Coyote to take the buckskin sacks and throw them where the sun comes up. Coyote took them and ran there, but he did not throw them all. He threw only the largest. "I want the Indians to be around here," said Coyote. Mountain Lion told Coyote what he wanted him to do, but Coyote would not. "My uncle, I did what you said." Mountain Lion said, "We do not want to stay here at this house. We will go two miles nearer and listen for the Indians. We do not want to stay here."

Mountain Lion and Coyote went away and lay down. After a while, somebody walked around. Coyote said, "Oh, my uncle, there is someone walking around my house; someone is talking." "No," said Mountain Lion, "No Indians are there. Flies are talking." Mountain Lion said, "There are no Indians around here. I want you to look at my head. There are many bugs there." Coyote said, "There are many Indians around my home. I hear them making a noise. I want to see the Indians very much. I shall run over." "No," said Mountain Lion, "I won't let you go," and Mountain Lion held Coyote. Coyote said, "I want to go see the Indians." Coyote pulled away from Mountain Lion and ran.

Coyote ran nearly to his camp where the Indians were already playing. Mountain Lion ran after Coyote; when Coyote saw him he stopped. Coyote hollered when he was close to his camp, "I see many Indians playing at our house; it is full. My uncle, come and see the Indians." Mountain Lion said, "Oh, you are no good; you never do what I tell you. You did not obey me. I do not think you hear me when I tell you things. You have no ears to hear what I say."

After a while Mountain Lion came up and saw the Indians. He saw that there were not enough playing the game, only half of them. Mountain Lion stood there and watched the game. Mountain Lion said to Coyote, "Well, I am thinking of the sun who killed the Indians, and perhaps he will kill these again." Mountain Lion sent Coyote to Habu,[3] where two brothers lived. They were Indians, these squirrels who lived there. Squirrel knew everything, all of the games. He could beat the sun. Coyote went after him. "Squirrel can do the best. Maybe he can beat the sun. Coyote, I want you to go get him to help us beat the sun," said Mountain Lion.

Coyote went to get Squirrel. Coyote started and made a fire at Wigawu'ula. Then he ran and made a fire again at Wigagwaθa. Then he started and made a fire at Aweodji'. Squirrel saw Coyote's fire; he sat up in a tree, tanning a buckskin, and said to his brother, "I see a fire. Someone is coming. I think my nephew, Coyote, is coming. He runs the fastest." Coyote ran to Flagstaff and made a fire there. He turned around and made a fire at Awega'asava. Squirrel saw that and told his brother, "Cook meat, for he is coming. Coyote is coming. Come up and see the fire. I am telling you the truth." The brother down on the ground said, "There are no Indians around here. I do not know what you see." Squirrel saw the fire again. "I see it close by. Maybe he is coming here," Squirrel said to his brother. "Maybe there is trouble over there," said Squirrel. "I saw the fire. I saw him; I saw the man who is coming. I think that my nephew, Coyote, is the best runner. He is the only one who can run fast," said Squirrel. "There he comes," Squirrel said.

Squirrel called to Coyote and asked what was wrong. But Coyote just came up, sat down, and said nothing to Squirrel. When the sun had nearly set, Squirrel went home and sat down in his house. But Coyote said nothing; he just sat there. Squirrel cooked meat, they ate and drank water, but still Coyote said nothing. In the night Squirrel asked Coyote, "I thought you would tell me some news from over there where you live. I thought someone killed the Indians and I thought you would tell me. You just came to eat. You say nothing to us." But Coyote told nothing. Then Coyote said, "My uncle, no, I did not tell you anything. I just liked the meat and I ate it; that is all I came for." "I thought you would tell me something because you made fire and ran as fast as you could. My nephew, I want you to tell me." Squirrel asked two or three times, but Coyote said nothing; he just slept there.

In the morning Squirrel cooked meat and they ate it. When they ate Squirrel said to Coyote, "You help yourself. We have plenty of meat and we can kill more. I thought you would tell me of some trouble over there. But all must be well and I am glad to hear that."

Squirrel and his brother hunted deer. They got two deer and brought them home. After a while his brother wore [made?] buckskin. When they were home they cooked meat again and ate that. In the night Squirrel asked Coyote, "How are the Indians doing over there? Please tell me right just what they are doing. I like to know about them. My brother and I both stay here, but we have no woman to cook for us. Deer is all that we have to eat here." Coyote said, "I cannot tell you anything. I just came here to eat meat."

In the morning Squirrel cooked meat and they ate it. Then the two brothers went hunting again. Coyote stayed there. Both brought two deer to the house. Squirrel asked Coyote again about the Indians. "I know you have something to tell me. There must be some trouble. Please tell me; I want you to tell me."

Coyote said, "All right, I will tell you something. Mountain Lion is over at our camp. The sun killed all the Indians. Mountain Lion told me to tell you to come over there and see the sun. That is what my uncle, Mountain Lion, sent me over here for, because you know all the games and everything. That is what I want to tell you." Squirrel said to Coyote, "I wanted to hear sooner. I had to ask you so many times. That is what I wanted to know. Tell me now."

Next morning the squirrels went hunting deer again. Then each brother brought two deer home. They brought them to the house on their backs. Squirrel said, "What is the trouble? I want you to tell me. Maybe enemies killed them. I want you to tell me." Coyote said, "The sun killed all of the Indians. That has been the trouble. The sun killed the Indians. In playing games he beat all the Indians and he killed them all."

Squirrel said, "The sun is the best player; perhaps nobody can beat the sun. Neither I nor my brother play shinny or the hoop-and-pole game, because only we two live here, and we have no Indians to play with." "But Mountain Lion wants you to come and help us. Mountain Lion said you know the games and everything. We think you can beat the sun." "But I do not know the game they play. We just run after deer and catch and eat them. That is all we do. There are no Indians around here and we cannot play," Squirrel said. "The sun is the best. I do not think I can beat him," said Squirrel. "When the Indians come along there, sun makes them feel bad and kills them quickly. All right, I will go to see him. Take all of our things and hang them in the trees; then make a shinny stick, and a hoop and pole." Coyote made them. "If the sun beats me he may kill me. Maybe I will not come back to see this again. You hang my things up in the tree."

Coyote made a ball for shinny. Squirrel told Coyote to go first and carry the load. Coyote went a long way and tried to play the hidden ball game. Squirrel stayed home for a time, and when Coyote had played, the two squirrels started. Squirrel said to his brother, "You find the ball. I cannot do it." The big brother went and found the ball. "Sun cannot do that; you are the best," Coyote said to Squirrel.

The squirrels stopped while Coyote went along playing the hoop-and-pole game. "Maybe we do not do it right and we cannot win much. We are going back." Coyote sat down and saw Squirrel playing and getting the hoop all the time. He said, "You can do it best. I think you will beat the sun."

Squirrel started another game after Coyote had gone on ahead. This time he played shinny. He ran as fast as he could and hit the ball all of the time, never letting it drop on the sand. Coyote saw him and said, "Oh, you are the best." Coyote went ahead again, and Squirrel ran a race with his brother. Squirrel had a stone and kicked it along, running as fast as he could.[4] Coyote said, "You are the best I ever saw. Maybe you will beat the sun." Squirrel said, "These are all the games I can play."

They all went on together, Coyote carrying all their things on his back. They went where the Indians' camp was. Many Indians camped there. They wanted to kill the sun. When they came, the Squirrel just lay down and did not talk. Mountain Lion talked to Squirrel, saying, "I am glad you have come to help me. I should like to beat the sun because the sun won from the Indians and killed them all. I am glad you have come."

Where the Indians camped there was no water, and the Indians became thirsty. Mountain Lion said, "Oh, we have no water near here." He put his stick on the sand and water came out. Mountain Lion went back to the Indians and said, "Now we have water."

In the morning Mountain Lion said, "All right, now we will go to see the sun." The Indians said, "All right, we will start to go." Squirrel said, "No, we cannot go while the sun sees us. Sun might see us and kill us all." The Indians stayed there, sitting about. Squirrel talked to the Indians, "I want you to make a road under the sand, and then we shall start to go." Prairie Dog made a road under the sand, intending to come out in Sun's house. Prairie Dog said, "I have finished the road." They started to go, Squirrel first. He saw that Prairie Dog had not made the road right. He had just made a straight hole which did not lead to Sun's house. Squirrel sent Chipmunk to make a road under the sand. Chipmunk started to go to work. He started to make a straight hole, but then he went off to one side. He came back and said to Squirrel, "I made the road and finished it." The Indians and Squirrel went through the road to where Chipmunk stopped working. He had not finished the road, but had told them a lie. So they came back. Squirrel said, "Now, I want you to do just as I told you. I do not want to come back two or three times. If I went down the road the sun might see and kill me; that is why I want to go through the sand. Then I might get there and beat the sun. That is what you want." Then he sent another to make the road. He sent Gotu's to make the road again. He went in and made the road. He was gone a long, long time and came back with sand all over him. He looked as though he had worked very hard. The Indians saw that he had been working a great deal and that he had been gone a long while. When he came back he said, "I finished it and I came through into the sun's house. I saw the Indian skin that Sun uses to cover his floor. But I did not take it away. I made a hole under it."

They started; Squirrel went ahead. Gotu' had made a good tunnel.

They went through it to where he had made the road into the house of Sun. Squirrel took the Indian skin on the floor of the house and threw it away. Then Indians went into the house. Sun said to his family, "Oh, my family, what makes that noise like a horse coming, or someone coming on the road? I want you to go and see." Sun was lying on the roof of his house. His family said, "No one is around here." They had not seen the Indians. Sun had many daughters. The Indians made a noise in the house. One of the girls looked around in the house and saw many Indians there. "Oh, you are blind; you never see Indians when they come. Many Indians are in your house," she said to her father.

Then Sun did not talk. After a while he came down and stood by the door. "Oh, what kind of children are you, here in my house?" he said. "My house is not a good place. There are many tarantulas (ʔni'sita) in my place and they will sting you pretty badly."

He stood by the door, took a big buffalo horn, and said, "If you can break this you can beat me." He threw it to the ground. Sun stood by the door with a stone knife to kill the Indians if they should fail. The Indians all wanted Squirrel to take the horn and break it. But Squirrel said to Sun, "Well, I like to come here. Why do you want to kill me? I thought you would give me something to eat or water to drink, but you just want to kill me." Coyote said, "I will try to take that and break it." But Squirrel said to Coyote, "If we cannot break that, Sun will kill all of the Indians." Squirrel stepped on the horn, broke it to pieces, and threw it on the ground.

Sun stood by the door and said, "Well, I thought you were a little boy." Sun told his daughter what Squirrel had done and said he was afraid of Squirrel. Sun told his daughter to give water to the Indians and something to eat. She started to give them water from a huge bowl. The Indians wanted to drink it, but Squirrel said to them, "That is not water; when you drink that he might beat you. That water is his tears, which he uses for water." And Coyote took the water and threw it away.

Sun said to his daughter, "I want you to make some mush for the Indians. I do not know what kind of Indians they are. They throw water away. I am afraid they will kill me. Make them some mush." Sun's daughter made the mush and put it in four flat baskets. She set them down where the Indians sat. Coyote wanted to eat it, but Squirrel said, "That is not good. When Sun killed the Indians he made that mush from their eyes. If you eat that, he will beat you." And Coyote took the mush and threw it away.

Sun said to his daughter, "Try to cook another mush of corn and see if they will eat that. I do not know what Indians they are. I am afraid of them." When she cooked it, she put it in three big, flat baskets and set these before them. Coyote wanted to eat it but Squirrel said, "That is made of the whites of the eyes, and if you eat that, Sun will beat you. He made corn of the whites of Indians' eyes. You saw no garden; he made corn that way. He wants to beat you." And Coyote threw away that mush and said, "I always eat that; I did not know about it."

Sun's daughter tried to cook prickly pear fruit for the Indians. Squirrel said, "That is not prickly pear fruit; he made that drink from the blood of Indians. I want you to throw that away." But Coyote said, "I have always drunk all those things." And Coyote threw it away.

An old woman came to where the Indians sat. She wanted to give them something to eat and drink. Squirrel took her water bottle, for that water was good. Squirrel said, "Now, that is water, my nephew. I want you to drink first." Coyote drank first and passed the bottle around. They all drank but there was just as much water as when they began, no less. They gave the bottle back to the woman.

Sun said, "You try cooking other things for the Indians. I do not know what tribe they are; they throw everything away that you cook. Now you cook beans for them." She cooked beans and took them to the Indians. Coyote wanted to eat them, but Squirrel said, "Those are not beans; they are *tcimpa'va*."[6] And Coyote threw it away.

"Those Indians know everything we cook. I do not know what we will do. They throw everything away. You cook something else for them," Sun said to his daughter. Sun's daughter cooked pumpkin and gave it to the Indians. Coyote wanted to eat it, but Squirrel said, "That is not pumpkin; that is intestines."[7] There is no garden here to raise pumpkin. I want you to throw it away again." And Coyote threw it away.

Sun said, "Oh, he knows what we cook; he always throws it away. But you cook something more for the Indians. We have dried mountain sheep meat; cook that for the Indians." She cooked it, put it in a basket, and gave it to the Indians. Then the Indians saw the meat and wanted to eat it, but they listened to Squirrel. He said, "That is not meat; you see no skin lying around here. That is Indian meat. If you eat that, he will beat you." Coyote took it and threw it away.

Sun said to him, "My nephew, Coyote, you said that you knew the pole and hoop game. I want you to play." Sun's nephew, Coyote, and Sun's family were already playing, when Squirrel and his brother went over to them. Squirrel said, "You just sit and watch. I and my big brother will play with Sun's family." Squirrel and his brother took their poles and went to see Sun's family playing. Sun's family used Indians' shin bones for poles and Squirrel saw that. Sun's hoop was made of Indian skin and Squirrel saw that. Squirrel took those things and threw them away. He gave them his pole and hoop. "We do not want to use bone; we shall use this thing." So Squirrel's brother and one of the Sun's family played and the squirrel was beaten. Sun won half of his things. Squirrel did not play hard; he just teased the Sun, but now he played hard and won his things back and beat Sun. Sun told his family, "It looks as though he is going to beat us. Try another game. Hide the ball."

Then Sun's family hid the balls. They were not balls, but Indians' ankle bones. He had a bundle of sixteen ribs [as counters]. Squirrel took them all and threw them away. Squirrel made counters and a ball of soapweed. He threw them on the sand, saying, "Here, you play with those."

Then Sun's nephew hid the ball under the sand, but Squirrel did not play hard. Sun's nephew beat the Squirrel again. Sun said to his daughters, "It looks as though we are going to beat Squirrel. I want you to go into the water to clean yourselves, paint yourselves with red, and comb your hair; then sit and watch Squirrel as he plays." The three girls went into the water and washed themselves clean. They painted their faces and their bodies, and sat to watch the game. Sun's family had beat half the Squirrels when it was nearly daylight. Now Squirrel got the ball and hid it in the sand and again he beat Sun. He won everything Sun had. Sun's family said to him, "We have nothing more to give Squirrel."

Sun said to his daughter, "My daughter, you marry whichever Indian you want." Sun's daughter took an Indian and wanted to go away with him, but Squirrel said, "No, perhaps she will kill you. I will go first and see how I get along." Squirrel took the girls away and found that they had toothed vaginas. He used a mountain sheep bone. The girls cut it right off, but their teeth all came out with the bone. Squirrel said, "All right, my nephew, I made them all right."

Sun said, "I am very sorry; they are going to beat us. I do not know what kind of Indians these are. I thought you [i.e., his family] were going to kill those men. In the morning we will run a race with Squirrel." Squirrel said to his people, "I do not think that any of you Indians can run as fast as I and my brother. We will run a race with Sun. You stay here. When we beat Sun's family and you see us returning, try to kill the sun. Take his arms off, take his heart, and put out his eyes. When you take the heart, run with me. I do not want to stop here."

Sun's family started to run. The squirrels just walked along, but did not run. They went around the mountains four times. Squirrel went slowly and in going around he met Sun's family. He passed them and went around the mountain four times; then he came back. Sun climbed up on the mountain and saw Squirrel and his people moving along. He said, "I want them to come back; I want to eat their brains." Then Squirrel ran as fast as he could and passed Sun's family. Squirrel taunted Coyote, Sun's nephew [sic]. "Now you run as fast as you can. You look as though you were just walking, not running." Squirrel had a little stone at his feet for a kicking-stick. Sun's family slipped on their kicking sticks and could just walk along. Squirrel beat the Sun's family. He ran as fast as he could.

Squirrel's people saw him coming. Mountain Lion, Wolf, and Coyote pounced on Sun and tried to kill him. They threw him on the ground, cut one arm off, and put out his eyes. They did not heed what Squirrel said and did not take the heart. They walked along with Squirrel. He asked them, "Did you do what I told you?" "No, we did not do it. We stuck something in his eyes and we just took one arm." "Did you bring the heart with you?" "No, we did not do that." "I thought you would obey me. The Sun will kill everybody again now. I told you to take his heart; then Sun could kill no more. Now Sun is going to kill everybody," Squirrel said.

When they started to go Sun woke up and asked his daughter for his fire drill. He had only one hand, so he rubbed the drill on his cheek to make fire. The fire burned the house and all about it. Squirrel grew angry as he walked along. He said to the Indians, "Turn around and see what Sun has done." They saw the big fire. Rocks and everything else were burning. Squirrel said, "We will all die now."

As Squirrel went along, he asked the tree, "Do you burn?" "Yes, I burn." He asked the rock, "Do you burn?" "Yes, I burn." He asked the sand, "Do you burn?" "Yes, when they made a fire on me I grew very hot." Then he asked water, "Do you burn?" "Yes," said the water, "when they put a fire on me I grow hot and boil."

The fire came close to the Indians and they all cried. Squirrel saw an ant and asked, "Where do you live?" "Just a little way over here." "I want to go and live with you, for the fire is coming and will burn me up." "The fire cannot go where I live. It will not go down there." The ant took the Indians into her house. The rabbit did not get in; the fire came to his shoulders and almost burned him. Then he ran into the ant's house and stayed down there. The ants cooked for the Indians.

They lived there two or three days. They cooked *sile'e* seeds for the Indians. Then Squirrel sent Ant out to see how it looked. Ant went out and saw that the ground was burned up. There were no trees; all were in ashes. They all came out and camped by the ant hill. In the morning Squirrel said, "You Indians go where you live, to your own camps. Our camp is all burned up but we can go over there and we will make ourselves squirrels." And they were no longer Indians.

| NOTES |

1. Told by Manakadja; interpreted by Lillie Burro; recorded by E. G., 1921.
2. Not translated.
3. Six or eight miles from Grand Canyon station.
4. The kicking-stick race of the Pueblos; unknown to the Havasupai.
5. A burrowing rat, living on the plateau.
6. "Little things near the heart."
7. Pumpkin is prepared in long, curling strips.

37. Porcupine and Coyote (first version)[1]

PORCUPINE HAD NO ARROW. HE THOUGHT HE WOULD GO HUNTING. He thought he would get materials to make arrows. So he got them, made stone arrowheads and fastened these on the arrows. When he had finished he carried them to hunt, stuck everywhere into his body. He traveled on until he saw a deer browsing. He sat hidden under a bush for a little while, watching the deer lying in the shade. Porcupine crawled little by little toward the deer. Soon he was quite near. Porcupine was then so small that the deer could not see him. So he crawled through the deer's anus right into his belly. There he became a porcupine, so that the quills stuck into the deer everywhere. The deer jumped up and ran, but he only went a little way before he fell dead.

Porcupine came out of the deer's mouth. He had no knife with him. He talked to himself as he looked around on the ground for a sharp piece of stone: "I ought to find a good piece of stone in order to skin the deer." He repeated this many times. Coyote was hiding under a tree; he heard what Porcupine said. Coyote came out and asked, "What are you talking about over here?" "No, I did not say anything." Coyote said, "Yes, you did. I heard you say, 'I wonder where I could get a good piece of stone to skin the deer.'" Porcupine said, "Yes, I killed a big buck. I have no knife. Yes, you heard me," and he showed the deer to Coyote. When Coyote saw it, he said, "You and I will have a contest. Whoever jumps over the deer will be the victor and can skin the deer." Coyote said, "Porcupine, you run first so I can see if you jump over. If you leap over you can skin it; if you do not, but I do, I win." Porcupine started to run and tried to jump. He leaped only halfway and fell back. Then Coyote jumped over and said, "I beat you. I am going to skin it." Porcupine let Coyote have his way and skin the deer. Coyote carried the skin away and laid it on a big branch of a tree. Coyote tied the two kidneys together and hung them from the tree so that they swung low. Porcupine sat down at a little distance while Coyote went home to tell his wife and sons.

"I was out hunting and killed a big buck. I left the meat over there. I want two of our boys to start running right here at the house and race over to the deer. Whoever gets there first can have the two kidneys." The boys felt glad, so they started to run toward the deer. One of them got ahead and reached there first, but he did not find anything; all the meat was gone from the tree. The boys saw tracks on the ground where somebody had come and taken the meat. The tracks led to a high pine tree, to which Porcupine had carried the meat and put it on top.

The two boys went home and told their father, "Porcupine has carried it all away. It is on top of a tall pine tree." The father and mother went with all their children to the tree where Porcupine was. They all stood close to the pine tree and looked up at him. Coyote called to Porcupine, "We want some of your meat. Give us some." Coyote repeated this several times. Then Porcupine said, "All right, I will give you the shoulder." He took it in his hand and stood there. Looking down at the coyotes, he said, "All stand together in one place. Do not scatter. If you scatter and I throw this from such a height, I might hurt you." So he lied to them. Coyote said, "All right, all stand together in one place." Porcupine pretended to throw the meat out where all the coyotes could get it, but instead he threw it right at them and killed them all.

Only a little baby was left live under the pile of dead. Porcupine heard the baby crying and, looking down, saw it. The baby said, "Porcupine, I want you to come down and get me, and carry me up to your house." The baby said this several times before Porcupine descended and carried it up. He boiled meat for it, making soup. He put the deer blood in the paunch and, pouring it in the meat soup, stirred it up. The baby ate it all and asked, "Where is the place where you defecate?" Porcupine said, "Right up at the tip of this branch; not this strong one, but just at the tip of this weak one. That is my place." The baby crawled out on the end of the weak branch. Then Porcupine grasped it with both hands and shook it until the baby fell off and smashed into fragments on the ground. The paunch containing deer blood, which the baby had not entirely consumed, also fell to the ground. Bursting open, its contents flowed out and became the opuntia cactus.

| NOTES |

1. Told by Sinyella; interpreted by Jess Chickapanega, 1919.

38. Porcupine and Coyote (second version)[1]

PORCUPINE CAMPED ALL ALONE. HE MADE MANY ARROWS with very sharp points. He went to hunt deer. He saw two big deer. He lay down and crept along until he was right by the deer. He shot it in the shoulder. The deer ran a short distance and then fell dead. He started to butcher it with a large arrow because he had lost his knife.

He kept looking for his knife and had followed his track back two or three miles when he saw Coyote burning trees to fell them. Coyote heard Porcupine talking, so he said, "What are you talking about?" At first Porcupine would not answer Coyote. Then Porcupine said, "I did not talk. I was just walking along." "Oh yes, I heard you talk close to me. You said, 'What did I do with my knife? I lost my knife? How can I butcher my deer?' That is what you said." And Porcupine said, "I did not say that. I said, 'I want to make an arrow; I lost my knife.'" Coyote said, "No, you did not say that. You said, 'I want my knife. I killed a deer and I want to butcher him.' I want you to tell me. I have a knife and I will cut up the deer for you." Then Porcupine said, "Yes, I was hunting near here and saw two big deer. I shot one dead. I want to cut it up but I lost my knife." Coyote said, "All right, we will go over there. I have a knife. We will go over and cut up the deer."

They started to go, when Coyote said, "Where did you kill the deer?" "I killed it over there," Porcupine replied. Coyote said, "I want to see it pretty quick." They saw the deer lying on the ground. Coyote said, "Porcupine, will you run a race with me? Whoever jumps over the deer first can cut it up." But Porcupine said, "No, we cannot do that. I want you to cut it up for me. I will not do anything with you. I just want you to butcher it and skin it for me." Coyote said, "I want you to run a race with me." "No," said Porcupine, "we will just cut it up and eat it." Coyote said again, "We will run and jump over the deer." So Porcupine said, "All right, we will try it." Coyote said, "We will not go together. You go first; run up to the deer and jump over it." But Porcupine could not jump. He tried to climb over the deer but fell down again. Coyote was very glad and laughed. He said, "Porcupine, I want you to stand there and watch me." And Coyote ran as fast as he could and jumped high over the deer. Then Coyote said, "I beat you and I will cut up the deer." So he started to cut up the deer while Porcupine sat and watched him. Coyote cut it up and took everything. Then Coyote cut a little piece of intestine off and threw it to Porcupine. Then Coyote wrapped up the meat in the skin and carried it off. He took the fat too. The blood was left on the ground and Porcupine just tasted that.

The meat Coyote carried off he put up in a tree and then set out to his camp. He defecated near the tree and said to it, "When you hear Porcupine coming, I want you to call me." Coyote went to camp. Then Porcupine followed Coyote's track and came to the tree with the meat in it. Coyote's feces called out. Coyote came right back, killed Porcupine, tore him all to pieces, and threw him away. Then he took the meat down, went on, and put it in another tree. He defecated again and told it to call him when Porcupine came. Porcupine got up and followed Coyote's tracks. Coyote was warned and came back and killed Porcupine again. Coyote carried the meat further, put it in another tree. He defecated again and talked to it. He went almost as far as his camp. Porcupine followed his tracks again. He saw the meat. This time Porcupine saw what Coyote had done, and it wanted to warn Coyote, Porcupine picked up a rock and threw it in its mouth. Porcupine killed Coyote's excrements and took all the meat. He saw a tall pine tree, which he climbed, and lived there. He made a fire up there and cooked the meat.

Coyote listened but heard nothing calling him. He went to his camp and slept there. He had two little boys to whom he said, "I want you to run a race to where I left some deer meat, and whoever gets there first can have the kidneys (? *tcimpava*)." So the boys ran away. Coyote said to his wife, "We will move to where the meat is and camp there. You go ahead; after a while I will be there." The two boys ran along but saw nothing. They hunted around in the trees. Coyote came and searched too. Coyote said, "Oh, Porcupine took my meat away!" He saw the tracks of Porcupine. Coyote had many little children. Coyote followed the tracks to the pine tree and could not find the tracks going on beyond. He looked up into the tree, where he saw the fire high up. He stood under the tree and said, "I want you to give me some meat." But Porcupine would not talk. He sat in the tree and cooked and ate. Coyote asked many times for meat. Porcupine did not reply. Coyote, his wife, and children all asked for meat.

Porcupine said, "I want you all to stand over there so that I will not hurt you; then I will throw some down. Stand together away from the tree." Then Coyote and his family all stood together, and Porcupine threw the deer's shoulder down. He hit them all on the head and killed them all, except one little coyote baby. It said, "Porcupine, I want you to take me up there." It kept on repeating this. Finally Porcupine put sand on the tree trunk to make it easy for the baby to walk up the tree to where Porcupine was.

Porcupine cooked plenty of meat and made blood mush for the baby, who just ate and ate without stopping. It got very large. Porcupine said to the baby, "I want you to eat everything I give you." The baby said, "I want to go out and defecate where you do." Porcupine said, "I go far up in the tree and hang down." The baby said, "Up there?" "No, up higher." So the baby went on up, holding onto the tree. "Go far up. If you do not, I will smell it." Porcupine made the baby go further and further up. When the baby hung far up in the tree Porcupine shook the tree and the baby fell down. The baby's blood became prickly pear. Porcupine came down with a basket, picked up prickly pear, and ate and dried some.

| NOTES |

1. Told by Manakadja; interpreted by Lillie Burro; recorded by E. G., 1921.

39. Coyote and Wolf Kill Bear[1]

WOLF AND COYOTE CAMPED SOMEWHERE. THEY HAD NOTHING to eat. They wanted something to eat very much. Coyote went to where Bear lived with her two children. Bear had not come home; only the two little children were there. Coyote put them on the bed and covered them up. Then Bear came home and put tobacco in her pipe and smoked. Bear warmed herself by smoking. Coyote stayed back of the children's bed so that Bear did not see him. Coyote saw Bear doing this and said that he would like to do it too. Coyote embraced Bear, and Bear clawed flesh off his back. When the little bears woke up, Bear held up the flesh from Coyote's back. Coyote said, "That is not my back; that is your paint sack."

Coyote ran back to his camp and was very sick. Wolf watched him but did not say anything. When daylight came, Wolf said to Coyote, I told you to go to my aunt, Bear, for something to eat, but you did not mind when I told you. You did something wrong over there." He asked Coyote what he did to her. Coyote said, "I did nothing to her, but she wanted me to get wood for her and I fell down and hurt my back." Wolf said, "No, you did something wrong over there, I think." Coyote said, "No, I just went after wood and I fell down while I was holding a big piece."

Then Wolf took a deer's back and put it on Coyote, making it smooth. After he fixed the back and the piece had remained there a long time, Wolf said, "Now, Coyote, you go again and ask my aunt for something to eat, but you must do nothing wrong over there."

Then Coyote and Wolf took some deer blood and broke up small rocks and crystals, put them in the blood, and roasted it in a big fire. They took this to Bear to kill her. When they brought this to Bear's house, Bear was away getting seeds. The children were at home when Coyote came. Coyote killed the two babies and laid them on the bed and covered them up. Coyote got deer meat and the deer blood he had used to kill the babies. Wolf had told Coyote, "When Bear comes home you give her the things you brought to her."

Coyote stayed there until the Bear came home. Then Coyote gave her the things which he had and said, "My aunt, I have some things for you this time." Bear took the things. When she swallowed the mass, the sharp fragments cut her throat and killed her. She lay down and died. Wolf said, "When they are killed you must not spill the blood, but bring them all right here and we shall eat them." Coyote butchered them and, throwing away the entrails, carried the rest away.

While Coyote was going away, he thought of the things he had thrown away, so after he had gone a mile he came back to get them. He could not find them. He ran all around and still he could not find them. He saw only his own track. He ran back, but he had lost all he had and had only the rope he had used for tying. Coyote said to Wolf when he came home, "I did what you told me. I killed everybody. I cut something over there and I ran back to get it and I lost it." Wolf did not say anything; he just slept. When daylight came, Wolf said, "I told you something and I thought you would mind me. You got into trouble again."

Then Wolf did not say anything; he just stayed there. Then he said, "I do not know what we are going to do with Bear." Wolf said, "We want to make arrows and make them sharp. We shall try Bear; call to her. We will make a deep hole in the sand. Well, we shall try to do that." They made a very deep hole and they put an arrow down in it. Wolf told Coyote, "The Bear will come south, for there is snow and it is pretty cold. You stand here by the hole. Do not warm yourself by a fire. Stand there and whistle and dance."

They stood there and whistled. The wind and snow was on their faces. Coyote said, "I want to go into the house." But Wolf said, "No, you stay there to watch for Bear and whistle, for after a while Bear will come after you." Coyote said, "Now there comes Bear. I am afraid. I want to go into the house." Wolf said, "No, you stay there." Then Bear came and Coyote jumped over the hole. Bear jumped after him and fell into the hole. When Bear fell into the hole, Wolf came out and shot Bear with an arrow. "We want to kill you and eat you," he said. He killed Bear then. When they had killed Bear, they roasted her flesh and ate it all. They took the claws and strung them together to make a belt. Wolf said to Coyote, "You make yourself a dress." Wolf made himself one too. They were all dressed up.

"I want you to make a hat and put it on your head. Then run around and tell everybody that I want a dance here," Wolf said. "Now you go after the Indians around here and tell them to come to dance with me, but do not tell them we killed Bear," Wolf said.

Wolf and Coyote went around making everything clean. Then Coyote went after the Indians. He went everywhere and then went home. He said, "All the Indians are coming. All said they would come to play and dance with Wolf." The same day the Indians came, many Indians, and they began to dance. They did not tell that they had killed Bear, for Bear was grandmother to all of the Indians. Wolf had hidden the belt of Bear's claws and did not show it to Coyote. He put it under sand where they made the fire. Wolf put it there and made a fire over it. The Indians commenced to dance. They were all dressed up and wore pretty things. Coyote said, "Oh, I want a belt; I want to dress up." He looked for something and found the belt Wolf had hidden. He took it to wear in the dance.

When Coyote got the belt the Indians saw it. They said, "Oh, those are our grandmother's claws and we are dancing here." They all stopped dancing and did not dance again. In the morning they were all gone. When they had all gone, Wolf said to Coyote, "You never heed me. You showed them the belt. Do you want the Indians to kill me?" Wolf said to Coyote, "You run away. Take all our buckskins on your back. Go to the mountains and lie down there, while I will stay here. The Indians will all come back after me. I will stay here alone when the Indians come. You stay there. You showed the Indians that we killed Bear when you wore the claws; that is why they are coming after me." Then Coyote ran away and lay down to sleep there.

When the sun came up the Indians came with things to kill Wolf. They came after Wolf and shot arrows all around his house, but they could not kill him. Coyote up on the mountain said, "Kill him quickly. Shoot him in the back." The Indians killed Wolf. When they killed him they took his skin off and ran back home. When the Indians went back they made no noise.

Coyote came back and saw Wolf killed. His head was off and his skin was off. Coyote put Wolf's body on his bed and left it there alone. Coyote was all alone in the house now. He thought of Wolf dead and said, "Oh, Wolf is killed. I must kill somebody because Wolf is killed. It is not good that I stay here all alone." So he went after the Indians.

He went along the road and danced where the Indians had danced and camped where the Indians camped. In the morning he went to the Indian camp. They were all gone, except an old woman who carried a basket [by its packstrap] on her head. He went with the woman. Coyote said, "I should like to see the Indians. I have not seen the Indians for a long time." The woman said, "Where have you been? You have not heard that Wolf is killed? That is why we dance all along the road." Coyote said, "I have never heard about that. Wolf was the only one there when the Indians came and you killed him. Nobody was there to kill the Indians; Wolf was all alone. You ran away." "Yes," said the woman, "we heard about Coyote. We are afraid of Coyote." Coyote said, "Coyote is not good. He does not come after you but lies down where the sun is warm or where the fire is built." The woman said, "You sound like Coyote. I think you are Coyote." "No, Coyote just lies down. He does nothing," Coyote said. "What have you been doing?" The woman said, "When I went by there the Indians were already dancing. The women danced inside the circle and the men outside." Then Coyote killed the woman. He jumped all over her, took her bones out, and put on her skin and took her basket. Then he looked just like a woman.

He went along to where the Indians stood. They said, "Here comes our grandmother." Coyote went to where the women sang and joined the dance. When Coyote went in the circle they all danced around. Coyote danced inside. He saw Wolf's head at the center. He took a stick and caught the head on it and danced with it. Then Coyote ran away with Wolf's head.

He ran toward his home. The Indians went after Coyote. Coyote ran fast and made himself look like a dry tree. The Indians could not find him. They looked around for his tracks, but they could not find them. Coyote ran away. When he ran, many Indians ran after him and came near. He ran into the woods and made himself into a cactus. They could not find him. They looked around and saw his track. He ran fast. He took the Wolf's head and ran as fast as he could yet the Indians nearly got him. Coyote made the wind blow the sand hard so that they could not see him. And Coyote made himself light so that the wind could blow him away. The Indians could not find him; they saw no tracks, while the wind kept blowing Coyote away. The Indians did not see Coyote.

Coyote reached home and put the head on Wolf's body again. He lay down until daylight. In the morning Wolf woke up and Coyote, too. Wolf got up. He was angry at Coyote and would say nothing to him. Then one day he said to Coyote, "You go over there and get wood, plenty of it, and put it on your back. Bring it here and we will cook. We will cook deer bones in a large bucket [basket or pot?]." Wolf was angry with Coyote, very angry. He said, "I do not want to stay with Coyote. He makes trouble all the time." He stood up and looked around for something to cook. Coyote went after wood. He came back and put it on the fire. "Where is Wolf now?" he said. He looked for his track but did not see it anywhere. He looked around, but he did not find him. He only saw where they had stood to cook. Coyote said, "Where has he been? I think he went in here." But Coyote was afraid to go in where they boiled.

He left there and went down the road where he saw Wolf living. Wolf had a wife and lived there. When Wolf and his wife lay down to sleep, Coyote lay down nearby. He went over the see Wolf's wife. In the morning Coyote went to get sticks to make a fire. The stick flew on the wife's dress and the stick said, "I always burn everything." Coyote made a fire and the stick flew on Wolf's blanket. Coyote saw Wolf's wife and lay down with her. Coyote said to himself, "Wolf has a pretty woman for a wife." Coyote liked Wolf's wife because she looked very nice.

He saw a mountain sheep laying down under the rocks. He came back and told Wolf. They went together to the mountain sheep. Wolf wanted to shoot him. Wolf got an arrow. Coyote held him over the rocks. When Wolf started to shoot, Coyote pushed him over the rocks to kill him again. Then Coyote ran back to where the woman waited. Coyote wanted her, but Wolf's wife did not like him. She went into a little hole in the rocks. Coyote was afraid to go there. Wolf came back. He saw Coyote on the rocks and pushed him over.

Coyote and Wolf lived together for a while.

Then Coyote made a nice red bird. Wolf liked the bird. Coyote said, "You like the bird. Come after it." Wolf took an arrow and went after the bird. Wolf almost shot the bird, but the bird flew away. Wolf followed the bird to where many Indians lived. The Indians got arrows and killed the bird. They gave it to Wolf. Wolf went back home. (That is all of this story.)

1. Told by Manakadja; interpreted by Lillie Burro; recorded by E. G., 1921.

40. Wolf and Coyote Catch Fish (first version)[1]

WOLF AND COYOTE LIVED IN THE MOHAVE COUNTRY, WHERE they planted corn, beans, squash, sunflowers, and other things. That is what they did in order to eat. Wolf thought about it; he did not like that country. He thought he would leave to hunt for another and better country to live in. "There is no game in this country; no deer or antelope. I would like another country where there is plenty of game," he said. "I think I will leave here after about four sleeps, and I want you to play the hoop-and-pole game, shinny, and the hiding game, so that I can lose all my things, and my shell beads." Wolf said, "Coyote, my older brother's son, I told you I wanted to go in four sleeps, but I really meant four summers."[2] He sang, "I want you to roast [?] the squashes, so we can eat them all. After four sleeps I will go. I know the place where there are plenty of deer. I want to go to that place. I always wear moccasins made of jackrabbit feet; that sort of skin is no good. And jackrabbit sinews are not long enough to sew moccasins, or to tie arrows. I will go to a place where there are plenty of deer. I want to get big buckskins and long sinews. That is where I want to go. I want to make leggings, shirt, and moccasins so that I can start."

Coyote thought that the four sleeps were up, so he said, "It is four sleeps now. We ought to go right now." But Wolf said, "I did not mean four sleeps, I meant four summers." Wolf sang, "The place I want to go is named Hua'lgasiya'va [Pine Point; Powell's Plateau in the Buckskin Mountains]. I like that place. There are plenty of deer there. I want to stay at that place, where I will have abundant meat and plenty of buckskin clothing. This country where I am now is no good. All I do is plant all the time." Wolf said, "The Havasupai country contains plenty of game. I am going to stay at that place, living like those people."

Wolf said, "It is time now; four sleeps have elapsed. We have been playing games with the hoop and pole, the hiding game, and shinny. We have lost all our belongings to some other people. It is all right now, Coyote, my older brother's son. Go right to the bank of this river [the Colorado] and follow it closely upstream. When the sun has nearly set, dig a hole in the ground, fill it with wood and some little stones, and let it burn until the stones are hot. Then when the hole is ready I will come. I will walk upstream in the water. While I walk in the water a fish will bite me and hang on, another will bite me and hang on, and another and another, until they cover my whole body." Thus he directed Coyote and then he went into the water. Coyote did as he was told. He dug a hole and built a fire, and then Wolf came. He came out of the water, walked to the hole, and stripped the fish off his body onto the ground. They picked them up and threw them into the hole to roast them. Then they slept. In the morning, they dug the fish out and ate them.

Again Wolf said, "Coyote, my older brother's son, you go first and prepare a pit in the same way, build a fire and get the stones hot, while I walk in the water in the same way to get more fish." Coyote went ahead again, prepared a roasting pit and built a fire. Then Wolf came with fish clinging all over his body, and again he brushed them off and roasted them. Again they slept, and in the morning they took the fish out and ate them. Wolf said, "We have no provisions with us. I will just walk through the water again, while you go ahead and prepare. I will come with the fish and we will roast them; that is what we will do as we are traveling." Wolf said, "You go ahead again in the same way and prepare. I will come with fish." So Wolf did this, bringing fish, and they roasted them in the same way while they slept. Every morning they ate them, and when the sun had risen a little way they went on. They did as Wolf said every day.

Wolf said, "It is not very far from here to that place; perhaps we are near there now." Wolf said, "I think I want to change. I want you, Coyote, to walk in the water, while I go ahead and do as you did. I will dig a hole, build a fire in it, and prepare the camp; then you should come." When Coyote walked in the water, the fish did as before. They bit into his body all over and clung there. When he had nearly reached camp, some of the spots where they were biting hurt very badly. Coyote did not like this, so he came out of the water and pulled the skin off his penis. When the fish smelled that they fell back into the water, so that he lost them all. He had none left when he came into camp.

Wolf sang, "We have nothing to eat, so we will camp, and in the morning we will go on. I told you many times; I thought you had ears to hear what I told you. If you intend to come out of the water like that, we will have no food. The place I want to go to is not at just a little distance; it is still pretty far away. Soon you will be starved." So both kept on traveling, following the river up the canyon. That night when they made camp, they had nothing to eat. In the morning both walked along but neither went into the water, and again they made camp and slept, but they had nothing to eat.

In the morning they went on again. After going a short distance, Coyote said, "My father's younger brother, I want you to do as you did before. I want you to walk in the water and get some fishes for me to roast and eat. I am very hungry now." But Wolf sang, "I told you many times, but you would not listen to what I said to you. You have done wrong. What you wanted to do in the water was wrong. I will not help you. We will just walk along. You are starved and trail behind. You are very starved, but just keep walking behind me as we travel." Next morning they went on. When the morning was half gone, Coyote said to Wolf, "I am very hungry; I am nearly dead now. Do you know of anything growing here that can be used for food? Tell me and I will eat it." Wolf said, "No, I do not remember how to prepare these things to eat. I do not know what these things are that grow about here." So they continued walking up the canyon.

Coyote looked up at the cliff and saw many mountain sheep. He asked Wolf, "Are those animals up there eaten by men?" Wolf said, "No, nobody eats those. I do not know what they are." He did not want to be bothered to kill them, so he said, "No, no, no." They kept going up the canyon. Coyote saw many more mountain sheep close by; they continually neared sheep. Coyote said, "I am going to kill one and eat it." Wolf said, "No," and went on. When they were just a little way below where our canyon [Cataract Canyon] joins the river, the sun had nearly set. Then Coyote saw another flock of mountain sheep. He said, "It looks to me as though people used mountain sheep meat to eat. I think I won't live through this night; I am nearly dead of hunger. I want you to kill one, so that we can eat it at this camp where we will stay overnight." Wolf said, "I am dying of hunger, too," so then he went and shot one. Coyote built a fire, butchered the sheep, threw the meat into the fire, and ate it. They stayed at that spot for three or four nights, and then they moved on.

They continued until they reached this [Cataract] canyon. Then Wolf said, "This creek is called *ʰhavasu'* [water blue; Cataract Creek]. Then he crossed this creek and continued up the canyon [of the Colorado]. Again they camped and the next morning they went on again. That night when they camped again, Coyote said to Wolf, "Have we nearly reached the place you want to go?" Wolf said, "Yes, we are nearly there now." They kept traveling up the canyon, and made another camp. In the morning they went on again; that night they made another camp. Wolf said, "We are now nearly to the place where I want to go." When they were just a little below Θodof'he'e [spruce or fir tree; Indian Gardens on the Bright Angel trail], Wolf said, "We are there now," and he climbed out on the north side way up on top of the [Powell] plateau. When they were on top, Wolf said, "This is the place to which I wanted to go. I am glad we arrived. Do you not see lots of deer running around? Now it will be good to build a house for ourselves." So they built a house and lived in it.

Wolf said, "Coyote, my older brother's son, you now see how this place is situated; there are plenty of deer here. That is why I thought I would come over there. You stay at the house, while I go out to hunt." Then he went hunting. He had not gone far when he killed two big bucks, carried both to the house, and skinned and butchered them. He spread the hides on the ground and laid the sinews carefully to one side. Then Wolf said, "You see what the sinews and buckskin are like. The buckskin is a very large skin and the sinews are very long. These will be good to make moccasins, leggings, shirts, and other things to wear. This is pretty good. I am glad." Then they called that place their own country, and lived there hunting all the time. They stayed a long time, and got lots of buckskin and plenty of meat. They scraped and tanned the hides, and made moccasins, leggings, shirts, and everything to wear. That is what they did all the time they lived there. Wolf and Coyote stayed there until they became wolf and coyote.

(The place is the same way yet; there are plenty of deer on the plateau, as thick as sheep.)

| NOTES |

1. Told by Sinyella; interpreted by Jess Chickapanega, 1919.
2. This seems out of place here; see below the opening of the second paragraph.

41. Wolf and Coyote Catch Fish (second version)[1]

THE PLACE WHERE WOLF AND COYOTE HAD THEIR HOME WHEN
they were men was Wamakovan_yawa [Mohaves' house] at Needles.
All they had to eat was corn, beans, and sunflowers. They had only
rabbit, jackrabbit, and fish as game to eat. Wolf thought and said to
Coyote, "I always use the rabbit and jackrabbit sinew, but it is not long
enough. It is too short. It is not strong enough to use to make moccasins. It does not last long. I think I will go to search for a country
where there are a lot of deer, so I can have long sinews." Wolf sang to
Coyote: "Coyote, my nephew, I think we will move and look for good
long sinew. When we stay here, we always use jackrabbit fur to make
robes for bedding; that is not good. We use the rabbit skins to make
moccasins, but they wear out quickly; they do not last long. I do not
like it. I know a place where there are plenty of deer. The name of the
place is Hualgasia'va [pine point; Powell Plateau]. There are plenty of
deer. I think that when we get there we will have lots of meat and lots
of buckskin. I think we will leave here after four sleeps." (This was not
really four sleeps; it was four years.) Coyote said, "Wolf, my uncle,
it's all right now. It is four sleeps now; we are ready to go." Wolf said,
"No, I meant four years, four summers (*hopadja aduya*). I have lots
of things which we can wager at the hiding ball game, shinny, and
the hoop-and-pole game. You can play until you lose all my abalone
shell and necklaces (*apu'g*). If you wager these and someone wins all
our things, then we can go in a hurry." Coyote did this. He wagered
the necklaces and abalone until they were all lost. Coyote said, "All
your necklaces and abalone have been won by someone. It is all right;
let us go." Wolf said, "We have plenty of corn, beans, and pumpkins.
We have plenty of those left. Hurry, grind the corn, cook it. Cook

the beans and squash. We must eat all our food. We must not leave any behind." Coyote used to play with the Mohave people at shinny, hiding ball, and hoop and pole. The Mohave won all Wolf's things; nothing at all was left. They ate all the corn, beans, and all their other food. All was eaten. Then Wolf said, "It is just time now; four summers have elapsed. We will leave now. We will not go directly; we will follow the river. We do not have to have any provisions with us. If we follow the river, we can catch fish. When we stop overnight we can use them for food." (When the Walapai tell this story, they tell it longer, but when the Havasupai tell it, it is shorter.)

Wolf sang, "Coyote, my nephew, you go first, following the river bank. When you find a good place to camp overnight, dig a hole, gather sticks and put them in it, place little stones on top of this, and let them burn until they are quite hot. I will walk up in the river, and when I come out where you are, we will see what we can find on my body that we can use to roast overnight." When Wolf was ready to go into the river, he stripped off all his clothes. He walked along upstream in the river. The fish bit him everywhere, all over his legs and trunk. He came out at sunset where Coyote was. Coyote had already prepared the fire. He came close to the fire, and brushed the fish off onto the ground. He picked up the fish and threw them into the fire in order to roast them overnight. Wolf said, "We will use these to eat in the morning." They camped overnight. Next morning Wolf sang, "Coyote, you can go ahead, just as you did before. Dig a hole, make a fire; make it very hot. We will do just the same. I will walk upstream in the river to get more fish to roast in the same way we did here. If we both go together, we would not have any food to eat. We might starve and die." They left next morning [sic]. Wolf sang, "I think that the place I want to go is Hualgasia'va. That is the place I like. You should go to where we will make our next camp. Prepare the camp, dig a hole, and make a fire. I will walk in the river and the fish will bite all along my legs and trunk, and when I arrive where you are waiting I will come out." When he said this, Coyote went. Coyote carried just two rabbitskin blankets, nothing more. Wolf came out where Coyote was waiting. He did just as he did before, and put the fish in the hole to roast. He covered them and left them all night until morning. Wolf said, "That is what we will do if we keep following the river. We can eat them."

They came up the river, until they reached a spot I do not know, when Wolf said to Coyote, "You can walk in the river so the fish can bite you just as they did me. I will go to prepare the camp, just as you did." Coyote said, "I am afraid to walk in the river. I do not want to do that." Wolf said, "I want you to walk in the river so that you can catch some fish." He said it to Coyote two or three times, but Coyote did not do it. Wolf said, "All right, I will go in again." So Wolf walked in the river as he did before. Coyote went and fixed the place to camp. Wolf walked in the river and the fish bit him all over, even his penis and buttocks. When he arrived where Coyote had prepared the fire, he cooked them, staying over another night.

Next morning when they were ready to start upstream, they changed about. Coyote walked up in the river. Wolf just went ahead and prepared the camp as Coyote had done. Coyote walked in the river, and the fish bit him just as they had done to Wolf. When Coyote reached the place where Wolf waited, the fish were clustered all over his legs and trunk. Coyote did not like the sensation of fish hanging all over his body. When the fish bit, they bit so hard they hurt too much. So Coyote rubbed his penis. When the fish smelled the bad odor, they fell off at once into the water. Coyote then walked right on up the river, but no more fish clung to him. The fish no longer bit on his body. He had none when he came out where Wolf waited. Wolf was waiting. He thought they were going to have roasted fish again. He had the ground all heated for them, but Coyote brought none at all.

Wolf did not say a word; he was angry because Coyote had caught no fish. They stayed overnight. Next morning they both went along the canyon together. Wolf no longer walked in the river. He did not say a word. They stopped another night. Next morning they went on the same way; Wolf said nothing. They stopped another night. Next morning they just went along. Another night, making four nights, Coyote said, "My cousin (? Nᵧanyadjau widj), you will have to walk in the river again to catch more fish." Wolf said, "No. Perhaps you do feel hungry, but you didn't get any before."

Next morning they started again. Coyote looked about and said, "That thing looks as though it might be used for food. If you know about it, tell me, so that I can prepare it to eat." Wolf said, "No." But Coyote, whenever he saw anything, asked Wolf about it. Wolf always said, "No." Coyote said this as they were coming along the riverbank. They saw mountain sheep. Coyote asked Wolf, "Is their meat good for people to eat?" Wolf said, "No." Coyote said, "It looks like it. I am quite starved. I want you to kill one so I can eat it." Wolf said,

"No." Coyote asked wolf about something else, agave [*via laha'na*, 'good mescal'; larger than mescal, very sweet]. "It looks as though food could be made out of it." Wolf said, "No, I do not know what it is." They kept on, and saw another flock of mountain sheep rams. Coyote said, "You kill one." Wolf felt pretty hungry too, but he said nothing. Wolf went after the sheep and killed one. They built a fire, cooked, and ate it. Wolf said, "We have plenty of meat. I think we will stay here for two or three nights. I will dry some, and we can eat all the rest. The place where I want to go to live is Hualgasia'va. There are plenty of deer there. I would like to have good big buckskins to make good moccasins. Though you feel tired and sore from walking, just keep on." Wolf said, "Coyote, my nephew, tie up the sheep meat and we will go. I think we are quite close to the place I want to reach. Though you feel tired and your feet are sore, just keep walking. We will arrive at that place some one of these days." They came close to where Havasu [Cataract Creek] joins Hagataia [Colorado River], and crossed it [the creek]. They continued upstream. Wolf said to Coyote, "We are quite close now. Walk a little faster." As they went on up the canyon Wolf said nothing.

They reached a place, perhaps Bass's camp or below Bright Angel, where they climbed up on the plateau. They reached the top. "That is the game I thought I wanted," Wolf said. "There are plenty of deer, just like flocks of domestic sheep. That is what we wanted to have, so we came here. Coyote, my nephew, you stay here at the camp. I will go out alone to hunt deer. Every day I will go out and get two bucks; every day I will do this." Coyote stayed at camp, drying the venison, scraping the hides, tanning the skins just as the Indians do. He threw all the buckskins together. It was a large pile; he had a great many. When Wolf had lots of buckskin soft-tanned, he made a shirt and leggings to wear. Wolf said, "That is what I wanted to do. We like this. That is why we came here. I am glad." Wolf said, "We have lots of buckskins tanned here. I think we will take them all over to the other side of the Colorado River where there are many people, my relatives, to trade with. That is what I will do." So he took all his buckskins, shirts, and leggings over there. (I do not know where that place was, where there were a lot of people. They say it was on the other [east] rim of Coconino Basin.) He arrived there with his possessions. He traded them for blankets. (They do not say when they tell this story what sort of people those were who had the blankets to trade.) After they traded for blankets, both returned to the other side to Powell Plateau. They returned to their own house to stay. Wolf said, "I am going to be a wolf; in the same way you are going to be a coyote. You will not have to kill anything. You will just travel around; perhaps you will find a dead animal, or steal something. You can do this." He said to himself, "I am going to be a wolf. I will be a hunter and kill deer and all sorts of large animals. I will do the same as you, just travel around, but I will kill big animals. I will be a wolf."

| NOTES |

1. Told by Sinyella; interpreted by Jess Chickapanega, 1921.

42. TURKEY[1]

MANY INDIANS WERE LIVING TOGETHER. TURKEY HAD A WIFE. He went hunting cottontails and jackrabbits which he roasted. The next day he hunted again. Turkey's wife said, "Our house is too cold; we cannot stay here. When it is cold, I feel sick." Every morning she went to another camp while Turkey went hunting. She always told Turkey at whose camp she stayed. One day she went to the camp of Tadi'θa [a small yellow bird]. She roasted some seeds; then she said, "I want to go to another camp. It is too cold for me here," and she went away. But Turkey stayed at home and thought how his wife went away every day. He thought he would go to see how she went around to the Indians' camps all day. Then Turkey went to Tadi'θa's camp and looked in through the roof. He saw that there were many women in the house, and Tadi'θa had intercourse with all of them, Turkey's wife among them. When Turkey saw this, he ran back home. He lay down in his camp and did not go hunting any more. After a while Turkey's wife came home. She brought some seeds and made mush for him. Turkey refused to eat it. In the morning he ate nothing but went off to hunt. He neither ate nor talked. His wife cooked for him, but he did not eat, so she threw away the food. Then she said, "What is the matter with you that you do not eat what I cook? I always throw it away." Turkey said, "You always go away to other camps. You never stay at home to work for yourself. You always go to Tadi'θa's camp; I saw what you did there. That is why I do not eat what you cook." And Turkey said, "I saw you in Tadi'θa's house. I do not like to have you here when you do that. You go to Tadi'θa and marry him." "Oh no, I do not do anything in Tadi'θa's house. I just work there." Then Turkey got very angry and said, "I will go away. I will not stay any longer."

He tied up his things and got ready to leave. When he had gone about two miles his wife came up with him. He said, "You stay and marry the Indians," but she walked along with him. Turkey killed a few rabbits and roasted them when he camped for the night. He ate it all and gave his wife none. Next morning he went on and his wife walked along behind him. In the evening he killed a rabbit and camped overnight. The next morning he said to his wife, "You had better go back and cook something for those Indians. I am going a long way; you might die." "All those Indians, my nephews, will not do anything to [for?] me," his wife said. The next morning before he started he said, "You go back to the Indians." But she would not go, she followed Turkey. He killed a jackrabbit but he gave none to his wife. The next morning he set out again. He killed a cottontail and a jackrabbit. He camped somewhere, roasted and ate them, but he gave none to his wife. After eating, Turkey lay down. His wife wanted to sleep with him but Turkey would not let her. His wife was cold; she made a fire and sat by it. She had nothing to eat; she was very hungry. The next morning he started out and said to his wife, "I want you to go back. They might kill me." And again he killed some rabbits but he gave none to his wife. Again he would not let her sleep with him.

Turkey said to his wife, "I want you to go back. I will get into much snow now. You might get cold and die there. You see those big clouds over there? I am going where it is very cold. You might die." The next morning he went along again and killed a rabbit, but he gave his wife nothing. He always told her to go back but she always went along with him. And still he gave his wife no food. At night when he lay down, his wife wanted to sleep with him, but he wrapped up in his blanket and would not have her. Turkey came to Red Butte and slept there. Again his wife wanted to sleep with him but he would not let her. In the morning he saw snow and clouds; when he started again he found snow everywhere. It was very cold. He made a fire because his wife looked very cold. But he did not stay with her very long. Turkey made himself into a turkey; he was no longer an Indian. He climbed up into a pine tree, leaving his wife below. Her fire had gone out; the snow covered it up. Then Turkey could see his wife, for she was down in the snow. It was very cold and the wind was blowing. The snow covered all the firewood. The woman was almost dead. She said, "Oh, my husband, take me up where you are." But Turkey would not listen.

She could not sleep all night. When daylight came she stopped talking. Turkey thought she was dead.

His wife was pregnant. In the morning Turkey flew down and saw that his wife was dead. When he came to the ground he brushed away the snow and made a fire. He pushed his wife over to the fire. She was frozen. When he put her by the fire he cut her open and found her full of small snakes, lizards, tadi'θas, all kinds of birds, and one baby turkey. He took that but killed all the others. He took care of the little turkey. He carried it on his back and went over to Hua'lagasia'va [Powell's Plateau]. Then he went near Grand View to live.

| NOTES |

1. Told by Manakadja; interpreted by Lillie Burro; recorded by E. G., 1921.

43. THE BUNGLING HOST STRIKES HIS HEAD[1]

WOLF WAS CAMPING ALONE WHEN COYOTE CAME TO SEE HIM. Coyote said, "My uncle, I wanted to see you very much, so I came. I am glad to see you." Wolf said "I am very glad to see you, too. You may stay here, but I have nothing to eat. I have no woman to gather wild seeds to cook. But stay here." After a while Wolf took a bowl, which he filled with water. Then he took a big stone and, pounding his head behind the ear, made seeds fall into the water. He gave this to Coyote to drink. Coyote drank it up and lay down to sleep with Wolf.

In the morning he started for his own camp. Wolf pounded more seeds out of his head, put them in a sack, and gave them to Coyote to take home. Coyote left. When he had gone but a little way, he stopped and said, "My uncle, I want you to come to my camp to see me after four days." Wolf remained there. After four days he said to himself, "I want to go to see my nephew; that is what he told me to do." Wolf set out looking for Coyote's camp. When he arrived he sat with Coyote, who, after a time, said, "I have nothing to eat at my camp. I have nothing to give you to eat." After a while Coyote took a bowl, filled it with water, and pounded his head with a stone. He fell dead in the water. Wolf saw him lying dead. Then he picked him up, put him in the fire, and returned home.

| NOTES |

1. Told by Manakadja; interpreted by Lillie Burro; recorded by E. G., 1921.

44. The Bungling Host Is Stepped On[1]

COYOTE CAMPED ALONE WHILE SUWA'GIDJIGWI'NA CAMPED about eighteen miles away. Coyote said, "I think I will go to see my uncle." He went there, where he saw that his uncle had plenty of mountain sheep meat hung to dry. His uncle cooked some for him and said, "I am glad you came to see me." Coyote slept with him. In the morning he started home, taking a quantity of the meat which his uncle gave him. After Coyote had gone but a short way, he turned and asked, "How do you kill the mountain sheep?" His uncle replied, "I go to the waterhole where the mountain sheep drink. There I lie down. When the sheep come they step on my back, but it is as slippery as ice, so they fall off on the rocks, and I can club them to death." Coyote said, "All right, we have a little waterhole near my camp. I will do that there. We have plenty of mountain sheep. Come to my camp after four days and eat meat."

After four days the uncle set out to visit his nephew, Coyote. He wanted to see him. When he arrived at Coyote's camp, he found no one there; it looked like an old camp. He looked for Coyote's tracks and found some two or three days old. He came to the waterhole where he found Coyote in pieces, for the mountain sheep had stepped on him. The uncle collected them, put them in the fire, and returned to his camp.

| NOTES |

1. Told by Manakadja; interpreted by Lillie Burro; recorded by E. G., 1921.

45. The Bungling Host Fires the Brush[1]

PORCUPINE LIVED SOMEWHERE. HE CLEARED THE GROUND for races and games. He wanted to build a fire with a bundle of tinder (*tcakaya'l*). There were many deer about; he thought he would kill them with fire. Fire burns all trees; the deer cannot escape through it, but must run into the camp and fall dead. So Porcupine built fires all around the deer. The fierce blaze came near. Porcupine ran back to the clearing. He wanted to go under the ground to escape burning. He scraped at the ground; it was quite soft and water came out of it. The fire came close to the spot where the water was coming out. When the water had all come out Porcupine went into the hole. The deer were all killed in the clearing. After a while Porcupine came out. The fire was out. Porcupine saw that he had plenty of deer. When he cut the deer up he dried the meat on the trees. He lived there cooking the deer meat.

After a while Coyote came from a great distance and said, "Well, I have to go see my uncle." He found Porcupine living there and saw that he had plenty of meat drying in the trees. Porcupine cooked for Coyote and Coyote slept with him. In the morning Coyote returned. Porcupine gave Coyote a quantity of meat and fat. Coyote tied it on his back and started to return. He went a little way and asked, "My uncle, how do you kill the deer?" "Oh, I make a fire in a wide circle and clear a place in the middle. Then I scrape a hole and go under the ground so the fire does not touch me. That is how I killed the deer," said Porcupine. "Oh, so you do that," said Coyote. "There are plenty of deer around my camp. I will do that too. My uncle, I want you to come and stay with me after four sleeps. You will have plenty of meat there, just as here." After four days Porcupine thought of his nephew and said, "Well, my nephew said he was going to kill deer. I will go over and see." Porcupine went to Coyote's camp, but found that he was not there. He thought, "Perhaps he is off hunting somewhere." He looked around for his tracks but found that they were old. He saw that Coyote had made a fire just as he had done, but that Coyote had not gone into the ground as he had. Coyote had burned up and died. Then Porcupine went back to his house and stayed there.

| NOTES |

1. Told by Manakadja; interpreted by Lillie Burro; recorded by E. G., 1921.

46. Deer Tricks Coyote[1]

COYOTE SAW THAT DEER HAD TWO FAWNS COLORED WHITE and dark all over. They looked very pretty. Coyote asked Deer, "How did you make your fawns like that? They look very pretty." Deer answered, "Oh, I made a fire with plenty of smoke. The smoke colored them."

Coyote went home. After a while she gave birth to three whelps. Then Coyote made a fire in a hole, put her babies in it, and sealed it up. The little coyotes in the hole were being suffocated and they cried, "Ka, kaka." Coyote said, "Stop your crying. I will make you look pretty." In a little while the coyotes stopped crying, so she took the fire away and pulled the babies out. They were all dead. Coyote said, "That is a very bad deer. She told me a lie and I killed all my babies."

| NOTES |

1. Told by Manakadja; interpreted by Lillie Burro; recorded by E. G., 1921. Compare *Havasuapi (Yuman) Texts*.

47. Bat[1]

BAT HAD THREE WIVES WITH WHOM HE CAMPED. AT DAYLIGHT
he went hunting deer and came home at night. When he came home
he said, "Put sand on the fire. I do not want you to make a fire." He
went hunting again. When he came home at night, the women wanted
the meat. Bat said, "You keep the fire away from me." He said, "I
have grease for you." In the daylight he went again while the women
stayed home. They said, "We do not know what is the matter with
him; he does not want fire." They shredded some bark for tinder and
put it by the fire in order to start it when he should return so that they
could see what he had been doing. When he came home he said, "I
bring the grease again. Put sand on the fire." The women all put sand
on the fire. He came in, put down his pack, and after he had stayed
a while the women built a fire. They saw Bat; he was very ugly. They
were afraid so they ran out and flew into the sky where they became
stars. Then they saw Bat no more.

| NOTES |

1. Told by Manakadja; interpreted by Lillie Burro; recorded by E. G., 1921.

48. Song Series[1]

ONE MAN, VATI'MA, WATCHED THE SUN ACROSS THE SKY. WHEN it was about set he said, "I am going to make a song about the sun. Just as the sun sets I am going to sing a lot of songs about it." So he sang two songs:

inya'a	ya'moghonove'		(repeat)
sun	the place where it sets		
inya'a	sako'mik	n ionyapu'k	(repeat)
sun	to travel across	the edge of the sky	
ki'lheee[k]			(repeat)
fall down jingling[2]			

The second song he sang was:

inya'aha	ya'hamo
sun	the place where it sets
oove'gwi'i	soma'nya igwe'
	spirit some song
soma'nya	igwe'ee
inya'aha	ya'ahamo

"I am going to leave my ground, my rocks, my country," he sang, and he sang many songs about the things he saw.

awi'inama'aga
rocks I leave

a'amo'tnama'aga nama'aga
ground I leave

djo'o ya'amaga'a
I go

nama'aga   djo'o   ya'a'maga'a

When he reached another country where there were plenty of people, he wanted them to clear the ground, so that they could sing and dance. They cleared the ground well and he sang:

mi'kidjokwodiii   ko'nomahaawe'e novowi'i   konomaha'awi
place cleared good   I am doing it

That man went to the dancing ground where all the men stood in a circle, and went right into the dance:

vawe'egini'ima   vawe'egini'ima
I am standing to sing now

i'djogwo'diθa'na   vawe'enyi'ma
at the cleared ground

Right in the center of the dance circle stood a pole with a man's intestines on its top. He sang:

pa'vahasao'no   e'emi'iega'aha
man guts stuck up (on something)   yes, it is

apa'vahasab'no'o

When they danced each one shuffled his feet sideways. He sang:

matapu'nya   maθa'agama'ne'e
dirt dust-cloud   dirt push to one side

(repeat)

gama'nee gama'nee gama'nee

They all had their fingers intertwined with those of their neighbors. When the man saw this he sang:

mi'iso'lmapai'hage	mivatciitu'mhage
ha'aya'ahahani'ihime	
hands clasped together	hands clasped (?)

ha'aha'ahahani'ihime

Next the married women danced with the unmarried men, and
their husband[s] outside the dance ring became angry and soon came
in. Dragging them out, they beat them. Then the man sang, "I see
them fighting with their wives."[3] All the women who had babies tied
them in their cradles, and left them here and there in the camp while
they came to the dance. The man heard the babies crying, so he sang,
"I hear the babies crying." Next the man sang about his older brother's son who had left the dance with a woman. "I cannot see my
nephew." Next he sang about the eagle tail feather he wore in his
headband: "I am an eagle." . . .

(I do not know any more of this story; it is a long one.)

| NOTES |

1. Told by Sinyella; interpreted by Jess Chickapanega, 1919.
2. This is onomatopoetic.
3. The songs that follow were not recorded.

APPENDIX

HAVASUPAI (YUMAN) TEXTS

By Leslie Spier.

The Havasupai of Cataract Canyon, Arizona, are the most easterly Yuman speaking group. These texts in their language were obtained incidentally during a field trip for the Southwest Society of New York in 1921. The first was told by Sinyella, the second by Mark Hanna ; both were corrected and translated by Jess Checkapanyega. Due to my interpreter's imperfect command of English, I am uncertain at some points of the tense, and even occasionally of the sense. It is offered only because there is little Havasupai material in print. Other versions of the stories were recorded.

The phonetic scheme is as follows :

a	as in father
ä	hat
e	fate
i	pique
o	note
u	rule
ą	but
ĕ	met
ï	pin
ŏ	not
ŭ	put
ω	law
g	velar g

The remaining symbols follow the " Phonetic Transcriptison of Indian Languages " [1]. Kʳ probably corresponds to ʈ (cerebral t) but for lack of certainty as to its exact character, the strong trill is indicated as shown. Some

1. Smithsonian Miscellaneous Collections, v. 66, n° 6, 1916.

words are given with several spellings ; the differences may be significant. Primary and secondary accents were not disguished in recording the text. Glottalization is weak. Final vowels are habitually elided.

WOLF'S BOY

hatagwilahadj   ku'dą ąpai'ïtïg   θŏknue'vigą
Wolf   long ago was a man. He was living

hąwil wiŋagwa' n̦awe'vïg   n̦aluwa' pe'mïg
   mountain camp.   " My wife I lack.

ąsi'taŋig vŏkwa'θąm ha'nàtąopigą pąkʳi'ⁿ
Alone   being   not good.   Woman

ąluwe' vąmą vąkwŏ'k gwenąwi'dąm ąma'hagą
   married   stay   something to eat cook.

ąsï'taŋïg   vagwa'θïg   gwenąwi'dïg
Alone   I stay   something to cook

ąsapo'tąo'pïg iya'mŏg   sãsavąsω'ha
I don't know.   I went   (a small piñon bird)

vądjai'⁗ą ąsi'tąm iyo' iya'mïg iyu'g sãsavąsω'ha
daughters one   to get.   I went many times
                 Piñon Bird's

n̦awa'ha va'mŏg   pąkʳi'ⁿąsi'tąθąm   aiyŏ'k
   house   women one   I get

ãluwe'higą pąkʳi'hidj o'pągą ya'mąyi'tao'pąg
for a wife. Woman   not   want to come.

e   mao'pïgmimo'me   avo'mhïg'iu
Yes,   if one don't want to go   I return. "

hatągwiląhĕdj   vo'gŭg yug   hatągwiląhą
   Wolf   returned.   Wolf

n,in,awa'ha   n,iva'g   kavạyu'm
his house   arrived.   "I wonder why

sǎsavạsωha   vidjai'ạhědj   inya"ạkokn_y-
Piñon Bird's   daughters   me   no

aạha'notạo'pig   ï'mo'ï   wa'ạsi'vạg vakwǒ'g
good   say.   Thinking of it stay.

hàwai'ạvidj   vag'yǔ'm   halạgata'pạ
Pool   I know where   abalone shell

valdjạwǔ'g   halạgata'pạ   ạha'vil   muwa'
put in.   Abalone shell   water   leave in.

tạwai' ạ tạo'pïtïg   miya'apě'
Not very long   appear to be alive.

apa'n,ạmạvạluwi'hagwïgï'ï   ạsitạsma'm
It will be alive like a man.   After one sleep

ạva'hěg'iu   hatạgwi'lạ   va'mǒg hạwai'ạ
I will return."   When Wolf   got to the pool

va'mǒg halạgata'pạ ug   k'ě'djạm apa'n_y-
abalone he looked at.   A little it looked

avạluwi'g   u'θạm   yu'ïg
like a man.   When he looked   appeared

ha'nạg valuwǒ'g   halạgata'pạ ïtcawo'widj
good inside.   Abalone where he left it

maha'nạ   miy,nï'wïgmiu   towai'ạ tạo'pïtïg
good   progressing.   "Not very long

ïnya'   apa'vạ   mạvạluwi'miy,nï'wïgmiu
like me   a man   it will appear.

sạsavạsω' vidjai'ạhěg madj miya'mạhïgmiu
Piñon Bird's daughters you   go over."

hatạgwila   yǒg   θǒ'kdjạwǒ'g   djạθu'lǔg
Wolf   took it   from there   washed

paiạma'tvạya''aha'nǒg   wi'vïdjǒkθạvạtï'm
all over the skin good.   Rock hole

valdjạwǒ'g taǒ'mǒg   kạθǒdhědj '
place inside close with something.   Coyote

1. The ǒ has deep pitch.

ya'mǒg hama'n'ạ   yǔgạ   pa'pǔg
went. Child   he took. Carrying it on his
back

vo'gǔg ạwa'hag vag   n,ïva'm   hatạgwi'lạhědj
he arrived at the   When they   Wolf
house.   arrived,

ug   kạθǒdhedj '   ïg   in,a'home'vidju
looked. Coyote   said,   "This is my son."

hatạgwi'lạhědj   gwawǔg   o'pạ   kạθǒd '
Wolf   spoke,   "No,   Coyote,

mohome'vạdju'tạ   tu'yạvïdju   in,a'a
that is not your son,   not at all.   Mine

hatạgwi'lạvạ home'vïdju magạθǒ'dn,ědj ' madj
Wolf's   son.   You, Coyote,   you

mïdjạθu'lig   miạ'ha'nạ   hatạgwi'lạ gwa'wǔg
wash him   good".   Wolf   spoke,

in,ahome'vïdj ya'mǔg sạsavạsω'ha vạdjai'ạha
"My son   is going Piñon Bird's daughters

ạsi'tạm yo'mihigui yo'mạm   vǒkwǒ'g
one   to fetch. Fetch   to stay here

teya'djta'g   sǔmkwï'nạm   ama'djạ
grinding corn, stirring it,   we will eat it.

mạ   miya'mạ   sạsavạsω vidjai'ạha miyǔ'g
Now,   go,   Piñon Bird's daughters get,

n,a'ạluwa"mi   halạgata'pạ apai'ïg
say 'You be my wife."   Abalone was man

ạha'nïga hatạgwi'lạ home' ka'umě'ě mạ
real.   Wolf's son was Kaume. "Now,

miya'mạ   sạsavạsω'han,ạwa'ha   mava'mạ
go.   Piñon Bird's house   go.

mạva'mǒg   mạu'   sạsavạsω'ha vạdjě'hïdj
Go there to look.   Piñon Bird's daughter

makaumě'mě'nyạ   n,ïma   ạha'nogạθo
you, Kaume, likes,   when she   likes you

in,aluwa'   mi'hig'mi   va'mạm
'My wife,   you say.'   When you arrive

nᵧi'u'giθᶏ pᶏkʳi'hïdj kaumē'nyᶏ nᵧīmu'gᶏθᶏ
she will see woman Kaume see,
you

e nᵧamᶏ'ᶏha'nogᶏθᶏ ya'mᶏhig
'Yes, I feel well disposed to want to go.'

pᶏkʳu'yᶏvidj hᶏwō'gig iya'mïdjᶏ kᶏumē'
Women two will go to be Kaume's

luwa'vidj ᶏpa'vᶏ ᶏha'nïdjog'iu ᶏha'nïgiu
wives. Man both like, 'Good,

iya'mdji'hig'iu hatᶏgwi'lᶏ homē'vïdj
let us go together'" Wolf's son

sᶏsavᶏsω'ha vïdjai'ᶏ hᶏwō'gam yūg
Piñon Bird's daughters two took'

sᶏsavᶏsωhïdj gwa'wūg ma'ᶏpa'vïdj kaumē
Piñon Bird spoke, "Our men with

nyūm matē'nᶏmō'govᶏ te'nᶏma'govūg
Kaume will run races. Run races with him

mᶏmō'didjᶏ ma paᶏtē'θig pai'yᶏ ma'hïg'i
for his stakes. Now, many men all everyone

iya'mīg'iūg kaumē'hēdj ᶏsi'tᶏθig mata'vūg
should go." Kaume alone north

teya'vūg ya'mūg yu'ūg'i kaume'vᶏ
that way went did. Kaume

nᵧamō'gᶏdjigᶏ yā'djmigᶏ ya'mūg viyū"ē
many run ahead kept going this way

nᵧato'povagᶏ satu'lūg sᶏsavᶏsω'hïdj ha'mūg
sunset place west. Piñon Bird looked :

pagatau'ᶏ inᵧa'nᵧawe'widj wi'hïlau'ᶏ
"Our men, my relatives Moon Mountain

hopa'djᶏ toka'vagūg θiyu'idjïg kaume'widj
four times around turn back." Kaume

kavᶏyu'g ᵔc'vīg yu'gyumω'yu
looked weak they look as he went far.

θeyu'wï'θag kaume'vᶏ nᵧama'gᶏdjïg
He was coming Kaume they were beating

ᵔθiyu'g kaumē'widj yuᶏta'mūgiu
him one coming. Kaume he was returning

wihalau'ᶏ hopa'djᶏ tᶏka'vōgūg
Moon Mountain four times round

yuita'migiu kaumē'widj yu'ig pagᶏha'-
returning. Kaume come back about

vōgta'mōgui swa'dōg katē'nᶏma'-
to get to many men, he sang, "Many foot

govᶏdidj paᶏhami'lādj mᶏvᶏyō'mōgᶏ
racers 'Brother-in-law, keep running'

yᶏvᶏmi'djïg miyu'tᶏ kamᶏyu'djïgmiu'
say to one another do not say at all.

inᵧa'itcïka'vōdj mᶏvᶏya'mogᶏ miyutᶏ kavᶏyu'-
My cousins are running they do

g'miu inᵧakaumē'vïdj iya'mᶏg ᶏhà'
not run fast. I, Kaume, to go fetch water

gwema'vᶏ ᶏgana'vᶏm ᶏpa'mᶏgōvgau'widjω
food will tell them. Fetch to meet the men

gïdjōvgau'vᶏ gina'vē gapē" ya'mïgiug
lots of food I will tell them. Ball go

sᶏsavᶏsωha inᵧawa'ha avᶏ'mᶏg'iug
Piñon Bird's house I will get there.

pᶏk·u'yᶏ hᶏwō'gam sᶏsavᶏsω' vïdjai'ᶏ
Women two Piñon Bird's daughter

yug ᶏgwēinya'djᶏka'vᶏhi'g'wi ḡwa'gᶏ
come. I will put up as stakes buckskins

kavūg no'hovūg sᶏsavᶏsω' homai'ᶏ
wager hiding game Piñon Bird's sons

vïdjai'ᶏ inya'tᶏk'ipᶏm sᶏsavᶏsω'ha vïdjai'ᶏ
daughters at night." Piñon Bird's daughters

kaumē'hēdj pama'djigᶏ ᶏgwa'gᶏ ᶏgwe
Kaume won. "Buckskin various things

pai'yᶏ inyadjᶏpa'ma'dᶏ sᶏsavᶏsω'ha
everything I, from the men, win." Piñon
Bird said,

ᶏgwe' gwiinya'djᶏ ḡwa'gᶏ mᶏga'vūg
"Anything blankets buckskin show as
stakes

mątŏ'covą ta'cąvąta'mŏθig wĩ'θig
play at shinney". Playing shinney trying

kaumĕ'hĕdj pai'yą pama'ṭig sãsavąsѡ'hĭdj
Kaume all won. Piñon Bird

gana'vŭg'ĭg mądu'dŏvą
told them to play hoop and pole game.

ma mui'dją kaumĕ'nĭdj kaviyu'tavŏg
Let us do it. Kaume looks like a good
player

gwĭ'mowi pai'yą pama'ṭig
going to do it. From everyone won all,

kaumĕ'hĕdj pama'ṭig kaumĕ'hĕdj sãsavąsѡha
Kaume won all. Kaume, Piñon Bird's

vĭdjai'ą huwŏ'gąm yŭg va'mŭgiu
daughters two taking, arrived.

n,iya'mŭm pąk'u'yąvĭdj pai'yą atĕ'ką
While going women all many

ya'djminyĭgą sãsavąsѡ'hĭdj gwau'ig'i
followed. Piñon Bird spoke,

pagątau'ą ĭnyąwe'wĭdj ma miya'djmĭg
"Men, run faster my own. Let us go

kaumĕ'ha mągąha'vŭg mątągwa'nĭdją
Kaume catch up with kill him."

kaumĕ'hą gia'θig kŏkdjĭna'lĭdjątąo'pĭg
Kaume shot at did not hit him.

pąk'u'yiyą hapi'dą paiyą pa'gĭdjmuwa'-
Women only all kill humans

djidjĭgwi kaumĕ'hĕdj swa'dĭg paiyą'apai'-
repeatedly. Kaume sang, "Unnatural

yą ąha'novĭdj iyu'tĕ hatągwĭ'ląhĕdj
birth not good myself. Wolf

paiyą'apai'yą ąha'ną n,iyo'vąvĭdj iyu'tĕ
unnatural birth not good make me myself.

kŏkyu'tąg ya'ątu'vŭg ąmądjai'ĭgą ąθu'-
I am not thirsty hungry feeling

inyąvŭm mątągwa'nĭdją miyi' tau'mąmi'i
weak they cannot kill me can never do it.

mãvau'djimą ąma'nąma'gĭdjim iya'-
Many going back let me alone, I will

mąhĭ'g'iu vąkŏ'k iyu'ṭig ĭgia'gą idja'mąhĭg
go." He was doing it he shot hitting

wi'hĭgwĭg'itą pai'yą panyągamąwa'djĭg
every time. All men he killed

panyąwi'dĭhig'iwi tŏtgwa'ųig atĕ'k
completely. He killed them many

pu'yĭg wigwĭ'tĭg inya'hŏtc
immobily dispersed. While he sunset
did this,

to'pi'hĭgu yu'hĭdj ąpai'ątig θo'kva'g
sank behind. Owl, who was like there
a man,

va'θąm kaumĕhĕdj o'pŭg'ĭgig kamiyu'hŭg
arrived. Kaume said, "No, no, why

mąva'g miu'momiu yu'tąg mątągwa'-
do you come here? " Perhaps someone

nĭdjąhimĭ yu'hĭdj gwau'ig pa'ągya'-
will kill you." Owl said, "I am going to

hŏg'iu tu'yą vąvąte'yąmiu'djig
shoot someone." Nothing fluffed his feathers.

sãsavąsѡ'ha homai'yą iyu'hą kya'θig
Piñon Bird's sons at owl shooting

vŏṁvątumu'ĭgą kąsso'k ka'ka'ka' gwe'-
grazed him. Crow said, "Ka, ka, ka, what

miyu'djinŭgmiu n,imiyu'djiθąm miyu'tąg
are you doing? If that is what
you do,

apa'manne'hĭdj'djihĭg'wi apakya'hŏgyugi'i
men killing you. I know which man
I will shoot.

miya'vŏg yug ąpakya'gwi
From the air I come shooting men."

sãsavąsѡ' homai'ą kąssã'ką kya'k ne'hĭdjiga
Piñon Bird's sons Crow shoot killing.

inyato'pŏkĭgiu inya'tąk'ĕ pigiu kaumĕ'hĭdj
The sun had set a little dark Kaume

gwau'ig   apa'yu'   matahai'a   amatinyä'dja
said,   "You Owl   of the wind   sand
     man,   black

agisima'vidj   iyu'mämigmi'nya   vaswa-
are a shaman,   that is what you said.   Tear

vami'wa   inya'tak'i'pa   kaumë'hidj
some off   and make it dark."   Kaume,

yu'hŭm   pak'u'yavidj   hawö'ga   ya'mŭg
Owl,   and women   two   going

hatagwi'laha   n,awa'ha   nava'mŏg pak'u'ya
Wolf's   house   arrived.

hawo'ga   wa'ha   va'migiu   pak'u'ya
House   he arrived   women

hawö'gam wa'ha   pagami'migwi   n,ahami'djima
two   house   bringing.   "My relatives,

ha'nigiu   pak'u'ya   hawö'gam   miyŭ'g mava'm
good   women   two   he took arrived

ha'nigiu   adiyĕ'giu   teya'dj   tag
all right   I am glad.   Corn   you grind,

sŭmkwi'nidjima   mag   ha'nigiu   ig'i'i
stir it, and   eat it;   it is good;   I say it."

kwa'ga   n,ig   ne'hog   hage'g
Deer   they hunted,   caught it,   carried it
                                     on the back,

vókvami'nvai'g'ig   kwa'gamat matau'lam
and dropped the load.   "Venison we will boil

amä'dja   hatagwi'lahĕdj   luwa'äpe'mig'iu
and eat it."   Wolf   had no wife

tu'asi'taθig'iu   kaumë'widj   pak'u'ya   hawö'gam
entirely alone.   "Kaume,   women   two

muwi'djig   asi'tam   amaë'nya   asi'taθig
you have,   one   give to me.   Alone

vókwa'θam   aha'natao'piga   gweinyi'nig
to stay here   is not good;   something to
                                    fornicate

wa'laiyi'gyug'i'i   kaumë'hidj   gwau'-
I like to do", he said.   Kaume   did not

wŭgtao'pig   vakŏ'k   pak'i'va   asi'tam
speak :   refuse   woman   one,

n,ae'gwa'layi'tao'pig   kaumëhidj   waiya'älai'g
he felt he would not.   Kaume   angry

wiya'migiu   vakŏ'kvahatao'piga   sma'mŭg
went away.   He did not return   for many

sma'mŭg sma'migiu   n,iva'g   asi'tinyasma'g
sleeps.   After(?)   one sleep

hatagwi'lahidj   gwau'ig   home'widj   vatao'-
Wolf   said,   "My son   does not

pigiu   iya'mŭg   inyä'dj   ahaatagwi'lovidj
return. I am going.   I,   Wolf,

iya'mag   aa'mdjigaha'me   kaumë"ĕ
am going   to walk about to   Kaume's
              look around."

yu'woha   misi'k n,iya'mag   yu'tam
tracks   he followed.   The erstwhile

kaumë'hĕdj   amuti'wŭgiu   hatagwi'lahĕdj
Kaume,   had become a   Wolf
             mountain sheep.

yu'tag ug   vama'dji'wŭg   kwa'va
saw him   and seized him.   Horns

yïlhlu'yïlhlu'yïg   wiwi'mŭg   ma
he pulled off   and cast away.   "Now,

kaumë"ĕ   vo'mïdja   kamiyu'g   vókmaa'-
Kaume,   come with me.   Why   do you

mdjig   maiyumω'miu   aha'natao'pig'iu   ma
wander   you ?   That is not good,   let

avo'mïdja   va'mïdjïg   wa'ha   n,aäluwa
us go."   They reached the house.   "My wife

aha'nigiu   pak'u'yadj   kaumë"ĕ   vókmuwó'm
all right   woman.   Kaume,   you stay
                                       with us

aha'na
all right."

****

WOLF'S BOY.

Long ago Wolf was a man. He was living at his mountain home. "I have no wife", he said. "Living alone is not good. I want to marry a woman who will stay here and cook something to eat. I stay here alone : I do not know how to cook. I will go to get one of Piñon Bird's daughters. I will go repeatedly to Piñon Bird's house. I want to get one of the women for a wife. The women did not want to come with me. 'Yes, if one does not want to go with me, I will return.'" Wolf returned. Wolf arrived at his house. " I wonder why Piñon Bird's daughters say I am no good. I will stay here and think about it. I know where there is a pool in which I can put abalone shell. I will leave the abalone shell in the water. In a short time it will appear to be alive. It will be alive like a man. I will return after one sleep". When Wolf reached the pool he looked at the abalone. It looked a little like a man. When he looked at it appeared good as it lay in the pool. The abalone was progressing where he had left it. "In a short time it will resemble a man like myself. You will go over to Piñon Bird's daughters", he said. Wolf took it from there and washed the skin well all over. He put it in a cave which he closed. Coyote went there. He took the child. Carrying it on his back, he arrived at the house. When they arrived, Wolf looked at them. Coyote said, "This is my son". Wolf said, "No, Coyote, that is not your son at all. It is mine, Wolf's son. You, Coyote, you wash him well". Wolf said, "My son is going to fetch one of Piñon Bird's daughters. He will fetch one to stay here grinding corn and mixing it for us to eat. Now, go, get one of Piñon Bird's daughters, saying, 'Be my wife' ". The Abalone shell was now a real man. Wolf's son was named Kaume. "Now go ; go to Piñon Bird's house. Go there to look. You,

Kaume, if Piñon Bird's daughter likes you, call her 'my wife'. When you arrive, Kaume, the woman will see you, and say, 'Yes, I feel well disposed to go with you'. Two women will go as Kaume's wives. If both like the man, they will say, 'Good, let us go together' ". Wolf's son took two of Piñon Bird's daughters. Piñon Bird spoke, "Our men will run races with Kaume. Run races with him for his stakes. Now all the men, everyone should go". Kaume went alone to the north. Many kept running ahead of Kaume this way toward the place where the sun sets, the west. Piñon Bird looked (and sang), "Our men, my relatives, are turning back after four circuits of Moon Mountain". They looked at Kaume who seemed weak as he ran far off. They were ahead of Kaume as he came alone. Kaume was returning after four circuits of Moon Mountain. When Kaume had nearly reached the many men on his return, he sang, "Many racers say, 'Keep going, brother-in-law', to each other, but now they do not say it at all. My cousins are running, but they do not run fast. I, Kaume, will go to tell them to fetch water and food. I will tell them to bring an abundance of food. I will get to Piñon Bird's house while kicking the ball. Two women, Piñon Bird's daughters, will come. I will wager buckskins against Piñon Bird's sons and daughters at the hiding game at night". Kaume won from Piñon Bird's daughters, "I shall win buckskins and all sorts of things from the men". Piñon Bird said, "Anything, blankets or buckskins, may be wagered when you play shinny". Kaume tried and won everything playing shinny. Piñon Bird told them to play the hoop and pole game. "Let us do it. You, Kaume, look like a good player". Kaume won everything from all the others. Kaume, taking two of Piñon Bird's daughters, arrived there. As he went off, all the women, a great many, followed him. Piñon Bird spoke, "My own men, run faster than he. Let us go, catch up with Kaume and kill him". They shot at Kaume but did not hit him. All they kept killing were the women. Kaume sang, "I am no good, because I am unnaturally born. Wolf did not create me properly by that unnatural birth. They can never kill me by weakening me by thirst and hunger. They are returning and leaving me ; I will go". He shot and hit every time. He killed them everyone. He killed many who lay scattered stiff everywhere. The sun sank while he did this. Owl, who was a man, arrived there. Kaume said, "No, no, why do you come here ? Perhaps some one will kill you". Owl said, "I am going to shoot someone". He fluffed his feathers with empty spaces between. Piñon Bird's sons shot and grazed Owl. Crow said, "Ka, ka, ka, what are you doing ? If that is what you do, you will be killed. I know which man I will shoot. I am coming down shooting at the man". Piñon Bird's sons shot killing Crow. When it was a little dark after sunset, Kaume said, "Owl, you said you were a wind- and black-sand shaman. Tear off some (of the black sand) and make it dark". Kaume, Owl, and the two women arrived at Wolf's house. He arrived at the house bringing the two women. (Wolf said to the women), "I am glad he took you two women and arrived, my relatives. Grind corn, stir it, and eat it ; it is good, I say". They hunted deer, caught one, packed it home on the back, and let the load drop. " We will boil venison and eat it". Wolf had no wife ; he lived quite alone. "Kaume, you have two women ; give me one. It is not good to stay here alone ; I would like something to fornicate", he said. Kaume did not speak : he felt that he would refuse to give him a woman. Kaume went away angry. He did not return for many nights. After one night Wolf said, "My son does not return. I, Wolf, am going to travel about in search of him". He followed the tracks of the erstwhile Kaume who had become a mountain sheep. Wolf saw

him and seized him. He pulled the horns off and threw them away. "Now, Kaume, come with me. Why do you wander about : that is not good : let us return". They reached the house. "My wife, woman, it is all right(?) Kaume, you stay with us : it is all right".

BUNGLING HOST.

Aqwaga	θŏknue'vagu'ĭdjĭga	θaùnudigu'-
Deer	her residence	offspring,

ĭdjĭgī	yum	kạθŏdhĕdj ' θiu'ĭdjĭga
spotted, seen	and then	male coyote yonder, coming
		approaching

θag	vagiu'gạ	Qwagaθạu nudĭg hanạta'-
there	come here.	" Fawns spotted very

vạm	n̦ĭu'gạ	Gamowi'm nu'dĭgiu
good	looks.	How did you make spotted ?

N̦a'aθạuạ	gagạha'ndjạĕta'o'bĭmạn̦a'aĭ'mĭg.
My offspring	not very good, I say. "

Gwĭθạvạdi'avạl	nyä'äpü'k.	Ahuwai'ĭg
" Small cave	put them in.	The smoke enters

n̦ạĭ'äwi'm	nu'dĭgiạ. E ha'nĭgiu n̦a'avo'magĭθạ
I do it	spotted. Yes, good I return

wi'higuĭ	hopa'djĭn̦ĭsma'gĭθau miạ'-
I will smoke them	four sleeps come

mĭgĭmạ'u.	Miăha'nĭki'ĭgi'ĭ. Hopa'djĭn̦ĭsma'm
over to see ".	" Do it properly ", Four sleeps
	he (she ?) said.

yamĭgiu'ĭg'ĭ.	Kạθŏdθáuạ ²	gwĭθạvạdi'ạvĭl
she goes.	Coyote whelps	little cave

pŭg	huai'ĭgwi'gĭ	huaiampu'ĭgiu'ĭgạ
put	in smoke	suffocate them,
them	many of them	they (he?) said.

Paiạpĕmgĭu'ĭgạ	Vămbŏ'ŏ'kiu
All gone, they (he ?) said.	That is all to tell.

---

1. The ŏ has deep pitch.
2. The ŏ has deep pitch, the á high pitch.

BUNGLING HOST.

Deer had spotted fawns at her home and Coyote came there. " Your spotted fawns look very nice", he said. " How did you make them spotted ? My whelps are not very good, I say". — "I put them in a small cave. (I built a fire at the entrance, so that) the smoke entered (their mouths and nostrils), and made them spotted". — " Yes, good : I will return to my home. I will try smoking them. Come over to my house to see them after four sleeps". Deer admonished, " Do it properly". After four sleeps had elapsed, Deer went to visit Coyote. Coyote said, "I put my whelps in the little cave to smoke them, but they suffocated. They were completely consumed". That is all to tell.

University of Washington,
     Seattle.

BIBLIOGRAPHY

Abram, David. *The Spell of the Sensuous: Perception and Language in a More-Than-Human World*. New York: Pantheon Books, Random House, 1996. Vintage Books paperback edition, 1997.

Aguilera, Miguel Olmos. *El viejo, el venado y el coyote. Estética y cosmogonía*. México, El Colef/Fondo Regional para la Cultura y las Artes del Noroeste, El Colegio de la Frontera Norte, 2005.

Allport, Gordon. *Becoming: Basic Considerations for a Psychology of Personality*. New Haven: Yale University Press, 1955.

Andrews, Lori B. "Havasupai Tribe Sues Genetic Researchers." *Law and Bioethics* 4, Report 10, 2004.

Arrieta, Olivia. "Religion and Ritual among the Tarahumara Indians of Northern Mexico: Maintenance of Cultural Autonomy through Resistance and Transformation of Colonizing Symbols." *Wicazo Sa Review* 8, No. 2 (Autumn, 1992): 11–23.

Arizona State University Library Archives. "People of the Blue Green Water Enter the 21st Century," 2001. http://www.asu.edu/lib/archives/Spring2001.htm#PEOPLE

Bahr, Donald. "Native American Dream Songs: Myth, Memory and Improvisation." *Journal de la Société des Américanistes* 80, No. 80 (1994): 73–93.

Bahr, Donald. "Dream Songs." In *Handbook of Native American Literature*, ed. Andrew Widget. London: Routledge, 1996.

Basehart, Harry W., and W. W. Hill. "Obituary: Leslie Spier." *American Anthropologist* 67 (1965): 1259–77.

Benedict, Ruth. Research Proposal 2. Ruth Benedict Papers, Vassar College, Poughkeepsie, NY, 1924.

Biggs, Bruce. "Testing Intelligibility among Yuman Languages." *International Journal of American Linguistics* 23, No. 2 (April 1957): 57–66.

Birenbaum, Harvey. *Myth and Mind*. Lantham, MD: University Press of America, 1988.

Boas, Franz. "Tsimshian Texts." *Bulletin* 27, Bureau of American Ethnology, Washington, D.C.: GPO, 1902.

Boas, Franz. "Tsimshian Mythology," *Thirty-first Annual Report of the United States Bureau of American Ethnology*. Washington, D.C.: GPO, 1916.

Braatz, Timothy. "The Question of Regional Bands and Subtribes among the Pre-Conquest Pai (Hualapai and Havasupai) Indians of Northwestern Arizona." *American Indian Quarterly* 22, No. 1/2 (1998): 19–30.

———. "Upland Yuman (Yavapai and Pai) Leadership across the Nineteenth Century." *American Indian Quarterly* 23, No. 3/4 (1999a): 129–47.

———. "[Bands of Gardeners: Pai Sociopolitical Structure]: Response to Dobyns and Euler." *American Indian Quarterly* 23, No. 3/4 (1999b): 175–76.

Brenzinger, Matthias. "Language Diversity Endangered." *Trends in Linguistics*, Studies and Monographs, 181. Berlin: Mouton de Gruyter, 2007: 101.

Broder, Patricia Janis. *Shadows on Glass: The Indian World of Ben Wittick*. New York: Rowman and Littlefield, 1990.

Bunzel, Ruth. "Zuni Origin Myths." *Forty-Seventh Annual Report of the Bureau of American Ethnology*, 1929–1930. Washington, D.C.: GPO, 1932: 547.

Burrus, Ernest J., and Félix Zubillaga. *El Noroeste de México, documentos sobre las misiones jesuíticas (1600–1769)*. Mexico: UNAM, 1986.

Campbell, Joseph. *The Hero with a Thousand Faces*. New York: Pantheon Books, 1949.

———. *Creative Mythology*. Vol. IV ("The Masks of God"). New York: Viking Press, 1968.

———. *The Mythic Image*. Princeton: Princeton University Press, 1974.

———. *The Inner Reaches of Outer Space: Myth as Metaphor and as Religion*. New York: Harper and Row, 1985.

———. *Historical Atlas of World Mythology*. New York: Harper and Row, 1988.

Campbell, Lyle. *American Indian Languages: The Historical Linguistics of Native America*. New York: Oxford University Press, 1997.

Carmony, Neil B., and David E. Brown. *The Wilderness of the Southwest: Charles Sheldon's Quest for Desert Bighorn Sheep and Adventures with the Havasupai and Seri Indians*. Salt Lake City: University of Utah Press, 1993.

Cleland, James H. "The Sacred and the Mundane—Cultural Landscape Concepts and Archaeological Interpretation in the Colorado Desert." *Proceedings of the Society for California Archaeology*, Vol. 18 (2005): 131–36.

Cline Library, Northern Arizona University, Digital Exhibit. Indigenous Voices of the Colorado Plateau, Northern Arizona University, Flagstaff, Arizona. N.D. http://www.nau.edu/~cline/speccoll/exhibits/indigenous_voices/havasupai /overview.html

Cohen, Morris, and Ernest Nagel. *Logic and the Scientific Method*. New York: Harcourt, Brace and World, 1934.

Cook, Roy. 2nd Annual Yuman Language Family Summit Conference Review, Colorado River Indian Tribe, Parker, Arizona, 2003. http://www.american indiansource.com/yuman.html

Corbusier, William F. "The Apache-Yumas and Apache-Mohaves." *American Antiquarian* No. 8 (1886): 276–84, 325–39.

Cordell, Linda S. *Prehistory of the Southwest*. New York: Academic Press, 1984.

Coues, Elliot, ed. *Garces, Francisco. On the Trail of a Spanish Pioneer: The Diary and Itinerary of . . . In His Travels Through Sonora, Arizona, and California, 1775–1776*. Trans. by Elliot Coues. New York: Harper, 1900.

Cozzens, Peter. *The Struggle for Apacheria: Eyewitnesses to the Indian Wars, 1865–1890*. Mechanicsburg, PA: Stackpole Books, 2001.

Curtin, J., and J. N. B. Hewitt, "Seneca Fiction, Legends and Myths." *Thirty-second Annual Report of the Bureau of American Ethnology*. Washington, D.C.: GPO, 1910–1911.

Curtis, Edward S. *The North American Indian*. [Seattle, WA] New York: H. Blackwell and Whitman Bennett, 1907–1930. Now available at http://curtis.library.northwestern.edu

Cushing, Frank Hamilton. "The Nation of the Willows." *The Atlantic Monthly* 50, No. 300 (October 1882): 541–59. http://cdl.library.cornell.edu/cgi-bin/moa/moa-cgi?notisid=ABK2934-0050-98

———. "Myths." *Thirteenth Annual Report of the Bureau of Ethnology, 1891–1892*. Washington, D.C.: GPO 1896: 375.

Densmore, Frances. *Yuman and Yaqui Music*. Washington, Smithsonian Institution. Bureau of American Ethnology, *Bulletin* 110. Washington, D.C.: GPO, 1932.

Dever, D. R. "Town and Hinterland: Kingman and Mohave County, Arizona 1860–1940." Ph.D. diss., University of Nevada, Las Vegas, 2000.

Dobyns, Henry F. "Prehistoric Indian Occupation within the Eastern Area of the Yuman Complex." M.A. thesis, University of Arizona, 1956.

———. "Historic Havasupai Population Trends." In *From Chaco to Chaco, Papers in Honor of Robert H. Lister and Florence C. Lister*, ed. Meliha S. Duran and David T. Kirkpatrick. Albuquerque: Archeaological Society of New Mexico, 1989.

Dobyns, Henry F., and Robert C. Euler. *The Ghost Dance of 1889 among the Pai Indians of Northwestern Arizona*. Prescott, AZ: Prescott College Press, 1967.

———. *Wauba Yuma's People: The Comparative Socio-Political Structure of the Pai Indians of Arizona*. Prescott, AZ: Prescott College Press, 1970.

———. *The Havasupai People*. Phoenix: Indian Tribal Series, Northland Press, 1971.

———. "The Nine Lives of Cherum, the Pai Tokumhet." *American Indian Quarterly* 22, No. 3 (Summer 1998): 363–85.

———. "Bands of Gardeners: Pai Sociopolitical Structure." *American Indian Quarterly* 23, No. 3/4 (1999a): 159–74.

———. "Pai Cultural Change." *American Indian Quarterly* 23, No. 3/4 (1999b): 148–58.

Doty, William G. *Mythography: The Study of Myths and Rituals.* 2nd Edition. Tuscaloosa: University of Alabama Press, 2000.

Du Bois, Constance Goddard. "The Religion of the Luiseño Indians of Southern California." *University of California Publications in American Archaeology and Ethnology,* Vol. 8, No. 3, 1908.

Eliade, Mircea. *Cosmos and History: The Myth of the Eternal Return.* New York: Harper Torchbooks, 1959.

Erdoes, Richard, and Alfonso Ortiz. *American Indian Myths and Legends.* New York: Pantheon Books, 1984.

Euler, Robert C. "Walapai Culture-History." Ph.D. diss., University of New Mexico, 1958.

———. "Ethnographic Methodology: A Tri-chronic Study in Culture Change, Informant Reliability, and Validity from the Southern Paiute." *American Historical Anthropology, Essays in Honor of Leslie Spier.* Carbondale: Southern Illinois University Press, 1967.

———. *The Paiute People.* Phoenix: The Indian Tribal Series, 1972.

———. "Havasupai Historical Data." In *Havasupai Indians, an Ethnohistorical Report,* ed. Robert A. Manners. New York: Garland Publishing Inc., 1974.

———. "The Havasupai of the Grand Canyon." *The American West* 16, No. 3 (May/June 1979): 12–65.

———. "The Grand Canyon Anasazi, Their Descendants and Other Claimants." Paper prepared for the Anasazi Cultural Affiliation Workshop, Fort Lewis College, Durango, CO, February 20–21, 1998.

Euler, Robert C., and Frank D. Tikalsky. *The Grand Canyon: Intimate Views.* Tucson: University of Arizona Press, 1992.

Ewing, Henry F. *The Pai Tribes,* ed. Robert C. Euler and Henry F. Dobyns. *Ethnohistory* 7, No. 1 (1960): 61–80.

Farish, Thomas Edwin. *History of Arizona.* San Francisco: The Filmer Brothers Electrotype Company, 1915 (vol. VII, 1918). http://southwest.library. arizona.edu/hav7/front.1_div.2.html

Ferguson, T. J., and E. Richard Hart. *A Zuni Atlas.* Norman: University of Oklahoma Press, 1985.

Fix, A. G. "Rapid Deployment of the Five Founding Amerind mtDNA Haplogroups Via Coastal and Riverine Colonization." *American Journal of Physical Anthropology* 128, No. 2 (October, 2005): 430–36.

Fontana, Bernard L. *Of Heart and Little Rain.* Tucson: University of Arizona Press, 1989.

Forbes, Jack. *Warriors of the Colorado: The Yumas of the Quechan Nation and Their Neighbors.* Norman: University of Oklahoma Press, 1965.

Forde, C. Darryll. "A Review of Havasupai Ethnography by Leslie Spier." *American Anthropologist,* New Series, Vol. 32, No. 3, Part 1 (July–September, 1930): 553–56.

———. "Ethnography of the Yuma Indians." University of California, *Publications in American Archaeology and Ethnology,* Vol. 28, No. 4, 1931.

Frazer, James G. *The Golden Bough: A Study in Magic and Religion.* New York: Macmillan Publishing, 1922.

Freud, Sigmund. *Totem and Taboo* (in *The Basic Writings of Sigmund Freud*). New York: Modern Library, 1936.

Garduño, Everardo. "The Yumans of Baja California, Mexico: From Invented to Imagined and Invisible Communities." *Journal of Latin American Anthropology* 8, No. 1 (2003): 4–37. http://www3.interscience.wiley.com/journal/120183753/abstract

Georges, Robert A., ed. *Studies on Mythology*. Homewood, IL: Dorsey Press, 1968.

Gifford, E. W. "The Northeastern and Western Yavapai Myths." *Journal of American Folklore* 46 (1933): 347–415.

———. "The Cocopa." University of California, *Publications in American Archaeology and Ethnology*, Vol. 31, No. 5. Berkeley, 1933.

———. "Northeastern and Western Yavapai." University of California, *Publications in American Archaeology and Ethnology*, Vol. 34, No. 4. Berkeley, 1936.

Gill, Sam, and Irene F. Sullivan. *Native American Mythology*. Oxford: Oxford University Press, 1994.

Goldfrank, Esther. "Notes on an Undirected Life: As One Anthropologist Tells It." *Queens College Publications in Anthropology*, No. 3. Flushing, NY: Queens College Press, 1978.

Graves, Charles. *The Asian Origins of Amerindian Religions*. Bochum, Bochumer Universitätsverlag, Bochum. *Bochum Publications in Evolutionary Cultural Semiotics* (BPX) Vol. 37, [1995] 2002.

Grimm, Jacob, and Wilhelm Grimm. *Kinder und Haus Maerchen*. Gottingen: Dieterich, 1819.

Gumerman, George J., ed. *Themes in Southwest Prehistory*. Santa Fe, NM: School of American Research Press, 1994.

Halpern, A. M. "Sex Differences in Quechan Narration." *Journal of California and Great Basin Anthropology* 2, No. 1 (1980): 51–59.

Harrington, John Peabody. "Yuma Account of Origins." *Journal of American Folklore* 21 (1908): 324–48.

Havasupai Tribe, Tribal Website, "About Us." http://www.havasupaitribe.com/aboutus.html

Heizer, R. F., and M. A. Heizer. *Whipple, The California Indians: A Source Book*. Berkeley: University of California Press, [1951] 1973.

Hinton, Leanne, and Lucille J. Watahomigie. *Spirit Mountain: An Anthology of Yuman Story and Song*. Tucson: Sun Tracks and the University of Arizona Press, 1984.

Hinton, Leanne. *Havasupai Songs: A Linguistic Perspective (Ars linguistica)*. Philadelphia: John Benjamins Publishing Co., 1984.

Hirst, Stephen. *I Am the Grand Canyon*. 3rd Edition. Grand Canyon, AZ: Grand Canyon Association, 2006. Originally published as *Life in a Narrow Place: The Havasupai of the Grand Canyon*, D. McKay, 1976; and as *People of the Blue Green Water, Havasupai Tribe*, Supai, Arizona, 1985.

Hitt, William D. "Two Models of Man." *American Psychologist* 24, No. 7 (1968): 651–58.

Hualapai Tribe, "We Are Hualapai." http://www.azcentral.com/culturesaz/amindian/tribes/hualapai_amind.html

Hubert, Howe B. "Myths and Languages." In *The Native Races of the Pacific States*, Vol. III. San Francisco: Bancroft and Co., 1883.

Iliff, Flora Gregg. *People of the Blue Water: A Record of Life among the Walapai and Havasupai Indians*. 3rd edition. Tucson: University of Arizona Press, 1990.

Indian Claims Commission. Findings of Fact, Vol. 20, Docket 210, December 30, 1968: 226–29. http://digital.library.okstate.edu/icc/v20/iccv20p222.pdf

Ives, Lt. Joseph C. *Report upon the Colorado River of the West*. [1861] Reprint, New York: Da Capo Press, 1969.

Jacobs, James Q. A Brief History of Havasupai Political Organization, 1999. http://www.jqjacobs.net/southwest/havasupai.html

Jacoby, Karl. *Crimes against Nature: Squatters, Poachers, Thieves and the Hidden History of American Conservation*. Esp. Ch. 7, "The Havasupai Problem." Berkeley: University of California Press, 2001.

James, George Wharton. *In and Around the Grand Canyon*. Boston: Little, Brown and Company, 1900.

Joël, Judith. "Another Look at the Pai Pai-Arizona Pai Divergence." In *Studies in American Indian Languages: Description and Theory*, ed. Leanne Hinton and Pamela Munro. Berkeley: University of California, *Publications in Linguistics* No. 131, 1998: 32–40.

Jones, A. T., and Robert C. Euler. *A Sketch of Grand Canyon Prehistory*. Grand Canyon, AZ: Natural History Association, 1979.

Jung, Carl G. *Psychology of Religion*. New Haven: Yale University Press, 1938.

———. *Von Den Wurzlen Des Bewusstseins*. Zurich: Rascher, 1954.

———. *The Basic Writings of C. G. Jung*, ed. Violet Staud De Lazio. New York: Modern Library, 1959.

———. "Archetypes of the Collective Unconscious." In *The Collected Works of C. G. Jung*, Bollingen Series XX, Vol. 9, Part I, ed. H. Read, M. Fordham, and G. Adler. Princeton: Princeton University Press, 1959.

———. "Symbols and the Interpretation of Dreams." In *The Collected Works of C. G. Jung*, Vol. 18, Part II.

Jung, Carl G., and C. Kerenyl. *Essays on a Science of Mythology*. New York: Pantheon Press, 1949. (New material copyright, Princeton: Princeton University Press, 1963).

Kelly, William H. "Cocopah Ethnography." *Anthropological Papers of the University of Arizona* 29. Tucson: University of Arizona Press, 1973.

Kendall, Martha B. "Yuman Languages." In *Southwest*, ed. Alfonso Ortiz, 4–12. *Handbook of North American Indians*, William C. Sturtevant, general editor, Vol. 10. Washington, D.C.: Smithsonian Institution, 1983.

Kluckhohn, Clyde. "Myths and Rituals: A General Theory." *Harvard Theological Review* 35 (1942): 45–79.

Kroeber, A. L. "A Preliminary Sketch of the Mohave Indians." *American Anthropologist* 4 (1902): 276–85.

———. "Yuman Tribes of the Lower Colorado." University of California, *Publications in American Archaeology and Ethnology*, Vol. 16, No. 8, pp. 475–85, Aug. 21, 1920. http://www.archive.org/stream/yumantribesoflowookroerich/yumantribesoflowookroerich_djvu.txt

———, ed. *Walapai Ethnography*. Menasha, WI: American Anthropological Association Memoir No. 42, 1935.

Laird, Carobeth. *The Chemehuevis*. Banning, CA: Malki Museum Inc., 1976.

Langdon, Margaret. "Bibliography of the Yuman Languages." *Survey of California and Other Indian Languages* 9 (1996): 135–59.

———. "Animal Talk in Cocopah." *International Journal of American Linguistics* 44, No. 1 (January 1978): 10–16.

Laylander, Don. "The Linguistic Prehistory of Baja California." In *Contributions to the Linguistic Prehistory of Central and Baja California*, ed. Gary S. Breschini and Trudy Haversat. Archives of California Prehistory 44. Salinas, CA: Coyote Press, 1997.

———. "The Regional Consequences of Lake Cahuilla." San Diego State University Occasional Papers, Vol. I, 2006. http://soap.sdsu.edu/Volume1/LakeCahuilla/cahuilla.htm

Levi-Strauss, Claude. *Structural Anthropology*. New York: Anchor Books, 1967.

———. *The Savage Mind*. Chicago: University of Chicago Press, 1966.

Levy, Jerrold. *In The Beginning: Navajo Genesis*. Berkeley: University of California Press, 1998.

Lord, Albert B. "The Singer of Tales." *Harvard Studies in Comparative Literature*, 24. Cambridge, MA: Harvard University Press, 1960.

Luthin, Herbert W., ed. *Surviving Through the Days: Translations of Native California Stories and Songs*. Berkeley: University of California Press, 2002.

Malinowski, Bronislaw. *The Father in Primitive Psychology*. New York: Norton, 1927.

———. *Myth in Primitive Psychology* (1926). In *Magic Science and Religion*, ed. Robert Redfield. Boston: Beacon Press, 1948.

———. *Myth in Primitive Psychology*. New York: Garden City Press, 1954.

———. *Argonauts of the Western Pacific*. New York: E.P. Dutton and Co., [1922] 1961.

Manakaja, Roland, and Jeff Manakaja. *Havasupai* [CD of traditional songs]. Oyate Online/Many Kites Press, 2006. http://www.oyate.com/artists/manakaja39/manakaja06.html

Manners, Robert A. *Havasupai Indians: An Ethnohistorical Report*. New York: Garland Publishing, Inc., 1974.

Martin, John F. "The Havasupai." *Plateau* 56, No. 4 (1986). Flagstaff: Museum of Northern Arizona.

———. "The Prehistory and Ethnohistory of Havasupai-Hualapai Relations." *Ethnohistory* 32, No. 2 (Spring 1985): 135–53.

———. "On the Estimation of the Sizes of Local Groups in a Hunting-Gathering Environment." *American Anthropologist* 75, No. 5 (October 1973): 1448–68.

Matson, R. G. "The Spread of Maize to the Colorado Plateau." *Archaeology Southwest* 13 (1999): 10–11.

Mead, Margaret. *Culture and Commitment*. New York: Doubleday and Co. Inc., 1970.

Meigs, Peveril. *The Kiliwa of Lower California*. Berkeley: University of California Press, 1939.

Messersmith, Dan W. *Camp Beale's Springs: A Short History*. Kingman, AZ: Mohave Museum of History and Arts, 2002. http://www.citlink.net/~mocohist/museum/beale.htm

Michno, Gregory F. *Encyclopedia of Indian Wars: Western Battles and Skirmishes 1850–1890*. Missoula, MT: Mountain Press Publishing Company, 2003.

Mithun, Marianne. *The Languages of Native North America*. Cambridge: Cambridge University Press, 2001.

Mixco, Mauricio. "Kiliwa Texts: 'When I have donned my crest of stars.'" *University of Utah Anthropological Papers*, 1983.

———. "Etnohistoria paipai de Baja California," *Meyibó* 5. Mexico: UBAC-UNAM, 1985.

Morford, Mark, and Robert Lenardon. *Classical Mythology*. New York: David McKay, 1971.

Morris, Clyde Patrick. "An Analysis of Upland Yuman Myths with the Dying God and Monster Slayer Stories." Unpublished Ph.D. dissertation, Arizona State University, 1974.

———. "'Monster Slayer' among the Upland Yumans: A Folk Theory on the Evolution of Hunting Cultures." *American Indian Quarterly* 10, No. 3 (Summer 1986): 199–221.

Muñiz, Gloria Bock. "Indigenous Language Preservation Programs and Language Policy in Education: A Web-Based Intertextual Analysis." Unpublished Ph.D. dissertation, Oregon State University, 2007.

Murray, H. A. *The Manual of Thematic Apperception Test*. Cambridge, MA: Harvard University Press, 1943.

National Research Council. *River Management in the Grand Canyon*. Washington, D.C.: National Academy Press, 1996.

Native Languages of the Americas: Hokan Language Family. St. Paul, MN: Native Languages of the Americas, N.D. http://www.native-languages.org/famhok.htm

Ochoa Zazueta, Jesús Ángel. *Los kiliwa y el mundo se hizo así*. Mexico: Instituto Nacional Indigenista, 1978.

Ogás Sánchez, Yolanda. *A la orilla del Río Colorado. Los Cucapá*. Mexicali, Baja California: Salcar, 2001.

Olavarría, María Eugenia. "Mitología cosmogónica del noroeste." In *Mitos cosmogónicos del México indígena*, ed. Monjarás-Ruiz. Mexico: INAH, 1979.

Ong, Walter J. *Orality and Literacy: The Technologizing of the Word*. London: Methuen and Co. Ltd, 1982.

Parezo, Nancy J. *Hidden Scholars: Women Anthropologists and the American Southwest*. Albuquerque: University of New Mexico Press, 1993.

Parsons, Elsie Worthington Clews, ed. *American Indian Life*. New York: B. W. Huebsch, Inc., 1922.

Piñón, Iraís. "Los mitos de tradición yumana en Baja California," presented in the seminar, "El mundo místico y mágico de la cultura prehispánica en el Noroeste de México y Sur de los EUA," *Encuentro Yoreme de Sinaloa*, photocopied document, 2003.

Reichard, Gladys A. "Franz Boas and Folklore." *American Anthropologist* 45, No. 3 (1943): 52–57.

Roberts, David. "Below the Rim." *Smithsonian* 37, No. 3 (2006): 54–65.

Rogers, Malcolm J. "An Outline of Yuman Prehistory." *Journal of Anthropology*, Vol. 1 (1945): 167–98.

Round, Phillip H. "'There Was More to It, but That Is All I Can Remember': The Persistence of History and the Autobiography of Delfina Cuero." *American Indian Quarterly* 21, No. 2 (Spring 1997): 171 (23). (A Yuman [Kumayaay] woman caught between traditional tribal migratory survival patterns and twentieth-century Mexico and America).

Schwartz, Douglas W. *On the Edge of Splendor: Exploring the Grand Canyon's Human Past*. Santa Fe, NM: School of American Research, 1989.

Scientific American Supplement. "A Miniature from the Past: Dwellers in Arizona Today Who Appear to Be Left-overs from the Stone Age." New York, May 24, 1919: 324–25. Available at Cline Library Archives, Northern Arizona University, Flagstaff, Arizona. (A report on Spier's visit to the Havasupai.)

Segal, Robert A. *Jung on Mythology*. Princeton: Princeton University Press, 1998.

———. *Theorizing About Myth*. Amherst: University of Massachusetts Press, 1999.

———. *Myth: A Very Short Introduction*. New York: Oxford University Press, 2004.

Shaul, David Leedom, and Jane H. Hill. "Tepimans, Yumans and Other Hohokam." *American Antiquity*, 63 (1998). http://www.questia.com/PM.qst?a=o&d=5001365900

Shermer, Michael. "Demon-Haunted Brain." *Scientific American* 288, No. 3 (March 2003): 47.

———. *The Science of Good and Evil*. New York: Henry Holt and Co., 2004.

Shlain, Leonard. *The Alphabet versus the Goddess: The Conflict between Word and Image*. New York: Penguin Group, 1998.

Sinyella, Juan. "Havasupai Traditions." Ed. J. Donald Hughes. *Southwest Folklore* 1 (Spring 1977): 35–52.

Smithson, Carma Lee. "The Havasupai Woman." *Anthropological Papers*, Department of Anthropology, University of Utah, No. 38: April, 1959. Reprint, New York: Johnson Reprint Corporation, 1971.

Smithson, Carma Lee, and Robert C. Euler. "Havasupai Religion and Mythology." Salt Lake City: University of Utah Anthropological Papers 68, 1964. Reprint: Smithson, C. L., and R. C. Euler. Republished as *Havasupai Legends: Religion and Mythology of the Havasupai Indians of the Grand Canyon*. Salt Lake City: University of Utah Press, 1994.

Sosis, Richard. "The Adaptive Value of Religious Ritual." *American Scientist* 92 (2004).

Sperry, T. J., and H. C. Myers. "A History of Ft. Union, Kansas." Kansas Heritage.org. http://www.kansasheritage.org/research/sft/ft-union.htm

Spicer, Edward H. *Cycles of Conquest.* Tucson: University of Arizona Press, 1962.

Spier, Leslie. "The Havasupai of Cataract Canyon: A Tribe of Indians in the Gorges of the Grand Canyon of Arizona Preserve Their Primitive Life." *American Museum Journal* 18 (December 1918): 637–45.

———. "Havasupai Days." In *American Indian Life,* ed. Elsie W. C. Parsons. New York: B. W. Huebsch, 1922.

———. "Havasupai Texts." *The International Journal of American Linguistics* 3 (1924): 109–16.

———. "Havasupai Ethnography." American Museum of Natural History, *Anthropological Papers* 29. New York, 1928.

———. "Problems Arising from the Cultural Position of the Havasupai." *American Anthropologist* 31, No. 2 (April–June): 1929.

———. "Historical Interrelation of Culture Traits: Franz Boas' Study of Tsimshian Mythology." In *Methods in Social Science,* ed. Stuart A. Rice. Chicago: University of Chicago Press, 1931.

———. *Yuman Tribes of the Gila River.* Chicago: University of Chicago Press, 1933.

———. "Some Aspects of the Nature of Culture." First Annual Research Lecture. Albuquerque, University of New Mexico, April 23, 1954. *New Mexico Quarterly* 24, No. 3 (1954): 301–21.

Strenski, Ivan. *Four Theories of Myth in Twentieth Century History.* London and Iowa City: Macmillan and University of Iowa Press, 1987.

———. *Malinowski and the Work of Myth.* Princeton: Princeton University Press, 1992.

———. "Morality and Myth." *International Journal of Religion and Philosophy* 1 (1996): 1–12.

Taylor, Walter W. "Leslie Spier, 1893–1961." *American Antiquity* 28, No. 3 (January 1963): 379–81.

Thrapp, Dan L. *The Conquest of Apacheria.* Norman: University of Oklahoma Press, 1967.

Underwood, Jackson. "Pipes and Tobacco Use among Southern California Yuman Speakers." *Journal of California and Great Basin Anthropology* 24, No. 1 (2002): 1–12. http://escholarship.org/uc/item/0q33llgh

U.S. Government Printing Office. *Walapai Papers: Historical Reports, Documents, and Extracts from Publications Relating to the Walapai Indians of Arizona.* Washington, 1936.

Wallace, W. J. "The Dream in Mohave Life." *The Journal of American Folklore* 60, No. 237 (July–September 1947): 252–325.

Waters, Frank. *Book of the Hopi.* New York: Viking Press, 1963.

Waterman, Thomas Talbot. "The Religious Practices of the Diegueño Indian." University of California, *Publications in American Archaeology and Ethnology* 8 (6): 271–358. Putnam and Kroeber, eds., Berkeley, 1910.

Wilken-Robertson, Miguel. Una Separación Artificial: Grupos Yumanos de México y Estados Unidos. *Estudios Fronterizos* 31/32 (1993): 135–59.

Wilken-Robertson, Michael. "Yuman Indian Peoples of the Western Borderlands." *Borderlines* 62, vol. 7, No. 11 (December 1999). http://americas.irc-online. org/borderlines/1999/b162/b162comp_body.html

Winter, Werner. "Yuman Languages II: Wolf's Son. A Walapai Text." *International Journal of American Linguistics* 32, No. 1 (January 1966): 17–40.

White, Leslie A. *Pioneer in American Anthropology: The Bandelier-Morgan Letters.* Vol. I and II. Albuquerque: University of New Mexico Press, 1940.

———. "History, Evolutionism and Functionalism." *Southwestern Journal of Anthropology* 1 (1945): 221–48.

———. *The Science of Culture.* New York: Farrar, Strauss and Co., 1949.

———. *The Evolution of Culture.* New York: McGraw-Hill Book, Co. 1959.

———. "The Ethnography and Ethnology of Franz Boas." *Bulletin of The Texas Memorial Museum*, No. 6 (April 1963): 5–76.

Whitener, Henry Carroll. *Havasupai Songs. Havasu suwatiji.* [n.p.] 1934. Available at Princeton University, Department of Rare Books and Special Collections, Western Americana Collection.

Whiting, A. F. "Is the Cultural Pattern of the Havasupai Applicable to the Cohonina?" Unpublished, undated manuscript, Culture Change Vol. 2, Havasupai Vol. 9, pp. 282–305. Cline Library Archives, Northern Arizona University, Flagstaff, Arizona.

———. *Havasupai Habitat: A. F. Whiting's Ethnography of a Traditional Indian Culture*, ed. Steven A. Weber and P. David Seaman. Tucson: University of Arizona Press, 1985.

———. "Ethnography of the Havasupai." Cline Library Archives, Northern Arizona University, Flagstaff, Arizona. Unpublished, undated manuscript.

———. "Whiting, Havasupai Indian Astronomy and Calendrical Observations." Cline Library Archives, Northern Arizona University, Flagstaff. Unpublished, undated manuscript.

———. "The Fixed Stars." Cline Library Archives, Northern Arizona University, Flagstaff. Unpublished, undated manuscript.

Xochime, Citalin. *People of the Red Brown Earth: Along Genetic Trails of Humankind in the New World.* Forthcoming in print; online 2001–2002. http://nahuatl.info/research/genetics.htm

Zolbrod, Paul G. *Diné Bahané: The Navajo Creation Story.* Albuquerque: University of New Mexico Press, 1984.

BIOGRAPHIES OF CONTRIBUTORS

CATHERINE A. EULER, PH.D.
Born in 1963, she lived in Havasu Canyon for parts of two summers as a child while her mother was collecting and recording memories of Havasupai elders in 1969–1970. She worked on the Prescott College Black Mesa Archaeological Project excavating Anasazi sites during the 1970s, and supervised archaeological fieldwork on Cerbat and Cohonina sites near Ashfork and Kingman for the Office of Contract Archaeology, University of New Mexico, in the early 1990s. She obtained a Ph.D. in European history from the University of York, England, in 1996, after which she taught European history, gender studies, and sociology at two English universities before returning to her native Prescott, Arizona, in 2002. For two years she served as the Tribal Anthropologist for the Yavapai-Prescott Indian Tribe. In 2008 she worked for EcoPlan during the excavation of the Hohokam "Antler House Village" in Cordes Junction, Arizona. She is currently an Adjunct Professor of Gender and Women's Studies at the University of Arizona in Tucson.

ROBERT C. EULER, PH.D. (1927–2002)
Born in 1927 in Brookline, New York, he moved to Colorado at a young age and became interested in archaeology after seeing sites near Manitou Springs. After receiving a Purple Heart following his

service as a lieutenant in the U.S. Marine Corps (4th Div.) at Iwo Jima in World War II, he became an anthropology student at the University of New Mexico and studied under Leslie Spier. His dissertation focused on the Hualapai, a people who before conquest were a different band of the same overarching tribal grouping as the Havasupai. The research involved extensive fieldwork in rock shelters in the Kingman area. He was awarded his Ph.D. in 1958. His early career included jobs as curator of anthropology at the Museum of Northern Arizona (1952–1956), chair of the anthropology programs at NAU (1956–1964) and the University of Utah (1964–1966), and founder and chair of the Center for Man and the Environment at Prescott College (1966–1972). He served briefly as president of Prescott College (1972–1973) before taking up a teaching position at Fort Lewis College (1973–1974). The remaining years of his career were spent as a research anthropologist with the National Park Service briefly in Tucson and then within and near the Grand Canyon National Park, where he recorded, researched, or excavated over eight hundred prehistoric Native American sites, including Stanton's Cave, thus making an invaluable contribution to our overall understanding of North American prehistory. He always advocated for a holistic rather than narrow view of anthropology.

ERNA GUNTHER, PH.D. (1896–1982)
Gunther graduated in 1919 as a student of Franz Boas and received her M.A. in anthropology from Columbia University in 1920. She formed part of the core of the newly formed anthropology program at the University of Washington in the 1920s, along with Melville Jacobs and Leslie Spier. She conducted field studies focusing on the Havasupai (1921) for the Museum of Natural History in New York. She was married to Leslie Spier, though the pair separated in 1930. In that same year the Washington State Museum named her as director. As head of the university anthropology department, she built the faculty from two in 1930 to over ten residents in 1955. In 1966 she moved to the University of Alaska, Fairbanks, becoming chair in 1967. An American Indian specialist, her later research focused on the Salish and Makah peoples of western Washington State, with publications on ethnobotany, ethnohistory, and general ethnology.

MANAKAJA (HMAAN GJAAH, "GUARDS THE CHILDREN")
  (1850?–1942)
Traditionalist, rather than accommodationist, leader of the Havasupai.
Born around 1850, he had been formerly called Wii Maya ("Little
Mountain"); he became head chief in 1900 at the age of fifty after the
death of Navajo, his uncle, and adopted his new name, "Guardian of
the Children," at that time. He is one of the two main storytellers in
this volume, having recounted all the traditional tales known to him
to two anthropologists, Spier and Gunther, who visited his canyon
home and recorded this oral tradition between 1918 and 1921, when
Manakaja was between sixty-eight and seventy-one years old. He was
one of the Havasupai's most respected leaders and spokesmen until
his death in 1942. His persistent traditionalist belief was that "the
white man and the Indian cannot live on the same ground; each must
have his own, and there can be no encroaching, one on the other"
(Iliff 1954: 193, quoted in Hirst 2006: 83). Manakaja once rode the
entire boundary of traditional Havasupai lands, around the plateau
and down to Indian Gardens, visiting family camps as he went.

JOHN NAGEL, M.D.
Born in 1944, he is a board-certified psychiatrist and a thirty-year par-
ticipant in the ethnomedicine program at the University of Colorado,
as well as a friend and colleague of Robert C. Euler. He currently
practices in Ft. Collins, Colorado.

DOUGLAS W. SCHWARTZ, PH.D.
He received his Ph.D. from Yale in 1955 after what he remembers
as four memorable years. The first two years included classes from
Ben Rouse, Wendell Bennett, Ralph Linton, George Peter Murdock,
Floyd Lousbury, and Cornelius Osgood. His third year was spent
doing archaeological research in the Grand Canyon. The next year
he returned to write his dissertation, "Havasupai Prehistory: Thirteen
Centuries of Cultural Development" (1959) with Ben as his major
advisor and Bill Sturtevant as a reader. He then spent ten years at the
University of Kentucky as a professor of anthropology and director of
its Museum of Anthropology. In 1967 Doug moved to Santa Fe, New
Mexico, to become president of the School of American Research, and
over the next thirty-four years developed it into a well-funded, pro-
ductive international center for advanced study in anthropology and

Native American art. He is currently a Senior Scholar at the School of American Research.

SINYELLA (1848?–1933)

This Havasupai headman is the other principle storyteller in this volume. He was between seventy and seventy-three years old when he told Spier, between 1918 and 1921, all the Havasupai stories he could remember. He was also the main source for Leslie Spier's *Havasupai Ethnography* (1928). He told Spier he remembered a Yavapai raid into the canyon in the 1840s, and another in 1855, when he helped to repel twenty Yavapai raiders from Havasu Canyon. The last Yavapai raid in the canyon, according to Sinyella, was in 1862, when two hundred attacked and were again repelled. In 1869 or 1870 Sinyella's father was visiting the Hopi at the same time as some Yavapai, and he said his father, the head chief (Wa Sgwiivma), took the opportunity to make a peace with the Yavapai which was never broken. Sinyella also remembered when Navajo refugees hid in Havasu Canyon following the murderous attacks in their country by U.S. Army Lieutenant Kit Carson in 1864. Sinyella's family camped sometimes on the plateau near a piñon grove past Big Catchment (Moqui Tank?), and he was there once when the government agents evicted all the Havasupai and told them they were restricted to living in the canyon bottom even in the winter (Hirst 2006: 118–19).

LESLIE SPIER, PH.D. (1893–1961)

Leslie Spier was born on December 13, 1893, in New York City. His career in anthropology started in 1915 when he began his graduate studies at Columbia University under Franz Boas. From 1916 until he obtained his doctorate in 1920, Spier worked at the American Museum of Natural History, where he became interested in Native American cultures. He was the first anthropologist to do a scientific ethnological study of the Havasupai, from 1918–1921. While Spier brought vast amounts of knowledge to the field of anthropology through his fieldwork, his greatest contributions were probably through his literary achievements and his students. In 1920 he began teaching at the University of Washington, where he established the Anthropology Department. In 1939 he transferred to the University of New Mexico where he remained until he retired in 1955. He made important contributions to sherd collection and seriation through his work in the

Zuni country, always advocating for a holistic, rather than a narrow, view of anthropology. At UNM he founded the *Southwestern Journal of Anthropology* and the University of New Mexico *Publications in Anthropology*. He edited both until his death in 1961. While Spier spent most of his tenure at these two universities, he also taught for several years at Yale University and visited many other academic institutions.

FRANK D. TIKALSKY, ED.D.
Born in 1932, Tikalsky retired in 1996 from the Los Alamos National Laboratory, Los Alamos, New Mexico, where he was occupational medicine psychologist and employee team leader. Tikalsky was honored with the Distinguished Alumnus Award from the Los Alamos Laboratory. He received his Ed.D. in educational psychology from the University of Northern Colorado. He is a licensed psychologist. Tikalsky's professional positions included full professor appointments at three colleges and universities. He is professor emeritus of the University of Montana–Western. He also served as director of mental health services for Mono County, California. Tikalsky served many years as a consultant to Native American cultures including the Navajo, Havasupai, and Ute. He assisted Dr. Robert C. Euler in studying traditional land use patterns of the Havasupai. Tikalsky has received important professional honors including the Certificate of Commendation from the International Congress of Psychology.